Management and the Arts

Third Edition

William J. Byrnes

Foreword by Dan J. Martin

Focal Press

An Imprint of Elsevier

AMSTERDAM   BOSTON   LONDON   NEW YORK   OXFORD   PARIS
SAN DIEGO   SAN FRANCISCO   SINGAPORE   SYDNEY   TOKYO

Focal Press is an imprint of Elsevier

Library of Congress Cataloging-in-Publication Data

Byrnes, William J.
    Management and the arts / William J. Byrnes.—3rd ed.
      p. cm.
    Includes bibliographical references and index.
    ISBN-13: 978-0-240-80537-5 ISBN-10: 0-240-80537-2 (pbk. : alk.paper)
     1. Arts—United States—Management.   I. Title.

NX765 .B87   2003
700′.68—dc21   2002043078
ISBN-13: 978-0-240-80537-5
ISBN-10: 0-240-80537-2

British Library Cataloguing-in-Publication Data
A catalogue record for this book is available from the British Library.

The publisher offers special discounts on bulk orders of this book.
For information, please contact:
Manager of Special Sales
Elsevier
200 Wheeler Road
Burlington, MA 01803
Tel: 781-313-4700
Fax: 781-313-4882

For information on all Focal Press publications available, contact our World Wide Web home page at: http://www.focalpress.com

Transferred to Digital Printing 2008

Contents

Foreword by Dan J. Martin   xiii
Preface   xv
Acknowledgments   xix

1   Management and the Arts   1

The Entertainment Business   1
  Profit-Making Ventures in the Arts   3
  Growing Businesses   3
  Concerns about the Future   5
Managers and Organizations   6
  The Manager   6
  The Organization   6
  The Process of Organizing   7
  Levels of Management and Types of Managers   7
  Common Elements in an Organization   10
  Arts Organizations as Institutions   11
The Management Process   12
  Planning   12
  Organizing   13
  Leading   13
  Controlling   13
  Functional Areas   14
Key Terms and Concepts   15
Questions   15
Selecting a Project Organization   16
References   16

2   The Evolution of Arts Organizations and Arts Management   18

The Artist-Manager   18
The Arts as Institutions   18
A Brief Historical Overview   19
  Ancient Times   19
  The Middle Ages   20
  The Renaissance   21
  The Seventeenth through Nineteenth Centuries   22
  The Twentieth Century   23
The Modern Nonprofit Arts Organization   24
  Legal Status and Financial Statements   24
  Incorporation   25
  Tax Exemption   25
Profile of the Arts Manager   28
  Updating the Profile   29

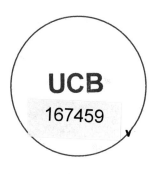

Jobs for Arts Managers Today   30
The Manager's Personal Mission   31
The National Endowment for the Arts   31
Government Support   32
Budget Battles and Censorship   33
The NEA and the Arts Manager   34
State Agencies   35
The Education Revolution   35
The Slowdown in Growth   36
Conclusion   36
Summary   36
Key Terms and Concepts   38
Questions   38
Case Study—Wanted: Art Scholar. M.B.A. Required   38
References   42
Additional Resources   44

3   Evolution of Management   45

Management as an Art and a Science   45
On-the-Job Management Theory   46
Evolution of Management Thought   47
Preindustrialization   47
A Change in Philosophies   47
The Industrial Revolution and Early Pioneers of Management   47
Changes in America   48
Management Trends to the Present   50
Classical Management Perspectives   50
Administrative Management (1916 to Present)   51
Human Relations Management (1927 to Present)   53
Modern Management   55
Scientific Management Today—Quantitative Approaches   55
Systems Theory   56
Contingency Approaches   56
Arts Application   56
Emerging Views   57
Conclusion   58
Summary   59
Key People, Terms, and Concepts   60
Questions   60
References   60

4   Arts Organizations in a Changing World   62

Changing Environments   64
Managing Change   64
Growing into Change   65
Content Analysis   66
Where to Look for Arts Content   67
Environments   67
Economic   68
Political and Legal   68
Cultural and Social   71
Demographic   72
Technological   73

       Educational   75
   Information Sources   75
       Audiences   75
       Other Arts Groups   76
       Board and Staff Members   77
       The Media   77
       Professional Meetings and Associations   78
       Consultants   78
       Other Sources   78
   The Impact of Future Trends on the Arts   79
   Summary   80
   Key Terms and Concepts   80
   Questions   81
   Case Study—A Cultural District for Downtown Atlanta   81
   References   83

5   Planning and Decision Making   84

   Relationship of Planning to the Arts   84
       The Necessity of Planning   85
       The Organization's Map and Leadership   85
   Planning Terminology   85
       Short-, Intermediate-, and Long-Range Plans   86
       Strategic and Operational Plans   86
       Single-Use and Standing-Use Plans   87
   Developing a Planning Process for the Arts   87
       The Mission Statement   87
       Situation Analysis   90
       Resource Analysis   91
       Formulating Strategies   91
       Goals, Objectives, Action Plans, and Evaluation   93
   Other Planning Approaches   94
       Developing a Formal Business Plan   94
       Top-down and Bottom-up Planning   95
       Contingency Planning   96
       Crisis Planning   96
   Limits of Planning   96
   Decision Making in Planning   98
       Choices, Decisions, and Problem Solving   98
       Steps in Problem Solving   98
       Problem-Solving Techniques   99
       Decision Theory   100
   Conclusion   100
   Summary   101
   Key Terms and Concepts   102
   Questions   102
   Case Study—Arizona Opera Education Long-Range Plans 2000–2005   102
   References   106
   Additional Resources   107

6   Fundamentals of Organizing and Organizational Design   108

   The Management Function of Organizing   108
       Four Benefits of Organizing   109
       Organizing for the Arts   109

Organizational Design Approaches   109
  Organic and Mechanistic Organizational Design   110
  Bureaucracy   111
  Organizational Structure and Charts   112
  Informal Structure   117
Structure from an Arts Manager's Perspective   118
  General Considerations   118
  Departmentalization   119
Coordination   121
  Vertical Coordination   121
  Horizontal Coordination   124
Organizational Growth   125
Corporate Culture and the Arts   125
  Theory versus Reality in Organizations   125
  Application to the Arts   126
  Five Elements of Corporate Culture   126
  Corporate Cultures and the Real World   130
Summary   130
Key Terms and Concepts   130
Questions   131
Case Study—An Arts Institution's Management Overhaul   131
References   135

7 Staffing the Organization   136

The Staffing Process   137
  Job Analysis   137
  Job Description   139
  The Overall Matrix of Jobs   141
  Constraints on Staffing   142
  Recruitment   143
  Selection Process   145
  Orientation and Training   147
  Replacement and Firing   148
Volunteers in the Arts   149
  The Board of Directors   150
Unions and the Arts   151
  Definition and Purpose   151
  Disputes   152
Maintaining and Developing the Staff   154
  Career Management   155
  The "Right Staff"   155
Summary   155
Key Terms and Concepts   157
Questions   157
References   157
Additional Resources   157

8 Fundamentals of Leadership and Group Dynamics   159

Leadership Fundamentals   159
  Formal and Informal Leadership Modes   160
  Theory X and Theory Y Approaches to People   160
Power: A Leadership Resource   161
  Sources of Power   161

Limits to Power   162
Guidelines for Using Power   163
Approaches to the Study of Leadership   164
Trait Approaches to Leadership   164
Behavioral Approaches to Leadership   164
Contingency and Situational Approaches to Leadership   165
Transactional and Transformational Leadership   168
Applications to the Arts   169
Future Leadership?   169
Motivation and the Arts Work Setting   170
Theories of Motivation   170
Need Theories   170
Cognitive Theories   172
Reinforcement Theory   174
Theory Integration   176
Group Dynamics   177
Group Management Activities and Forms   177
Dysfunctional Group Activities   179
Strategies for Making Groups More Effective   180
Distributed Leadership   182
Communication Basics and Effective Leadership   182
The Communication Process   182
Perception   183
Formal and Informal Communication   184
Conclusion   184
Summary   185
Key Terms and Concepts   186
Questions   186
Case Study—Cooper-Hewitt Shake-up and Layoffs Reverberate   187
References   190
Additional Resources   191

9 Organizational Controls and Budgets   193

Control as a Management Function   193
Elements of the Control Process   194
Management by Exception   197
Management by Objectives   198
Performance Appraisal Systems   198
Summary of Control Systems   199
Management Information Systems   200
Data and Information   201
Management Information Systems in the Arts   201
Computers and the Management Information System   203
An Effective Management Information System   203
Common Mistakes   204
Management Information System Summary   205
The Future   205
Budgets and the Control System   205
Budgetary Centers   208
Budgets as Preliminary Controls   208
Budgets as Top Secret Documents   208
Types of Budgets   208
The Budgetary Process   209
Budget Reality   210

Budget Controls   210
Budgets in Detail   210
From the Budget to Cash Flow   215
Summary   217
Key Terms and Concepts   218
Questions   218
Case Study—Radio Station Officials Got Free Cruises   218
References   221

10   Economics and Financial Management   222

The Economic Problems and Issues Facing the Arts   222
   The Cultural Boom from an Economic Perspective   223
   Trend Shift in the 1980s   223
   The Arts Audience   223
   The Productivity Issue   224
Basic Economic Principles Applied to the Arts   225
   The Economics of Making More than You Spend   227
   Economic Impact of the Arts   227
   Organizational Impact   227
   Fixed, Variable, and Marginal Costs   228
   Economies of Scale   230
Supply and Demand   230
   Law of Demand   230
   Market Demand and the Arts   232
   Law of Supply   232
   Supply, Demand, and Revenue Maximization   234
Summary of Basic Arts Economics   236
Overview of Financial Management   236
   Nonprofit Financial Management   237
   Financial Management Information System (FMIS)   237
   Developing a Financial Management Information System   239
   Accounting and Bookkeeping   239
   The Accounting System Overview   241
   Financial Statements   242
   Statement of Activity   243
   Investment   245
Summary of Financial Management   248
Managing Finances and the Economic Dilemma   248
   Reserve Funds   249
   Looking Ahead   249
Questions   249
Case Study—Creating a Financial Report   249
References   251

11   Marketing and the Arts   252

An Event in Search of an Audience   253
   A Means to an End   253
Marketing Principles and Terms   254
   Needs and Wants   254
   Exchange Process and Utilities   255
Evolution of Modern Marketing   256
   Modern Marketing   257
   Marketing and Entertainment   257

Marketing Approaches 258
    Product Orientation 258
    Sales Orientation 258
    Customer Orientation 258
Marketing Management 260
    The Four Ps 260
    Market Segments 261
    Market Research 261
    Other Arts Research 264
    Marketing Ethics 264
Strategic Marketing Plans 265
    Planning Process 265
    Marketing Audit 265
    Consultants 267
    Strategies 267
    The Competitive Marketplace and Core Strategies 267
    Project Planning and Implementation 269
    Evaluation 269
    Marketing Data System 269
Conclusion 270
Summary 271
Key Terms and Concepts 272
Questions 273
Case Study—Portrait of the Artist As a Focus Group 273
References 276
Additional Resources 277

12 Fundraising 278
Why Do People Give? 278
Fundraising and the Arts 279
Fundraising Plans 280
    Preparing Fundraising Plans 281
    Strategic Planning and Fundraising 281
    Profile and Audit 281
    Funding Pyramid 283
    Marketing and Fundraising 284
Fundraising Management 285
Background Work 285
    What Does the Organization Do? 285
    Staff and Board Participation 286
    Data Management 286
    Fundraising Costs and Control 288
Fundraising Techniques and Tools 288
    Individual Donors 289
    Corporate Giving 294
    Foundations 296
    Government Funding 296
Conclusion 298
Summary 299
Key Terms and Concepts 300
Questions 300
Case Study—Donors Increasingly Use Legal Contracts to
    Stipulate Demands on Charities 300
References 302
Additional Resources 303

13   Integrating Management Styles and Theories   304

Management Styles   304
 The Dysfunctional Arts Manager: A Model Rooted in Overextension   304
 The Analytical Manager: Changing the Culture   306
 The Systems Manager: Structure and Control   308
 The Organic Manager: Adjustment and Adaptation   309
Management Theories   309
 Process Management   309
 Human Relations   310
 The Open System   311
 The Contingency System: An Integrating Approach   311
The Management Functions   311
 Planning and Development   311
 Marketing and Public Relations   313
 Personnel Management: Staff, Labor, and Board Relations   314
 Fiscal Management   316
 Government Relations   316
Conclusion   317
Questions   318
Case Study—A Dramatic Disagreement: Did the Rep Have to Die?   318
Reference   323

14   Career Options and Preparing for the Job Market   324

Where the Jobs Are   324
Personal Choices and Selection Criteria   325
 Develop a Personal Plan   326
From the Employer's Perspective   326
Compensation Issues   326
Career Development Options   328
 Education   329
 Internships   330
Organizing Your Job Search   331
 Developing Your Résumé   331
 Developing Your Cover Letter   332
 Portfolios and Other Ways to Demonstrate Your Skills   334
 Interviewing   335
Getting Hired   335
Building a Career   336
 Career Goal   337
Career Development Work Plan   337
References   338

Index   339

Foreword

The process commonly thought of as "arts management" is, in essence, bringing artists and audiences together in as effective and efficient a manner as possible. As arts managers, we hope to provide opportunities for our artists to develop their work and flourish in a supportive and productive environment. We present the results of these labors to what we hope will be an audience eager and prepared well for the experiences.

It's not getting any easier. With each passing day, as new situations and new realities confront us, we need to eliminate the "hoped for" above and to produce results on a fairly consistent basis. As arts organizations face ever-increasing competition for attention, participation, and support on all fronts, arts managers are called upon to perform their roles at extraordinarily high levels of competence and to execute them as flawlessly as possible. The challenge can be overwhelming for ill-prepared or inexperienced managers. Today's best managers know not only the "nuts and bolts" of getting a performance onstage or an exhibition mounted; they also understand the theories and practicalities of the management process, the external and internal environmental challenges, the effect of organizational culture on operations, the challenge of change, and the opportunities and realities of strategic choices (as well as the consequences that come from not making choices). To be sure, many of us wish it were as simple as "Hey, Spanky, let's put on a show in the barn."

Management and the Arts is an important resource for today's arts managers, both inquisitive students of the field and seasoned managers. In this book, William Byrnes does more than simply introduce the fundamentals of management as they are applied to the arts and entertainment fields. He provides us with a context for the management process and helps us understand the implications of our actions as managers—the ripple effect on our institutions, our partners, and our stakeholders. As we have learned from other industries and our ever more connected and interdependent world, actions have impact far beyond the visible landscape and with more than the expected collaborators. This is no less true in the arts. And in this book Mr. Byrnes provides a well-constructed map for navigating through the intersecting, interwoven, and sometimes conflicting issues, strategies, and opportunities. Those interested in beginning a career in arts management could not ask for a better introduction to the field. Working professionals will develop additional confidence in their skills as they come to understand more of the theoretical underpinnings of their work.

As the struggle to fulfill our artistic missions without weakening institutional foundations intensifies, arts managers need every advantage they can get. *Management and the Arts* is a vital tool in confronting those challenges.

Dan J. Martin
Associate Professor, School of Drama
Director, Master of Arts Management Program
Carnegie Mellon University

Preface

When I first began teaching arts management, I had to use several textbooks to build the kind of interdisciplinary approach to the field I wanted. I set about writing this text with the goal of blending management theory and practice, economics, personnel management, marketing, and fundraising with the performing and visual arts. The focus of the book is on the process of managing an arts organization through integrating many different disciplines. After covering a brief historical perspective, we will examine all of the functional and operational areas involved in the business of running an arts organization. Our study will focus on performing arts organizations and museums.

This is an introductory text and is intended for use in an arts administration or theater management course. It is designed to give the student an overview of the evolving field of arts management while introducing key concepts in management, marketing, and fundraising. I have assumed that the student has had some course work in the arts, even if only at the introductory level. Although every topic may not receive all of the attention it deserves, it is hoped that the reader's interest in a specific topic will lead to an exploration of the other resources suggested at the end of most chapters. In the process of writing the third edition I found it necessary to revise and update many of the news items and illustrations. I have also reorganized the chapters on control, budgeting, economics, and financial management. Each chapter has questions that I hope will lead to more in-depth discussion on the material. I have tried to find case studies that offer thoughtful application of the material in many of the chapters. I have also added a chapter focused on issues related to developing a career in arts administration and management.

Finally, this text was written with the underlying belief that it is important to develop managers in the arts who have sensitivity, use common sense, and apply skills from disciplines such as business, finance, economics, and psychology. The central premise of this text is that an arts manager's specific purpose is to help an organization and its artists fulfill their mission and attain their articulated goals and objectives. This lofty-sounding purpose is grounded in the assumption that an effective arts manager helps bring to audiences or members the unique benefits of the arts experience. There are different ways to describe this experience. For example, when a musical note is sung or played perfectly, or a dance movement seems to defy gravity or triggers an emotion or creates a realization, we experience something unique. Sometimes a painting, sculpture, or photograph provides an indescribable pleasure as we stand there viewing it. When we go to the theater and witness a scene that is acted with such power and conviction that it gives us chills, we are enriched.

Working to bring these experiences to others is a worthwhile endeavor to pursue. Although this book makes no pretense of having all the answers about how best to go about maximizing the arts experience or operating the perfect organization, it is hoped that it will provide information and guidance about how an arts manager can be as effective as possible given the resources available. The information and ideas contained in this text are intended to be a springboard for developing your own schematic for leading and managing in the arts.

Organization of the Text

Chapter 1 provides an overview of types and levels of management found in arts organizations. The management process is also discussed.

Chapter 2 examines the historical origins of arts organization as well as profiles the evolution of arts management.

Chapter 3 introduces the reader to the evolution of management theory from ancient times to the present. The basic concepts of systems and contingency management are introduced.

Chapter 4 has been revised to reflect the many changes that have taken place in the world in the last few years. However, the focus of the chapter is still on the relationship of the arts organization to the many external forces that shape how our society functions today.

Chapter 5 begins the examination of the process of management by explaining strategic planning and the decision-making process. This chapter has been reorganized in an effort to better mirror the planning process.

Chapter 6 analyzes the principles of organizing and how organizations are designed. Organizational charts for several different types of arts organizations have been added. The concept of organizations as complex cultures is also discussed.

Chapter 7 integrates strategic planning with organizational design to show various methods for designing jobs, recruiting employees, selecting staff, and providing job enrichment.

Chapter 8 outlines the major concepts of leadership theory, including trait, behavior, and contingency leadership approaches, group dynamics, and behavior.

Chapter 9 has been revised and now covers management information systems and the budgeting processes required to effectively operate an arts organization. Concepts of control and resource allocation are introduced.

Chapter 10 has been reorganized and now includes what has been a separate chapter on financial management. This chapter examines basic economic concepts and financial management techniques as applied to the arts. Concepts in the areas of supply and demand are related to arts organizations. Current and classic studies of performing arts economics is also highlighted. Reading and understanding financial statements and the basics of financial planning are also discussed.

Chapter 11 reviews the basic principles of marketing. Marketing is related to the financial planning system and the overall strategic planning process of the organization. The concepts of a marketing audit, marketing management, segmentation, and audience development are discussed.

Chapter 12 focuses on ways that an organization can increase its revenues to meet its mission. The fundraising audit, strategic planning, working with different categories of funders, and the techniques of fundraising are discussed.

Chapter 13 develops approaches to integrating management styles, theories, and operations. Dysfunctional, rational, humanistic, and scientific management techniques are discussed.

Chapter 14 is new to this edition. An outline of strategies is provided to assist students with the process of developing a sustaining career in the field of arts management.

Most chapters conclude with a list of terms and concepts, discussion questions, a case study, and a list of references for further reading in related topics. Where possible I have tried to create illustrations that provide a visual map to the reader of the concepts discussed in the chapter.

A detailed course syllabus with additional project assignments is available by contacting me at wmjbyrnes@hotmail.com. I will also be happy to send instructors the answers to the dance company financial report used in Chapter 10. In addition, I always welcome suggestions, corrections, or questions about this edition of the book. Thank you.

Acknowledgments

Third Edition

I am once again grateful to many people who helped shape the third edition of *Management and the Arts*. First, I am eternally grateful for the support and patience of my wife, Christine, as I once again dove into four months of very intense writing and editing. The continuing support of the Florida State University School of Theatre for the Theatre Management MFA Program has also been invaluable. I'd also like to thank the many instructors from around the world who have sent me E-mail suggestions and requests for the assignment information. I hope I have been able to respond to your feedback with the changes in this edition. I particularly appreciate the assistance of Dr. Linda Donahue of Texas Tech University for her many suggestions for this edition. There is also a long list of people who helped with this edition. They include: Tony Archer, Susan Baldino, Stacy Dyer, Randi Goldstein, Kristen Mathias, Michelle McDaniel, Casey McEnelly, Joseph Patti, Jessica Sadowski, Ombra Sandifer, Russell Sandifer, Julie Shankle, Jean Simpson, Christine Stanley, and Tiffany Wilhelm. Finally, I want to thank Focal Press for their continued support of this book, and Diane Wurzel, Theron Shreve, Jodie Allen, and Harbour Hodder for actually turning all these words into a book.

Second Edition

First I'd like to thank the instructors and readers of the first edition for their feedback. I have tried to incorporate your many good suggestions in this new edition. The support of Florida State University and the School of Theatre has also been invaluable. Since arriving at FSU I have been fortunate to have the opportunity to serve as Director of the MFA Theatre Management Program and to work with many fine faculty and students in the Schools of Music and Visual Arts and Dance. The chance to teach graduate courses covering all aspects of operating an arts organization has proven very helpful in providing more depth to this edition. The assistance of the following FSU staff and students is deeply appreciated: Patricia Marshall, Dr. Deborah Martin, Dafna Kapshud, Randi Goldstein, and Jean Simpson. The United States Institute for Theatre Technology (USITT), one of the most successful nonprofit arts-related organizations in North America, also has provided a practical laboratory for applying the principles of managing an organization discussed in this book. In particular, I would like to acknowledge Christine Kaiser and Leon Brauner for their help as colleagues in what continues to be a very rewarding volunteer management experience. I'd also like to thank Marie Lee and Theresa Jadick at Focal Press for their guidance and assistance in navigating through the shoals of this edition.

First Edition

I would like to thank the people who assisted with this project. First, I owe much to my wife, Christine, for the many long hours she spent proofing my drafts and for her suggestions. My student assistant, Stephanie Goss, also was tremendously helpful in pulling together many of the sources used in this text and in handling the permissions. The ideas and suggestions of Steve Roth and Claudia Chouinard were a big help in the early stages of planning this book. I would also like to thank Professor James Zinser of the Oberlin College Department of Economics for his insightful advice; my daughter, Alison, for her help at the copying machine; Oberlin College for its help and resources; William Patterson and James Schempp for their many helpful comments on the early drafts; and last but not least, Sharon Falter, Kris Smead, and Pat McLaughlin and the staff at LeGwin Associates for their excellent work in producing this book.

Management
and the Arts

Management and the Arts

1

□ □ □ □ □

The Entertainment Business

By a unique combination of historical circumstances and the existence of what is often referred to as a market-driven or consumer-driven economy, the United States has created a multibillion-dollar entertainment industry that is a mix of large professional profit and many smaller professional and nonprofessional nonprofit fine arts businesses. Unlike many other nations, the federal government provides minimal direct support to the arts and entertainment industry in the United States. Some museums and many performing arts centers are owned by cities or states, but the vast majority of performing arts organizations, media companies, and sports teams are privately owned businesses, public companies with stockholders, or tax-exempt nonprofit corporations. Figure 1-1 provides an overview of the various types of organizations where one may find employment in arts management.

Both commercial popular entertainment and nonprofit businesses depend on admission sales and other investments for income and special tax breaks. For-profit arts organizations are able to take advantage of numerous laws that allow them legally to minimize their tax liability. Nonprofit organizations enjoy the additional benefits of being exempted from paying many taxes and being permitted to raise money through the solicitation of tax-deductible contributions.

The roots of the current system of profit and nonprofit arts businesses were established around the beginning of the twentieth century as advances in technology began to change the way people experienced entertainment. The new technologies created what would later be dubbed the *mass media audience*. People tuned in to the radio, went to the movies, and eventually stayed home to watch television, videotapes, and DVDs, or to be entertained by video games or computer software. In the later part of the twentieth century the concept of home entertainment centers built around ever-advancing computer technology allowed people even more entertainment options. In addition, family-oriented theme parks provide active entertainment experiences to millions annually with events and rides tied directly to film and television industry products. The profits attained by being able to package and distribute entertainment to millions of people led to the creation of an industry based on appealing to the broadest possible audience. Meanwhile, the live performing arts groups continued to face the inherent limitation of seating capacity and the rising costs of delivering the product. Fortunately, the rising levels of education, population, and income fed by unprecedented growth after World War II, along with contributions by individuals, foundations, corporations, and state and federal arts

1

Music
- Symphony Orchestras
- Choral Groups
- Music Festivals
- Chamber Groups
- College/University
- Community Groups

Theater
- Broadway
- Off & Off-Off Broadway
- Touring
- Regional
- Dinner Theater
- Children's Theater
- College/University
- Community

Opera
- Major Companies
- Regional Companies
- Touring
- College/University
- Community

Dance
- Major Ballet Companies
- Regional Dance Companies
- Modern Dance Companies
- Ethnic Dance Companies
- College/University
- Community

Museums
- Art/Science/History/Health/ Children, etc.
- Galleries
- College/University

Arts/Humanities Councils
- National
- State
- Regional
- Local

Presenting
- Booking Agencies
- Regional and Local Arts Presenters
- Colleges/Universities

Service Organizations
Representing and providing support
- Performing Arts Groups (Symphonies, Theater, Dance, Opera, etc.)
- Museums
- Arts Agencies
- Arts Presenters

Themed Entertainment
- Theme Parks Worldwide
- Regional and Local Theme Parks

Broadcast & Cable TV
- Major Companies and National Public TV and Radio
- Local Stations
- College/University Stations

Film Industry
- Major and Independent Companies
- Movie Theaters
- Distribution Companies
- Music Video Companies

Recording Industry
- Major Labels
- Independent Companies
- Recording Studios
- Popular Music Touring

These areas offer job opportunities for lower, middle, and upper level managers

Figure 1-1 Arts Managers and Administrators at Work

agencies, helped support the art forms abandoned by audiences for the mass media.

On paper, the future looks bright. For example, recent surveys by the National Endowment for the Arts (NEA), which has been responsible for helping to stimulate growth in the arts since its inception in 1965, found more than 12,000 performing arts organizations operating in America.[1] As recently as 2000, consumers spent more than $9.8 billion on admissions to performing arts events, $8.1 billion on tickets to motion pictures, and $9.3 billion on spectator sports in America.[2] According to the NEA, more than 2.1 million people were employed in artist or performer job categories in 2001.[3]

Profit-Making Ventures in the Arts

Much of this text is focused on the business of arts in the nonprofit structure. As you will see, managing effectively and being an effective manager is not determined by the type of organization where you work. As Figure 1-1 demonstrates, there are many different types of arts and entertainment organizations and companies seeking skilled managers. Popular music, theater, theme parks, television, multimedia companies, and the film and recording industry all need managers to help fulfill the primary purpose of the corporation. The entertainment industry is very concerned with this purpose—maximizing revenue and creating a profit. In fact, we live in a world that delivers the majority of the entertainment we watch or attend through a for-profit business structure. The example of the steps involved in producing a commercial theater production shown in Figure 1-2 is just one segment of a diverse and complex entertainment marketplace. Although the risks of failure are very high, there are still a substantial number of people willing to take the chance of making a profit from the hit show, popular event, or artist.

Growing Businesses

With the creation of new ways to experience live and prerecorded entertainment and the increase in wealth among the general population came the proliferation of both profit and nonprofit businesses designed to meet the rising demand for entertainment. Thousands of new jobs were created for managers as companies expanded their operations. Each of these enterprises needed people with special skills and knowledge to ensure that the product was created and distributed in a way that realized the organization's goals, as stated by the owners or boards of directors.

For-profit theater, film, television, videos, nightclubs, popular music, radio, and spectator sports are big businesses employing highly visible "stars" and hundreds of thousands of support people. A report published by Rand Research noted that over 20,000 companies were in the broadcast, publishing, or wholesaling business of delivering entertainment product in the United States.[5] The Rand total includes broadcasting and cable companies, film companies, and music stores.

Nonprofit professional arts organizations in theater, music, dance, and opera and nonprofit museums make up a great many of these organizations, providing year-round employment at all levels of management. There are also many smaller nonprofit amateur community groups in music, theater, and dance that often hire a manager to help administer the organization. As noted earlier, these two sectors of the entertainment market account for more than 2.1 million workers.

Producing Theater

As you can see in Figure 1-2, which is a schematic of the definitive text on the subject by Donald C. Farber,[4] there are six basic steps to producing a commercial theater production. First, you must decide why you want to do this production. This step is similar to the development of a mission and purpose statement in a not-for-profit organization. Next, you must obtain the rights to produce the event and develop the legal contracts with the author(s) or the holder of the rights to perform the work. At the same time that this is happening, you can be in the process of establishing your production company. Most theatrical ventures use the LLC or Limited Liability Corporation model to form a legally binding company. This model offers the best mix of tax advantages and simplicity. Of course, without the capital (the money) to produce the show, you will not go very far. There are dozens of contracts to be negotiated and signed with the actors, designers, and stagehands unions, and with the theaters. Eventually you complete the part of the process that most theater people are familiar with: casting, rehearsing, and designing sets, costumes, and the like.

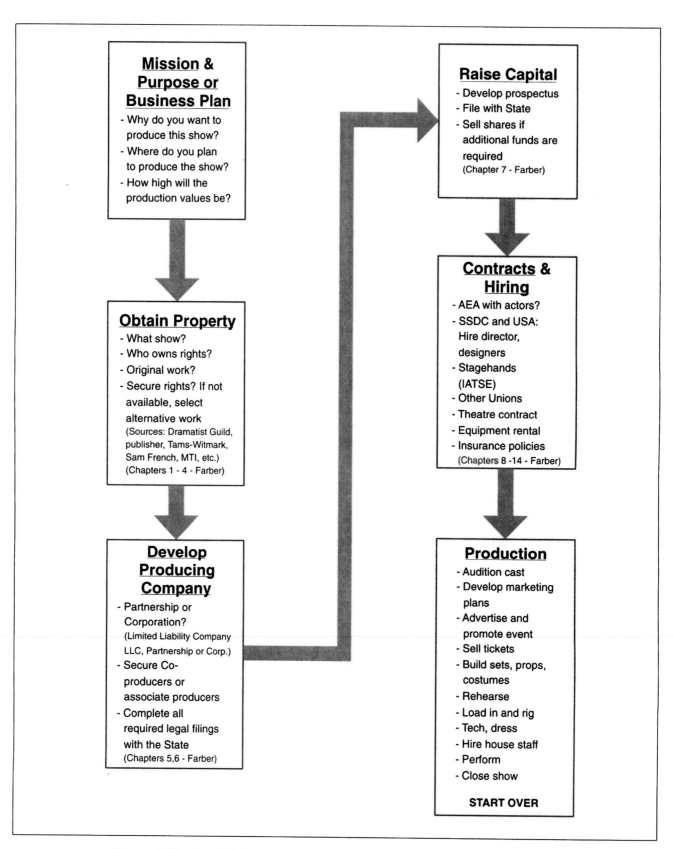

Mission & Purpose or Business Plan
- Why do you want to produce this show?
- Where do you plan to produce the show?
- How high will the production values be?

Obtain Property
- What show?
- Who owns rights?
- Original work?
- Secure rights? If not available, select alternative work
(Sources: Dramatist Guild, publisher, Tams-Witmark, Sam French, MTI, etc.)
(Chapters 1 - 4 - Farber)

Develop Producing Company
- Partnership or Corporation?
(Limited Liability Company LLC, Partnership or Corp.)
- Secure Co-producers or associate producers
- Complete all required legal filings with the State
(Chapters 5,6 - Farber)

Raise Capital
- Develop prospectus
- File with State
- Sell shares if additional funds are required
(Chapter 7 - Farber)

Contracts & Hiring
- AEA with actors?
- SSDC and USA: Hire director, designers
- Stagehands (IATSE)
- Other Unions
- Theatre contract
- Equipment rental
- Insurance policies
(Chapters 8 -14 - Farber)

Production
- Audition cast
- Develop marketing plans
- Advertise and promote event
- Sell tickets
- Build sets, props, costumes
- Rehearse
- Load in and rig
- Tech, dress
- Hire house staff
- Perform
- Close show

START OVER

Figure 1-2 Simplified Steps in Producing a Commercial Theater Production
References to chapter numbers in Donald Farber's *Producing Theatre*, 2nd rev. ed. (New York: Limelight Editions, 1997).

People working in the arts in turn contribute to the national economic system with their purchases of goods and services. The arts help to foster economic growth in communities across America. Chapter 10, "Economics and Financial Management," will elaborate on the economic impact of the arts.

Concerns about the Future

Despite a history of strong growth and development, many people in the arts are anxious about the future. Some of these concerns stem from the changing demographics in America and the preference among young people for recorded or electronic media as their source for entertainment. The question about where future audiences will come from is very much on the mind of arts managers. Others see the political pressure at the state and federal level to limit or reduce taxes as only further increasing the demand on limited resources. Government policy has become more focused on delivering essential services at the expense of what is often perceived as more marginal activities, such as supporting arts and cultural groups. Issues relating to censorship and conservative views about funding (see "Other Viewpoints") continue to have an impact on arts groups. The commercial entertainment industry is also concerned about the plethora of entertainment opportunities available

---

Other Viewpoints: The Arts Subsidy Challenged

As the following excerpt demonstrates, arts managers should not assume that everyone agrees that state, local, or federal governments should subsidize the arts. Dr. van den Haag has been a longtime critic of any subsidy for the arts.

Involuntary Patrons: Taxpayers' Rights versus Government Art
Dr. Ernest van den Haag

European governments have traditionally subsidized art and religion because both glorified God, king and country and helped governance: Art and religion were the principal means of indoctrination in social values before TV, radio and print. They were quite indispensable in forging the social bond that makes a nation. Subsidies have continued in Europe, although art and religion have become marginalized. It would be hard to imagine Italy without its cathedrals or its operatic performances.

They require subsidies; but they also bring in tourist dollars. In the United States art, mostly imported, never has become a central part of our social bond. Baseball is more like it—and does well without a federal subsidy.

Consider opera. (Exhibitions of paintings would do as well as an example.) Only a small proportion of Americans enjoy it. I do. Yet all taxpayers are forced to subsidize performances. I feel guilty every time I attend, thinking of the people whose taxes are used for my enjoyment, although they would rather use their money for their own enjoyment—perhaps to attend a Madonna concert (unsubsidized). Why is money taken from (low income) taxpayers to benefit (middle class) opera lovers? Congress forces taxpayers to subsidize my aesthetic preferences, because Congress thinks opera is good

for taxpayers (or paintings are) even if they don't attend (luckily they are not forced to).

Taxes are often spent on things individual taxpayers do not want. But defense, or police forces, unlike art, cannot be bought individually. They protect people whether they pay or not. To avoid "free riders" everyone must pay through taxes. However opera, concerts, paintings or poetry do not benefit those who do not attend, view, or listen. Why, then, should the voluntary non-beneficiaries be compelled to pay for those who benefit from art (or at least enjoy it)? Why should the non-beneficiaries, or non-enjoyers, not be allowed to spend their money on what they prefer?

SOURCE: Ernest van den Haag, "Involuntary Patrons," *Vantage Point* (the magazine of the Americans for the Arts) Spring 1990: p. 6. Excerpted with permission.

to consumers. In addition, rising production and salary costs are driving ticket prices up for live and recorded arts products.

New technology has permitted entertainment to become more personalized and miniaturized. The change from mass media to individual entertainment systems, coupled with the uncertain resources for arts in the schools, appears to many arts managers to be creating audiences with different attitudes about what they see and hear. Performers often note that people do not know how to "behave" at a concert, theater, dance, or opera event. Expanded education departments are now found in many arts organizations to help enhance the impact of the arts in a community.

The often-predicted dramatic increase in leisure time seems to have failed to materialize. With less leisure time available, consumers are making careful choices about how they spend their entertainment dollar. Many organizations also fear that too many arts groups are chasing too few patrons. Although many organizations agree that it is a sign of a thriving community to have many types of arts organizations existing side by side, they also recognize that their potential audiences only have so much money to spend on and donate to the arts.

In Chapter 4, "Arts Organizations in a Changing World," we will delve into a more detailed examination of the forces and trends that affect arts organizations. The development of trend analysis skills can prove to be very useful in plotting the future of an arts organization.

Managers and Organizations

This book will examine how the manager of the arts can use the processes of *planning, organizing, leading,* and *controlling* to facilitate the operation of an organization and fulfill its mission in these uncertain times. These *four functions of management* are the basis for the working relationship between the artist and the manager. Because most of the activity associated with the performing arts and with museums occurs through some type of organization, this text concentrates on management in a group environment.

Let's look now at a brief overview of the manager, the organization, and the process of organizing.

The Manager

In any organization, a *manager* is "a person who is responsible for the work performance of one or more people."[6] The manager's basic job is to organize human and material resources to help the organization achieve its stated goals and objectives. With this definition, a director, a stage manager, a lighting designer, a conductor, a choreographer, and a curator are all managers. The details of their job descriptions may differ, but the responsibility of getting others to do something is the same. Leadership skills are needed to effectively direct others to accomplish the work that must be done.

The Organization

Managers function within an *organization,* which has been defined as "a collection of people working together in a division of labor to achieve a common purpose."[7] This definition certainly describes the way we go about creating and delivering the artistic product in our world. Figure 1-3 shows how organizations interact with many external environments in a process of transforming their resources (inputs) to products or services. The output of an arts enterprise may be a performance or an exhibition. This *open system model*,[8] as it is called, is a graphic representation of how organizations interact with the world around them. The primary environments that affect all organizations are economic, political, cultural, demographic, and technological. Chapter 4, "Arts Organizations in a Changing World," examines the impact of each of these environments on organizations. As we will see, the survival and growth of an organization depend on its being able to adapt as these environments change. Managers of organizations must use all the skills and knowledge at their disposal because these environments are always presenting new opportunities and threats.

The Process of Organizing

As we will see in Chapter 6, "Fundamentals of Organizing and Organizational Design," the process of achieving the organization's goals and objectives requires that the manager actively engage in the process of *organizing*, which has been defined as "dividing work into manageable components."[9] Typical examples of organizing in the arts include a director working with a stage manager to develop a rehearsal schedule for a production, or a box office manager designing a staff schedule to cover the upcoming performances.

Levels of Management and Types of Managers

In any organization, there are different levels of management and different types of managers. Typically, organizations have operational, managerial, and strategic levels of management,[10] and line, staff, functional, and general managers or administrators.[11] (See Figure 1-4.)

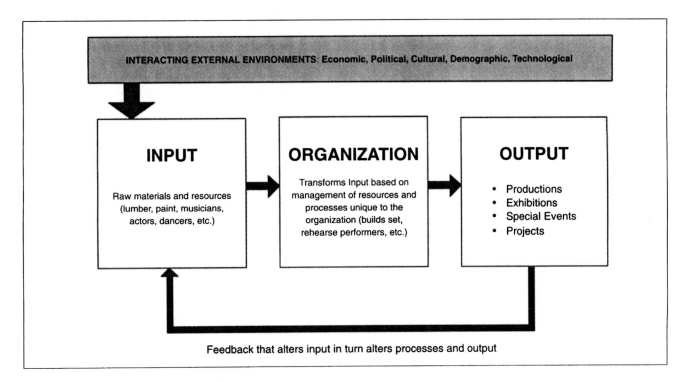

Figure 1-3 Organizations as Open Systems

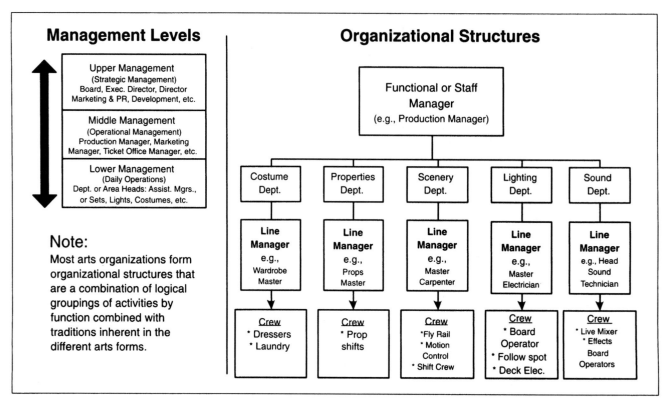

Figure 1-4 Management Levels and Organizational Structure

Levels of Management The *operational level* of management is concerned with the day-to-day process of getting the work done. The sets must be built, the museum guards must assume their posts, the rehearsal schedule must be posted, the membership renewals must be mailed, and the box office must sell tickets. The operations level is central to the realization of the organization's goals and objectives. Without the efficient and productive management of its operations, the organization faces extinction.

The *managerial level* is often called *middle management*, because it coordinates the operations and acts as a bridge between the operational and strategic levels of management. For example, the board of directors and the artistic director of a theater or dance company ask the production manager to evaluate the impact of adding a touring season to the company's schedule. If the plan is feasible, the production manager will have the task of coordinating the schedules, materials, and people required to initiate this program of activity. The managerial level usually functions in a one- to two-year planning cycle in the organization.

The *strategic level* of management, on the other hand, watches the overall operation of the organization with an eye toward constantly adjusting and adapting to the changing environments that affect the future of the organization while staying true to the mission. The goals and objectives are typically assessed annually. Planning also may extend into the future as much as three to five years, or beyond. The artistic director, general manager, general director, managing director, marketing director, or other similar senior level personnel are associated with this role.

In addition, strategic managers typically present these long-range plans to a board of directors. In most cases the board ultimately oversees the organization's mission and purpose.

Types of Managers   The arts have evolved unique types of managers to make organizations work. The types of managers listed in this section are found in different combinations in arts organizations, depending on the purpose and design of the organization. Each art form has specialized job titles and responsibilities.

The first type of manager is the *line manager*. This person is directly responsible for getting the product or service completed. The head carpenter, who supervises a stage crew, is a good example of such a manager. The head carpenter's job is to get the set up on stage and ready for the performance. The ticket office manager is another example of a line manager. This job typically entails supervising a group of staff responsible for the ticket and subscription sales for an arts organization.

Staff managers "use their special technical skill to support the efforts of the line personnel."[12] For example, the technical director in a performing arts group is usually given this responsibility. He or she coordinates the work of line managers such as the head carpenter or master electrician. Another example of a staff manager is the production manager. This person is given the responsibility of overseeing all of the production departments in an arts organization, such as scenery, lighting, costumes, props, and sound.

The *functional manager* has responsibility over a single area in the organization. For example, the production manager in a theater company oversees the production departments and therefore is both a functional manager and a staff manager. A company manager, who is responsible for the performers, is another example of a functional manager.

It is worth noting that because many arts organizations are understaffed, the roles played by the line, staff, and functional managers are often very blurry. As you will see in Chapter 7, "Staffing the Organization," job titles are often combined in arts organizations. For example, a manager may have the title of Marketing and Public Relations Director. These two functional areas are usually full-time jobs in themselves, but the lack of funds for managerial positions requires doubling up on work assignments. The lack of staff funding may also mean that there are no line managers or staff to work for the functional manager. For example, the Marketing Director and Public Relations Director may find themselves typing their own press releases and sending them to the media via E-mail.

General managers are found in more complex organizations with many functional areas. For example, the general manager of an opera company oversees production, marketing, fundraising, and administration for the organization.

Another managerial title often found in organizations is *administrator*. Although the administrator is really a manager, based on the definition of being responsible for the work efforts of one or more people, the title is often used in nonprofit or academic organizations to refer to someone empowered only to carry out functional tasks defined by others. Like the general manager, the administrator may not be given the authority to make plans or policies but is responsible for their implementation.

Management in Practice

The typical production process for a performing arts event provides a good example of management in practice. For example, a director or choreographer working to prepare a production or concert draws on many of the same techniques and principles applied every day in the highly competitive world of business. Practices such as teamwork, project management, and performance appraisal are fundamental ingredients in a show. The leadership skills of a director or choreographer determine how well the entire production will go. Preparing a production or concert is a group management effort and therefore requires careful attention to the changing, complex dynamics of the performers, designers, and production staff. Motivation levels must be maintained, conflicts must be resolved, and effective time-management skills are required if the show is to open on time and be of a high quality. In other words, the skills required to successfully create a performance event are the same skills required to run a successful business.

Common Elements in an Organization

Chapter 3, "Evolution of Management," examines the history and early management theories that influenced much of today's thinking about how to accomplish the objectives of an organization. Some of these theories apply to fundamental issues of organizational design and structure and are applicable to arts organizations.

A division of labor and some type of hierarchy exist in most organizations. The *division of labor* usually takes a form that matches the organization's function. A dance company has a different division of labor from an opera company for the simple reason that the processes and techniques used in preparing a performance are different. For example, many opera companies have a small permanent administrative and fundraising staff. The singers, orchestra, director, stage crew, and designers are hired to do a single show. Ballet companies, on the other hand, often have 30 or 40 dancers contracted for 40 weeks a year. They therefore require a different division of labor to meet the needs of a resident company of performers.

The *hierarchy of authority* in an organization is designed to ensure that the work efforts of the different members of the organization come together as a whole.[13] The typical hierarchy involves a vertical reporting, communication, and supervision system. Chapter 6, "Fundamentals of Organizing and Organizational Design," details various methods for organizing management systems.

In most arts organizations, which are small- to medium-sized businesses, the levels of management and the formality of the hierarchy are usually limited. However, as an organization grows in size and more staff are added, the levels of management increase, and the hierarchy tends to become more formal. A good arts manager is watchful of this development, especially if overly complex divisions of labor or a burdensome hierarchy begin to impede the accomplishment of the organization's goals and objectives.

An *informal structure* also exists in all organizations. No organizational chart or detailed plan of staff responsibilities is able to take into account all of the ways people find to work with each other. Employees often find new combinations of people to accomplish tasks that do not fit into the existing hierarchy or organizational design. Some organizations thrive on this sort of internal innovation; others become chaotic. Arts organizations often develop organizational designs aligned with functional areas. For example, the production staff, office staff, performers, and upper management develop structures to operate their own areas. The result is four organizations instead of one. At the same time, organizations, like people, can lapse into habitual behavior patterns. Tradition becomes the norm, and innovation is resisted. Again, the arts manager must keep an eye on the organization's formal and informal structure. Careful intercession can correct unproductive structures that develop.

Organizations are not neutral entities. They are microcosms of the society at large. Organizations are collections of individuals with beliefs, biases, and values. Unique myths and rituals are part of what is called an organization's *corporate culture* (see Chapter 6). Simply described, the corporate culture is how things are done in the organization. For example, the culture of the organization usually establishes values for such things as the quality and quantity of work expected. Some organizations have a positive culture that is communicated to employees. For example, managers might say, "Our stage crew is here to make things work, and their contribution is valued and recognized." In this situation, the overall culture of the organization values the labor of its employees. Other organizations have weak or destructive cultures. Phrases such as "The crew around here is always looking for a way to get out of work, and they are not to be trusted" signal a culture based on distrust and conflict. The founder-director organization, a model quite prevalent in the arts, can also help establish a strong culture imbued with the beliefs and values of one individual. Unfortunately, the departure of this person often leaves the organization adrift.

Any arts organization, no matter how small, is ultimately a complex mixture of behaviors, attitudes, and beliefs of the people who work there. Because people are the major resource used in creating an arts product, an organization will continue to be influenced and changed in ways that no one can predict. Interaction with external environments also affect the way people inside the organization think, feel, and behave. For example, changes in laws and the social system have led to the addition of multicultural programming and the hiring of more minorities in many arts organizations. (See Figure 1-5.)

Arts Organizations as Institutions
Arts organizations are learning to effectively integrate long-term strategic thinking while developing sensitivity to the changing environments that shape the beliefs and values of the entire culture. (See Figure 1-5.) Because the performing and visual arts are dependent on the creative explorations of individuals for the new material they present, the design and function of these institutions should be focused on looking toward what will be and not at what was. However, many artists perceive arts organizations as institutions that are more comfortable with the past. The creation of organizations in the performing and visual arts that look like imitations of corporations with executive directors, vice presidents, and associate directors is not universally seen as a good sign. Many artists are asking organizations to examine such fundamental questions as "What is our mission?" "Just what is it we are doing?" "What things are really essential to our mission?" "Whom do we serve?" "What do people think we do?" and "What are we really contributing to the

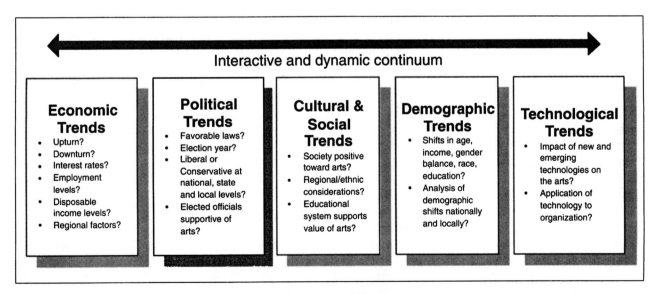

Figure 1-5 External Environments

community and our culture?" In some cases, artists are seeking a more entrepreneurial environment in which to work. They are finding that rigid structures and corporate models are not the most effective way to bring the audience and artist together.

The continual seeking of answers to artistic questions needs to be factored into the design and operation of the arts organization. The unique pursuit of an artistic vision, and the successful presentation of that vision to the public, needs as much attention and thought as any commercial business enterprise in the world.

The Management Process

The organization and systems described thus far are predicated on the assumption that there is an artistic product to manage. How does this product come into being? In many cases, an individual or a small group of people have the drive and energy to create something from nothing. For example, a playwright and director may team up to interest other people in a script. If people with money can be found to back the show, they hire performers and designers to bring the work to life. Sometimes, much less often than anyone cares to consider, the show is a hit. A long-standing love for opera may drive someone to start a regional opera company. Two dancers may decide that it is time to start their own company. They are tired of dancing someone else's choreography, and they have some ideas of their own that they would like to see performed. A group of visual artists may start a cooperative exhibition gallery and operate it themselves.

Whatever the circumstances, the success or failure of these artistic ambitions will be directly related to how well the four functions of management are fulfilled. Without proper planning, good organization, creative leadership, and some control over the enterprise and its budgets, the chance of success is greatly diminished. Obviously, projects and programs succeed in this world that do not master these four functions. Poorly planned, badly organized, weakly led, and inadequately controlled events happen all the time. The events that suffer from various forms of dysfunctional management make for great stories, but the human toll taken by such examples of bad management is precisely why good managers are needed in the arts. There is no benefit to the art form or the community if the very people who love the arts are destroyed by it.

It is important to remember, however, that a bad play, opera, musical, ballet, symphony, or exhibition cannot be made good by excellent management. If people do not respond to a work after all the rewrites and extra rehearsals, it does not matter how well it was managed. Ultimately, if there is no artistic vision behind the enterprise, then the chances for long-term success are greatly diminished.

We will take more time to examine the evolution of the arts and how arts managers fit into the entire process in Chapter 2. For now, let's consider the four functions and relate each of them to an arts application.

Planning

This first function of management is the hardest. Deciding exactly what it is we want to do, setting realistic goals (what the organization wants to accomplish), and then determining the objectives (the specific steps to take and the timetable for completing the tasks) to be used in meeting the goals are hard work.

The Four Functions of Management

- *Planning* is deciding what is to be done.
- *Organizing* is deciding how it is to be done and who is to do it.
- *Leading* is deciding how other people are to get it done.
- *Controlling* is deciding if it is or isn't getting done, and what to do if it isn't.

There are various sorts of plans. Some are short-range plans: What am I going to do tomorrow? Short-term plans usually don't present too much of a challenge for people. On the other hand, planning five years ahead can be an intimidating, if not impossible, task.

Organizations and people must plan because the world is constantly changing. Audience tastes and values change over time. The arts manager's job is to recognize the elements in the world around the organization that may pose new opportunities or may be a threat. Then the manager must work with the board and the artistic leadership to chart a course of action designed to guide the organization into the future.

For example, the artistic director of the ABC Opera Company reads in the newspaper that state funds for arts organizations to visit schools will soon be available. A goal is established to seek the funding and then implement a touring program in the next year because it relates directly to the organization's mission of bringing opera to the widest possible audience. The staff researches costs and benefits. A plan and the goals are drawn up and reviewed with the board. The board approves the idea and the company establishes a pilot program.

Organizing

Organizing is the process of converting plans into a course of action. Getting the people and resources together, defining the details, creating a schedule and budget, estimating the number of people needed, and assigning them their jobs is all part of organizing.

The ABC Opera Company, for example, sets up a special touring department. With the grant it obtains the company hires a director of touring and puts into place the details of the plan. For the first year, the company will have a small group of six singers tour 10 schools to perform scenes and hold opera workshops. Detailed schedules, contracts, and evaluation methods are established.

Leading

The third function of management requires getting everyone in the organization to share a vision of what can be accomplished if everyone works together. Leadership skill and effectiveness are highly prized attributes in any situation. For the arts manager, working with the highly self-motivated, independent-minded people often found in the arts offers a unique leadership opportunity.

After the ABC Opera Company touring staff is hired, the artistic director meets with everyone to clarify the project's purposes and goals. The director provides an overall timetable and explains where this new operation fits into the organization. The company's mission is recalled, and a challenge is issued to make this a quality touring program. The leader of the tour group provides the day-to-day guidance needed to make the project a success.

Controlling

The fourth function of management is concerned with monitoring how the work is proceeding, checking the results against the objectives, and taking corrective action when required.

After six months, the artistic director reviews the activities of the ABC Opera touring company and finds that bookings are down, singer turnover is high, and the budget for the year is almost gone. Meetings are held to pinpoint problems and consider solutions. Staffing changes are made, and the project is monitored on a weekly basis. After a year, many of the problems have lessened, and the touring project is having a positive impact on the community.

Functional Areas
When engaged in planning, organizing, leading, and controlling there are seven basic functions an arts manager fulfills:[14]

1. Planning and development
2. Marketing and public relations
3. Personnel management

Sample Statements of Core Values, Purpose, Mission, Goals, and Strategies

The Alliance Theatre Company is a professional resident theater organization located in Atlanta, Georgia. This 1998 document is an example of an arts organization articulating its mission, values, purpose, and goals. Kenny Leon, Artistic Director from 1989 to 2000 at the Alliance, played a key role in helping to shape this plan. Susan Booth, his successor, has continued to commit to diversity in her role as leader of the company.

Alliance Theatre Company Long-Range Plan

Core Values
Excellence, Creativity, Integrity, Diversity, Responsibility

Core Purpose
Connecting human beings through the live theatrical experience.

Mission Statement
The Alliance Theatre is dedicated to celebrating our diversity by building bridges, which can connect us as human beings through the development and production of exciting, entertaining, and stimulating plays, nurturing and enriching both the art, artists, and audience.

Goals
1. Artistic
  • Present a mix of classic and contemporary plays

which speak to the heart and illuminate the human condition.
  • Create an artistic environment that is rich, challenging, and alive through the research and development of new works.
  • Provide opportunities for individual artistic growth.

2. Audience
  • Increase paid attendance for all performances to 400,000.
  • Develop our core audience to consistently reflect the diverse multicultural profile of Metro Atlanta's five core counties (Fulton and contiguous counties).
  • Build a loyal and diverse subscriber base of 20,000 with an annual renewal rate of at least 75%.

3. Financial
  • Generate an annual operating surplus equal to at least 2% of total operating revenues.
  • Build our cash reserves up to $1.5 million by the end of FY03.
  • Add to our endowment funds an amount equal to

the Robert W. Woodruff endowment gift by the end of FY03.

Strategies
  • Produce and develop plays of consistently high artistic quality that attract our targeted audiences.
  • Use the income from the Robert W. Woodruff Foundation endowment gift and the additional funds raised to exclusively support our artistic product.
  • Provide maximum financial resources to develop "best-in-class" marketing and development activities.
  • Attract and develop competent, well-trained artists and professional staff, an active board, and a strong corps of volunteers that reflect the diverse, multicultural profile of Metro Atlanta's five counties.
  • Continue to develop strong education, outreach, and training programs that support and feed the company's overall programming.
  • Through Theatre for Young Audiences (TYA) identify, attract, and build a young, diverse, multicultural audience that is our audience of tomorrow.

SOURCE: Alliance Theatre Company, May 28, 1998. Used with permission.

4. Fiscal management
5. Board relations
6. Labor relations
7. Government relations

Planning and development are linked because arts organizations are always seeking ways to increase revenue to fund new programs and to pay for the inevitable increases in operating costs. Marketing and public relations provide the organization's most visible link to the community. Without a strong connection to the community the arts organization will find it difficult to attract audiences and donors. Good personnel management and labor relations are essential if the organization is to be productive. Neglect or abuse of the human resources available to a manager can disrupt the entire enterprise. Good fiscal management is critical if the organization's planning, marketing, and fundraising efforts are to succeed. In addition, donors prefer to make contributions to organizations that show they know how to manage their financial resources. As with personnel relations, an arts manager must effectively work with and report to a board of directors. The board and the management may sometimes have a different set of priorities. Until the differences are resolved, the organization will find it difficult to meet its goals and objectives. Finally, government relations, which includes the local, state, and national levels, grow more complex each year. New laws are passed or court rulings are enforced that change the way an organization does business. These types of changes typically add to the expenses of the organization.

Throughout this text, we will examine how external environments and internal organizational dynamics make the task of being a manager in the arts a challenging and demanding job. The almost endless variety and changing circumstances in the world around the arts organization keep the manager's job from ever getting dull or routine.

Key Terms and Concepts

Review these terms from the chapter and begin to incorporate them into your day-to-day thinking about management and the arts.

Manager
Organization
Organizing
Open system model
Levels of management: operational, managerial, strategic
Types of managers: line, staff, functional, general, administrative
Division of labor
Hierarchy of authority
Formal and informal structures
Corporate culture
Functions of management: planning, organizing, leading, controlling
Functional areas of work for an arts manager: planning and development, marketing and public relations, personnel management, fiscal management, board relations, labor relations, government relations

Questions

1. Are you aware of any arts organizations that have been particularly successful or have faced difficulty in your community? Outline

the situation, and explain why you think the organization did well or faltered.

2. Can you recall a particular work situation you have been in that was either positive or negative as a direct result of the manager in charge? What type of manager was this person (line, staff, functional)? What made this manager effective or ineffective?

3. Do you agree or disagree with the author of the "Involuntary Patrons" article? Why? Do you agree that art "never has become a central part of our social bond" in America? The author argues that because the arts are not available to everyone, subsidies are inappropriate. What is your opinion?

4. List some examples of how you "manage" your life. Have you used any combinations of the management functions of planning, organizing, leading, or controlling to achieve objectives you have set for yourself?

Selecting a Project Organization

Over the course of the semester select an arts organization and request (or download) a copy of its mission statement, bylaws, and other relevant planning documents (for example, a five-year plan) for a discussion in class. Based on the topics covered in this chapter, answer the following questions:

1. Is the organization fulfilling its stated mission? If yes, how? If no, why not?

2. Is the organization facing financial problems? Did it have a deficit or surplus in the last budget year?

3. Based on the information gathered, is it possible to ascertain if this is a well-managed organization? If yes, what evidence supports this position? If no, what are the management areas that need improvement (planning and development, marketing and public relations, personnel management, fiscal management, board relations, labor relations, government relations)?

References

1. NEA Research Division Note #62 (Washington, D.C., 1998).
2. NEA Research Division Note #79 (Washington, D.C., April 2002).
3. NEA Research Division Note #80 (Washington, D.C., May 2002).
4. Donald C. Farber, *Producing Theatre* (New York: Limelight Books, 1997).
5. Kevin McCarthy, Arthur Brooks, Julia Lowell, and Laura Zakaras, *The Performing Arts in a New Era* (Santa Monica, CA: Rand, Inc., 2001), p. 68.
6. John R. Schermerhorn, Jr., *Management for Productivity*, 2nd ed. (New York: John Wiley & Sons, 1986), p. 7.
7. Ibid., p. 8.
8. Ibid., p. 8.
9. Ibid., p. 161.
10. James H. Donnelly, Jr., James L. Gibson, and John M. Ivancevich, *Fundamentals of Management*, 7th ed. (Homewood, IL: BPI-Irwin, 1990), pp. 28–29.

11. Schermerhorn, *Management for Productivity*, pp. 13–15.
12. Ibid., p. 13.
13. Ibid., p. 12.
14. Paul DiMaggio, *Managers of the Arts*, Research Division Report #20, NEA (Washington, D.C.: Seven Locks Press, 1987).

2

□ □ □ □ □

The Evolution of Arts Organizations and Arts Management

In 1826 John Turnbull, President of the American Academy of the Fine Arts, proposes to President John Quincy Adams a "Plan for the Permanent Encouragement of the Fine Arts by the National Government."

From the NEA, "Brief Chronology of
Federal Support for the Arts," 2000

In this chapter, we review the evolution of arts organizations. After examining the basic model used to establish a nonprofit arts organization in America, we will study the evolution of the job of an arts manager. We explore how the responsibilities have changed to meet the increasingly complex demands placed on arts organizations and artists, and we also touch on the impact the National Endowment for the Arts has had on the arts scene in the United States. The chapter concludes with an examination of the national network of performing arts centers in communities and on university campuses in the United States.

The Artist-Manager

For more than 2,000 years, the artist-manager has been the person who created and arranged the meeting of artist and public. Creative drive, leadership, and the ability to organize a group of people around a common goal remain the foundation on which all arts management is built. The traditional role of the artist-manager has been split into separate jobs to better cope with the increasingly complex demands placed on managers. However, this split does not mean that a division or barrier must be erected between these two roles. Instead, the separation should be viewed in much the same way as the human brain functions: the two hemispheres are linked and communicate with each other while each side continues to do what it does best.

The Arts as Institutions

One result of the political and social upheaval of the last 400 years has been the establishment of institutions designed to provide continuing support and recognition for the artist and the arts. In much of the world, the performing arts are part of a state-supported system and are operated by resident managers with extensive administrative staffs. Performing and visual arts centers for opera, dance, theater, and music as well as museums reserved exclusively for art, history, and science are integral parts of many communities in the world.

In the United States, token governmental backing for the arts is a recent phenomenon. Fund-matching grants, special project support, and a taxation system designed to promote deductible donations by individuals and corporations continue to be the extent of government involvement in the arts. More recently, in the last hundred years, the U.S. government opted for an alternative system that encouraged the creation of tax-exempt, nonprofit corporations to supply and distribute the arts and culture in society.

The increasing complexity of an industrially based society hastened the shift from the artist-manager as the dominant approach to organizing and presenting the arts. As many communities began to establish arts institutions late in the nineteenth century (e.g., museums, symphony orchestras), year-round management experts began to emerge. Many arts institutions now appear to be organized along patterns similar to large business corporations.

Today, the role of the artist and the manager and the degree of control each has over his or her respective domains vary from art form to art form. Many small arts organizations are still created and managed by artist-managers. However, the norm is a corporate structure with a board of directors and multiple levels of staff arranged in a hierarchy.

A Brief Historical Overview

Let us examine some selected points in Western history to trace the development of the management function in the arts. As has been noted, the artist-manager is a well-established pattern in the arts. Although this pattern of management has not changed much in the last 2,000 years, the demands placed on this individual have increased to the point where the artist-manager position is now only one of many ways to organize the presentation of arts events.

Ancient Times

As the centers of civilization grew, so did those functions we associate with the arts. The first examples of performance management were the public assemblies associated with religious rites in early societies. These performances were "managed" by the priest and were enmeshed in the fabric of a society. The theatrical trappings of costumes, dramatic settings, music, movement, and so on, all supported and heightened the event. Ultimately, though, these events were not an expression of the creative drive of a people, but rather a way of controlling and molding a culture. However, these staged events did provide a model for organizing large-scale public gatherings.

The beginnings of a system of state-sponsored play festivals can be traced to the Greeks around 534 B.C.E. These festivals required the management skills of planning, organizing, leading, and controlling, much as they do today. Typically, a principal magistrate, the *archon eponymous*, supervised the production of the play festivals sponsored in Athens. Financial support came from the richer citizens (*choregoi*), and the cities provided the facilities. The playwright functioned as the director and had something akin to total artistic control over the show.[1]

Museums were very much a part of the Greek culture. The word *museum*, in fact, comes from "the Greek *mouseion*, a temple of the muses."[2] Neil Kotler and Philip Kotler note that the early museums in places like Alexandria "functioned as a scholar's library, a research center, and a contemplative retreat."[3] Ancient Rome often displayed collections of items taken through military campaigns. The Catholic Church also amassed a considerable collection of art.[4]

The Romans produced state-sponsored arts festivals as part of an overall cycle of public events throughout the year. City magistrates were responsible for screening and coordinating the entertainment for their communities. The managers (*domini*) acted as producers, bringing the play and the performers to the festivals. These early managers arranged all the elements needed for the production with the financial support of the local magistrate. According to research in theater history, as many as 100 days a year were committed to the various theater festivals of ancient Rome. If this schedule is indeed true, a great deal of managerial skill must have been required to coordinate and produce these events.[5]

With the decline of Rome came the dissolution of the state-sponsored festivals. The breakup of the Empire did not mean that all artistic activity came to a halt. However, the transition into the Middle Ages left society without a developing dramatic literature to generate works for performance. The disappearance of organized financing and facilities also made it impossible to sustain an ongoing arts community. Performance groups therefore resorted to touring as a means of survival. The management of the troupe was done by a member of the performing group. Smaller-scale community festivals helped provide opportunities for the itinerant artists to eke out a living. On the whole, Western history has not provided much evidence of significant artistic activity in Europe during this time.

Other cultures were, of course, developing indigenous forms of music, dance, and theater. The arts were very much a part of Byzantium, India, and China. While Europe was struggling, other cultures were establishing forms of dance, theater, music, and visual arts that are with us today. Varying degrees of state and private sponsorship were involved. The role of the manager did not radically differ in these cultures because the functions required to organize and coordinate arts events were the same.

The Middle Ages

The Church was the producer of many sanctioned performances during the Middle Ages. The performance of liturgical drama, which served as a type of religious instruction, originally resided within the management structure of the Church. As communities developed and the overall economic environment improved, this drama moved outdoors and became part of public pageants and festivals, using stages mounted on portable wagons. Nonliturgical drama and various forms of popular entertainment, such as jugglers and mimes, were part of a rebirth of performance.

By the fourteenth century, the Church had little control over the proliferating performances. A system of patronage and sponsorship by the trade guilds led to an expanding role for the manager-director.

Historian Oscar Brockett notes that during the fifteenth and sixteenth centuries:

> Complex productions required careful organization, for the handling of casts that sometimes included as many as 300 actors, of complex special effects, and large sums of money could not be left to chance. Consequently, the director (or stage manager, or pageant master) was of considerable importance. Often this position was given to a member of the guild, but in some instances a "pageant master" was put under contract for a number of years at an annual salary. The pageant master secured actors, arranged rehearsals, and took charge of every phase of production.[6]

The Renaissance

The continuing surge of the arts was dramatic throughout the Renaissance. The social, political, economic, and cultural environments were undergoing changes that fundamentally altered people's perceptions of the world. The rediscovery of the Greeks opened up the creative spirit of the times. During the fourteenth to sixteenth centuries, neoclassical theater began to flourish, opera and ballet were born, and the role of the arts manager burgeoned.

In opera, theater, and dance, the expansion of literature was accompanied by the construction of performance spaces that took advantage of the new stage technology of the time. This in turn led to the rise of stage crew specialists in such areas as rigging, lighting, special effects, and costumes. The coordination required of the increasingly complex productions helped solidify many of the traditional roles in backstage operations and management.

In the late sixteenth century, opera was born in Italy out of the *intermezzi*, which was a form of entertainment that occurred between the five-act dramas of the time. In 1594, the first opera, *Dafne*, authored by Ottavio Rinuccini and Giulio Caccini, music by Jacopo Pevi, premiered and laid the foundation for an entire art form.[7]

The court dance of the thirteenth and fourteenth centuries helped forge a path for the creation of ballet. The court "dance masters of the [fourteenth and fifteenth centuries] began to develop a theory of dance instruction that systematized its various movements and styles."[8] The first ballet, *Ballet Comique de la Reine*, was performed in 1581 in the court of Henry III of France.[9] As with opera, specialized production and management techniques evolved over the centuries to support the art form.

Private collections of art work and artifacts were being built during this time. However, access to the collections was very limited. Public museums did not become popular until the eighteenth century.[10]

As is the case today, finding financial support was an ongoing activity of the early artist-managers. Church support, royal patronage, and shareholder arrangements were the chief means of financing work. The shares sold to people helped provide the resources needed to pay for salaries and production support. Management functions were expanded to include overseeing the distribution of any profits to the shareholders.

The other major problem that managers and artists grappled with was censorship. Throughout history, the performing and visual arts have had to contend with varying degrees of control from both the church and the state. The selection of plays, the access to performance spaces, and sometimes even the selection of performers have been subject to severe constraints. The arts manager is often placed in the middle of the battle between an artist seeking an avenue of expression and a state or religious group attempting to suppress the work. We see the legacy of the sometimes uneasy relationship between the arts and society in the continuing controversy over the reauthorization of the National Endowment for the Arts.

The Seventeenth through Nineteenth Centuries

In many European countries during this time, the arts continued to grow and flourish. Playwrights, directors, composers, musicians, dancers, and singers found work in newly created companies and institutions. In France, the theater, opera, and ballet companies were being organized in state-run facilities, and the performers received salaries and pensions. Germany established a state theater by 1767. It became the foundation for a national network of subsidized arts institutions. England also had a thriving performing arts community. The Education Act of 1870 and the Local Governments Act of 1888 helped promote the growth of museums and performing arts facilities throughout Great Britain.[11] British support for museums was well-rooted in the nineteenth century. However, the first Arts Council in England was not created until 1945.[12] Throughout the seventeenth to nineteenth centuries, especially on the Continent, the formalization of management structures and systems to operate the state theaters solidified the role of the arts manager.

In the United States, theatrical presentations were made up of touring groups performing varied programs in cities across the nation. The development of the railroad system in America assisted with the spread of touring groups and artists in the eighteenth and nineteenth centuries. The local theater venue often contained stock sets that were used by the performers, who brought their own costumes. The expanding rail system of the mid-nineteenth century helped support an extensive touring network of performing groups. Companies were formed and disbanded almost constantly, and no permanent theater companies were established. The management structure was dominated by the producers and booking agents who arranged the tours. The control of most theaters eventually fell into the hands of these booking agents. A monopoly known as *The Syndicate* controlled what was available for viewing around the country. This monopoly was supplanted by another group of theater owners, the Shuberts. The Shubert brothers created a management dynasty that lasts to this day.[13]

Unlike the impermanent theater, symphony orchestras and opera companies began to secure a more stable place in the larger metropolitan areas in the United States. For example, the support of wealthy patrons made it possible to establish symphony orchestras in New York City (1842) and Boston (1881). Opera, which had been performed in the United States since early in the eighteenth century, found its first home in the Metropolitan Opera in 1883.[14] Dance was often included in touring theatrical productions in the eighteenth and nineteenth centuries. European dance stars also regularly toured the country. However, permanent resident dance companies were not a regular part of the arts scene until the twentieth century.[15]

Museums developed in a uniquely American style according to Kotler and Kotler. As they point out, "The great majority of U.S. Museums, by contrast, were created by individuals, families, and communities to celebrate and commemorate local and regional traditions and to enlighten and entertain people in the local communities."[16] They point to a city like Charleston, South Carolina, as a site of an early American museum (1773).

The Twentieth Century

The role of management increased as the continued growth of the arts accelerated. Despite two world wars, European arts institutions expanded into smaller communities, developing national networks of performing spaces and providing jobs for managers and artists. Seasons expanded, repertories grew, and new facilities were constructed—especially after World War II—in an overall environment of support from the government. As noted, England eventually established a state-supported system for the arts after the war.

In Europe and the United States, the new technologies of radio and film significantly changed attendance patterns at live performance events. The theater in the United States, for example, saw a rapid decline in attendance by the 1920s.[17] Because there were no resident theater companies, it was difficult to keep a loyal audience base such as existed for the few opera and symphony groups in the country.

The rise of the off-Broadway and regional theater system helped renew the theater and, at the same time, helped build a base for what were to become established organizations. The more experimental, but still profit-driven, off-Broadway system was born in the early 1950s. The nonprofit regional theater network was built from the Barter Theater in Virginia (1932), the Alley Theatre in Houston (1947), the Arena Stage in Washington, D.C. (1950), and the Actor's Workshop in San Francisco (1952). These theaters formed the nucleus of the new distribution system for theater in America.[18] The need for good managers escalated in the professional world, and because of the unprecedented baby boom after the war, the educational system—especially colleges and universities—expanded offerings in the arts. Community and campus performing arts centers helped establish a new network for touring and provided local groups with venues to use. Managers were needed to operate the new multimillion dollar complexes and to book events throughout the year.

Opera first spread beyond New York into the major metropolitan areas of Chicago, San Francisco, Philadelphia, St. Louis, and New Orleans. However, after the Great Depression, only New York and San Francisco were able to hold onto their companies.[19] The support in the 1950s from the Ford Foundation helped bring opera to the American arts scene. By the early 1970s, 27 opera companies were in operation.[20] Today, the Central Opera Service reports that there are over 110 major opera companies in existence. Part of this growth was due to the NEA's matching grant programs, which enabled many companies to professionalize their management.

Until the early 1960s, dance companies were in limited supply in the United States. The American Ballet Theatre, the New York City Ballet, and the San Francisco Ballet topped the list of professional companies. Ballet West in Utah and Ruth Page's dancers, who were associated with the Chicago Lyric Opera, offered regular programs with their semiprofessional companies.[21] At the same time, modern dance companies were being operated on very tight budgets by such pioneers as Martha Graham, Alvin Ailey, Merce Cunningham, José Limon, and Paul Taylor. Their staff resources and their seasons were very limited.

The Ford Foundation in the 1960s and the NEA in the 1970s helped create a new national support system for ballet and later for modern dance. Although these groups still struggle, there are now more than 400 dance groups that operate, according to data collected by the NEA in 1992.[22]

Symphony orchestras have also grown in number over the last 30 years. According to the NEA, in 1992 there were 349 symphony orchestras and 130 chamber music organizations in the United States.[23] It is also estimated that in 1992 there were 3,105 U.S. museums and art galleries, 2,749 of which were tax-exempt.[24]

In 1846 Congress accepted a bequest of the late James Smithson that led to the establishment of the Smithsonian, one of America's premiere museums.[25] Business leaders and later philanthropists such as Andrew Carnegie, Marshall Field, and Julie Rosenwald helped found museums and libraries in the late nineteenth century in cities such as New York and Chicago. These museums continued to evolve and grow in the twentieth century to become the major cultural institutions we know today.[26]

The expansion period in the arts seems to be slowing now that most communities have established visual and performing arts institutions. The long-term struggle for operating funds has been accelerated in recent years as competition for support has increased. Additional funding from the state and federal government appears to be an unrealistic expectation. Demand is increasing for resources to assist with social programs, medical research, and education. Foundation, corporate, and individual support is being tapped by increasingly sophisticated fundraisers from hospitals to day-care centers. Meanwhile in Europe, the government subsidy is being reevaluated. Ironically, the model being adopted is the U.S. approach of private and public support for the arts. Performing and visual arts organizations are scrambling to develop the expertise to become successful fundraisers to maintain their current levels of operation. In England, for example, bitter battles have been fought over the level of government support for the arts. England has recently shifted funding to the arts from lottery sales. In some cases this has proven to be a boon to arts organizations. Lottery funding has also gone to support projects that extend beyond the traditional scope of fine and performing arts funding.

The Modern Nonprofit Arts Organization

In the twentieth century the development of arts organizations was fueled by changes in the tax laws and requirements for establishing businesses that were designated to serve a public good or fill a need not met by the overall economic system. Let us take a look at the steps required for starting a nonprofit business, and then focus on what is required to establish an arts organization. The sidebar "In Practice: Writing a Business Plan" provides a practical example of how to go about starting an arts organization.

Legal Status and Financial Statements

When a business or arts organization starts up, it may be owned and operated by one individual. The founder-director often operates from home—or even from a car. However, once the operation grows to the point that a staff and office space are required, it may be time to incorporate the enterprise. Individual artists may also incorporate to gain some specific tax advantages. In many areas of the country, the group Volunteer Lawyers for the Arts helps individuals and organizations with the incorporation process. (For more information, go to http://www.starvingartistlaw.com.)

Incorporation

The major reason why an individual or organization decides to legally incorporate is to provide protection for the people who operate the business. Without the protection of incorporation, the owner is legally responsible for all debts incurred and may be sued personally. A legal settlement against an individual might mean that all personal assets would have to be sold to pay the organization's debts.

In the case of most arts organizations, filing for incorporation as a nonprofit business (or any business, for that matter) is fairly straightforward. Provided that the proper papers are filed, the state bestows upon the organization the legal right to operate. Filing for exemption from state and local taxes requires additional paperwork. Filing for incorporation is usually covered under the operational procedures established by the Secretary of State. Forms and detailed instructions on filing are usually available on the Website for the Secretary of State. Typically, you need to provide the following:[27]

- Official name of the organization
- Purpose or purposes of the organization
- Scope of activities (if you are filing for tax exemption, it will limit what you can and cannot do)
- Membership provisions (if any)
- Name of the person registering the incorporation and the place of business
- Names and addresses of the incorporators and the initial board of directors (if any)
- How any assets will be distributed when the corporation is dissolved

Additional legal regulations may affect nonprofit corporations, including business or occupation licenses and state or local charitable solicitation licenses. Incorporation and nonprofit status, if accompanied by tax exemption, empowers the organization to raise funds. Vending licenses may also be required if you plan to sell items through a gift shop.

Tax Exemption

Exemption from local, state, and federal taxes does not automatically come with nonprofit incorporation. The Internal Revenue Service (IRS) Code, section 501(c)(3), exempts charitable organizations and public and private foundations from paying taxes on net earnings. However, an organization must still pay some taxes. In addition to payroll taxes, for example, a sales tax must be collected if the organization operates a gift shop. The IRS has many tax-exempt categories that cover social welfare organizations such as the League of Women Voters (501,c,4), and even cemeteries (501,c,19).

When applying for tax-exempt status, financial data for the current fiscal year and the three preceding years will be requested. If the organization is just getting started, the current year's budget and a proposal for the next two years will be accepted. A form that fixes the organization's fiscal year (e.g., July 1 to June 30) is also required.

To qualify for tax-exempt status, the organization must be operated for a purpose allowed by tax law. The exemption status is bestowed upon organizations that fulfill some of the following purposes: religious, charitable, scientific (research in the public interest), literary, educational, or testing for public safety.

Arts organizations typically are founded under the education category. The organization purpose is typically stated in terms such as "Increase appreciation and awareness of" the arts form such as chamber music, Shakespeare, or ballets. In addition, there are restrictions pertaining to making a profit from enterprises not directly related to the exempted purposes of the organization. These activities will be subject to the *unrelated business income tax* (UBIT). For example, if an arts organization starts acting as a travel agent and sells bookings for cultural cruises, the IRS might rule that this is unrelated to the organization's stated mission, and any surplus revenue from this activity would be subject to income taxes. Certain lobbying and propaganda activities are also prohibited by law.

A 501(c)(3) organization is not restricted from making a profit. As long as the profit-making relates to the stated purpose of the organization, net earnings (profit after deducting expenses for operations, programming, salaries, and benefits) may be accrued and retained. However, these earnings may not be distributed to members of the organization or the board of directors. Net earnings are usually placed in endowment funds or a restricted account and then put to use in a manner that helps fulfill the mission of the organization.

As should be expected, the rules and regulations contain a significant amount of fine print. Hiring a lawyer, using legal services donated by a board member, or contacting the Volunteer Lawyers for the Arts is a prerequisite to filing the incorporation papers.

Once an organization has attained the legal status to operate, it is obligated to provide reports and documentation to local, state, and federal agencies. The organization is also required to file forms related to Social Security taxes and withholding taxes, and to file tax forms with the IRS that list revenues, expenses, and changes in net assets (the nonprofit organization's equivalency of worth, which is often called a Fund Balance). The details of the organization's liabilities, assets, programmatic activities, revenues, donations, and expenses for the previous four years must be filed every year. We will review these business operation details in Chapter 9, "Organizational Controls and Budgets," and Chapter 10, "Economics and Financial Management."

A financial management information system and a person designated to oversee this important area become vital once the organization reaches the level of legal incorporation. The preparation of required reports—such as a balance sheet, a statement of account activity, and a financial statement of the worth of the organization—is also required. (See Chapter 10.) In addition, the organization's finances must be in order to the degree that an outside auditor can analyze the financial operation. A complete audit, which can be very costly, is often required.

In Practice: Writing a Business Plan

What steps do you need to take if you want to start up an arts organization? The following is a sample of an arts-focused business plan. The business section of your local bookstore will contain sources on writing a business plan. Potential financial backers or donors from the business community know what a business plan is and have expectations about how the document should be organized.

The area covering the financial plan is typically most important and is critical to developing the initial support to build your board of directors and to secure startup donations.

Business Plan for an Arts Organization
Outline of a Modified Business Plan

1. Title Page

2. Table of Contents

3. Executive Summary—Summarize the major points of the entire plan so that prospective board members, donors, and community or government members will be able to grasp what is being contemplated (two pages maximum, if possible).

4. Vision/Mission/Goals Statement
   • Vision Statement
   • Mission Statement
   • Major goals and objectives for years 1 through 5 (3 to 5 goals maximum)
   • How will the organization serve and enhance the quality of life in your community?

5. Organization Overview
   • Describe how you will be organized (a small business operated in a house, etc.).
   • Incorporation papers as per your state.
   • Bylaws—use standard bylaws customized for your organization.
   • Organizational chart.

6. Market Analysis and Marketing Plan
   • Present your research about how your organization is uniquely qualified to provide what is missing in your community.
   • Who are the "customers" for what you have to offer?
   • What is the demographic profile of your potential audience?
   • Expectations you have about who and how many people will purchase tickets, subscriptions, or memberships.
   • How will you advertise (through expenditure) or publicize (for free) who you are and what you do? How will you develop your audience or membership base, attract customers, or develop new audiences for your organization?

7. Operations Plan
   • Overall description of how the organization will run on a daily basis.
   • Job descriptions of management and staff.
   • Employee Policy Handbook.

8. Financial Plan
   • Explanation of sources of revenue and description of expenses. How will you finance the startup of the organization? (For example, donations, grants, special local economic incentive supports, small business loans, and so forth.)
   • First-year Operating Budget—Your startup budget may have large capital outlays for equipment, or you may need to detail donations of equipment and space you anticipate receiving.
   • 12-month cash-flow statement for year 2.
   • Projected operating budget for years 2, 3, and 4.

9. Appendix (optional)—You may need to supplement your plan with additional supporting materials or research that helps make the case that your organization is needed and that your organization is uniquely capable of solving the problems you have identified as needing solutions. Information (probably from the World Wide Web) should be clearly organized for the reader to look up your sources.

Profile of the Arts Manager

The growth in the arts over the last 30 years has created a tremendous demand for managers at all levels and in all disciplines. Unfortunately, arts managers are not clearly identified as a work group when counting the over 2.1 million people employed in all aspects of the arts. The Census Bureau counts performers, architects, composers, printmakers, and instructors in the arts but does not include people in arts management, sales, consulting, or promotion or public television employees.[28] Whether or not the people who do not directly make art were counted in the census data, they are obviously a central part of the culture industry in the United States.

One source that provides substantial information on the arts manager is Paul DiMaggio's 1987 book, *Managers of the Arts*. Originally created for the NEA under the official title *Research Division Report #20*, the book outlines the background, training, salaries, and attitudes of arts managers in theater, orchestra, and museum management and community arts associations.

Unfortunately, DiMaggio does not include data about opera or dance managers. In addition, the survey was conducted in 1981, which may make the data somewhat irrelevant to today's market. DiMaggio's book only samples a limited number of people. With these limitations in mind, let us take a look at some of the highlights of this report (Figure 2-1).

DiMaggio's book reveals the following profile of arts managers: they are upper-middle class, highly educated individuals who either majored in the subject they are managing or were humanities majors in English, history, or foreign languages. DiMaggio found that a limited number of managers had management or arts management degrees. The upper management jobs tended to be held by men in museums (85 percent), theater companies (66 percent), and orchestras (66 percent), but women held the majority of positions in community arts associations (55 percent).[29] The data also indicated that there were a wide variety of ways to enter the career path in arts management, thus making it a fairly open system.

The section of DiMaggio's report on training offers some interesting insights into the opinions of those surveyed regarding their preparation for their jobs. Figure 2-1 shows the results of a survey that asked how well prepared participants felt to handle various aspects of the job, including fiscal and personnel management, planning, and board, labor, and government relations. The data indicates that "few managers felt they were well-prepared to assume many of [the] functions" required for their jobs.[30] Labor relations consistently stood out as an area for which respondents felt poorly prepared. The survey results show that in many areas, less than 40 percent felt that they had "good preparation" for budgeting and finance, planning and development, personnel management, and government relations.

DiMaggio also asked arts managers how they learned to do their jobs. An overwhelming number of the respondents indicated that they learned how to manage while on the job. These managers included 95 percent in theater and orchestra management, 90 percent in museum management, and 86 percent in community arts agency (CAA) management.[31] Typically, around 20 percent said they had learned through university arts administration courses.

	Fiscal Management	Personnel Management	Board Relations	Planning and Development	Marketing and Public Relations	Labor Relations	Government Relations
THEATERS							
Had good preparation	27.45%	42.57%	30.69%	37.62%	39.60%	20.00%	NA
Had poor preparation	25.49	13.86	29.70	23.76	16.83	16.83	
(Respondents)	(102)	(101)	(101)	(101)	(101)	(95)	
ART MUSEUMS							
Had good preparation	25.60	30.40	45.83	32.52	29.27	15.25	21.95
Had poor preparation	40.80	24.00	14.17	23.58	30.89	55.00	43.09
(Respondents)	(125)	(125)	(120)	(123)	(123)	(118)	(123)
ORCHESTRAS							
Had good preparation	26.42	36.89	43.14	33.33	47.06	22.00	NA
Had poor preparation	23.58	15.53	23.53	19.61	20.59	49.00	
(Respondents)	(106)	(103)	(102)	(102)	(102)	(100)	
ARTS ASSOCIATIONS							
Had good preparation	29.46	39.84	42.64	52.71	53.13	11.02	37.01
Had poor preparation	20.16	13.28	17.83	14.73	11.72	50.85	25.20
(Respondents)	(129)	(128)	(129)	(129)	(128)	(118)	(127)

NOTE: NA = Not asked/not applicable

Figure 2-1 Self-Evaluation of Preparedness at the Time of First Managership by Function
Source: Paul DiMaggio, *Manager of the Arts*, Research Division Report #20, National Endowment for the Arts (Santa Ana, Calif.: Seven Locks Press, 1987).

Updating the Profile

A recent survey of 641 professionally managed performing arts organizations, undertaken by J. Dennis Rich and Dan J. Martin, examined the role of education in arts administrative training.[32] The authors identified 26 management skills ranging from accounting to trustee and volunteer relations. Respondents provided their ratings of the skills needed to be an effective arts manager. (See Figure 2-2.) The top skills, not surprisingly, included leadership, fundraising, communication and writing, marketing and audience development, and budgeting. The survey also identified skills employers thought best learned in the classroom versus those learned on the job. Interestingly, the respondents could not seem to agree about whether classroom or on-the-job training was better. For example, the authors noted:

- Arts managers want more training in marketing and fundraising (executive education).
- Arts managers prefer to hire marketing and development directors with formal arts administration training.
- They believe that marketing and fundraising is, by and large, best learned "on the job."[33]

In the 1990s, the diversification of arts institutions continued to increase the opportunities for women and minorities in the field of arts management. As a result, today's arts manager profile is somewhat more representative of our society. The National Study of Arts Managers (NSAM) conducted in 1996 found that "67 percent of the upper-level (management) positions are held by males, whereas 33 percent of upper-level positions are held by females."[34] The percentage of males to females was quite different at the middle-management level: 24 percent male and 76 percent female. The survey also found significant differences in salaries. "The average salary for a male arts manager is $56,936; however, the average salary for a female arts manager is $41,368."[35]

Jobs for Arts Managers Today

When scanning a publication like *ArtSEARCH*, an employment service bulletin that is issued 23 times a year by the Theatre Communications Group (TCG),[36] it is possible to gain an overview of the job market for arts managers. The job listings also reveal the expectations of organizations about staff qualifications for an arts manager in today's workplace. For example, a typical issue of *ArtSEARCH* will list openings for exec-

NOTE: 10 being the highest	Median	Mean	High	Low
Leadership	10	9.12	10	1
Budgeting	9	8.82	10	4
Team Building	9	8.82	10	1
Fundraising	9	8.79	10	1
Communication Skills/Writing	9	8.76	10	3
Marketing/Audience Development	9	8.49	10	4
Financial Management	9	8.41	10	3
Aesthetics/Artistic Sense	9	8.23	10	1
Trustee/Volunteer Relations	9	8.12	10	1
Strategic Management	8	8.18	10	3
Grant Writing	8	8.01	10	1
Public Relations/Press Relations	8	7.89	10	3
Organizational Behavior	8	7.69	10	1
Public Speaking	8	7.66	10	1
Etiquette/Social Grace	8	7.62	10	1
Information Management	8	7.52	10	1
Community Outreach/Education	8	7.41	10	1
Accounting	7	7.10	10	1
Expertise in One Arts Discipline	7	6.91	10	1
Political Understanding	7	6.50	10	1
Knowledge of Many Arts Disciplines	7	6.48	10	1
Personnel Relations/Unions	7	6.26	10	1
Contract Law	6	5.61	10	1
Statistical Analysis	6	5.38	10	1
Collective Bargaining	5	5.39	10	1
Computer Programming	5	5.08	10	1

Figure 2-2 Critical Value of Management Skills

Source: J. Dennis Rich and Dan J. Martin, "The Role of Formal Education in Arts Administration Training," from *The Guide to Arts Administration Training and Research 1997–1999* (Washington, D.C.: Association of Arts Administration Educators [AAAE], 1997). Used with permission.

utive directors, managing directors, administrative assistants, box office managers, development directors, education directors, general managers, public relations managers, and telemarketing managers.[37] The qualifications often noted for executive directors, for example, include skills in areas such as administration, communication, planning supervision, fundraising, and fiscal management. Obviously, executive director positions require previous experience or, as is often indicated in a job posting, "a proven track record."

Depending on what part of the United States the job is in, and the overall operating budget of the organization, the salaries for entry-level assistants may range from as little as $18,000 to $24,000. Middle management positions may start at $22,000 and range up to $48,000, and upper management dues could start at $30,000 and go up to $60,000 and beyond. The benefits will vary with the resources of the organization. Most offer health insurance through a group policy and may require the employee to pay a percentage of the benefit costs. Larger organizations and institutions (such as colleges and universities) offer more comprehensive benefit packages. The reality about employment in the area of arts management is that there are jobs available. However, many of the smaller nonprofit arts and culture organizations simply do not have the resources to offer salaries that are competitive with the private sector. Please refer to Chapter 14, "Career Options and Preparing for the Job Market," for more information about a career in arts management.

The Manager's Personal Mission

An essential ingredient in the mix of the knowledge, skills, and abilities that a person brings to any arts management job must include a passion for what he or she is doing and a strong sense of purpose. The challenges in this field are many. Therefore, a strong personal mission and sense of purpose is an important part of the profile of an arts manager. Although it is difficult to quantify and list often intangible attributes, nonetheless, one must be prepared to offer a clear point of view about the value and contribution the arts make to a community. As you will see in Chapter 7, "Staffing the Organization," and Chapter 8, "Fundamentals of Leadership and Group Dynamics," there are many related issues that a successful arts manager must tackle.

The National Endowment for the Arts

The role of the arts manager in the United States was further defined by the passage of legislation establishing the National Endowment for the Arts and Humanities on September 15, 1965.[38] The struggle to create a modest system for promoting growth and excellence in the arts took several years, numerous congressional hearings, and incredible dedication by a few people. Since its establishment, the NEA has helped shape the arts scene in the United States by organizing an identifiable arts constituency, stimulating donations through matching grants, and providing guidance to arts groups on ways to manage their limited resources effectively. Although the NEA appropriation was only $115.2 million in 2002, or roughly $0.41 per person in the United States,[39] the endowment regularly generates millions more through various matching grants.

The NEA's vision and mission statements are worth noting, because they help shape the numerous grant categories created to support the arts. The following is from the NEA's current website:

Vision
A nation in which the arts play a central role in the lives of all Americans.

Mission
The National Endowment for the Arts, an investment in America's living cultural heritage, serves the public good by *nurturing* the expression of human creativity, *supporting* the cultivation of community spirit, and *fostering* the recognition and appreciation of the **excellence** and **diversity** of our nation's accomplishments.

Goal 1—Access: Broaden public access to the excellence and diversity of the arts.

Goal 2—Creativity: Foster opportunities for the creation and presentation of artistically excellent work.

Goal 3—Arts Education: Strengthen the role of the arts in our nation's educational system and encourage lifelong learning in the arts.

Goal 4—Preservation: Preserve our nation's cultural heritage for the twenty-first century.

Goal 5—Organizational Stability: Strengthen the organizational and financial capabilities of America's arts organizations.

Goal 6—Community Arts Development: Help address the concerns of America's communities through the arts.

Goal 7—Partnerships: Strengthen the Endowment's partnerships with the public and private sectors.

Goal 8—Strengthen the NEA as an innovative, efficient, and effective organization.[40]

The creation of the NEA has led to the development of a support system for performers, performing arts organizations, museums, and film, design, and humanities projects for nearly 40 years. Currently the NEA grants funds to individuals in the form of fellowships in literature and national heritage as well as sponsoring grants for an American jazz masters program. Grants are also made for special programs such as Leadership Initiatives, Save America's Treasures, and Challenge America. Grants to organizations fall under six categories: Creativity, Organizational Capacity, Access, Education, Heritage and Preservation, and Arts on Radio and Television.[41] In addition, the NEA provides funds to regional arts agencies, who in turn distribute funds regionally and locally.

The typical application process moves through a system of staff screening, review by a committee of peers in the discipline, review of the peer group recommendation by the National Council on the Arts, and a final decision by the Chair of the endowment. Applications can take from six months to a year to work their way through the system. The chance of receiving funding is dependent to a large degree on how well the proposed project matches the criteria the NEA has set for the funding area. For example, in 2000 the NEA recorded 2,599 applications and 1,487 grants awarded, which translates to a funding rate of about 57 percent.[42]

Government Support

The pros and cons of government support for the arts have not changed significantly since the inception of the NEA (see "Involuntary Patrons" in Chapter 1). The supporters of the legislation that led to the creation of the

NEA saw it as an opportunity to make the arts more available to people throughout the United States and to enrich the nation's cultural life. Programs were designed to promote a type of cultural democracy through very modest grants to a wide range of projects and institutions. It was deemed important to support the creative spirit and at the same time promote new work. The preservation of a cultural heritage was a high priority, and the support of work that might not otherwise exist in a market-driven economic system was thought to benefit everyone.

The critics of the legislation believed that the establishment of a government subsidy system would eventually result in general mediocrity creeping into the arts. There was fear that centralizing the power of the subsidy in the hands of a few would lead to less, not more, creative work in the country. Others believed that it was wrong to give the taxpayers' money to projects and programs with no appeal beyond a limited number of people. Some people argued that a type of cultural dictatorship would result from the peer review system. Others argued that if the government started subsidizing the arts, private and corporate philanthropy would dry up.

Budget Battles and Censorship

In the end, the astute shepherding of the legislation through the House and Senate by Livingston Biddle, who became chairman of the NEA in 1977 to 1981, and others helped neutralize critics in the early days of the endowment. The NEA flourished and survived the annual congressional budget hearing process until 1981. Under the budget planning guidance of White House aide David Stockman, the new Reagan administration proposed a 50 percent cut in the NEA budget for 1982 and additional cuts in 1983–1986.[43] The new administration saw in the NEA an example of the government creating a disincentive for private support for the arts. When confronted with the increase in private giving that had been generated by the endowment, the Reagan administration backed away from massive budget cutting, and reductions of 6 percent were adopted by Congress. The political spotlight shifted off the endowment, and the budget actually continued to increase up until 1992 (see Figure 2-3).

The budget battles of the early 1980s were minor in comparison with the firestorm that erupted with reauthorization legislation in 1989 and 1990. The reauthorization of the NEA became the focal point for a political struggle over censorship and the whole concept of funding for the arts. In the fall of 1990, arts lobby groups pleaded with arts groups across the country to support the NEA's reauthorization. Telegrams and letters were sent to Washington to show members of Congress that there were constituents who supported the arts.

The compromise legislation eventually enacted required grant recipients to return their grant monies if the work they produced was found to be obscene by the courts. This compromise did not sit well with the artistic community. Controversy continued to follow the NEA as artists and organizations sued over the obscenity pledge. Several organizations, among them the Public Theater in New York City, turned down substantial grants rather than agree to the terms that the NEA established.

Censorship charges continued to be leveled at the NEA when grant recommendations by the National Council on the Arts were overturned by the acting director of the endowment in the spring of 1992. The resignations of peer review panels and key staff have disrupted the operations of the endowment.

From the Bookshelf

Livingston Biddle's comprehensive personal history of the NEA, *Our Government and the Arts: A Perspective from the Inside*, is filled with hundreds of facts and anecdotes about the struggle to establish and maintain what may be one of the most cost-effective organizations in government. In addition to telling interesting stories, Biddle takes the reader inside the legislative system as well as the early management structure of the endowment. The book was published in 1988 by Americans for the Arts (One East 53rd Street, New York, NY 10022).

For a more current insider's perspective on the NEA you would do well to read Jane Alexander's book, *Command Performance: An Actress in the Theater of Politics* (New York: Public Affairs, a Perseus Books Group publication, 2000). The book offers a fascinating look into the strategies used by Alexander to help insure the survival of the NEA at a time when its very existence was being threatened. In addition to offering a wealth of information about how the NEA met these challenges and survived, the book provides arts managers with valuable lessons on the fine art of working with the political system in the United States.

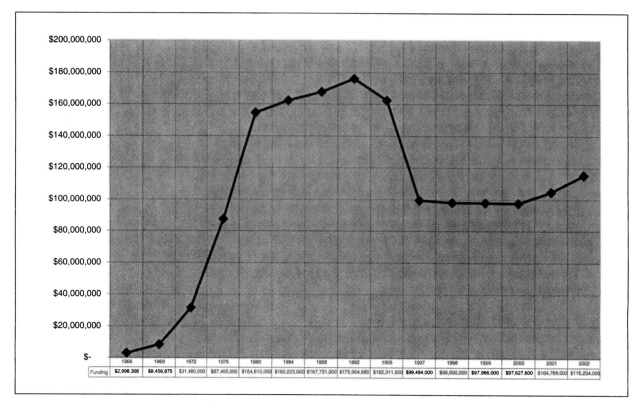

	1966	1969	1972	1976	1980	1984	1988	1992	1995	1997	1998	1999	2000	2001	2002
Funding	$2,998,308	$8,456,875	$31,480,000	$87,455,000	$154,610,000	$162,223,000	$167,731,000	$175,954,680	$162,311,000	$99,494,000	$98,000,000	$97,966,000	$97,627,600	$104,769,000	$115,234,000

Figure 2-3   NEA Funding 1966–2002
Source: Summary of Appropriated Funds 1966–2002, National Endowment for the Arts, May 2002.
Not adjusted for inflation.

The remainder of the 1990s saw more trouble for the NEA as it went through further reauthorization hearings. The shift to a Republican controlled House and Senate kept the NEA on the budget hot seat. Proposals to completely shut down the NEA found favor in the House, and the eventual budget compromise process led to the agency being funded for only $98 million in 1998.[44] A casualty of the political struggles of the NEA has been funding for individual artists. In 1996 the NEA revised many of its grant categories and for the most part limited individual grants to fellowships. The hard work of Clinton appointee Jane Alexander, NEA Chair from 1993 to 1997, helped keep the agency stable. William Ivey was appointed Chair in 1998, and he was to be succeeded by Michael Hammond in 2002. However, Hammond, former Dean of the Shepherd School of Music at Rice University, passed away suddenly in January 2002. The agency appointed an interim Chair soon thereafter.

The NEA and the Arts Manager
The granting process implemented by the NEA in the late 1960s helped to stimulate the growth of many careers in arts management and to hasten the professionalization of the field. The specialized skills required to seek out grants were in great demand. Because all organizational grants were at least a one-to-one match, meaning that for every federal grant dollar a matching dollar of other money must be found, fundraising staffs and development experts began to be hired. Typically, grants to large organizations required three dollars of private money for every dollar of federal money over a three-year period. This further necessi-

tated establishing a staff support system to run the initial campaign and to continue bringing the money in after the grant expired.

The development of the now-common structure of a board of directors and management staff was a product of the new accountability that arts organizations faced. Organizations had to prove that they could responsibly manage the funds they were given. Annual reports, financial statements, and five-year plans became standard operating procedures for organizations that wanted to be considered by the federal, corporate, and foundation funders. The net result was an increase in staff openings, which provided jobs for the baby boomers graduating from the colleges and universities across America in the 1970s and 1980s.

State Agencies

The original NEA legislation provided funds for the creation of state agencies to distribute 20 percent of the endowment's overall budget. The state and local arts agencies created another network of funding opportunities for artists and arts groups as well as staff positions for arts managers. The NEA is mandated to provide a percentage of its budget to the partnerships funding program with the states.[45]

The Education Revolution

Arts managers became an integral part of the unprecedented growth in the higher education industry. The baby boom and the resulting expansion programs undertaken by many schools to accommodate the incoming students led to the creation of numerous fine arts programs that were integrated into the overall mission of the institution.

There are more than 1,800 administrative heads of university or college theater programs in the United States today.[46] In 1990 Stephen Langley and James Abruzzo listed 961 music programs, 409 opera programs or workshops, 1,622 visual arts programs, and 266 dance programs graduating future artists each year.[47] The Association of Arts Administration Educators (AAAE) listed over 30 graduate degree programs and a dozen undergraduate programs in arts administration and theater management around the world.[48] In addition, certificate programs in arts administration and museum management are now found around the world.

In many larger university graduate programs, the performing arts evolved into preprofessional training programs in the late 1960s and 1970s. The number of management jobs grew as fine arts centers were built to house the visual and performing arts programs across the country. In many cases, at least one large facility was constructed to serve the dual purposes of supporting the academic programs and providing a venue for community events. Subscriptions to various arts series were offered to the community and to students and provided the performance experience that arts students needed. Even small college and university programs adopted more professional approaches to producing shows, due in part to the influx of faculty trained in the graduate programs of the large universities. The late 1970s and early 1980s were a period of tremendous growth in the smaller performing arts programs.

Educators within the arts community began to recognize the need to develop trained managers as well as performers, designers, and technicians. Several schools, such as Yale, Northwestern, University of Wisconsin, and University of California at Los Angeles, created training programs that became models for developing arts managers.

By the early 1970s, the network of facilities managers and sponsors had developed into an organization now known as the Association of Performing Arts Presenters (APAP). APAP produces an annual conference that is an important booking opportunity for theater groups, dance companies, music ensembles, and soloists. Student associations also hold annual meetings to book acts on campuses around the country.

The Slowdown in Growth

The educational boom began to slow at the end of the 1980s as the number of college-age students dropped. The consolidation of arts programs and the outright elimination of arts departments began to be discussed. By the early 1990s the talk had turned to action. Budget cuts, little or no facility maintenance, and staff reductions began to sweep across U.S. campuses. Many programs experienced difficulty filling their graduate classes even when they offered full scholarship support. As the 1990s progressed, the pressure of rising tuition costs and the increasing overhead costs of operating colleges and universities brought issues of resource redistribution to the forefront. Arts programs are particularly costly to support. The need for small classes and one-on-one instruction makes the unit cost per student very high in comparison to departments that can deliver their subject matter in large lecture classes. The needs for efficiency and maximizing resources will continue as the next wave of college students come in to the system in the new century.

Conclusion

The evolution of the role of the arts manager continues as thousands of arts organizations undergo the arduous process of adapting to the changing cultural environment. As we will see in Chapter 4, "Arts Organizations in a Changing World," arts groups must constantly assess the opportunities and threats that present themselves in the world around them. In theory, at least, an arts manager should be trained to serve the needs of his or her particular discipline by effectively solving the problems of today and anticipating the significant changes of tomorrow. Unfortunately, the day-to-day struggle for financial survival that goes on in most organizations leaves little time for planning for the future.

Whatever changes take place in the next 20 years, arts managers working with artists, boards, and staffs will play a central role in the future of the arts in the United States. Dynamic vision and articulate leadership will be required if the arts are to build on the growth of the last 50 years.

Summary

Over the last two thousand years, the basic functions of the artist-manager have remained the same: to bring art and the public together is the continuing objective.

In ancient times, simple religious ceremonies evolved into full-scale state-sponsored arts events that lasted from several days to a few weeks. The functions of management (planning, organizing, leading, and controlling) were distributed between artist-managers and the public officials who acted as arts managers. The rise of the Church and the decline of Rome created a shift away from state-sponsored events.

The late Middle Ages produced economic growth that allowed for the expansion of population centers. The rise of guilds and community-sponsored celebrations helped fuel changes in the overall arts climate. Complex pageants often needed people with management expertise to organize the large casts and the various sets associated with the productions.

Continued changes in society and the birth of more democratic forms of government eventually led to changes that became the foundation of many modern organizations. The Renaissance fostered the rebirth of drama and contributed to the development of the first operas and ballets. Problems with financing, patronage, and censorship also accompanied the growth in the arts. The additional art forms created additional jobs for arts managers.

In the seventeenth and eighteenth centuries, some countries began to establish national dance, opera, music, and theater companies. Permanent staff members and performers received salaries and pension benefits. By the nineteenth century in Europe and the United States, the arts had expanded into smaller population centers. However, there were no state-recognized arts institutions in the United States comparable to those of Europe. As communities became cities, orchestras, opera companies, and museums became permanent institutions. Most were supported by a small group of philanthropists. The role of the arts manager in the United States expanded with the continued development of touring, which was made possible by an extensive rail system. Monopolistic enterprises took control of many of the theaters at the end of the nineteenth century. The invention of movies and radio contributed to a decline in attendance at arts events by the 1920s.

The last 90 years have been shaped by major wars, slowly improving economic conditions, the new technologies of television, videotape, and computers, and a population boom. At the same time, legislation and tax laws have helped artists and managers to establish nonprofit organizations to carry out their artistic vision. The process for establishing nonprofit, tax-exempt arts organizations is a well-established process widely used in America.

As a profession and a recognized field of work, arts management is a product of changes in U.S. national policy since the 1950s. Ford Foundation funding and, beginning in 1965, the National Endowment for the Arts helped make private and public support for the arts a priority. The expanding arts market resulting from the population increase and the education boom has also contributed to the creation of thousands of new jobs in the arts.

The typical arts manager profile in the 1980s was of a highly educated, upper-middle-class person with a background in the humanities. A limited number had done course work in management while in school. Survey results show that many arts managers had to learn the functions of their positions on the job. The growth in training programs in the 1980s and 1990s has created a more diversified group of arts managers.

The NEA was created in 1965 to promote excellence, broaden the availability of the arts, and preserve work identified as part of the United States' national heritage. The political environment has reshaped the NEA, and the resulting changes have reduced the budget by nearly 50 percent since 1992. The NEA has assisted many groups in organizing and professionalizing their staffs. In addition to promoting the growth of the arts at a national level, the NEA also supports numerous state and local arts agencies.

The field of arts management has also grown as a result of the boom in arts programs at colleges and universities across the United States. Degree programs, new facilities, and often-extensive staffs have created a national network of arts centers with jobs for arts managers. Recent shifts in demographics have placed more pressure on the higher education field to deliver its product more efficiently.

Key Terms and Concepts

Artist-manager
Archon eponymous
Choregoi
Domini
The Syndicate
The NEA, and its mission

Questions

1. Summarize the major arts management activity associated with the following time periods:
   a. Ancient Greece
   b. Ancient Rome
   c. Middle Ages
   d. Renaissance
   e. Seventeenth through nineteenth centuries
   f. Twentieth century

2. What are the seven steps typically required to incorporate a nonprofit arts business?

3. What changes have taken place in the job market that might alter DiMaggio's profile of the arts manager?

4. How much control should management have over the artistic product of an organization? For example, how much input should management have when it comes time to select the season's titles? Can you think of a situation in which too much or too little control was exercised by the management of an arts organization? What were the results?

Case Study

The following article from the early 1990s presents a model for change in the world of museum management. As you will see, not everyone agrees that this change is good.

Wanted: Art Scholar. M.B.A. Required
Alexander Stille

When Jack Lane took over as director of the San Francisco Museum of Modern Art three years ago, one of the first things he did was shut his office door. "The previous director's door was open to everyone who wanted to talk to him," Mr. Lane explains. "That just seemed unworkable. I wanted to clarify the chain of command, so we divided the museum into four major areas, and the heads of those areas report directly to me."

It was that kind of tough-minded decision the museum's trustees had hired Mr. Lane, who holds a master's degree in business from the University of Chicago as well as a Ph.D. from Harvard, to make. They wanted a director with a degree in business as well as art to lead the museum through a period of major expansion.

Their choice is representative of a growing perception that leadership at museums requires business acumen as well as connoisseurship. Although business management techniques have been used in museums for at least two decades, in the last few years those skills have been more heavily emphasized—to the dismay of some in the art world.

While many cultural institutions have long had business departments to take care of marketing, public relations and accounting functions, the emphasis at the top had been on scholarship. But now, at some major museums, even directors are being chosen for their business training as well as for their fine arts backgrounds.

Perhaps the most conspicuous and controversial appointment has been that of Thomas Krens at the Guggenheim Museum in New York. The 43-year-old director, who has a master's degree from the Yale School of Management, has come under criticism for his plans to create a multinational museum with branches in this country and abroad, and for selling paintings from the museum's permanent collection to buy newer works.

Museums run by art historians are also making increasing use of modern management techniques. "You have to know how to negotiate with unions, hire contractors, run a restaurant and a bookstore," says Patterson Sims, associate director of the Seattle Art Museum, who does not hold an M.B.A. "Those are not issues that connoisseurship prepares you for."

To help meet the demand, several of the country's best business schools—Harvard, Yale, Stanford, and the University of California at Los Angeles—offer courses in arts management. And the American Federation of Arts, a New York–based service organization that offers both exhibitions and professional training to 600 member museums, runs a summer program to train museum curators in business administration.

Perhaps not surprisingly, this mingling of art and business tends to polarize the museum world. "Administrative imperatives are taking precedence over artistic judgments," says Hilton Kramer, art critic and editor of the *New Criterion*, a magazine of cultural criticism. Others disagree. "A well-run operation should free the curator," counters Graham W.J. Beal, director of the Joslyn Art Museum in Omaha, who made the jump from curator to administrator after participating in the American Federation of Arts' training program.

Whether they see it as a blessing or a curse, there is widespread agreement that a business orientation in a museum is here to stay. "It's not a question of whether it will happen," says Roger M. Berkowitz, deputy director of the Toledo Museum of Art. "It is happening."

The Changing Profile of the Curator
According to museum professionals, the trend is linked to the increased size and complexity of many arts institutions.

"Museums are demonstrably more complex," says J. Carter Brown, director of the .National Gallery in Washington and perhaps the first museum head to combine a joint

M.B.A.–art history track as a calculated career strategy. He decided to take a business degree from Harvard while pursuing a master's degree in art history at the Institute of Fine Arts in New York. "When I became director in 1970," says Mr. Brown, "we had 350 employees. Now we have 1,000. Back then the museum was all in one building; we have doubled the space. Our budget was $5.9 million in 1970; today it's $53.9 million.

"My predecessor's fund-raising activities were simple," he continued. "He had lunch with Ailsa Mellon, and if he needed a Leonardo she would write a check." During Mr. Brown's tenure, the National Gallery has raised $40 million from 92 corporations.

As a result of such changes, the profile of the typical museum director has changed since the mid-70s. Directors of the old school tended to be socially prominent connoisseurs, as knowledgeable in wooing wealthy collectors as in evaluating art. "It was a hobby," says Thomas Hoving, director of the Metropolitan Museum from 1966 to 1977 and now editor in chief of *Connoisseur* magazine. "When I first got out of graduate school, people told me that the biggest prerequisite for becoming a curator was an outside income."

Although Mr. Hoving has no degree in business (nor does his successor, Philippe de Montebello), many credit—or blame—him for starting the focus on business in museums. "It was during Hoving's tenure at the Met that museums became broad, popular institutions, with blockbuster shows, expanded education programs, gift shops, bookstores and restaurants maximizing income," says Mr. Lane, who has raised more than $65 million for the San Francisco museum and will double its exhibition space with a new building.

Last year the Minneapolis Institute of Art hired Daniel E. O'Leary as deputy director, in part because of his experience turning around a financially troubled museum. After earning a joint Ph.D. and M.B.A. at the University of Michigan, Mr. O'Leary became director of Artrain, a Michigan-based regional museum that presents traveling exhibitions in a railroad car. "I applied classical business school analysis," he says. "We booked exhibitions of greater appeal, extended the touring schedule to create a greater economy of scale. We managed to more than double the revenues and cut expenses by a third, and audiences went from 40,000 annually to 130,000."

One of the first things he did at Minneapolis was to conduct a market survey. "We live in a competitive world. We have to justify ourselves to government, to foundations, to corporations."

Some critics of the trend toward a business mentality fear that museums' preoccupation with attendance is inimical to their artistic purpose. "Museums are market-driven," says Hilton Kramer. "Museum directors have become salesmen."

Others insist that ignoring the bottom line can jeopardize a museum's artistic mission.

"A number of museums have become more or less insolvent," says Myrna Smoot, director of the American Federation of Arts. "They reduce their hours, they don't change their collections, they reduce maintenance and security, stop paying to conserve the collection, in order to keep the doors open."

Does "Thank You" Mean Forever?

The problem of continual growth is one that preoccupies Mr. Krens at the Guggenheim, the most outspoken advocate of the so-called M.B.A. revolution, who has sought to challenge the assumptions on which museums have traditionally operated. "It's increasingly expensive to store and preserve works of art," he says. "When you accept an object into your collection, do you take on an obligation to preserve the work forever?" Older museums, he says, are at a critical juncture; they cannot continue indefinitely as both custodians of the past and purveyors of the new. Do you go on collecting forever? And if not, where do you stop?"

Mr. Krens clearly answered his own question with his decision to sell a Kandinski, a Modigliani and a Klee last year to pay for a major collection of Minimalist art from the Italian Count Giuseppe Panza.

Most M.B.A. curators warn against taking this trend too far. "If M.B.A.'s are running museums without an art history background, we're in for a grim future," says Mr. Nash.

For the moment, anyway, the low wage scale of the not-for-profit world ensures to some degree that the M.B.A.'s entering the museum world will have to be passionate about more than money.

SOURCE: Alexander Stille, "Wanted: Art Scholar. M.B.A. Required," *New York Times* (January 19, 1991). Copyright © 1991 by the New York Times Company. Reprinted with permission.

Case Study Follow-Up

NOTE 1: In the spring and summer of 1998 the Guggenheim hosted an exhibition of motorcycles that attracted thousands of new visitors to the museum. Thomas Krens, the Guggenheim's director, was the show's curator. Bikers and motorcycle club members from across the country flocked to see the exhibition. Some of the critics of Mr. Krens doubted the audience attracted to BMW and Harley-Davidson classic motorcycles would be coming back to the museum on a regular basis.

NOTE 2: A related article about Thomas Krens may be found in the *New York Times*, April 19, 1998, Section 2, Arts and Leisure. "The Global Straddler of the Art World" provides an interesting profile about Mr. Krens, who celebrated his tenth year as the Guggenheim's director on July 1, 1998.

NOTE 3: In a critical article entitled "When Art Puts Down a Bet in a House of Games," published on April 14, 2002 in the *New York Times*, Herbert Muschamp wrote the following about the Guggenheim's latest venture:

The two Las Vegas satellites launched last year by the Guggenheim Museum will disappoint those who have been hoping to have their faith in the mother institution restored. Lodged in the base of the Venetian Hotel, an architectural collage of vapid scenographic effects, the two pavilions are not disgraceful. Rem Koolhaas, who designed them, has brought some architecture into the picture. More, in fact, than was strictly necessary.

Probably no design could redeem the vanity behind this venture. Far from "bringing art to the masses," the Guggenheim has brought corporate branding to an anticipated public that has thus far failed to show up. But the enterprise has delivered a crisis for the museum itself. The Guggenheim's efforts to remake itself in the image of a multinational corporation—with outposts for culture consumers in Spain, Germany, Austria, Japan, Brazil and elsewhere around the world—have reached the point of philosophical collapse.

Questions

1. List at least two reasons why a museum curator needs business management skills.

2. Do you agree or disagree with Hilton Kramer's judgment that museums have become "market-driven" and museum directors have become "salesmen"? Explain.

3. What alternatives can museums pursue to increase membership other than high-visibility exhibitions?

4. Do you agree with the notion of selling off museum holdings to raise money for other works? What should museums do about preserving their holdings?

References

1. Oscar G. Brockett, *History of the Theatre*, 3rd ed. (Boston: Allyn and Bacon, 1977), pp. 15–47.
2. Neil Kotler and Philip Kotler, *Museum Strategy and Marketing* (San Francisco: Jossey-Bass, Inc., 1998), p. 11.
3. Ibid., p. 11.
4. Ibid., p. 11.
5. Brockett, *History of the Theatre*, pp. 51–73.
6. Ibid., p. 105.
7. Ibid., p. 136.
8. Richard Kraus and Sarah Alberti Chapman, *History of the Dance in Art and Education*, 2nd ed. (Englewood Cliffs, NJ: Prentice-Hall, 1981), p. 62.
9. Ibid., p. 67.
10. Kotler and Kotler, *Museum Strategy and Marketing*, p. 12.
11. John Pick, *Managing the Arts? The British Experience* (London: Rhinegold, 1986), p. 23.
12. Ibid., p. 45.
13. William J. Baumol and William G. Bowen, *Performing Arts: The Economic Dilemma* (Cambridge, MA: MIT Press, 1966), p. 20.

14. Ibid., p. 29.
15. Kraus and Chapman, *History of the Dance*, pp. 93–95.
16. Kotler and Kotler, *Museum Strategy and Marketing*, p. 12.
17. Baumol and Bowen, *Performing Arts*, p. 29.
18. Ibid., pp. 27–28.
19. Martin Mayer, "The Opera," in *The Performing Arts and American Society*, ed. W. McNeil Lowry (Englewood Cliffs, NJ: Prentice-Hall, Spectrum Books, 1977), p. 45.
20. W. McNeil Lowry, ed. *The Performing Arts and American Society* (Englewood Cliffs, NJ: Prentice-Hall, Spectrum Books, 1977), p. 14.
21. Ibid., p. 11.
22. NEA Research Division Note #67, "Dance Organizations Report 43% Growth in Economic Census: 1987–1992" (Washington, D.C., May 1998).
23. NEA Research Division Note #68, "Classical Music Groups Report 22% Growth in Economic Census: 1987–1992 (Washington, D.C., May, 1998).
24. NEA Research Division Note #64, "Museums, Arboreta, Botanical Gardens and Zoos Report 18% Growth, 1987–1992" (Washington, D.C., May 1998).
25. National Endowment for the Arts, "1965–1995: A Brief Chronology of Federal Involvement in the Arts," edited by Keith Donohue (Washington, D.C.: NEA, 2000), p. 4.
26. Kotler and Kotler, *Museum Strategy and Marketing*, p. 12.
27. From Anthony Mancuso's *How to Form a Nonprofit Corporation*, 4th ed. (San Francisco: Nolo Press, 2001), summary of chapters 1–3, pp. 1.2–3.14.
28. NEA Research Division Note #80 (Washington, D.C., May 2002).
29. Paul DiMaggio, *Managers of the Arts*, NEA Research Division Report #20 (Washington, D.C.: Seven Locks Press, 1987), p. 12.
30. Ibid., p. 42.
31. Ibid., p. 46.
32. J. Dennis Rich and Dan J. Martin, *The Guide to Arts Administration Training and Research 1997–1999* (Washington, D.C.: Association of Arts Administration Educators, 1997), pp. 69–73.
33. Ibid., p. 72.
34. Donna G. Herron, Tamara S. Hubbard, Amy E. Kirner, Lynn Newcomb, Michelle Reisner-Memmer, Michael E. Robertson II, Matthew W. Smith, Leslie A. Tullo, and Jennifer S. Young, "The Effect of Gender on the Career Advancement of Arts Managers," *Journal of Arts Management, Law and Society*, Vol. 28, No. 1, Spring 1998, p. 30.
35. Ibid., p. 30.
36. *ArtSEARCH* is published by the Theatre Communications Group, Inc., 355 Lexington Ave., New York, NY 10017.
37. *ArtSEARCH* (May 1, 1998), pp. 1–11.
38. Livingston Biddle, *Our Government and the Arts* (New York: American Council for the Arts, 1988), p. 180.
39. The per-person cost was calculated by dividing the current budget for the NEA (fiscal year 2002) by the total U.S. population of 288 million according to the 2002 Census Bureau.
40. *Guide to the NEA*, Washington, D.C., http://www.arts.gov/learn/NEAGuide/Overview.html.
41. Ibid.

42. http://www.arts.gov/Learn/FACTS/2001Funding.html.

43. Biddle, *Our Government and the Arts*, p. 492.

44. NEA, Summary of Appropriated Funds 1996–2000, www.arts.gov/Learn/FACTS/2001Funding.html.

45. http://www.arts.gov/partner/index.html.

46. Association of Theatre in Higher Education (ATHE).

47. Stephen Langley and James Abruzzo, *Jobs in Arts and Media Management*, pp. 10–11.

48. http://artsnet.org/aaae.

Additional Resources

The *New York Times* covered the NEA extensively in "Washington's Stake in the Arts" (April 12, 1998), Arts and Leisure, Section 2. The article offers a great deal of useful background on the state of affairs of the NEA in the late 1990s and is recommended reading for arts managers.

The article "Leadership and Arts Management" in *The International Journal of Arts Management*, Volume 3, Number 3 (Spring 2001), provides an interesting point of view about artistic leadership and arts management.

Evolution of Management

3
◻ ◻ ◻ ◻ ◻

*Management facilitates the efforts of people in organized groups
and arises when people seek to cooperate to achieve goals.*
Daniel Wren

In this chapter, we scan the evolution of management thought. After a review of early management practices, we examine the management concepts that grew out of the shift to mass production during the Industrial Revolution. Finally, we will look at the impact of scientific management and the application of psychological theories to the workplace.

Little mention will be made of arts organizations in this chapter because the primary objective is to provide the reader with a general historical background on the field of management. Many of the terms and concepts noted in Chapters 1 and 2 have developed from classic and contemporary management theory and practice. If you have taken college courses in business or management, the terms, concepts, and people noted in this chapter should not be new to you. Before moving into the specific areas of external environments, planning, organizational design, and human resource management, it seems appropriate to explore the source of the current management systems used to operate all organizations.

Management as an Art and a Science

A basic assumption of this text is that management is an art. In this case, an *art* is defined as *an ability or special skill that someone develops and applies.* Studying the theories of management, synthesizing the application of these theories to a practical work environment, and then creating a workable system for a specific organization require a tremendous amount of thought and effort. It is often a lifetime job.

Management can also be considered to be a science. Although the idea of science in the workplace may not be very appealing to an aspiring arts manager, the reality is that applying some of the techniques noted in this chapter may help make a stronger arts organization. As we will see, the general concept of *scientific management* is not universally welcomed in the workplace. The term describes a particular approach to maximizing productivity by applying research and quantitative analysis to the work process. The creation of general and specific management theories to explain and predict how organizations and people behave is also integral to thinking of management as a science.

At the center of any theory is the ability to predict an outcome if given a specific set of circumstances. A scientist develops a theory, conducts experiments, establishes an outcome that can be repeated by others, and provides proof of the theory. Management theory tries to achieve the same goal: predictable outcomes given specific inputs. Unfortunately, the science of management, as with any social science, is sometimes subject to unanticipated outcomes. In management science, numerous other variables, including the behavior of employees in the work environment, can quickly undermine a theory.

On-the-Job Management Theory

When studying management theory and practice, which are often examined by using case studies, it becomes apparent that many managers enter into the practice of managing with virtually no theoretical background. Whether in the arts or business, not having formal training has never been a barrier to running an organization. For example, the late Katherine Graham, who once owned the *Washington Post*, had no formal training in business management. The sudden death of her husband thrust her into the role of chief executive officer. Nonetheless, she was able to successfully operate a major newspaper using her personal abilities and adaptability. She was able to learn on the job and to further develop her own operating theories and practices to maintain a successful business. For every Katherine Graham there are many other people in the workplace less successful at playing the role of manager. Your local bookstores are stocked with readings about how employees should deal with the boss or supervisor who does not seem to have mastered the art of managing.

In Paul DiMaggio's 1987 study for the National Endowment for the Arts, more than 85 percent of the arts managers in theaters, art museums, orchestras, and arts associations said that they learned from on-the-job training.[1] The university-trained arts managers surveyed claimed that their schooling did not adequately prepare them for many of the demands of running an organization. The numbers of university-trained arts managers has increased in the last few years, but it is still safe to say that the experience of the workplace is required to complete the education of any arts manager.

Regardless of how an individual learns the art and science of management, an effective manager must eventually be able to analyze variables and predict outcomes based on experience. In other words, the manager must find a set of operating principles that can be used. For example, an arts manager might have to say to the board, "If we raise prices, ticket orders will decline based on discretionary spending patterns of our audiences. If we change our subscription plans, fewer people will order because any change creates confusion. If we perform nothing but concerts of avant-garde music, a significant portion of our subscribers will stay home." These statements may all be true, but that does not mean the Board will follow the manager's recommendation. It may be perfectly appropriate, given the mission, for an organization to make a decision that will produce a negative outcome. A good manager should be able to articulate his or her expectations of outcomes based on an understanding of the effects of variables on particular decisions. Obviously, experience is and always will be a great teacher.

To be an effective arts manager one should have an awareness and appreciation of the overall field of management. The rest of this chapter focuses on some of the major theories and principles that shape management today.

Evolution of Management Thought

Preindustrialization

For the last several thousand years, organized social systems have managed the resources needed to feed, house, and protect people. The evolution of management is intertwined with the development of the social, religious, and economic systems needed to support cities, states, and countries. The church and state provided the first systems for planning, organizing, leading, and controlling. These management systems were predicated on philosophies that placed people within complex hierarchies.

History provides many examples of management systems established by the Egyptians, Romans, and Chinese. Many basic principles of supervision and control evolved from the projects undertaken by these societies. Building temples, pyramids, and other massive structures required extensive management and organizational skill. Organizing massive armies to go forth and conquer the known world required detailed organizational planning and logistical coordination. Many modern management concepts expanded on the skill needed to implement public works projects as the world shifted from an agrarian to an industrial base.

A Change in Philosophies

The decline of the Catholic superstate in the fourteenth and fifteenth centuries, and the subsequent religious struggles created by the rise of Protestantism, slowly changed the fundamental relationship of people to their governmental and religious systems. The seeds of the Protestant work ethic were planted in the new order. The expansion of trade and the creation of a permanent middle class grew out of the changes brought about by the national and international economic systems. The effects of the Renaissance and the Reformation extended far beyond rediscovering the ideas and philosophies of antiquity. The development of new political and social theories of government and management by such theorists as Niccolo Machiavelli, Thomas Hobbes, John Locke, and Adam Smith led to crucial changes in thinking about the individual and the society at large. For example, Adam Smith's *Wealth of Nations*, published in 1776, moved economic theory beyond the mercantile system with Smith's now-famous economic principles. The "invisible hand" of the marketplace is the core concept of the system of economic self-regulation that survives today.

The Industrial Revolution and Early Pioneers of Management

Four principal changes in the management of the workplace are often attributed to the Industrial Revolution:

1. Mechanization of work,
2. Centralization of production,
3. Creation of the labor class, and
4. Creation of the job of manager.

The elements of science and technology, changes in government policies, population growth, improved health conditions, and the more productive use of farmland were all part of the changes that occurred during the seventeenth, eighteenth, and nineteenth centuries. The early entrepreneurs who established manufacturing businesses using the new technologies of the time (e.g., the steam engine) needed others to supervise the laborers hired to operate the equipment. Essentially, the industrial manager was created to watch over the laborers. The problem of treating people as nothing more than extensions of machines and the subsequent abuses of labor—long hours, low pay, no job security, health and safety hazards, child labor, and so on—has left a legacy we still grapple with today. For example, the concept of "the carrot and the stick," which was used as a motivational management method in the factories, survives in the minds of many managers today. The positive inducement (the carrot) to earn more by working harder and faster was set off against a punishment (the stick), which included such things as a cut in wages or being assigned a more dangerous task, as a method of motivating people. However, not all owners and managers approached labor and production with the same attitude.

One of the early pioneers of a more enlightened approach to management was Robert Owen (1771–1858). At age 18, Owen operated and supervised a cotton mill, where he observed problems occurring in the manufacturing process. He tried to improve overall working conditions and changed the equipment to reduce the hazards to workers. However, due to a shortage of labor, he too hired children to work 13 hours a day.[2]

Charles Babbage (1792–1871), often cited as the inventor of the world's first computer (a counting machine) in 1822, is also credited with creating the first research techniques to study labor.[3] His early research was the forerunner of what is now called *scientific management*. In *The Evolution of Management Thought*, Daniel Wren notes that Babbage attempted to establish salary systems that reflected the mutual interest labor and management shared in the process of production: "Babbage's profit-sharing scheme had two facets: one, that a portion of wages would depend on factory profits; and two, that the worker should derive more advantage from applying any improvement he might discover, that is, a bonus for suggestions."[4]

Figure 3-1 provides a visual depiction of the major movements and the people involved in the evolution of management theory.

Changes in America

The early stages of the Industrial Revolution in the United States depended on borrowing management and organizational techniques from England and Scotland. However, by the mid-nineteenth century, U.S. manufacturers began to show the world how to mass-produce interchangeable parts for a variety of equipment.[5] The development of late-nineteenth-century America's management system was due, in large part, to the engineer. The mechanical, industrial, and civil engineers were the primary force behind the development of "systems" for doing work.

The railroads and the new technology of the telegraph created a climate for rapid business expansion in America. Daniel Craig McCallum (1815–1878), a manager for the Erie railroad, is credited with such things as creating a formal organization chart (it was shaped like a tree), matching authority with responsibility, and using the telegraph system to provide feedback about the location of trains.[6]

Henry Varnum Poor (1812–1905), the editor of the *American Railroad Journal*, wrote extensively about management organization and systems. Wren describes Poor's three-part philosophy as follows:

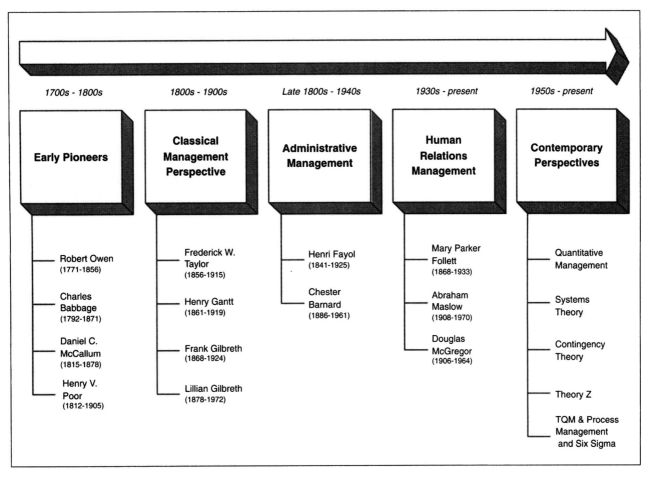

Figure 3-1 Management Time Line

[First,] organization was basic to all management; there must be a clear division of labor from the president down to the common laborer, each with specific duties and responsibilities. Second, communication was devising a method of reporting throughout the organization to give top management a continuous and accurate accounting of operations. Finally, information was "recorded communication." Poor saw the need for a set of operating reports to be compiled for costs, revenues, and rate making.[7]

As noted in Chapter 2, "The Evolution of Arts Organizations and Arts Management," the railroads played an important part in changing how entertainment was distributed in the United States. As we saw, the railroad brought to the arts the need for a specialist to manage the logistics of moving the company from city to city. The complexity of railroad schedules (time zones as we know them today were not in place until the late 1880s) also demanded a large portion of a manager's time.

Although management concepts may have been growing in sophistication and depth during this period, the treatment of employees lagged behind. The safety and well-being of workers were not high priorities. Child labor, extremely low wages, and a lack of job security were catalysts for the creation of powerful labor unions later in the nineteenth and early twentieth centuries.

Management Trends to the Present

Classical Management Perspectives

One of the founders of modern management is Frederick W. Taylor (1856–1915). Taylor is credited as the founder of scientific management. His efforts to change the workplace often faced bitter opposition. In 1912, Taylor stated his principles before a special congressional committee created to investigate the effects of scientific management on the worker. His words speak clearly of a management theory that is far different from the highly efficient assembly line many people imagine as the realization of his principles. Taylor's ultimate goal was to use his methods to achieve a "great mental revolution."[8] His testimony makes a convincing case:

> Scientific Management is not any efficiency device, not a device of any kind for securing efficiency; nor is it any bunch or group of efficiency devices. It is not a new system of figuring costs; . . . it is not holding a stop watch on a man and writing things down about him; it is not time study; it is not motion study nor an analysis of the movement of men. . . .
>
> Scientific management involves a complete mental revolution on the part of the working man engaged in any particular establishment or industry. And it involves the equally complete mental revolution on the part of those on the management's side—a complete mental revolution on their part as to the duties toward their fellow workers in the management, toward their workmen, and toward all of their daily problems.
>
> Frequently, when the management have found the selling price going down they have turned toward a cut in wages . . . as a way of . . . preserving their profits intact. Thus it is over the division of the surplus [or profits] that most of the troubles have arisen; in the extreme cases this has been the cause of serious disagreements and strikes.[9]

The drive toward making the workplace and the work process as efficient as possible by careful analysis of all phases of manufacturing continues into the present. Taylor's early time and motion studies, for example, are now regular fixtures in examining how an organization is accomplishing its tasks, from building cars to making hamburgers.

Some of the other pioneers of the scientific management field were Henry L. Gantt (1861–1919), Frank Gilbreth (1868–1924), and Lillian Gilbreth (1878–1972).[10]

Arts Application   Arts groups have limited use of the application of sophisticated scientific computer models in day-to-day operations. However, the fact is that whatever limited gains in organizational productivity are to be achieved will result from integrating specific quantitative techniques in the organization. As you will see in Chapter 9, "Organizational Controls and Budgets," the basic economics of the arts mitigates against productivity increases. However, there are components of arts organizations that do lend themselves to quantitative applications rooted in scientific management. For example, inventory and accounting systems can easily be computerized and linked to networked office computer systems. The process of assembling sets may be streamlined if time is spent analyzing how the work is being done. Often the way a task is done is based more on tradition than a detailed process analysis of the work. In fact, almost any routine procedure is worth examining. There is often a more efficient way to do almost any work, whether it is counting ticket stubs, building platforms, sorting color media, or hanging lights.

Administrative Management (1916 to Present)

Henri Fayol (1841–1925), a mine engineer, was a pioneer in the field of modern *administrative management*. The basic idea of this approach is that it focuses on principles that can be used to coordinate the work in an organization. Fayol's Fourteen Principles (Figure 3-2) helped to form the first comprehensive approach to management theory. Although many of Fayol's Fourteen Principles seem straightforward today, they broke new ground in 1917 by helping to establish a basis for administrative management.

Fayol also postulated that an individual with more skill in management than in technical expertise would not necessarily be bad for a company. In fact, he believed that an engineer with no aptitude for management would do more harm than good in an organization.[11] He also saw that management could be studied separately from engineering, and he noted that every organization required management: "Be it a case

1. **DIVISION OF LABOR**
   Work specializations can result in efficiencies in both managerial and technical functions. However, there are limits to how much work specializations can be divided.
2. **AUTHORITY**
   Managers have the right to give orders and exact obedience. With authority comes responsibility.
3. **DISCIPLINE**
   Discipline is necessary to develop obedience, diligence, energy, and respect.
4. **UNITY OF COMMAND**
   An employee should receive orders from one supervisor only.
5. **UNITY OF DIRECTION**
   All operations with the same objective should have one manager and one plan.
6. **SUBORDINATION OF INDIVIDUAL INTERESTS TO GENERAL INTERESTS**
   The interests of one employee or group of employees should not take precedence over the interests and goals of the organization.
7. **REMUNERATION**
   Compensation should be fair for employee and employer.
8. **CENTRALIZATION**
   The proper amount of centralization or decentralization should depend on the situation.
9. **SCALAR CHAIN (Hierarchical)**
   A clear line of authority should extend from the highest to lowest levels in the organization. Horizontal communication is encouraged as long as the employees in the chain are informed.
10. **ORDER**
    Materials should be kept in well-chosen places to facilitate activities.
11. **EQUITY**
    Employees should be treated with kindness and justice.
12. **STABILITY OF PERSONNEL TENURE**
    Because time is required to become effective in a new jobs, high turnover should be prevented.
13. **INITIATIVE**
    Managers should encourage and develop employee initiative to the fullest.
14. **ESPRIT DE CORPS**
    Harmony and union build organization strength.

Figure 3-2 Fayol's Fourteen Principles of Management
Source: Adapted from Henri Fayol, *General and Industrial Management*, trans., Constance Storrs
(London: Pitmanand Sons, 1949), pp. 19–42.

of commerce, industry, politics, religion, war, or philanthropy, in every concern there is a management function to be performed."[12]

Chester Barnard (1886–1961) is also frequently cited as another contributor to the field of administrative management theory. In 1938 he published *The Functions of the Executive*, which brought forward the notion of *acceptance theory of authority*.[13] Acceptance theory postulates that authority is derived from the acceptance of authority by the people being managed. The efficient day-to-day administration of an organization depends on the willingness of the employees to comply with directives given to them by managers. As long as these directives generally fit within the realm of the possible from the employees' perspective, they accept the control of the management structure. The successful Dilbert cartoon series often utilizes acceptance theory situations from the workplace. Humor is often found as the hapless employees receive directives from the manager that are often at odds with common sense. We will discuss the importance of acceptance theory in more detail in Chapter 8, "Fundamentals of Leadership and Group Dynamics."

Arts Application   Many typical work situations in the arts can be identified by a quick review of Fayol's principles (Figure 3-2). For example, labor is divided on stage into specialized departments for carpentry, props, lighting, and sound. A gap between authority and responsibility (Principle 2) may be found in some arts settings. An example would be the university student stage manager with a great deal of responsibility but very little authority in the organization. Unity of command (Principle 4) can be applied to arts organizations in the supervisor and employee working relationship. For example, a ticket office employee may be instructed in how to sell a ticket by a fellow student supervisor. The ticket office manager, who is usually a full-time staff person, later instructs the student employee to sell the ticket differently. Suddenly the student employee has two supervisors giving contradictory instructions. Which supervisor should be listened to? Who is in command? The idea of unity of direction (Principle 5) comes into play with the director, choreographer, conductor, or crew head leading the ensemble. For example, your event can quickly become disorganized if an assistant is providing contradictory information to the cast, ensemble, or crew. Principles 6 and 14 (subordination of individual interests and esprit de corps) describe what a choreographer, director, conductor, or crew chief is seeking to achieve with a group of dancers, actors, musicians, or staff: a group that works toward the greater good of the event over the personal interests of its members and, at the same time, achieves a unity or harmony as an ensemble. The idea of a clear hierarchy (Principle 9) is built into the structure of how many arts events are organized in the first place. The artistic leader assumes a place at the top of most arts organizations, and the basic structure of the organization includes people reporting to other people in a form that has evolved after hundreds of years of creating public performances. Other principles such as order (10), equity (11), and stability of personnel (12) are easily connected to the behavior of people in arts organizations. For example, you need to be able to efficiently find the prop chair in storage; cast and crew want to be treated with respect for their efforts; and having a stable workforce is key to the success of an arts event. Given the choice, no arts organization would want to profess to be disorganized, treat people poorly, or have constant staff turnover. Of course, you may have had direct personal contact with arts organizations that could benefit from applying Fayol's principles.

A good example of Barnard's theory of *acceptance of authority* is often seen in the process of managing volunteers. Typically, the volunteers in an organization are responding to the leadership of a manager based on the acceptance they have of the directives they are given. Since they do not have to be there, their willingness to work is based on their willingness to do what is asked of them. If "orders" exceed their usually unspoken sense of the scope of their volunteer effort, they will simply walk away. Anyone who has ever tried to work with an all-volunteer crew on a production understands the issue of acceptance of authority.

Human Relations Management (1927 to Present)

The Behavioral Approach   The major failure of the classic approaches to management mentioned thus far was their lack of understanding of the human factor in work. The most efficient way of accomplishing a task was often thwarted by what the scientific management theorists thought was employees' stubborn resistance to change. Researchers began to apply principles and concepts from what was then the new field of psychology in an effort to understand workers better and to make organizations and people more productive. The basic assumptions behind much of this research were that (1) people desire satisfying social relationships and derive satisfaction from accomplishing specific tasks; (2) they respond to group and peer pressure in their work output; and (3) they search for individual fulfillment in their work.

Mary Parker Follett (1868–1933), a Radcliffe graduate and social worker in the Boston area, articulated several ideas about group dynamics that still have a place in today's workplace. Follett noted that people working in organizations are continually influenced by each other and are very capable of accomplishing work in groups. In fact, her ideas are in use today as many organizations develop "teams" to accomplish tasks. Follett argued for a workplace in which management shared power with, not over, employees. She also developed the concept of *integrative unity* to describe how organizations could better reach their goals by coordinating group activities.[14]

A valuable piece of research involving people in the workplace, and a classic example of an unintended consequence, can be found in a project undertaken at the Hawthorne Wire Works in Illinois in the 1920s.

The Hawthorne Effect   In 1924, Vannevar Bush of MIT undertook a study of worker productivity at the Hawthorne Wire Works. The employees wound wires on motor coils or inspected small parts. Bush and his colleagues experimented with different lighting conditions on the assumption that different intensities of light would affect worker output. They found that the lighting level had no effect. Worker output increased despite wide variations in brightness.

Elton Mayo and Fritz Roethlisberger, professors at Harvard, began the second phase of the study in 1927. A group of workers was carefully monitored for five years using a special test facility built for the experiment. The researchers gave the workers physicals every six weeks, monitored their blood pressure, recorded weather conditions, noted their eating and sleeping habits, and so forth. No matter what changes were instituted, worker productivity kept increasing. It became clear to the researchers that other factors were influencing the employees' work behavior. Mayo and Roethlisberger surmised that the extra attention being paid to the experimental group combined with such things as changes in the supervision system, the creation of a small social system in the work groups, and the creation of a type of *esprit de corps* among the workers contributed to the increased output.[15] The Hawthorne Effect, as it is now called, stresses the importance of human interaction in the workplace.

Maslow's Hierarchy of Needs Another theory that helped shape the human relations approach to management was Abraham Maslow's hierarchy of needs. Maslow's 1943 paper, "A Theory of Human Motivation," was quickly incorporated into management theory and practice. Chapter 8, "Fundamentals of Leadership and Group Dynamics," discusses ways to apply his approach in the work setting from the leadership perspective. In summary, the theory suggests that part of the manager's job is to provide avenues leading to employee satisfaction, and that managers must work to remove obstacles that prevent employees from accomplishing their jobs. According to Maslow, people have various needs, including (from lowest to highest) physiological, safety, belongingness, esteem, and self-actualization. These needs can neither be fully met by nor ignored in designing the workplace. The goal is for a person to become self-actualized so as to lead a full and productive life.

McGregor's Theory X and Theory Y Douglas McGregor gave a speech in 1957 at the Sloan School of Management called "The Human Side of Enterprise." His presentation included an idea about work that changed the relationship of manager to employee. McGregor's theory is based on the concept that managers develop "self-fulfilling prophecies" about people that affect all of their interactions with employees.[16] He identified two major perspectives held by managers: Theory X and Theory Y. Theory X assumes that (1) people generally dislike work and avoid it when possible; (2) they must be coerced, controlled, and threatened with punishment to get them to work; and (3) they want to be directed and avoid taking responsibility. On the other hand, Theory Y assumes that (1) people are generally willing to work; (2) they are willing to accept responsibility; (3) they are capable of self-direction; and (4) they have creative and imaginative resources that are not effectively utilized in the work environment. The Theory Y approach to management has become a part of current trends toward what is called *participative management*. Companies are now asking employees what they think, rather than treating them simply as labor. McGregor believed that any enterprise can flourish if there is a partnership between the workers and the managers.[17]

Arts Application The whole idea of work being a social activity is common today. People working in arts organizations, like those in other professions, spend significant portions of their waking hours working with others. They develop complex patterns of interaction that are no different than any other business in our society. The very process of rehearsal in the arts is central to improving a person's eventual "performance." Therefore, the success of artist-managers is often tied to how well they can motivate the people around them. When we say the performance was "excellent," we are really responding to how well the people were managed and prepared for the performance. Follett's integrative unity is seen in bringing together cast and crew in the group effort of producing a live performance, special event, or exhibition.

The Hawthorne Effect can be observed in a work call involving a crew on a production. The work to be done (e.g., a stage light hanging and cabling project) can be made a more positive and productive experience if the manager supervising the work creates a positive and enjoyable situation for the people doing the work.

Maslow's theories have found their way into many aspects of contemporary arts organizations. Achieving success by navigating the levels in Maslow's hierarchy may lead a person to being described as self-actualized. Artists are often seeking a level of enlightenment or connection through their art that also results in reaching a state of self-actualization. But in order to accomplish that, artists must first have some basic needs met. For example, a performing ensemble that does not achieve a sense of belongingness may have a difficult time achieving the level of artistic excellence demanded of the art form. Individuals who do not feel a part of, or comfortable in, the ensemble may not be able to contribute their fullest in the enterprise.

McGregor's description of a Theory X manager might apply to directors, choreographers, conductors, designers, or crew heads who work with their cast, dancers, musicians, design assistants, or crew from a point of view assuming that people need to be coerced, controlled, and threatened in order to produce good work. The artistic director as a tyrant who must drive the talent to produce describes the Theory X manager to some degree. On the other hand, it is also possible to find artistic leaders who work with people from the Theory Y point of view. They see their job as carefully directing highly talented and self-motivated people to even higher levels of achievement.

Modern Management

Scientific Management Today—Quantitative Approaches

The rise of research universities and graduate schools of business and management, and the increased application of scientific management to the workplace, have come together in the last 60 years to form a strong theoretical base for the study of management. Wharton was the first undergraduate school to offer a degree in business (1881), and Dartmouth (1900) and Harvard (1909) were the first universities to offer graduate programs in management.[18]

Scientific management techniques have undergone further refinement with the assistance of computer models to help design the most efficient and productive workplace. The worldwide application of these techniques is well documented. Terms such as *operations research* (OR), the application of quantitative analysis to all parts of a business operation, are now common.[19] The critical path method (CPM) for scheduling and controlling work on projects is part of standard operating procedures in many businesses. Scientific management techniques have been applied by the Japanese in much of their manufacturing, and the resulting gains in productivity have advanced them to the forefront of world competition. Ironically, the processes to achieve this productivity were the result of the work of American quality expert W. Edwards Deming. Such concepts as "just-in-time inventory" (or Kanban), computer-aided design (CAD), computer-assisted manufacturing

(CAM), and computer-integrated manufacturing (CIM) are natural extensions of the work started by Taylor nearly 100 years ago.

Systems Theory

Systems theory assumes that organizations are composed of interrelated parts and activities that are arranged by design to produce goods or services. The open system model (see Figure 1-3) is an example of a systems theory application to an organization. It assumes that an organization functions in a complex world influenced by multiple environments as it goes about gathering inputs and transforming them into outputs in the form of goods or services. The "inputs" are the people who work for the organization, and materials, equipment, and money required to produce the organization's goods or services. The "output," or performance of the organization, is not the sum of its parts, but rather the result of the interaction of the parts. The process of management transforms the inputs to the output. Ideally, an organizational *synergy* results from the process, and the whole becomes greater than the sum of its parts.[20]

Contingency Approaches

The contingency approach to managing an organization works on the assumption that there is no one way that works best in all circumstances facing an organization. The management team must therefore be adaptable and capable of understanding the different mixes of management techniques that may be required at different times. This approach also recognizes that the people who make up the organization have differing styles of work and management. The top management must therefore expect that different work groups will have alternative ways of achieving the stated objectives. Rather than seeing this as a threat, diversity must be perceived as a strength. Synergy can once again be achieved if the management is capable of effectively coordinating the different work groups.[21]

Arts Application

One assumption this text makes is that arts organizations are open systems subject to internal and external forces that shape and change how they operate. The next chapter specifically discusses the larger world in which the arts organization must function. The system model allows a manager to create, revise, or remove subsystems that are not effectively supporting the mission. For example, a subsystem within an arts organization might be volunteer support. As a subsystem it may have goals, specific objectives, a staff member assigned to coordinate work, and budget resources allocated. However, if there is poor turnout by volunteers, or low-quality work is being done, then this subsystem is not effectively adding to the overall productivity of the organization. The arts manager then would step in, analyze the problems, and attempt to put in place changes that would help make the volunteer system work better.

The contingency theory assumes that the appropriate action to take by management should be driven by a careful analysis of the problem and situation. One assumes that there is no one universal set of principles that will work for all organizations. Situational factors should determine the best application of management solutions. For example, the solution to the volunteer problem may be a simple change in venues. Perhaps there is no problem with volunteer leadership, but rather it is too difficult to find a space big enough to have the group gather to work on their projects. So rather than delve into applying human relations theory solutions to the problem, a manager might apply a quantitative approach by studying the work processes of the volunteers and then improving the work space to facilitate what they do for the organization.

Emerging Views

It remains to be seen if there will ever be one theory that can be applied to how to best establish and operate an organization. The basis for effectively managing most organizations in the world in which we live recognizes that a contingency approach makes the most sense. Flexibility and adjusting to pressures applied to the organization from the outside, while carefully monitoring the inside processes of the organization, is paramount. The theories will continue to evolve. For example, we have *Theory Z*, proposed by William G. Ouchi and Alfred M. Jaeger, which attempts to take the positive management techniques from American and Japanese manufacturing and integrate them into a new system.[22] *Total quality management* (TQM), embraced by companies producing goods and services, is based on the assumption that an organization can better satisfy its customers if it is dedicated to continuously improving its product or service. (TQM is also called "*Kaizen*" in Japan; see http://www.kaizen-institute.com/kzn.htm for details.) The management and improvement of all of the processes an organization undertakes to accomplish its mission are very much a part of contemporary thinking about how to better manage organizations.

Another term added to the management vocabulary is *Six Sigma*. The phrase refers to a management system and philosophy that "focuses on eliminating defects through practices that emphasize understanding, measuring and improving processes."[23] Six Sigma grew out of the need to improve the quality and reliability of microprocessor chip manufacturing. From its beginnings in the early 1980s, it became a way of life for many organizations as they worked to compete in the global marketplace.

The management theorists often speak of major *paradigm shifts* and the *reengineering* of corporations today. [24] A current definition of a *paradigm* is a "set of rules and regulations (written and unwritten) that does two things: (1) establishes or defines boundaries, and (2) tells you how to behave inside the boundaries in order to be successful."[25] For example, we accept as a paradigm that a college education is best administered by gathering people together in large buildings, setting them down in neat rows of chairs, and imparting information from 9:00 to 9:50 A.M. Monday, Wednesday, and Friday for fifteen weeks a year over a four-year period. The emergence of distance learning is a good example of a shift in that paradigm. In a larger sense, this shift is really about the way in which information is imparted to people and who controls the classroom. The nineteenth-century paradigm of the schoolroom, and all that it involves, is undergoing change.

Arts organizations face similar challenges from shifting paradigms, as you will see in Chapter 4, "Arts Organizations in a Changing World." One of the most obvious paradigm shifts facing the live performing arts involves the change being brought about in how people interact with or experience what we do. The "digital age" is having an effect on how entertainment is delivered to and experienced by our audiences.

The impact of this change appears to be profound, but as yet it is unclear what new "rules" or "boundaries" will require adaptation in the performance process.

What does the future hold for management theories? One place to look is the business section of any bookstore. There you will find the latest trends in management thinking. So many good books are published each year that it is difficult to keep up with the output. Another good source is a book entitled *The Manager's Bookshelf* by Jon L. Pierce and John W. Newstrom. The sixth edition, published by HarperCollins College Publishers, covers a wide range of topics from management paradigms to ethics and management. The World Wide Web also offers a quick way to explore new ideas found in *The Manager's Bookshelf*. For example, if you search for information on the aforementioned Six Sigma concept, you will turn up dozens of websites on the topic. Be forewarned that there is a high degree of the "flavor of the week" syndrome to be found on the bookshelves. As Pierce and Newstrom point out, "These new terms feed the management world's preoccupation with quick fixes and the perpetuation of management fads."[26]

University business schools are also a source for ideas about future directions in management. The major research universities support faculty in the development of refined and new theories of management and organizational design. Many of the journals found in college and university libraries also provide an academic view of all of the major fields of management. Specialty journals are published regularly on such topics as operations, systems analysis, human resources, organizational psychology, and marketing.

Conclusion

Several thousand years of the evolution of management theory have led to the open system and contingency approaches to organizational management. During this time, societies have created organizations capable of accomplishing an incredible range of activities. Cities, roads, dams, hospitals, schools, and churches have been built by organized groups of individuals using the techniques and theories of management. At the same time, it is important to remember that management techniques have been and continue to be used to organize and implement unimaginable amounts of destruction and suffering.

Organizations and systems of management are still evolving today. The nineteenth-century organizational model, with its rigid hierarchy and complex chains of command, has been proved to be incapable of responding quickly enough to change. Newer information-based organizational models with fewer levels of management are forming. As we begin the twenty-first century, political and economic upheaval will continue in ways we cannot foresee. Change seems to be the only constant on which organizations and individuals can count. If change is managed wisely as part of the planning process, the resources needed to provide for the future of the organization will be available. However, it is also possible to envision a world that is overwhelmed by the problems of population, pollution, and hunger. The images of an unmanageable world that come to us from both science and fiction writers may provide the incentive people need to solve the problems around us. Ultimately, it will be the people who make up the organizations who will determine the type of future we all share. Cooperation and collective action among these people and organizations hold the key to the future.

In the next chapter, we will examine how all organizations are affected by the social and political systems within which they must function. These and other external environments shape how the organization defines its mission and what the people in the organization believe.

Summary

Management is an integral part of all social systems, from a family to a multinational corporation. Whether the objective is gathering food or taking over another corporation, managers are required to coordinate the interactions of people carrying out designated tasks. Although many people have learned to manage while on the job, a body of knowledge accumulated over the last 2,000 years constitutes management theory and practice.

Preindustrial societies developed laws, rules, myths, and rituals to control and direct people. The Renaissance and the Reformation created many new dynamics in the Western world. The opening of trade, the expansion of city centers, the rise of the middle class, and the major changes in political and social philosophy led to the formation of more sophisticated concepts of managing.

The Industrial Revolution produced fundamental changes in the nature of work and production, thus transforming Western societies. The mechanization of work in factories created the need for managers to supervise the activities of the factory workers.

The railroads, telegraph communication, manufacture of precise interchangeable parts, and other new inventions and advances in technology radically altered the workplace in the nineteenth century. As new production methods were devised, techniques for managing employees and organizing work began to be documented. The early systems of organizational design, production supervision, and data recording that were used in the railroads and factories became the basis of modern systems of scientific management.

Frederick W. Taylor was the first to document techniques for improving work output and streamlining antiquated manufacturing techniques. Scientific research was quickly adopted by the business world. Computer models and simulations are now used regularly to improve productivity and output in factories.

Other major management practices focused on organizational design and optimal ways to structure the operation. The basic principles expressed by Henri Fayol and others about such things as chain of command, lines of authority, and rules and policies in business were thought to be applicable to any organization.

Another branch of management theory falls under the heading of human relations management. The premise underlying this research is that people want socially satisfying work situations. The Hawthorne studies verified that work output increases if employees are given more control over their jobs. Mary Parker Follett's integrative unity, Abraham Maslow's hierarchy of needs, and Douglas McGregor's Theory X and Theory Y articulated many of the complex needs and interpersonal relationships people bring to the workplace.

Contemporary management practices are based on integration models. One model assumes that organizations are open systems affected by external environments in the process of transforming inputs into outputs. The other model, the contingency approach, assumes that there is no one best way to operate an organization; managers must therefore be flexible and find the best match between the resources available and the problems to be solved.

Key People, Terms, and Concepts

Robert Owen
Charles Babbage
Daniel Craig McCallum
Henry Varnum Poor
Frederick W. Taylor
Scientific management
Operations research
Critical path method
Computer-aided design, computer-assisted manufacturing, and
    computer-implemented manufacturing
Henri Fayol's Fourteen Principles
Human relations management
The Hawthorne Effect
Elton Mayo
Fritz Roethlisberger
Mary Parker Follett's integrative unity
Abraham Maslow's hierarchy of needs
Douglas McGregor's Theory X and Theory Y
Operations research (OR)
Systems theory
Contingency theory
Synergy
Paradigms

Questions

1. Describe examples from antiquity that demonstrate the use of the basic management functions of planning, organizing, leading, and controlling.

2. Describe some of the legacies of the Industrial Revolution in manufacturing today.

3. Which of Fayol's Fourteen Principles can be most easily applied in an arts organization? Which principles seem inappropriate?

4. Have you ever worked for a Theory X or Theory Y manager? To which theory do you subscribe?

5. How does a college or university fit into the open system model? What are the inputs? What happens in the transformation process? What are the typical outputs?

6. Do you think government, business, and social service organizations in the United States are capable of solving the problems facing society? If not, what changes must be made in these organizations to meet the demands?

References

1. Paul DiMaggio, *Managers of the Arts*, NEA Research Division Report #20 (Washington, D.C.: Seven Locks Press, 1987), p. 46.
2. Daniel Wren, *The Evolution of Management Thought*, 3rd ed. (New York: John Wiley & Sons, 1987), p. 56.
3. Ibid., pp. 58–62.

4. Ibid., p. 61.

5. Ibid., pp. 68–72.

6. Ibid., pp. 74–76.

7. Ibid., p. 78.

8. Michael T. Matteson and John M. Ivancevich, eds., *Management and Organizational Behavior Classics*, 4th ed. (Homewood, IL: Richard D. Irwin, 1989), p. 4.

9. Ibid., pp. 3–5.

10. Wren, *Evolution of Management Thought*, p. 132.

11. Ibid., p. 180

12. Henri Fayol, *General and Industrial Management*, trans. Constance Storrs (London: Sir Isaac Pitman and Sons, 1949), p. 15.

13. Chester Barnard, *The Functions of the Executive* (Cambridge, MA: Harvard University Press, 1938), pp. 165–166.

14. Kathryn M. Bartol and David C. Martin, *Management*, 3rd ed. (Boston: McGraw-Hill, 1998), pp. 47–48.

15. Wren, *Evolution of Management Thought*, p. 240.

16. Warren Bemis, Foreword, *The Human Side of Management*, by Douglas McGregor (New York: McGraw-Hill, 1960), p. iv.

17. Douglas McGregor, *The Human Side of Management* (New York: McGraw-Hill, 1960), pp. 33–57.

18. Wren, *Evolution of Management Thought*, p. 199.

19. Ibid., p. 397.

20. Kathryn M. Bartol and David C. Martin, *Management*, 3rd ed., pp. 54–57.

21. Ibid., p. 58.

22. Ibid., pp. 58–60.

23. Greg Brue, *Six Sigma for Managers* (New York: Briefcase Books, MaGraw-Hill, 2002), p. 2.

24. Michael Hammer and James Champy, *Reengineering the Corporation* (New York: HarperBusiness, 1993).

25. Joel A. Barker, *Paradigms: The Business of Discovering the Future* (New York: HarperCollins, 1993), p. 32.

26. Jon L. Pierce and John W. Newstrom, *The Manager's Bookshelf: A Mosaic of Contemporary Views*, 6th ed. (New York: HarperCollins College Publishers, 2002).

4

□ □ □ □ □

Arts Organizations in a Changing World

Museums are more crowded than ever, and these days they're more crowded with people wearing earphones or carrying "wands," gadgets that look like first-generation mobile phones but aren't. . . . MP3 players and wands . . . allow for "random access" [to exhibits].

USA Today (February 22, 2002)

The news highlight above is an example of organizations experimenting with ways of responding to technological changes that effect their operations. The Metropolitan Museum of Art borrows a new music recording format to make it easier for people to gain a richer understanding of the 2002 blockbuster exhibit entitled *Surrealism: Desire Unbound.*

Over at the Metropolitan Opera they rejected the popular practice of placing a supertitle projection screen above the stage in the mid-1990s. Instead, the Met custom-designed viewing screens in the seat backs.

The Metropolitan Opera's and the Metropolitan Museum's adaptations of enhanced presentation technology illustrate the ways that an organization can exploit an opportunity made available by the changing world in which it functions. The Met Opera solution was estimated to cost $1.25 million, but making opera in a foreign language more accessible to American audiences may have a long-term payoff for the opera company. The Met Museum's cost to provide MP3 players probably quickly paid for itself in rental fees to use the players. As we will see in this chapter, arts organizations need to be adaptable to the changes in many other areas of society if they are to continue to be successful in an increasingly competitive entertainment marketplace.

An arts organization, like any business, must work within changing external and internal environments. The term *environment* is used throughout this text to denote forces that interact with organizations. Here we examine six external environments: economic, political and legal, cultural and social, demographic, technological, and educational. We assess the impact of each of these environments on arts organizations and, later in the chapter, examine some of the trends that may reshape the arts in the near future. In addition, we study how arts organizations interact with these environments based on the information received from six major sources: audiences, other arts groups, board and staff members, the media, professional meetings and associations, and consultants.

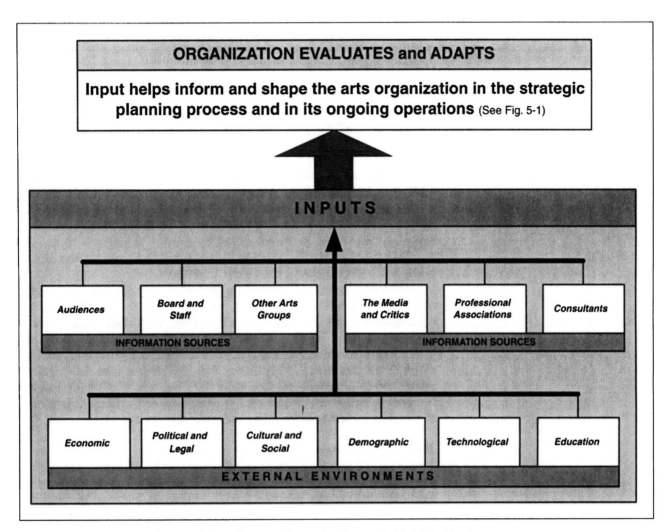

Figure 4-1 The Arts Organization and Multiple Environments

Figure 4-1 provides a graphic representation of the organization, the information sources (inputs), and the environments. An organization's relationship to information sources and to different environments may vary from organization to organization. Some organizations are more responsive to audiences and patrons, and others are more responsive to their boards or staffs. The process used in evaluating inputs from various sources and external environments will therefore vary with the predominant operating approach of the organization.

The information provided by the external environments and obtained from other sources help organizations in the vital process of strategic planning. The application of this information in the planning process is covered in Chapter 5, "Planning and Decision Making." The inputs noted in Figure 4-1 are used collectively to develop what in the planning process is often called a *SWOT Analysis* (Strengths, Weaknesses, Opportunities, Threats).

Nearly all of the activities that an arts organization undertakes may be related to the interaction between these environments and information sources and the functions of management: planning, organizing, leading, and controlling. Based on these relationships, a primary goal for an arts manager is to fulfill the stated mission of an organization by dynamically balancing all the various factors affecting it.

Changing Environments

As depicted in Figure 1-3, organizations are open systems that receive inputs from various sources; the inputs are then processed and transformed to outputs. In the broadest sense, this process applies whether it is an arts organization or a company that manufactures automobiles. Although there are substantial differences in these "businesses," arts organizations would be better served by coming to terms with the fact that they do not exist in isolation by accepting their similarities and by being more responsive to the public they serve.

The mission or purpose of the organization and its interpretation of the input it receives may differ, but these facts remain: If the enterprise does not adapt to changes in the world, it is likely to suffer or be less effective fulfilling its mission; if it is too rigid or too slow to change, it will cease to exist. Ultimately, the abstract "organization" will not suffer if the business is shut down. It is the people who work for the organization who will pay the price for the lack of adaptability and for poor management decisions. As should be self-evident, the process of managing change is an integral part of the manager's job.

Managing Change

A manager of an arts organization is responsible for more than helping to get the show or exhibition opened. He or she must be aware of the world around the organization: locally, regionally, nationally, and internationally. How does one go about monitoring and managing change? Developing a systematic process for monitoring key forces that may affect your organization is the first step. At the same time, the arts manager needs to appreciate that change will often happen in such a way that an organization has no choice but to be reactive. A good arts manager also needs to keep a sense of perspective on the rate of growth and development inside the organization while watching the changing world around it for opportunities and threats. Unfortunately, change is often difficult to monitor accurately because, like the hands of a clock, you only notice the movement after the fact.

In addition to navigating the organization through uncertain circumstances, the manager must also attend to internal organizational needs. In most organizations, people feel comfortable with a certain degree of routine or predictability. All organizations establish specific operating rules and detailed procedures for getting work done. Payroll procedures and basic work conditions are established as a routine part of the organization. People cannot function anywhere near their potential if they are worrying about whether they will be paid or about other conditions of their employment. Ironically, once conditions are stabilized, people have a tendency to become bored if their jobs assume a routine that seldom varies. Subtle changes in work patterns can be just as important to the long-term health of an organization as major shifts to new programs. An important part of the manager's job is to remain aware of the overall direction and mood of the organization while helping people do their day-to-day jobs.

Growing into Change

As we saw in Chapter 2, "The Evolution of Arts Organizations and Arts Management," arts organizations are often the result of a person or a small group of people who are willing to commit to the incredible effort it takes to bring a creative idea to life. The same could be said for many of the major corporations in existence today. It is possible to trace the founding of many businesses to one or two people with the drive, passion, and ambition to make it happen. Many of today's arts organizations are the product of the generation created by the post–World War II boom in births coupled with increased access to education and financial support from individuals, foundations, and the government. An unplanned mix of circumstances after World War II supported the unprecedented growth in performing and visual arts organizations across the nation. New theater, dance, and opera companies were founded, symphony orchestras spread throughout the nation, and museums opened in large and small cities. The support and vision of the Ford Foundation helped establish many arts organization in the 1950s and 1960s. Once established, the arduous task of maintaining what became arts institutions took center stage.

Let us examine a hypothetical example. A founder-directed opera company with an annual budget of $35,000 in the early 1970s grows to become an arts "institution" in its community with a budget of $4.5 million in the early part of the twenty-first century. As the organization evolves, a board of directors is added and new staff members are hired to do what the original founder and one or two volunteers were doing. The tiny storefront office becomes a large storefront office, and when that space is too small, a suite of offices is leased in a high-rise. Slowly, but inevitably, the small opera company begins to function at a scale that requires longer-term planning and careful analysis of its future. In other words, the company begins to move from daily, weekly, and monthly planning to year-to-year planning, and then on to what may be three- to five-year plans.

As any organization matures, it begins to take on characteristics that make it less responsive to change. After all, when a company finds something that works, it continues making more and more of that product. Our hypothetical opera company, for example, finds that a particular pattern of performances (two grand operas, two operettas, one musical) sells well, and so it repeats that cycle with different titles every year. Suppose now that the same community also becomes home to a professional theater company, a ballet company, and a symphony orchestra. The creation of each new organization will have an impact on the opera company. It will find itself competing for arts revenues because audiences have more choices. The theater company, for example, may decide to do two or three musicals each season. The change in the cultural environment of the community requires that the opera company's decisions about programming be made in the context of three other groups struggling for entertainment dollars.

To better adapt to its new circumstances, a process of continual evaluation should become the opera company's operating norm. Asking questions about where the opera company stands with respect to the six environments and the other arts groups, and sifting through the feedback from its information sources, should become as critical as mounting a season of high-quality productions.

Does adopting this process offer any guarantee that the opera company will fare better than a business that does not? Unfortunately, no;

but it can give the opera company an edge if the board, management, and artistic team cooperate in a process of evaluating what is happening in their community and the world.

It is important to remember that the process of continual evaluation is nothing more than a tool that will only be as effective as the managers and artists who use it. If the managers are not skilled at using the process, they may chart a course for the organization that leads to ruin. On the other hand, successful assessment and planning should lead the opera company to develop at a pace that fits well within the parameters of the community and the six environments.

Organizations discover that a process of monitoring the organization through ongoing assessment requires the development of techniques for gathering and analyzing information. Technique, as any performer will tell you, is acquired through long hours of rehearsal and disciplined practice. Just as dancers, singers, musicians, and actors learn to master their art through developing techniques for approaching a role, analyzing a musical score, or examining a play text, so too can an arts manager master the art of organizational evaluation. Once mastered, this technique can then be applied to the four functions of management. For example, to avoid duplication or conflicts, the opera company could consult with the theater company on upcoming titles and dates. This may seem obvious, but many organizations don't think of their work as part of a larger cultural context in their community.

Before discussing techniques for exploring individual environments, let us examine a general approach to organizational evaluation and assessment. As we will see, the biggest problem in assessing the opportunities and threats to an organization is the conflicting information facing a manager.

Content Analysis

An arts manager can start gathering vital information from books, newspapers, magazines, broadcast media, and the Internet. The basic methodology, which is called *content analysis*, simply involves identifying key sources for clues about current practices and possible future trends. Gathering input from sources external to the organization is complicated by the cyclical patterns of the print, electronic, and digital media. Topics come and go from the front page and TV news or websites with incredible speed. The key factor in an arts manager's quest for information through content analysis is to find enough trustworthy sources for facts and trends. This is not an easy task, as more and more of media control has become concentrated in the hands of a few conglomerates.

The manager must also differentiate between trends and fads. For example, shifts in population growth establish trends that ripple through a society for years: more people, more services, more houses, more apartments, and so forth. Fads, on the other hand, tend to die out more quickly. Arts organizations that react to fads sometimes find themselves scheduling programming that is out of step with current topical stories. In the time between the decision to produce a particular program and its actual production, a new hot issue may arise to take its place.

The arts manager must therefore use caution when trying to sort through what the future may bring. For example, it is not unusual to find contradictory opinions expressed about a particular topic. One futurist predicts a grand vision of a world where people will be able to use their computer to navigate through thousands of options for entertainment and information. Another pundit sees us becoming more isolated from each other as we spend our limited free time exploring these endless entertainment and information options in ways other than attending arts events.

Where to Look for Arts Content

If nothing else, the development of the Internet and the World Wide Web has made it possible to access information much more quickly than in the past. Being selective about where you go for information is probably even more critical than it was before one could type in a few words and send a search out to the Web. Online access to sources such as the *New York Times*, the *Wall Street Journal*, and *Business Week* are an integral part of the information base that a manager can use to begin building a manageable source for content analysis activities. These are not the only sources for general news of the world or the trends that are developing in our society, but having such content delivered to you electronically every day is a boon to someone trying to keep up to date.

The need to stay current in your arts discipline has been aided by website development in the last ten years. The number of sources is overwhelming. The words "arts organization trends" typed into a search on MSN, for example, returned 131,129 responses. Obviously, narrowing such a Web search is required, but narrowing it to what? Focusing on your discipline area as well as seeking information from organizations that specialize in research can help narrow your sources to a more manageable level. The Direct International Cultural Exchange is such an organization. Its homepage (http://www.euclid.co.uk/dice/) describes DICE as:

> DICE is the first international online information exchange system providing an opportunity for policy makers, planners, researchers and other interested parties in the cultural sector across the globe, to receive and contribute regular updates on policy initiatives, research, surveys, reports and studies, data analysis, training projects, conferences and seminars, and other relevant information. In addition, there is a facility for the circulation of immediate news and announcements to all subscribers.

Reports by the NEA, Americans for the Arts, and sources such as the Rand Institute, a nonprofit research firm, can be of great assistance to a manager trying to stay informed about the possible trends affecting the arts. Another helpful source for service organizations may be found at http://www.artslynx.org/colorado/webs.html. This website for the group Artslynx helps sort through the alphabet soup of organizational titles.

Environments

To effectively manage change, the arts manager must identify the environments that will have the most direct impact on an organization. A recognition of the biases and preconceptions of the manager and the readiness of the organization to change influences each environment and its potential impact on the organization. Let us review some of the environments that interact with arts organizations and establish some basic guidelines about what constitutes significant input.

For Further Consideration—The Value of Predictions

William A. Sherden's 1998 book *The Fortune Sellers* (John Wiley & Sons, Inc.) offers some interesting insights into our seemingly obsessive focus on trying to predict the future for businesses. It is as true for the corporate world as the small arts organization that effectively using content analysis to project the future for an arts organization may be affected by our own biases and the biases of our board and the staff. For example, he notes, "barriers . . . obscure our view of the future, such as 'situational bias': the phenomenon by which our thinking is so obscured by present conditions and trends that we cannot begin to see the future." He goes on to note, "Situational bias has continually been a major barrier in envisioning future technology. We have tended, and still tend, to imagine future technologies as mere extensions of things that already exist."[1]

FYI—The Arts and the Economy

A May 2001 report issued by the University of Arizona entitled "Arts in Tucson's Economy: An Economic and Tax Revenue Impact Study" provides a local arts manager with the kind of information that is helpful in understanding the place an arts organization has in the regional economy. The study noted that Tucson's major arts organizations had a 1999–2000 payroll of $27.6 million and employed 1,747 people, and that major arts organizations generated more than $5.8 million in tax revenues. Such studies are done on a regular basis and may already exist in your community. If such a study does not exist, then this type of report gives the arts manager a good sample to take to the local business community in support of gathering this impact data. Developing a working relationship with and contacts in the local economic development office can be an important first step to helping an arts organization become part of the business community in its region.

SOURCE: University of Arizona, Office of Economic Development, "Arts in Tucson's Economy," prepared by Tucson Arts Odyssey 2001. The report is available in a format that can be downloaded free from the University of Arizona's website: http://www.oed.arizona.edu.

Economic

Arts organizations, as part of the economic system, experience the effects of expansions and contractions in the national economy. In addition, regions, states, and cities exhibit different reactions to changes in the national and international economic environment. Some of the factors that may have an impact on an arts organization include the federal banking system (raising and lowering interest rates), new tax increases or cuts, revisions in existing tax legislation (which may promote or hinder donations), the balance of trade (international exchange rates), and inflation (price increases). This last factor can be the most destructive to an arts organization in the long run. When the cost of doing business continues to escalate, the organization faces tremendous pressure to increase revenue from either more sales or more donations. Chapter 10, "Economics and Financial Management," reviews some basic principles of economics and explores the unique economic dilemma that increasing costs and limits on productivity impose on arts groups.

The process of evaluating the economic environment is often subject to contradictory reports by experts in the field. One expert may issue a news release announcing that the recession is over, while another says it will continue for six more months. If a manager is trying to plan a budget based on projections of income and expenses in uncertain economic times, the most practical approach is to plan with contingency budgets. In other words, the organization's budget would be subject to constant revision depending on whether the economy is growing, stable, or slowing down.

One of the enduring myths of the entertainment industry is that when times are tough, people seek escape by spending on entertainment. The facts indicate that when the economy goes into a recession, people in the middle income levels reduce their spending, people in the upper income levels do not radically change their spending, and people in the lower income levels curtail what little spending they do on the arts.[2] Donation frequency seems to follow similar patterns. If a recession extends beyond a year, arts organizations will generally also see a slowdown in ticket purchases and donations from upper-income patrons. In more severe economic conditions, such as a depression, all spending and donation activity at all levels will slow dramatically. Knowing this, arts organizations can plan for reduced revenues, plan to increase fundraising activity, or both. The key to working with the economic environment is to have alternative budgets ready to implement should conditions change.

The impact of such extraordinary circumstances as the 9/11 terrorist attacks on the U.S. economy in general and arts organizations in particular, coupled with a recession already in place in the early 2000s, had a substantial effect on arts organizations. New York City arts organization felt the impact first and hardest. The aftereffects of the attack on the World Trade Center were felt in many different external environments beyond the economy. Not only did people forgo attending arts events in the period immediately after the attacks, but the loss in tax revenue to the city of New York reduced grant funding months later.[3]

Political and Legal

The arts in the United States today are very much a part of the political scene. However, with the heightened visibility of the arts has come the added responsibility of artists and arts organizations to lobby continually to protect the support gained over the last 30 years. Up until the creation of the NEA in 1965 the arts were only minimally involved with the political system. The only other time that the government and the arts had joined forces was during the 1930s when work projects that employed actors, singers, dancers, painters, and others became part of the U.S. economic recovery plan. The Federal Theatre Project, for example, burst onto the scene in 1935; by 1939, it was gone in a maelstrom of political struggle. The fear of Communist infiltration of theater groups sent the whole program into budgetary limbo. The productions produced by the Theatre Project often challenged the mainstream political environment to the point that it lost its base of support in Congress.[4]

The input from such sources as professional associations, consultants, board members, and the media can help shape how an organization will adjust to changes in the political and legal environment. The board and staff of an arts organization, whether they like it or not, face increasing scrutiny when they receive public funds. It is unlikely that the next few years will lessen the pressure on arts groups to justify their needs against the needs for the poor, the ill, and the homeless.

The current trend at state and local levels seems to be to privatize many services. In addition, many states are pursuing the politically attractive path of downsizing—or to use a business jargon term, "rightsizing"—state government payrolls. The theory is that more efficient and cost-effective private sector firms can do such jobs as run prisons, issue licenses, and so forth. The savings can then be passed along to the public in the form of either no tax increases or lowered tax rates. The goal of lowering taxes while delivering the same services typically can only be met by cutting funds for what are termed "nonessential" activities. The arts, unfortunately, fall under this category of activity. Arts managers who are active in the community and who have clearly made the case for the place of the arts and culture in the quality of life of the region can often counteract the effects of this trend.

Changes in the legal environment are carried out through federal, state, and local enforcement agencies. For example, the Occupational Safety and Health Administration (OSHA) and similar state agencies issue regulations that have a direct impact on the operation of the technical production shops and museum preparatory facilities in the United States. Employees have sometimes reported unsafe conditions and practices to these agencies as a way to force unresponsive arts managers to make the workplace safer. The impact of laws that affect the design of public spaces and the workplace by mandating access for people with disabilities must be taken into account. Issues relating to smoking, sexual harassment, medical and retirement benefits, maternity leave, and other needs and concerns have had an impact on arts organizations over the last ten years. Although it is true that many arts organizations fall below the minimum size required to comply with federal regulations, many state and local lawmakers have expanded the scope of the legal requirements to cover smaller businesses and organizations. In most cases, changes in the legal environment have a price tag attached, and the implementation of new laws translates into expense items that appear in the operating budget.

More arts organizations are adopting an active rather than a reactive approach to coping with changes in the political and legal environment. In fact, the word "proactive" has replaced "active" and has become a part of the arts managers' vocabulary. For example, arts organizations extend personal invitations to politicians to arts events that are accompanied by high-visibility social activity. Trips to Washington, D.C., the state house, or city hall for one-on-one discussions with the legislators, governor, or mayor have become mandatory. In their regular communication with lawmakers, arts managers stress that the people who attend the arts are also voters. The excerpt from the Americans for the Arts Web page illustrates an aspect of the lobby process regarding the issues of artists entering the United States with visas (see "Lobbying for the Arts"). In addition, lobbyists representing arts organizations are now a regular fixture on the national scene. One of the lobbyist's jobs is to keep abreast of pending legislation that may have an effect on the arts.

Lobbying for the Arts

The active presentation of information about the impact of government legal policy on arts organizations can be an important activity for an arts organization. In this example, Americans for the Arts is working to make legislators aware of the costs for presenting organizations in bringing guest artists to this country based on a decision made by the Immigration and Naturalization Service (INS).

Improving the Visa Approval Process for International Artists—2002

Making the Case to Congress

Background   Arts organizations are encountering increasing difficulty getting visa approval for international guest artists. The Immigration and Naturalization Service (INS) on June 1, 2001, began implementing a premium processing service, by which petitioners paying an additional $1,000 are guaranteed processing within 15 days. This fee, which is unaffordable for most arts organizations and many U.S. arts management companies, applies to a number of visa categories, including the O & P categories used by foreign guest artists. [Note: O category visa is for

workers with extraordinary abilities in Sciences, Arts, Education, Business or Athletics, and the P category is reserved for Athletes and Entertainers. For more information go to http://www.ins.usdoj.gov/graphics/services/visas.htm.] Since the implementation of the fee, regular visa processing has lengthened to between 60–120 days—far too long to accommodate many performance schedules.

Congress was expected to pass a major immigration reform bill in 2002, providing an opportunity to address the arts community's difficulties with the O and P visa categories.

Action Needed   As Congress considers immigration reform measures this year, require the INS to:

- Reduce the regular processing period for O & P petitions to a maximum of 30 days.
- Specify that failure to comply with this deadline automatically moves the petition to Premium Processing Service, at no additional cost.
- Require that the INS establish uniform procedures for processing "traditional

expedite" requests, which are available, free of charge, only in emergency situations.
- Clarify that when for-profit agents petition on behalf of nonprofits they are to have access to the regular expedite.

Talking Points
- Nonprofit arts organizations cannot routinely afford the $1,000 Premium Processing fee, but require timely processing.
- Allowing non-profit organizations to continue to pursue the regular expedite process is not a solution; most nonprofit petitions do not qualify for the expedite, and procedures for processing eligible petitions are currently unreliable.
- Perhaps now, more than ever, it is important that American arts organizations continue to facilitate international cultural exchange. The INS must provide a reliable and affordable process for bringing guest artists to the United States.

SOURCE: The Americans for the Arts website—www.artsusa.org—"Americans for the Arts is the nation's leading nonprofit organization for advancing the arts in America."

Cultural and Social

The cultural and social environment in the United States in the twenty-first century is heavily influenced by the economic, technological, and political environments. The traditional social structures (family, schools, and religious organizations), though undergoing change, still play major roles in the transmission of social values and beliefs.

Some of the changes affecting the cultural and social environment include two-income households, single-parent households, attitudes about gender roles and race, health care, and leisure time. The potential impact of these changes on arts organizations is far too complex to predict accurately.

Another major force in U.S. socialization processes is the broadcast media. Television and radio are the major sources of information and entertainment for millions of people. Unfortunately, the commercial broadcast media do not focus much attention on the fine arts. An interest in opera, the symphony, or the fine arts is often the source of humor, if mentioned at all, in the TV shows watched by millions every night. An appreciation for the arts is often depicted as the act of a snob.

The arts, which are a leisure time activity for most people, face difficult times ahead as the cultural and social environment of the United States continues to diversify. The generation that created the baby boom and contributed greatly to the growth of the arts has not been replaced in equally large numbers. In fact, the trend seems to be toward a generally lower standard of living for Americans under 30. An article in *Business Week* pointed out that in a typical American family, heads of household who are under 30 are making less money today than their counterparts in 1973. Families headed by college graduates are the only segment making more money than in 1973. Education level, which consistently correlates with attendance at arts events, also correlates with income level. In all cases, families headed by individuals with some or no college were making less than their peers made in 1973. The same applies to African-Americans and Hispanics.[5] These lower numbers may make it harder for arts groups to diversify their audiences, because these groups will probably spend any extra money on less expensive entertainment options.

The arts manager must also recognize that alternative living arrangements have created new definitions of "families" and have led to new arts consumption patterns. The high cost of housing has meant that many young people have not moved out of their family homes and established their own independent living arrangements. Single-parent families are also common today. In many communities, a greater number of people are living alone. Career pursuits also contribute to fewer leisure hours for a large segment of the highly educated population. Finding creative ways to reach these potential audiences with special discount ticket plans or through the types of programs offered will mean rethinking marketing and fundraising strategies for many organizations.

Peer group influence is another social factor identified in research about potential audiences. The Ziff Marketing, Inc. Survey undertaken for the Cleveland Foundation in 1985 found a strong correlation between arts attendance, education, and peer attendance. People will often try attending an arts event because a friend invites them. They may find they like the experience of attending the arts and become a regular consumer of the arts form they enjoy the most. The arts manager's energies are probably best directed toward developing, maintaining, and increasing a positive public awareness of and interest in the performing and visual arts. These objectives can best be met by working with artists to shape the audience of the future.

Artists are often at the leading edge of change in a society. For example, much of the content of the traditional and, of course, popular titles in the repertories of theater and opera companies reflects gender roles that were much different than they are today. Increasingly, the dominant culture is changing to reflect more diverse points of view as directors and producers seek out other perspectives. Women, African-American, Hispanic, and Asian-American artists are seeking to change cultural values to reflect a broader vision than that of the white Eurocentric world view. Many arts organizations are proud of the programs they do for Black History Month. However, for many African-Americans this special month of programming begs the question, "What about the other eleven months of the year?" In addition, contemporary marketing techniques focus on the segmentation of audiences as a way to reach new people. This approach may only further divide the audiences into smaller and less cohesive supporters of the arts. Ultimately, arts organizations have to address the issue of whether it is worth trying to be all things to all people in their quest for audiences and donors.

Changes in the cultural and social environment will continue to present major challenges to arts organizations in the future. As noted in the Rand report discussed later in this chapter, people are seeking entertainment through enhanced technology and not necessarily in person. Of course, not all changes in the cultural and social environments may be negative. The excerpt in this chapter from Richard Florida's *The Rise of the Creative Class* speaks to a complex mix of economic, technological, and social changes that may bode well for the arts.

As society becomes more diverse, audience tastes and preferences will continue to change to the point where arts groups need to reexamine their mission and fundamental choices in titles and programming options.

Demographic
The arts manager must closely monitor the demographic environment, which comprises the vital statistics of a society. Factors such as gender, age, race, income level, occupation, education, birth and death rate, and geographic distribution influence organizations. The more that is known about a community and the surrounding region, the better able the organization's ongoing assessment process will be to address community needs. For example, the baby boom generation will create a large number of elderly in the first quarter of the twenty-first century. Together, the boomers and the current elderly population account for a significant portion of today's arts consumers. Trying to anticipate the changing taste and attendance patterns of aging boomers will be a high priority for arts managers over the next 20 years.

The arts manager must also be concerned about the lower birth rate since the 1970s. Arts attendance may drop in direct proportion to the population base. This will have devastating consequences for organizations facing what will no doubt be greater financial pressures in the next 30 years.

The Creative Class

In 2002 Richard Florida's book *The Rise of the Creative Class: And How It's Transforming Work, Leisure, Community and Everyday Life* was received with much interest and favorable press. Richard Florida is the H. John Heinz III Professor of Regional Economic Development in the Heinz School of Public Policy and management at Carnegie Mellon University. His book, as its subtitle indicates, encompasses a wide range of topics. Professor Florida has done extensive research into the complex interaction of the rise of the creative class and its effect on America. Central to his premise is the recognition that creative activity isn't limited to artists and that expanding our understanding of how adaptable we are as a society is critical to our development as human beings. His book goes on to identify the geography of the creative class and its impact on the communities that foster and support its growth.

The New Class

The economic need for creativity has registered itself in the rise of a new class, which I call the Creative Class. Some 38 *million* Americans, 30 percent of all employed people, belong to this new class. I define the core of the Creative Class to include people in science and engineering, architecture and design, education, arts, music and entertainment, whose economic function is to create new ideas, new technology and/or new creative content. Around the core, the Creative Class also includes a broader group of *creative professionals* in business and finance, law, health care and related fields. These people engage in complex problem solving that involves a great deal of independent judgment and requires high levels of education or human capital. In addition, all members of the Creative Class—whether they are artists or engineers, musicians or computer scientists, writers or entrepreneurs—share a common ethos that values creativity, individuality, difference and merit. For the members of the Creative Class, every aspect and every manifestation of creativity—technological, cultural and economic—is interlinked and inseparable.

SOURCE: Richard Florida, *The Rise of the Creative Class* (New York: Basic Books, 2002), p. 8.

It is probably safe to assume that with an aging population health care costs will continue to take up a greater portion of the financial resources of society. This demographic trend is already being noticed by arts organizations as state funding for the arts is cut due to the pressure of financing federally mandated health care support. In addition, artists and arts organizations have also had to face ever-increasing medical insurance costs.

Demographic trends in the next 25 years will require arts organizations to adapt to a more ethnically diverse audience that spans a greater age range. One strategy that arts groups can take is to adjust programming choices to the audience, rather than expecting the audience to adjust to the program. For example, an older crowd might have its own special symphony series, while a younger audience might have a series tailored to its tastes. This is the equivalent of the "narrowcasting" of cable television companies.

Technological

As noted in Chapter 2, "The Evolution of Arts Organizations and Arts Management," the invention and distribution of film, radio, and television had a profound effect on the arts around the world. In the United States, the new technologies were quickly adopted for commercial profit-making purposes. The displacement of live performers with film, for example, put thousands of actors, dancers, singers, musicians, and technicians out of work in the 1920s and 1930s. New jobs were

Research Tool

A 1996 NEA report offers an in-depth study of demographic trends and arts participation (NEA Research Division Report #34, *Age and Arts Participation with a Focus on the Baby Boom Cohort*). The findings of this report raise questions about the attendance patterns of what is commonly called the baby boom generation. At issue is the lower attendance percentage of this generation at performing arts events. Despite being highly educated, many of the baby boomers seem to be seeking their entertainment from electronic and not live events. This report is published by Seven Locks Press of Santa Ana, California, and is worth adding to your management library.

created, of course, but many of the older performers in the larger metropolitan areas were permanently put out of work by the movie screen and the sound track. As the job market adjusted to the new technology, the live performing arts have adapted and grown since the end of World War II.

As we have seen, the arts boom was due in large part to the combination of the birth rate, economic growth, and increased levels of education. Through the 1960s and 1970s, arts centers and performing arts groups came into existence even though television sets and movie screens could be found nearly everywhere. By the 1980s, the home videocassette recorder (VCR), video disc, and compact disc player created a new demand for program material. Home computers further expanded the market for entertainment in the 1990s.

In the twenty-first century the VCR is losing its dominance to the DVD format, and the issues of control and the illegal distribution of media is a major problem facing distributors. Overall, the video and digital technology has provided more opportunities for viewers to rent or purchase programs of opera, theater, and dance performances or to see museum collections. The Internet and increasingly sophisticated websites have further enhanced the opportunities for arts organizations to share who they are and what they do with wider audiences.

One example of the technology affecting distribution may be found in the music industry. The issuance of thousands of classical titles on compact discs, coupled with improved sound quality, has helped keep the limited classical music industry alive. At the same time, the costly economics of recording classical music is changing the dynamics of the industry. As the Rand study *The Performing Arts in a New Era* points out, the recording industry is clearly dominated by for-profit businesses.[6] (See discussion under "The Impact of Future Trends on the Arts" later in this chapter.) Classical music recordings that often lose money, therefore, present a challenge to most music businesses owned by larger corporations. The degree to which a few classical "hit" recordings subsidize the remainder of the music line has not gone unnoticed by these companies. The music technology industry appears to be headed toward a content delivery system using the digital capabilities of the Internet. Opportunities may exist to extend the reach of the classical musical niche if distribution, marketing, and packaging costs can be reduced.

Some of the developments expected in the future offer further opportunities for the arts. For example, high-definition television (HDTV) will eventually make the home entertainment center a reality for millions of consumers. Integrating advanced computer systems with these entertainment centers may make possible home versions of the new virtual reality technology. Virtual reality (VR) is an interactive computer technology that allows the individual to enter into an electronic world that not only appears real to the viewer but also allows direct interaction in an environment. As the current technology keeps improving and the cost of equipment continues to fall, the application of VR will continue to expand. The technology is moving us toward the point where a person will be able to be part of a performance, rather than simply viewing it.

Although we may take comfort in the thought that people will want to continue to gather with other people and witness live performances, as they have done for thousands of years, we cannot assume that it will always be this way. New technologies seem to present opportunities rather than threats to arts organizations. It remains to be seen, of

In the News—Houston Opera Invests in Plasma TVs

A *New York Times* article entitled "Going to the Opera in Houston, But Watching It on TV" (September 18, 2002) offers evidence of an arts organization adopting technology to enhance its traditional presentation format. David Gockley, general director of the company, had large screen plasma monitors installed in 1999 in the upper balconies of the 2,346 seat Brown Theater. One stated goal for installing the monitors included increased ticket sales. The special video feed utilizes a director who selects close-ups of the singers. The article noted that an audience survey indicated strong support for the monitors, but 27 percent found fault with the innovation. The complaints focused on tampering with the traditional presentation of opera. The use of closed-circuit video feeds for latecomers has been common for years, but Houston is the first to bring the monitors into the auditorium.

SOURCE: Cynthia Greenwood, "Going to the Opera in Houston, But Watching It on TV," *The New York Times* (September 18, 2002).

course, how a product that is best delivered and experienced live will fare in an entertainment industry driven by a model that puts the choice of where and how to be entertained into the hands of end-users. In fact, the birth rate may have more to say about the future than technological advancements. It is possible that there will be a decline in attendance as the aging baby boomers and the digital generation stay home to be entertained by their own home theaters.

Educational

Studies show that education is one of the most significant factors in developing an arts consumer. Researcher Lynne Fitzhugh notes, "The socio-economic variable most often and most perfectly associated with cultural attendance is, not surprisingly, education."[7] Many surveys have found that more than half of the people attending arts events have college or graduate degrees. When considering how little focus is given to arts education in the United States, these numbers are all the more startling. One can only guess how much greater the attendance would be at cultural events if the arts were more integrated into the educational environment.

Arts organizations stand to gain the greatest long-term benefit from working in cooperation with local school systems. However, because the schools seldom have the resources to pay for the services of arts organizations, outside funding is required. Foundation and corporate grants to improve the quality of education may provide opportunities for arts groups to establish good community relations and to build future audiences.

The most effective methods for making the arts a significant part of the educational environment usually combine visits to the schools with planned lessons throughout the year. Transporting busloads of kids to an auditorium and putting on a show only offers a superficial connection to an arts event, and, in many cases, only acts to further alienate young audiences from the arts. Without a context for the experience, the concert, play, or opera is an isolated incident at best and boring at worst.

In the decades to come, schools will be the focus of much political attention. Performance standards, national testing, increasing budgetary pressures, and parental choice in selecting schools will be among the issues facing the 16,000 school districts across the United States. It will take aggressive action on the part of arts organizations to positively position themselves in this environment.

Information Sources

To effectively manage change and operate a useful evaluation and assessment system, arts managers must identify the sources they will use for gathering information and must develop an ongoing process for evaluating the opportunities and threats facing the organization. Let us examine the type of information each source generates.

Audiences

Smart arts managers want to know as much as possible about the people who expend the effort to go to a show or an exhibition or who give an organization money in exchange for a ticket, subscription, or membership. Why? For the simple reason that the organization's survival depends on establishing a long-term relationship with these people.

Unpredicted Change

There are also forces beyond the arts manager's control—such as weather. For example, in June 2001 Tropical Storm Allison dropped 36 inches of rain on the Houston, Texas, area causing widespread damage. One of the many arts organizations affected by the storm was the Alley Theatre. According to an Associated Press article published in the *Buffalo Evening News* on January 19, 2002, it cost $6 million to renovate the space after the playhouse was flooded. The Nuehaus Arena Stage was "buried under 3 million gallons of water from the storm last June." Other arts organizations in the Houston cultural district also sustained damage to their performance spaces as well as to their scenery, stage properties, and costumes. In these circumstances, having comprehensive insurance becomes part of an organization's crisis planning. Preparing for unplanned and unpredictable change can be as critical to the arts organization as planned change.

SOURCE: Michael Grayczyk, "Curtain Rises Again at Houston theater," Associated Press, *Buffalo Evening News* (January 19, 2002).

Within the bounds of an ethical system of gathering data, an arts manager would want to know (1) why this person made the purchase; (2) what he or she liked about what you presented; (3) what he or she didn't like; and (4) what other arts related "products" this person would be interested in purchasing. Members of the audience, patrons, donors, members—whatever they are called—are tremendous resources usually receptive to being asked what they think and feel. Exit surveys for museums, program insert surveys, phone surveys, or small discussion groups of randomly selected arts consumers are viable techniques for gathering information. Some techniques will be more effective than others, but regardless of the method, the arts organization that is able to provide detailed profiles of the consumers of its "products" will be better able to predict how a planned change will affect the relationship that exists between the individual and the organization.

Does this data-gathering process imply pandering to the audience's tastes? Hardly. The primary purpose of asking people what they think about your organization is to learn how to communicate better with them. Arts organizations forget that their audiences do not use the same vocabulary to describe the product and the process of the arts. In the open system, the arts manager designs the communication devices (brochures, letters, posters, and so on) to the outside world to reflect terms and concepts that effectively translate the organization's mission to the widest possible audience. Ineffective communication only raises barriers between the organization and repeat customers or future customers. (Chapter 11, "Marketing and the Arts," and Chapter 12, "Fundraising," discuss this topic in more detail.)

To summarize, then, establishing an ongoing communication process with your audience or members is essential to the long-term health of an organization. The importance of knowing as much as possible about who is interested in what you do and why cannot be stressed enough. Feedback from the consumers of your arts service is a resource that will shape the future of an organization.

Other Arts Groups

A community with several arts groups can achieve a synergistic boost from the combination of programs and activities. The term *synergy* is often used in management and marketing to describe the result of two or more organizations working together that results in the sum of their individual efforts being greater than the whole. When the different arts groups recognize that they can benefit from communicating with each other about their seasonal or exhibition plans, the local arts scene can flourish.

Strategic thinking and long-term planning should create a mutual understanding among arts groups that there is a complex arts audience, in addition to individual audiences for ballet, opera, theater, and so on. Research seems to indicate that a segment of the audience can be classified as users of different art forms, while other segments are loyal to one form and seldom go to see other events.[8] One strategy that seems to address these differences is the consortium approach. For example, many cities publish a quarterly arts calendar covering different arts groups and museums. These calendars give potential arts consumers an overview of all events happening in their area. Discount coupons and advertisements are often used to highlight special events. Multiple-page flyers can be widely distributed through a Sunday newspaper or a mass mailing. The net result of consortiums can be an enhanced awareness of the overall arts scene in a community and cooperation among the arts groups.

In addition to cooperative publications, different arts groups can work together to present new programming combinations that benefit both groups. The symphony and the ballet or the ballet and the opera can pool their resources on occasion to present larger-scale productions than either could mount individually.

If nothing else, a regularly scheduled meeting among the different presenting groups in a community offers an opportunity to share ideas about trends in the different art forms. The sharing of information ultimately helps a manager better understand the overall arts dynamic of the community.

Board and Staff Members

The board of directors and the staff of an arts organization are a vital component in the information-gathering process. The key to success is ongoing input via staff meetings, suggestion boxes, retreats, informal social gatherings, and formal planning sessions. When a board member asks about presenting a particular type of program or a staff member suggests a new procedure, the organization must have mechanisms for responding to the input. Some of the ideas may be very helpful and others may be driven by private agendas. Part of an arts manager's job is to actively sort through this input and try to adapt those suggestions and ideas that will more effectively support the mission of the organization. An open system depends on these suggestions and works from the assumption that there are always alternatives to what is currently being done. An organization that does not allow for input from the board or the staff will probably become stagnant and dysfunctional over time.

The Media

The print and broadcast media and the Internet provide the arts manager with up-to-the-minute information about many of the external environments that have an impact on the organization. It is also possible to gain some insight into the general mood of the country or region from polling conducted by the media. Trade publications in the arts as well as national and regional news sources and selected websites should be part of the arts manager's regular reading list. Although contradictory information is often generated by these sources, this is to be expected in a diverse society.

Cultivating and sustaining a positive working relationship with the press and the broadcast media can be of obvious long-term benefit to arts organizations. However, arts and nonprofit groups are often naive about the realities of media coverage. Column space in the print media or airtime on TV is an issue of money. For the print media, advertising sales space and news articles are always in a complex struggle with each other. For the local commercial television or radio station, ratings determine advertising revenue. Therefore, coverage that will generate ratings is often the focus of attention. Getting a feature story in the arts section of a newspaper or getting 30 seconds of airtime at the end of the six o'clock news can be a struggle. Attaining a level of visibility is critical for an arts organization's interactions with the external environments. No matter how good and noble the programs or projects of an organization may be, it is hard to establish credibility in the community without publicity.

One example of the ebb and flow of media coverage was the NEA struggle described in Chapter 2, "The Evolution of Arts Organizations and Arts Management." The media focused on the obscenity issue rather than on the larger questions of government support for the arts because the struggle of Congress with the NEA was simply more interesting than an abstract national policy issue. The net result was a great deal of publicity for the NEA, most of which, unfortunately, cast it in a negative light. Very few stories mentioned the thousands of grants made each year and the millions of people who benefit from grants and endowment services.

Arts organizations are in a very competitive situation when it comes to getting the attention of the media for the good work being done. However, a carefully designed public relations program will keep the arts organization in the news and help create a positive image.

Professional Meetings and Associations

Each of the arts has a professional service organization or trade association that provides regular information about issues of importance to its constituency. Many of the organizations and associations publish newsletters or magazines, and almost all hold annual conferences. The information-exchange process among members often focuses on current operational problems or topics related to new methods for raising money. The benefit for the arts managers of belonging to these associations or attending these conferences lies in expanding their knowledge of how other organizations are adapting to external forces.

Consultants

Consultants are another source for information about methods of keeping an organization functioning effectively. In theory, a consultant gives the organization a needed outside perspective. Of course, arts managers should never assume that consultants are always right any more than they would blindly trust any other source of information. However, because consultants usually deal with several organizations at one time, they can suggest new ideas and approaches that would not necessarily occur to the internal management staff. Consultants can also validate the staff's ideas about how best to manage change in the organization.

Other Sources

Depending on the art form, other input sources may provide valuable information to the manager of an open system. For example, the U.S. government regularly publishes statistical data from the Census Bureau and the Commerce Department that arts managers could apply. The local or regional chambers of commerce website or the convention and visitors bureau in a community are often very helpful sources of local economic and demographic information. This is especially useful when the data profiles a region of the country in which the arts organization resides. Another source of information might be found among the various suppliers of goods and services purchased by the organization. For example, the bank used by the organization could be an excellent source of local economic information. Printers or graphic arts firms could be a source of information about new trends and techniques in advertising. After all, the arts organization is a business in the community, and belonging to local groups that attract other businesses could prove helpful when seeking direct information about the economic health of the area.

The Impact of Future Trends on the Arts

Trying to anticipate change is a difficult if not impossible task. As we have seen from this brief overview of the major environments affecting arts organizations, complex forces can interact to produce unforeseen results. Seeking additional points of view and analysis is critical to developing a better understanding of how to respond to change.

Probably one of the most important recent studies about trends in the arts in America was a 2001 commission by the Pew Charitable Trusts. *The Performing Arts in a New Era*, published by the Rand Institute, will most likely be a source of a great deal of discussion by policy makers, arts leaders, and students in the next few years. This publication offers a comprehensive overview of the performing arts and is required reading for anyone trying to develop a better understanding of audiences, artists, arts organizations, and the financial state of the arts.

The introduction of the report notes that

> Our research offers evidence of a fundamental shift in the structure of live performing arts in the future. Specifically, we predict that the number of organizations supplying live performances of theater, music, opera, and dance will contract at the professional level and expand at the community level. Organizations that produce live professional performances face particular problems in many small and midsized cities across the country and could become increasingly concentrated in large metropolitan areas and important regional centers that can support high-budget nonprofit organizations with top-echelon performers and productions. For many Americans access to this level of performance arts will depend on touring productions. At the same time, Americans will have greater access to small, low-budget productions of greater cultural and artistic diversity performed largely by amateur artists (and professionals willing to perform for little or no pay) in their own communities. Also, as is true today, Americans will increasingly choose to experience the performing arts not through live performances but through recordings and broadcast media, the quality of which will continue to improve.[9]

This comprehensive report offers a less-than-bright future for organizations situated between the large institutions and the small arts organization. High fixed costs and limited earned and unearned income (e.g., fundraising and grants) potential seem to be having the most negative effect on middle-sized arts organizations. Larger organizations have the income and donation earning power and a scale of operation that help sustain them. Smaller organizations are not burdened with as many fixed costs and are able to be more flexible in their operational decision-making.

This study provides several recommendations for plans of action to meet the current and future problems facing arts organizations. Equally important, the report provides a forum for the kinds of policy discussions that seem to be lacking in all levels of government.

Summary

All organizations in an open system interact with changing environments that shape the transformation and output of the product. The economic, political and legal, cultural and social, demographic, technological, and educational environments interact to form a complex set of conditions that influence how well an organization will be able to meet its objectives. The evaluation of the six environments is a function of information gathered from audiences, other arts groups, board and staff members, the media, professional meetings and associations, and consultants. Since environments are constantly changing, managers must develop a process for continually evaluating input.

The economic environment is the most influential external force. General conditions such as inflation, recession, interest rates, and the taxation system determine the financial health of the operation.

The impact of the political and legal environment on an arts organization extends from the international scene to the local level. Cultivating positive communication and stressing the important part the arts play in the lives of voters can help build support from within the political arena.

The cultural and social environment is a combination of the values and beliefs of the society, as communicated through the family, the educational system, religion, and increasingly, the broadcast media. The changing family profile, increased racial diversification, expanding career and work choices for women, and gender role differences in U.S. society are creating a different profile of the potential audience member.

The distribution of the people in the United States is changing in terms of age, sex, race, income level, education, and location. The baby boom generation that fueled much of the growth in the arts is aging and is not being replaced in equally large numbers. The birth rate has been dropping since 1970. The impact of these demographic changes will have a profound effect on the arts well into the next century.

Technology, once a major threat to the live performing arts, is now helping artists reach a wider audience than at any time in history. New technologies have helped increase the distribution of the arts in the United States, and may make the experience of the live performance available to consumers in their homes.

The U.S. education system is undergoing tremendous pressure to increase its effectiveness through accountability measures. Because education levels are a strong predictor of later attendance at arts events, arts managers would do well to become part of the education revolution by working to incorporate the arts into the changing educational environment.

Key Terms and Concepts

Environments in the open system: economic, political and legal, cultural and social, demographic, technological, educational

Continual evaluation process

Content analysis

Demographic descriptors: sex, age, race, income level, occupation, education, birth and death rate, geographic distribution

Information sources: audiences, other arts groups, board and staff members, the media, professional meetings and associations, consultants

Questions

1. Do the six environments affect the various art forms in different ways? For example, are theater groups more or less influenced by changes in these environments than art museums? Explain.

2. This chapter focused on the influence of the environments on organizations. What influence do these environments have on the individual artist?

3. What combination of demographic descriptors would you use to outline why you and your family or friends are arts consumers?

4. What opportunities and threats will artists and arts organizations face over the next 20 years?

Case Study

As the article below indicates, creative solutions to developing cultural districts can take on many forms.

A Cultural District for Downtown Atlanta
by Arthur C. Brooks and Roland J. Kushner

Many U.S. cities have developed cultural districts not only to enrich the cultural experience of residents but also to stimulate economic growth and urban revitalization, increase the attractiveness and safety of the downtown area and attract tourism. At the request of the Fulton County Arts Council, Research Atlanta studied the experiences of cities comparable to Atlanta to determine the critical ingredients for a successful cultural district initiative. This report explores those ingredients, then assembles them into a blueprint for action should the community choose to create a cultural district in downtown Atlanta.

The key issues for developing a cultural district are the purpose; the location; the organizing authority; the content or attractions; the management or level of control over the district; and the funding. The most pragmatic and marketable argument for a cultural district in downtown Atlanta is to provide an enriching cultural experience that increases the quality of life for Atlantans. This framing forces debate of the project's own merits rather than of its economic return relative to that of other infrastructure or public amenities projects. Intown revitalization and economic development merit discussion as secondary benefits, not motivating factors.

Most successful cultural districts develop in geographically contiguous areas that already boast cultural amenities and have supporting transportation and commercial infrastructure to help concentrate demand and encourage traffic among cultural institutions within the district. For these reasons, the most appropriate area for the cultural district in downtown encompasses the Fairlie Poplar district and extends east along Auburn Avenue to Boulevard.

Three kinds of authorities typically organize and administer cultural districts: independent nonprofit organizations, consortia between the local government and an existing nonprofit organization, and government entities. An independent nonprofit created to develop and administer the district makes the most sense for Atlanta, because its funding, programming and development are less influenced by politics.

A coherent, long-range plan for content and programming, driven by the demand of consumers, has been the cornerstone of success in other cultural districts. Identifying the target audience(s), understanding their cultural tastes as well as their interests in related retail offerings, and then creating a theme for the district that satisfies those tastes tend to produce better results than trying to duplicate another city's success. Targeting the citizens of Atlanta rather than tourists suggests programming that embraces both the city's rich African American cultural heritage and organically growing high energy interpretations of the more classical arts for a district unlike any other in the U.S.

The level of administrative control in the surveyed cultural districts varied along a continuum from simply designating the district with signage to dominating all aspects of funding, programming and management. In between, some authorities focus on development or building support and encouraging action to develop the more physical aspects of the project; donation, i.e., recruiting outside sources to finance individual arts entities in the district as well as district improvements; or direction, i.e., attracting and directly funding cultural institutions in the district. Combining the responsibilities for designating, developing and donating activities seems most feasible for an administering body in Atlanta.

Funding for a cultural district may come exclusively from tax revenues, from private and corporate philanthropy, or from a combination of these. Atlanta can learn most notably from Charlotte and Philadelphia, both of which have stitched together corporate, private and non-subsidy government funding for their cultural districts while maintaining a consistent vision for the district's activities.

Effective tripartite leadership from the city, the corporate sector and the arts community is essential for success. As other cities found, government leadership in the form of supportive zoning and tax laws, seed money and outspoken public support for the project can help convince business leaders to commit their support and help insure long-term viability of the project. Finding such leadership will be especially important for Atlanta because zoning ordinances for the historic Auburn Avenue corridor prevent the kind of performance, hospitality and retail spaces necessary for a vibrant cultural scene.

SOURCE: Arthur C. Brooks and Roland J. Kushner, *A Cultural District for Downtown Atlanta*, Research Atlanta, Inc., Andrew Young School of Policy Studies, Georgia State University, 2002, used with permission. For more information: www.researchatlanta.org/arts_economy_in_20_cities.htm

Questions

1. Do you think there are any current trends in the various external environments discussed in this chapter that may

have a positive or negative effect on this idea for a cultural district?

   2. If such a district exists in your community, how did it come into being and how well is it fulfilling its stated mission?

   3. If no such cultural district exists in your community, do you think the idea might work? What factors may help or hinder the development of this idea in your community?

References

1. William A. Sherden, *The Fortune Sellers* (New York: John Wiley & Sons, 1998), p. 8.
2. Lynne Fitzhugh, "An Analysis of Audience Studies for the Performing Arts in America," Part 2, *Journal of Arts Management and Law* 13 (Fall 1983), p. 7.
3. Robin Pogreen, "Arts Groups in New York Brace for Cuts in City Funds," *New York Times* (Monday, May 20, 2002), p. B-1.
4. John O'Connor and Lorraine Brown, eds., *Free, Adult, Uncensored: The Living History of the Federal Theatre Project* (Washington, D.C.: New Republic, 1978).
5. "What Happened to the American Dream?" *Business Week* (August 19, 1991), pp. 80–85.
6. Kevin McCarthy, Arthur Brooks, Julia Lowell, and Laura Zakaras, *The Performing Arts in a New Era* (Santa Monica, CA: Rand Institute, 2001), p. 10. http://www.rand.org./ARTS_area.
7. Lynne Fitzhugh, "An Analysis of Audience Studies for the Performing Arts in America," Part 1, *Journal of Arts Management and Law* 13 (Summer 1983).
8. Ibid., p. 56.
9. McCarthy, Brooks, Lowell, Zakaras, *The Performing Arts in a New Era*, p. 3.

5

□ □ □ □ □

Planning and Decision Making

If you aren't thinking ahead, you'll be left behind.

As noted in Chapter 1, "Management and the Arts," planning is one of the primary functions of management. In this chapter, we define planning and look at strategic and operational planning and the decision-making process, which are examined as tools to assist with the planning process.

Before we can delve into the topic of planning, we need to step back for a moment and consider an important question: Why are we doing this concert, play, or exhibition? Are we trying to introduce our audiences to a new work or artist? Are we trying to raise money for a cause? Are we trying to make a profit or generate a surplus in our depleted operating budget? The planning we do must be driven by the answer to this important "why."

As we discovered in Chapter 4, "Arts Organizations in a Changing World," there are complex forces at work in the various environments in which arts organization must function. Artists and organizations have to adapt to the pressures of the external environments that are an integral part of our society. For example, solo artists unencumbered by a board of directors and an administrative staff may be able to achieve the goal of performing a new work through the sheer force of their energy and drive. However, they still face very practical issues related to the political and legal environments in the process of trying to present their work. A well-established orchestra, on the other hand, may debate for months over the conductor's desire to do a new series of modern music concerts. In this case, the probably differing attitudes of the members of the board enter into determining why an organization selects a new direction.

Relationship of Planning to the Arts

The creation and use of a planning process can be an excellent way to provide the overall framework needed to keep an organization headed in the same general direction. For these plans to be effective, they should be integrated into the daily operation of the organization. Does this ensure that the organization will be a success? No. In fact, many founder-driven arts organizations came to life and struggled to national prominence without any planning documents. However, it is difficult today for an arts organization to attain support from foundations, corporations, or government agencies without a published mission statement and a strategic planning document.

The Necessity of Planning

Over the last 30 years, arts organizations and artists have had to deal with ever-increasing accountability, especially when dealing with individual donations, public money, corporate donations, and foundation support. It is typical for arts organizations to provide three- to five-year plans in their funding applications. However, the need for arts organizations to remain flexible and open to change is also important. Planning that locks an arts organization into rigid thinking can be deadly to the whole enterprise.

The management of any arts organization must assume that change is a given. Opportunities and threats to the organization will constantly present themselves. Therefore, there is no choice other than to draw up plans detailing how the organization will respond to change. The key is to develop a planning process and planning implementation system that fits with the scope and scale of the organization.

The Organization's Map and Leadership

Most of us have had to read a map at some point in our lives. In effect, the planning document for an organization is the map to help it get to its ultimate destination. Although most of us have read maps, few of us create them. Arts organizations need the skilled assistance of managers who know how to develop a workable planning process for the organization.

Ultimately, planning cannot ensure success. Without dynamic and articulate leadership, an organization will probably be less likely to succeed. Board and management leadership that is not trained in developing and implementing plans must learn these skills if the organization is to remain healthy over the long run.

Planning Terminology

Let us begin our overview of planning by defining some of the basic terms used in the process. First, *planning* is a process of stating what you want to do and how you want to do it. Planning involves thinking about the future—even if that is only tomorrow. It requires imagination, careful thought, and, most importantly, time. This text uses the term *plan* to mean a statement of intended means for accomplishing stated results. A plan should answer five questions:

1. Why?
2. What?
3. When?
4. Where?
5. Who?

Here is an example of this approach:

In order to fulfill our mission of bringing new music to the community, we have set a goal for ourselves of attracting more patrons to our events. To achieve that goal we have set a specific objective for our marketing and sales staff to expand our subscription audience by 7 percent for next year's concert series in New Hall. To meet this objective the marketing and sales staff will contact corporate personnel departments and offer group discounts.

FYI—Other Resources for Planning

A source for highly systematized information about planning may be found in John M. Byron's *Strategic Planning for Public and Nonprofit Organizations*. Byron sets a benchmark for organizational planning. His approach is particularly helpful because it recognizes the unique elements of the nonprofit organization in a planning process. He also articulates a useful perspective about strategic thinking and acting as it informs strategic planning. Lastly, he provides concrete examples of successful and unsuccessful planning practices.

Another very helpful workbook, entitled *Strategic Planning for Nonprofit Organizations*, is published by the Wiley Nonprofit Series. Authors Michael Allison and Jude Kaye have created a very detailed and practical guide for planning.

As you can see, this plan answers all five questions: *why*—the organization's mission to bring new music to the area; *what*—meet our goal and objective to expand concert subscriptions by 7 percent through group sales; *when*—for next season; *where*—New Hall; and *who*—the marketing and sales staff.

In this text, a *goal* is defined as a desired outcome and an *objective* is the specific means to achieve the desired outcome. In our example, the goal is to attract more patrons (a desired outcome), and the specific objective is to increase the subscription audience by 7 percent next season by corporate group sales (specific means). The result of this process should be goals that are feasible to achieve and objectives that are realistic given the resources available. Clear, simple, direct language should be used to make it easy to understand what is being attempted and why.

Short-, Intermediate-, and Long-Range Plans

There are many different types of plans typically used by people and organizations. When we refer to short-range plans we mean one that is a year or less. Intermediate-range plans are usually one to four years, and long-range plans cover five or more years. Generally, long-range plans that exceed five years are of limited value because there are too many unforeseen variables. However, that does not mean an arts organization shouldn't plan that far ahead. For example, raising funds for a major building project often has five or more years associated with the entire process. As you will see in Chapter 12, "Fundraising," fundraisers may deal with gifts that will not come to the organization until far in the future; therefore, their planning horizon may be extended out well beyond 10 years.

It is important to consider how people within the organization perceive time as you start the planning process. Research on planning points out that most people are comfortable with thinking three to six months ahead. Once you get past one year, most people are only able to think in the most general terms. Therefore, it is not advisable to develop overly detailed planning objectives and documents that extend too far into the future. The age of an organization also determines perceptions of time. When you first establish an organization, four months can seem like a long time. However, if you are part of a long-standing arts organization, three- to five-year plans might not be so difficult to comprehend.

Strategic and Operational Plans

Any discussion of planning assumes that the organization has developed strategic and operational plans. For our purposes, a *strategic plan* is a set of comprehensive plans designed to marshal all of the resources available to the arts organization for the purpose of meeting defined goals and objectives derived from the mission statement. Another important element in the planning process involves formulating *operational plans*, which are usually limited to activities designed to support the day-to-day operations of the organization. You may have the strategic plan to become the largest arts organization in your region, but in order to do that you'll need operational plans to do the marketing and public relations needed to achieve that strategy. Therefore, your operational plan identifies and develops the resources you need to support components of the strategic plan.

Planning Proverb #1

"Planning is 80% thinking and 20% writing. Then 100% doing!"[1]

Single-Use and Standing-Use Plans

Single-use and standing-use plans are the most common in arts organizations. *Single-use plans* include a budget, a production schedule, and a project timeline, and *standing-use plans* include a policy, operating procedures, and rules.[2]

A *budget* is a single-use plan designed for the purpose of clarifying the organization's decisions about the distribution of resources. A budget that allocates more money for costumes than for scenery says something about the idea driving the production. An exhibition may allocate 80 percent of the budget for a full-color book and only 20 percent for mounting the exhibition. A symphony may decide to focus on national touring and reduce its home schedule by 20%. These choices ideally represent a plan agreed to by all of the people involved in putting on the show or concert or setting up the exhibition.

Another single-use plan would be a *schedule*. We are all familiar with a schedule as a list of deadlines for completing specific tasks designed to meet an overall objective. Most arts managers work with either weekly or monthly calendar formats. For example, when an opera company sits down to plan a season, it works from a single-use plan: the season production schedule. If the company knows it will perform *Aida* next season, it can plan for accommodating the animals for the triumphal march scene. The logistics related to this part of the plan can be arranged far in advance. (Budgeting and scheduling are discussed in more depth in Chapter 10, "Economics and Financial Management.")

A *standing-use plan* is designed to be used repeatedly. For example, an arts organization should have a standing-use plan dealing specifically with how the administrative offices will operate. The office operations plan would include such things as how the phones are to be answered, messages taken, mail opening, filing systems, and so forth. A theater box office should have a standing-use plan detailing the day-to-day operational procedures for processing orders and accounting for all revenue. Standing-use plans are also typically found in policy books, employee handbooks, or posted rules.

On the surface, these two planning components may seem less weighty than the grand strategic plans, but they are often critical for the success of an organization. As we will see in Chapter 7, "Staffing the Organization," employees depend on well-designed single-use and standing-use plans to do their jobs.

Developing a Planning Process for the Arts

Let us now examine in more detail how to develop a planning process for an arts organization. Most of us use a planning process of one sort or another to get through the day: "After class or work I have to go to the bank, then have lunch with Fred, and then head over to the library or the store this evening." When people make the transition to a formal planning process they can become bogged down in a level of detail that makes the idea of planning daunting. Planning should be approached as a practical and enjoyable journey, not a set of abstract tasks.

The Mission Statement

As you see in Figure 5-1, the first step in the planning process is to analyze your mission. A clear mission statement, which defines the organization's "reason to be," is the source from which all plans should

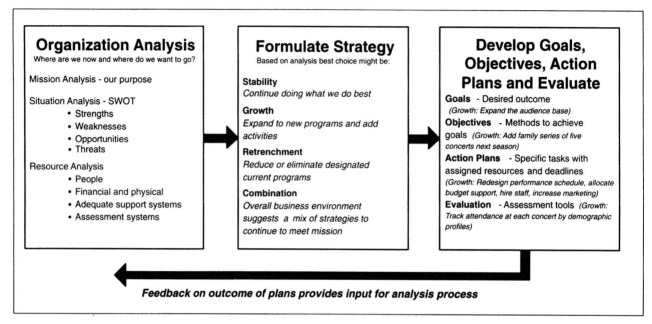

Figure 5-1   Strategic Planning Process

spring. For example, a theater company might be dedicated to presenting new works, or a ballet company might be committed to performing classical works. Groups of all sizes need a concise statement that communicates to the world who they are and why they exist. Here are six arts organization mission statements:

- The Actors' Guild of Lexington, Kentucky, states that its mission is to "create and present compelling contemporary theatre for the region."[3]
- "The Guthrie Theater serves as a vital artistic resource for the people of Minnesota and the region. Its primary task is to celebrate, through theatrical performances, the common humanity binding us all together. The Theater is devoted to the traditional classical repertoire that has sustained us since our foundation and to the exploration of new works from diverse cultures and traditions. The Guthrie aspires to the highest levels of artistic achievement and to reaching the widest possible audience with our work. The Guthrie Theater sees itself as a leader in American Theater with both a national and international reputation."[4]
- "The San Diego Chamber Orchestra's mission is to provide a resident orchestra of the highest professional caliber to San Diego County."[5]
- "Mission Statement:
   The Alliance Theatre is dedicated to celebrating our diversity by embracing our common humanity. Our work builds bridges to connect us as human beings through the development and production of exciting, entertaining and stimulating plays, and by nurturing and enriching the art, artist, and audience. The Alliance produces a mix of classic and contemporary plays that speak to the heart, provoke the mind, and illuminate the unlimited possibilities of the human spirit."[6]

- "The Museum of Fine Arts houses and preserves preeminent collections and aspires to serve a wide variety of people through direct encounters with works of art."[7]
- "Atlanta Ballet Mission:
  —To serve our community actively by providing enlightened arts education opportunities.
  —To inspire a diversity of audiences with a broad, stylistic range of dance repertoire.
  —To honor our past and contribute to the legacy of the art of ballet in an enduring way."[8]
- "The mission of the San Francisco Symphony is: Sets the highest possible standards for excellence in musical performance at home and around the world; Enriches, serves, and shapes cultural life throughout the spectrum of Bay area communities; Maintains financial stability and gains public recognition as a means of ensuring its ability to fulfill its mission."[9]

Readers of the mission statement of the Actors' Guild find a succinct phrase describing who it is, what it does, and where it is located. It is an active statement that is easy to remember.

The Guthrie Theater's statement is less accessible, but certainly sounds lofty. Although it is not readily evident what the mission of the Guthrie is, the second sentence seems to contain the core of its purpose: "to celebrate, through theatrical performance, the common humanity binding us all together."

The San Diego Chamber Orchestra elected to focus on providing a resident orchestra as its mission. Its statement essentially says that the purpose of the chamber orchestra is to provide a high-quality chamber orchestra. The chamber orchestra might be better served by a mission statement that focused on the works presented.

The Alliance Theatre's mission appears to be contained in the first sentence, although the reader is left with a great many words to process under the heading "Mission Statement." The bulk of the statement is really a description of what the theater group does. Interestingly, the phrase "common humanity" appears in this mission statement too.

The Boston Museum of Fine Arts has a compact and direct mission statement. The only thing preventing it from being 100 percent effective is its omission of the word "Boston." This museum mission statement could describe any number of organizations anywhere in the world.

The Atlanta Ballet appears to have three missions, which in fact read more like goals (desired outcomes) than the organization's "reason to be." After reading the ballet's mission statement one is left wondering what its primary mission really is.

Lastly, we have the mission statement from the website of the world-renowned San Francisco Symphony Orchestra. One is immediately struck with the lack of continuity between the phrase "The mission . . . is:" immediately followed by, "Sets the highest possible standards. . . ." This "mission statement" goes on to describe what the organization does. If its mission is to set high standards for excellent musical performance, then the other items listed are what the symphony accomplishes through that mission.

As you can see from this sampling, there are as many different ways to state a mission as there are organizations. Some missions are composed of one sentence, and others take a paragraph. A mission statement is your main tool for describing the organization to the world. Some of the mission statements cited do achieve that outcome, but others are less successful.

Perhaps the best advice about formulating a mission statement is to remember that this is an introduction of the organization to people who do not know what it is and have no idea what it does. A mission statement is directed at audiences, donors, funding sources, and other public agencies. Think about how easy it would be to introduce yourself at a reception or public function by saying, "I am with Actors' Guild of Lexington, and our mission is to create and present compelling contemporary theatre." The person you just met knows who you are, the name of your organization, and what it does. Try this exercise with the some of the other mission statements we examined, and you will see why staff often make up variations on the published mission statement in order to actually communicate about their organization when meeting the public.

Reading these sample mission statements may lead you to question the admonition that planning should be driven by the mission, since some well-known organizations publish mission statements that do not clearly present the primary purpose of the organization. Yet many of these same organizations still do quite well. The real world of how arts organizations function and the textbook models for how to accomplish certain activities—such as developing mission statements and planning—do not always match. Nevertheless, it is easier to plan and set priorities as an arts manager if the mission is clear and is widely communicated inside and outside the arts organization.

Situation Analysis

The process of looking at oneself and frankly assessing one's good points and shortcomings is as difficult a process for an organization as it is for an individual. The arts consulting business thrives on bringing the outsider's viewpoint into what too often becomes a self-congratulatory process. Organizations, like people, sometimes have a hard time seeing their flaws.

The next step in the process, then, is to undertake what is often referred to as a *SWOT* (strengths, weaknesses, opportunities, and threats) *analysis* (see Figure 5-1). One creates a detailed inventory list of items under each area to develop an overview of the organization in relationship to factors that may help or hinder the organization realize its mission. Being open and honest about the organization's current status is critical, as is recognizing that at times a strength can be a weakness and an opportunity may also be a threat. For example, an experimental theater company, with a mission of presenting *only* new works, may have the strength of very talented writers and an outstanding acting company. The company's weakness may also be its newness. It lacks experience working within the existing arts community in the area. It may also have an opportunity in the newness of its work, and thus may be able to capture more attention than one more production of *Hello, Dolly!* or *A Streetcar Named Desire.* Lastly, it may face the threat of censorship in the community if the work is controversial.

How do all of these factors shape planning for our experimental theater company? First, in doing a rigorous analysis of the situation it may discover that it might never thrive in this community and that relocation to a more conducive setting would be advantageous. Or, the company may decide that the challenge of presenting new works in this community is worth the effort, even if it never achieves widespread public and financial support. Or, based on its SWOT analysis, it could decide to change its artistic mission and produce a season of more accessible works along with new plays.

As you can see, a planning process can be directed at creating goals, objectives, and plans of action for the purpose of fulfilling a mission statement. This may seem like an obvious starting point for planning, but I have spent many hours in meetings where conflicting views of an organization's mission statement were never resolved. The planning went ahead, but conflicts always arose when the process led to the stage of deciding what was most important to the organization. A weak or contradictory mission statement is like an out-of-focus photograph. When people view the picture, they often see different things. They reach conclusions and make assumptions based on imprecise information. Actions are taken, and then questions are raised: "How does this project or program serve our mission?" Often it does not, but resources are allocated anyway.

Resource Analysis

The last step of an organizational analysis, as shown in Figure 5-1, involves a resource assessment. An important aspect of organizational self-analysis is to evaluate the organization's internal human, material, and technological resources and operating system. Questions such as the following must be posed:

1. Do we have the people with the skills we need to realize our plans?
2. Do we have the facilities, money, equipment, and other resources needed to make our plans work?
3. Do we have the ability to monitor progress and make corrections as we proceed?

These questions raise critical issues facing an arts organization. Many plans are never realized because the first question on this list cannot be answered in the affirmative. You may want to expand your telephone marketing sales for your season, but if you don't have the staff you can't engage in this activity. You may wish to have your museum staff engaged in more educational outreach activities, but not if staffers are already strapped for time to accomplish their existing task list. Even if you have the human resources available to support the plan, lack of space, equipment, or budget support can thwart those trying to achieve the goals you have all agreed need to be addressed. Lastly, plans that are made and then executed need to be monitored and often adjusted as they unfold. Having the time and energy it takes to keep your plans moving through to completion is also a critical part of the planning process.

Formulating Strategies

The next step in the planning process is to take the organizational analysis and shape a strategic direction for the organization (see Figure 5-1). Strategy defines the direction in which the whole organization intends to move. It also establishes the framework for the action to be taken to achieve the goals outlined in the strategy. We have noted that the strategy should relate to the environment in which the organization must function. In Chapter 4, "Arts Organizations in a Changing World," six

Another Point of View on the SWOT

In an article in *The NonProfit Times* of June 2002, Thomas McLauglin questions the SWOT approach in an article entitled "Swat the SWOT—Moving ahead is much better." He points out that a SWOT can do more harm than good and tends to focus too much attention on operational issues rather than long-range strategic issues. McLauglin also raises a good point about organizations honestly facing their weaknesses: "No matter how rational and balanced the SWOT model may seem to be, it defies common sense to expect any staff members, whose compensation or reputation are linked to a weak area, will be happy to explore that weakness publicly and honestly." As an alternative to being overly dependent on the SWOT analysis as a key planning factor, McLaughlin suggests looking "for key environmental trends and patterns." Weaknesses exist in all organizations, thus, he suggests, organizations would be better off focusing their planning energies on "external trends, internal strengths, and the opportunities that arise from the interaction between the two."

For more information about *The NonProfit Times* go to: http://www.nptimes.com/.

environments were outlined: economic, political and legal, cultural and social, demographic, technological, and educational. Depending on any number of conditions, one or more of these environments could be stable, undergoing change, or even be uncertain.

Strategic planning usually draws on one or more of the following approaches: stability, growth, or retrenchment. It is also possible to use some combination of all three of these strategies.

Stability Strategy   The basic thinking behind this strategy is, "We are doing pretty well with our current operation, and there is no reason to make any big changes." This does not mean that the organization is doing nothing about meeting its stated goals and objectives. It simply implies there is no reason to move off in new directions. Many arts organizations would probably feel comfortable adopting this strategy because so much of an arts organization's programming is set into an annual pattern. The major arts organizations in a community are often seen as institutions that are part of the basic fabric of the area. People cannot imagine not having the museum, the symphony, and so on.

Growth Strategy   This approach makes sense when expanding operations into new markets or if the organization is considering starting new programs. With this strategy, a company may diversify its product line or actively seek a bigger share of the market. Arts organizations may adopt growth as an overall strategy by doing such things as increasing the numbers and types of events that it produces. Another example of a growth strategy is to deliberately push for greater community involvement by adding a ballet school or an art school to the dance company or museum. With growth comes increased costs and, it is hoped, increased income. These elements should be carefully calculated in the overall strategy.

Retrenchment Strategy   The third strategy describes a slowdown, cutback, or elimination of some portion of the organization's activity. Because this process is often viewed as retreating, many organizations will go to great lengths to describe it as something else. For example, a music group might say, "We are engaged in a planned phase-out of our Tuesday night concert series." In other words, the group is retrenching and cutting back on its programming, probably to save money. Like the early 1990s, the 2000s have been marked by a great deal of cutting back and retrenching among many arts organizations.

Combination Strategy   An organization might use all three of these strategies at any given time. Again, the influence of the external environments will determine to what degree various strategies must be adopted. If the community is experiencing an economic slump combined with an uncertain political environment, the organization might need to retrench in some areas and expand in others.

To formulate an overall strategy, an honest appraisal of the organization's mission statement and the organization's strengths, weaknesses, threats, and opportunities must be made. Here again, the services of an outside consultant can help the board of directors and staff to keep a sense of perspective about what the organization will really be able to accomplish through its strategic plan.

Goals, Objectives, Action Plans, and Evaluation
The final phase of the planning process results in developing goals, objectives, action plans, and evaluation systems. The goals are shaped by the choice of strategy, and the objectives address fulfilling that goal with specific methods. The action plans develop concrete steps in the allocation of human, financial, and equipment resources to meet the objective. Lastly, a measurement or assessment process monitors how well the organization is achieving the goals and objectives it has set for itself.

In Figure 5-1, the example of a growth strategy goal of expanding the audience base is outlined. One objective is to add a series of concerts to the season. Some of the specific action plans required to achieve the objective and fulfill the goal include changing the performance schedule, establishing a budget to support the new series, hiring more staff to run the series, and devoting support for marketing the new series. Last, but not least, the example notes methods that will be used to evaluate how the new series did. This could include tracking sales and attendance and developing demographic profiles of the audiences.

A more detailed depiction of this type of planning process is shown in Figure 5-2. Please feel free to use this to organize your planning documents using a spreadsheet format. It really does not matter if you use a word processing, spreadsheet, or database application to assemble and track your planning effort; the key is to write it down.

Our Mission: To be an arts organization that makes a difference with its programs in our community.

Goals	Objectives	Action Plans	Responsibility	Budget Line	Status
STRATEGIC					
1. Actively pursue a more ethnically diverse audience.	1.1 Increase the total number of subscribers to 4000 as per budget projections for next fiscal year (7% net increase over previous year).	1.11 Develop overall subscriber development campaign plan by July 1.	Marketing Director, staff assisted by Marketing Committee of the Board.	Marketing & PR budget	In progress.
	1.2 Increase the ethnic diversity of our subscribers by the end of the next fiscal year.	1.21 Conduct subscriber survey to assess current diversity levels in Fall. Establish baselines.	Marketing Director and staff.	Marketing & PR budget	In planning process. Needs sign off by Managing Director and Board President.
		1.22 Develop and implement membership campaigns targeted to specific under-represented groups by Oct. Assess and report to Board in Nov.	Marketing Director and staff.	Marketing & PR budget	To be developed.

NOTE:
The basic structure of the planning document allows for multiple objectives and action plans to be developed by the staff after the Board and Executive leadership establish the goals.

Figure 5-2 Sample Planning Document

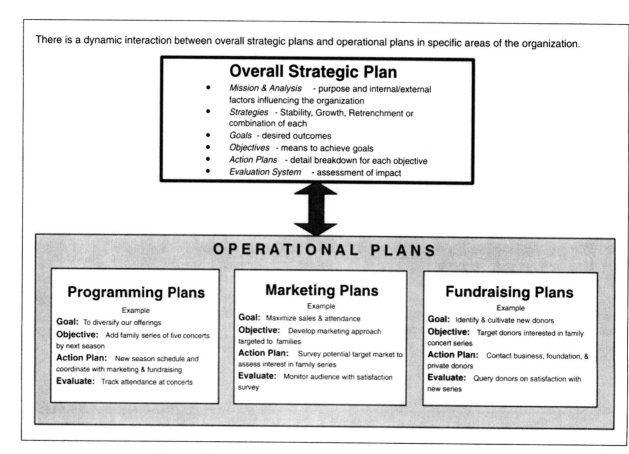

Figure 5-3 Operational Plans Related to Strategic Plans

Figure 5-3 demonstrates that within the overall strategic plan of an organization there are many component parts. It is not unusual to find plans for marketing, fundraising, programs, or facilities being driven by the overall strategic plan. The dynamic nature of planning, implementation, and assessment is difficult to impart in a diagram. As the diagram depicts, the flow of the process leads back to analysis and assessment. In order to have an effectively managed planning process it must be clear to the board, staff, artists, and potential supporters what you are trying to achieve. In general, plans that are expressed through diagrams are often easier for everyone to comprehend and implement.

Other Planning Approaches

The business world is filled with different approaches or combinations of approaches to take when planning. Arts organizations are usually not as bureaucratic in the planning process as businesses are. However, care must be taken not to fall into the trap of spending more time planning than actually doing the work that needs to be done.

Developing a Formal Business Plan

One of the fundamental approaches used to create a for-profit business involves creating a business plan. Chapter 2, "The Evolution of Arts Organizations and Arts Management," provides an outline for a business plan that can be adapted to an arts organization. As you will see,

Sample Decision Making and Planning Process

Let us assume that you manage a small professional chamber music group. You have decided that your mission is "To broaden the appreciation and understanding of chamber music in the tri-state area" and your overall goal is "To present quality concerts that will reach geographically diverse audiences." In order to fulfill your mission and realize your goal you are going to have to develop strategic growth plans to carry out specific activities. Let's walk through the process.

1. Define your objectives.

This key first step defines what you want to achieve. For example, "I want to have 40 bookings for my touring concert group by November 1, two weeks before we start our seven-month season." You must be specific in this first step. Specifying a quantitative achievement by a fixed date is one way to define your objectives.

2. Assess the current situation in relation to your objectives.

You must clearly assess where you are and just how far

you have to go. "I have 15 bookings, and it is September 1. I still have 25 to go in two months. It took me 4 months to book the first 15. I'd better be more aggressive in seeking out bookings, or I'll never make my target."

3. Formulate your options regarding future outcomes.

Now you must design specific options to choose from to reach your objective. "I will need three to four bookings per week over the next eight weeks. I can only devote two more hours per day to this project after I adjust my schedule. I could hire someone to help me, but I'll have to pay him or her. I could lower my target figure to 30 bookings, but our booking income will go down and we will not meet our revenue budget. I could extend the deadline to January 30 in the hope of reaching my original target figure."

4. Identify and choose among the options.

After creating and reviewing your options, you must select the option you assess as the most effective. For example, you might decide to hire a temporary assistant to help you se-

cure bookings. Your reason might be driven by financial need or by the fact that your musicians have other commitments and they need to know the final tour schedule by November 1.

5. Implement your decision and evaluate the outcome.

If this plan is to work, it will be critical for you to set up short-term measuring points to mark how well you are doing. You may find that you need to implement other options if the outcome still seems questionable. You may establish a weekly review of the bookings totals and further adjust the plans as needed.

These five steps may seem simple and straightforward, but more often than not, people and organizations fail to even make a detailed plan. It takes work and self-discipline to keep on top of this process. One of the most important skills you can develop as a manager is to master the planning process and effectively put it to use.

---

engaging in creating mission statements, setting goals, and developing objectives closely parallels the format we have discussed in this chapter. Answering the questions of why, who you are, and how you are going to accomplish what you say you are going to do is just as important in writing a business plan.

Top-down and Bottom-up Planning

Top-down planning simply refers to a process where upper-level management sets the broad objectives, then middle- and lower-level management work out detailed plans within a limited structure. *Bottom-up planning* begins with lower and middle management setting the objectives; upper management responds with final planning documents that reflect the input. Mixtures of these approaches make sense for most organizations.[10]

Top-down planning can fail if upper management does not consult with middle and lower management and labor when setting objectives. For example, suppose that the board and artistic director of a theater company plan to expand the season of a regional theater company from 24 to 36 weeks. Before trying to implement this plan, they should ask the people in the other levels of management (managing director, production manager, marketing and fundraising directors) to evaluate the impact of this change. Middle- and lower-level management will be asked to prepare reports showing the increased costs and increased revenue anticipated as a result of this plan. Upper management will then have the information it needs to assess the consequences of expanding the season. Modifications can be made in the plan before final implementation. (Given the number of anecdotal stories by staff people about never being consulted when sweeping changes are being made in their arts organizations, I surmise that an effective top-down planning process is only an ideal in many settings.)

Pure bottom-up planning is fairly rare because it is usually a very cumbersome process. Too much staff time is spent meeting and reviewing every detail of the planning documents. More typically, the process might begin with upper management requesting that middle and lower management draw up planning documents for their areas or departments. Difficulties may arise when middle and lower management are not well informed about the overall organizational goals and objectives. The fact is, if everyone in the organization doesn't understand the mission and the goals of the organization, this bottom-up planning process may actually be counterproductive.

Contingency Planning

As the name implies, *contingency planning* sets alternative courses of action that depend on different conditions. Contingency planning is most effective when trigger points are built into the process. For example, suppose that your season subscription campaign began in March. You expected to have a 70 percent renewal rate by July, but the box office reports only a 40 percent renewal by July 15. You would now activate your contingency plan for another mailing and a media blitz.

Crisis Planning

Crisis planning is an offshoot of contingency planning. Plans for dealing with a crisis do have a place in arts organizations. This is especially true when the organization must deal with the media, supporters, subscribers, or the general public. For example, an arts organization should have a plan ready to activate in the event of the death of a key person like a founder-director. It is also a good idea to plan for crisis if an organization decides to tackle a controversial project or programming choice. Arts organizations all too often go through months and years of chaos because no one took the time to map out a plan before a crisis struck.

Limits of Planning

One of the byproducts of the growth and development of the arts in the 1960s and 1970s has been the steady increase in organizations developing strategic plans. The NEA helped foster the process of organized

In the News

As this brief news item indicates, arts organizations can change course just as any business.

Opera Housing

The Washington Opera has abandoned plans to convert a former department store into a landmark opera house for the nation's capital. The company's board voted Tuesday to stay at its current home in the Kennedy Center; it signed a 15-year agreement that will allow it to expand its season from 74 to as many as 100 programs. The center agreed to a technical updating and renovation of its opera house in 2001.

SOURCE: "Opera Housing," *USA Today* (June 10, 1998), p. D-1. Copyright 1998 © *USA Today*, a division of Gannett Co. Inc.

planning as part of its funding process. In the 1980s and 1990s the term "visioning" was added to our planning vocabulary. In order to secure funding arts organizations had to demonstrate that they had a vision and a planning process in place for the funds they were requesting. Although the level of resources allocated to arts planning never reached the intensity that it did in the corporate world, many arts organizations generated thick tomes of strategic plans that took considerable time and effort to assemble. Unfortunately, many of these plans gathered dust on a shelf in an office because they lacked an operational relevance to the organization. The systematic application of these plans often failed to materialize for the simple reason that they were never fully integrated into the day-to-day operation of the organization.

In *Management for Productivity*, John Schermerhorn cites seven general reasons why organizational plans fail:[11]

1. The upper management fails to build a formal planning process into the general operating routine.
2. The people involved in planning are not very skilled in the planning process.
3. The data used in making the plans are incorrect [or incomplete].
4. The resources needed are not made available to execute the plans.
5. Circumstances change due to unforeseen events.
6. Staff members do not want to change, and they hold to plans that do not work.
7. Staff members become bogged down in the details and fail to reach the broader objective of the plan.

For many arts organizations a combination of these reasons may limit the success of the planning process. For example, months might be spent developing detailed planning documents with the help of outside consultants, only to have them become irrelevant because of a change in board or artistic leadership. In many cases the planning documents are too complex to implement given the limited staffing resources of the organization. Nello McDaniel and George Thorn point out in *Towards a New Arts Order* that planning often "places one more burden and distraction on an already overburdened organization."[12] Another writer in the field of management, Richard Farson, points out in *Management of the Absurd* that, "By and large, organizations are simply not good at changing themselves. They change more often as a result of invasions from the outside or rebellion from the inside, less so as a result of planning."[13]

Another point of view about planning was raised by Henry Mintzberg, a respected management author, in his book *The Rise and Fall of Strategic Planning*. It is Mintzberg's opinion that the term "strategic planning" is an oxymoron, and that strategy and planning are two different processes that do not work well together. He states:

> An organization can plan (consider its future) without engaging in planning (formal procedure) even if it produces plans (explicit intentions); alternately, an organization can engage in planning (formalized procedure) yet not plan (consider its future)....[14]

At the heart of Mintzberg's challenge to some aspects of the strategic planning process is the assumption that one can predict the future.

Murphy's Law and Planning: Bachman's Inevitability Theory

"The greater the cost of putting a plan into operation, the less chance there is of abandoning the plan—even if it becomes irrelevant."[15]

On the positive side, Mintzberg challenges many planning assumptions and offers good suggestions to all managers on how to develop a realistic planning process that will be more responsive to change.

When we sit down to "plan," do we really know what unforeseen events will occur and shape how an arts organization behaves? For example, would anyone have predicted the impact that an arts manager's decision to cancel Robert Mapplethorpe's exhibit would have on the arts in America? Canceling this exhibit of photographs in a gallery in Washington, D.C., in 1990 nearly led to the demise of the NEA a few years later. Politicians focused on what kind of work was receiving public funding and artists rallied against censorship. One of the results of this chain of events was a significant funding cut to the NEA in 1997 (see Figure 2-3). In fact, at one time in 1996, the House and Senate were considering motions to shut the NEA down.

Decision Making in Planning

For any planning process to succeed, the organization must have a well-defined decision-making process in place. A good arts manager (or any manager, for that matter) locates problems to be solved, makes decisions about appropriate solutions, and uses organizational resources to implement the solutions. Our discussion of planning was based on the assumption that the ability to make decisions was an integral part of the manager's background. Let us take a closer look at this key part of the entire planning process.

Choices, Decisions, and Problem Solving

You make hundreds of decisions every day. For example, you make a choice to wear your long coat after (1) identifying a problem (it's cold); (2) generating alternatives (wear no coat, wear two sweaters, wear short coat); and (3) evaluating the alternatives (wear no coat and freeze, or two sweaters and look bulky). This process leads to a problem being solved (keeping warm). *Problem solving*, then, is "the process of identifying a discrepancy between an actual and desired state of affairs and then taking action to resolve this discrepancy."[16]

Schermerhorn identifies three styles of problem solving: problem avoiders, problem solvers, and problem seekers.[17] The first two styles need little explanation. The third style describes the rare person who actively goes out and looks for problems to solve. At any given time, all of us have probably exhibited a little of each of these styles. Give some thought to whether or not one of these styles dominates your problem-solving approach.

When approaching problems, it is helpful to define whether you are dealing with *expected* or *unexpected problems*. For example, you should expect that from time to time an audience member will appear on Saturday night with a ticket for Friday's show. You should have a solution to this problem ready to be activated when the situation arises. An unexpected problem might be smoke pouring into the lobby from an overheated motor in the air circulation system. In this case, you must quickly assess your alternatives without creating a panic.

Steps in Problem Solving

The following example illustrates one way of proceeding through the problem-solving process:

1. Identify the problem

What is the actual situation? What is the desired situation? What is causing the difference? For example, suppose that your interns are always late and you want them to be on time. You must try to determine why they are late. Is it inadequate transportation, inappropriate work schedules, an unsafe workplace, the workload and expectations, or their supervisor?

2. Generate alternative solutions

This step is critical and often requires some imaginative thinking. Your investigation of the situation should allow you to gather as much information as possible to evaluate various courses of action. For example, you may discover that the interns are late because they do not like their supervisor. They feel the supervisor is disorganized and sometimes verbally abusive. Further investigation reveals that one of the interns also has an attitude problem. He has been rallying others to stage a work slowdown by showing up late every day.

3. Evaluate alternatives and select a solution

You consider replacing the supervisor, the interns, or both. You also assess the workload expectations and any other relevant information you gathered about the situation. Your solution may be to dispense with the assistance of the intern and reassign the supervisor. You may also enroll the supervisor in a two-day workshop on human relations skills.

4. Implement the solution

After consulting others within the organization (there could be some legal or interpersonal problems you had not foreseen), you implement your solution.

5. Evaluate the results and make adjustments as needed

You monitor the new supervisor and interns on a regular basis, conduct formal and informal talks with all concerned, and monitor the former intern supervisor. (See "Sample Decision Making and Planning Process on p. 95 for another example of how to approach the process.)

Problem-Solving Techniques

If problem solving were as easy as these five steps imply, then managing would be a much simpler task. In reality, problem solving is a difficult and demanding part of the manager's job.

Defining Problems, Making Hasty Decisions, and Accepting Risk   One of the many difficulties in problem solving is accurately defining the problem. People often incorrectly identify the symptom as the cause of the problem. For example, the lateness of the interns was the symptom for which causes were later identified. In the planning process, you may create many extra difficulties if you formulate objectives based on incorrectly identified problems. For example, a drop in subscription sales is a warning symptom of a whole host of possible problems. The ultimate cause may be show titles, prices, schedule, or even sales staff, among other things.

Another difficulty in problem solving is jumping to a solution too quickly. The first solution is not always the best solution. This is where trying out ideas on others can be helpful. A group brainstorming session may give you the added dimension you need to solve the problem.

Management texts frequently note that problem solving can take place in environments that are uncertain and risky.[18] The way you go about implementing the five-step problem-solving process depends a great deal on factors that you may have little control over. For example, if the intern supervisor happened to be the spouse of the artistic director of the theater company, there would be an added element of risk in your decision.

Analyzing Alternatives   Probably the best approach to analyzing your alternatives is to write them down. You can make an inventory of alternatives by simply listing all of the alternatives you have and writing out the good and bad points of each choice.[19] By forcing yourself to write your choices down, you may see other alternatives or ramifications of a decision.

Making a Final Choice   After you have written out all of the alternatives, you have reached the stage of making a decision. After all is said and done, you need to ask yourself, "Is a decision really necessary?" The intern may quit out of frustration, or the supervisor may ask for a transfer to some other part of the operation before you have finished gathering all of the evidence you need for a decision.

Decision Theory

In reality, the classic decision theory situation (clear problem, knowledge of possible outcomes, and optimum alternative) seldom exists.[20] Arts managers more commonly find themselves operating in the realm of *behavioral decision theory*. This theory assumes that "people only act in terms of what they perceive about a given situation. Because such perceptions are frequently imperfect, the behavioral decision maker acts with limited information."[21] According to this theory, people reach decisions based on finding a solution they feel comfortable with given their limited knowledge about the outcome. For example, when faced with the problem of the difficult intern, you may opt for dismissing the intern and tolerating the obnoxious supervisor. You may assess the risk of transferring the supervisor and in turn alienating the artistic director and find that it is too high.

Conclusion

Planning, as described in this chapter, is a series of logical steps that can lead to creative solutions to problems. One of the manager's most important functions is to solve problems. An excellent way of solving problems is to ensure that planning is integrated into all phases of an organization. For an arts manager, the organization's mission statement is a fundamental element in the planning process. The mission statement is not some historical relic to be taken off the shelf once a year and dusted off for a board meeting. Rather, it is a statement of the purpose of the organization, and, therefore, the force behind all decision making. The distribution of resources to performance, production, marketing, fundraising, and administration should be traceable back to the mission statement. When this link is broken, an organization finds itself in a struggle to make sense of why it is doing what it is doing.

Planning is a tool that any organization can put to good use. As Robert W. Crawford writes in his introductory chapter to *No Quick Fix*

(*Planning*), "Planning is, in reality, a commonsense way of defining what it is that one wants, when one would like to attain it, and how one goes about attaining it."[22] Crawford makes an excellent point about how people misconceive what planning really involves:

> It is fascinating how difficult it often is for individuals to transfer their understanding of planning in their own lives, and its flexibility, to organizations of which they are a part. More often than not, when organizational planning is brought up or initially discussed, psychological blinders appear. It often is assumed that planning is a restrictive process, that the organization and its creative leadership will be locked into a plan which may well not be good for either; that a plan must be adhered to rigidly once it is formulated and approved; that change is impossible, or at the very best, difficult; that it forces people to do things when they realize from further experience that doing something else would be better; that because one doesn't know what is going to happen in the future, one is precluded by a plan from taking advantage of opportunities which may arise unexpectedly. To put it succinctly, such perceptions of planning are ridiculous.[23]

Later in this text, we will focus on planning as it relates to the areas of finance (Chapter 9), marketing (Chapter 11), and fundraising (Chapter 12). All three areas rely on and should come from the work done in the strategic planning process.

Summary

Planning is a primary function of management. For arts organizations, creating a mission statement that defines their "reason to be" is an important first step in the planning process. A plan is a statement of means to accomplish results. The entire process of planning should clearly state the organization's objectives and help determine what should be done to achieve those objectives. Short-range plans (under one year), intermediate-range plans (one to four years), and long-range plans (five to ten years) are used to reach the stated objectives.

The overall master plan, called a strategic plan, supports the mission of the organization. Strategic plans may stress stability, growth, retrenchment, or some combination of these. The strategic planning process analyzes the organization's mission, reviews external environments, and examines the organization's strengths and weaknesses. Within the strategic plan, various operational plans are designed to achieve specific objectives. Operational plans include single-use plans (budgets and schedules) and standing-use plans (policies, rules, and regulations).

There are five steps in formal planning: defining objectives, assessing the current situation, formulating options, identifying and choosing options, and implementing the decision and evaluating the outcome. Planning approaches include top-down and bottom-up planning, contingency planning, and crisis planning. Organizations can benefit from formulating plans in case a crisis occurs.

For the planning process to be effective, an organization must have a decision-making system in place. Problem solving is the process of identifying a discrepancy between an actual and a desired state of affairs and then acting to resolve this discrepancy. There are five steps to the process: identifying the problem, generating alternative solutions, evaluating the alternatives and selecting a solution, implementing the solution, and evaluating the results. You must assess the risks involved in your decision and carefully analyze alternatives.

Key Terms and Concepts

Planning
Goals
Objectives
Short-, intermediate-, and long-range plans
Strategic plans
Operational plans
Single-use and standing-use plans
Top-down and bottom-up plans
Contingency and crisis plans
Mission statement
SWOT analysis
Decision making
Inventory of alternatives
Decision theory

Questions

1. Analyze the mission statement of an arts organization you are familiar with. Is it clear and to the point? What changes would you make to the mission statement to improve its clarity?

2. What would be a good strategy for an arts organization to adopt if the national economy is in a recession?

3. Use the five steps of the formal planning process to plot out your own personal short-range plans (for the next year) and intermediate-range plans (for the next two to three years).

Case Study

The following document gives you a working model of a planning document for a major regional opera company. The structure of the document shares many of the attributes of planning documents talked about in this chapter. The use of some planning terms differs from this chapter, but the basic meaning still applies. For example, the Goals (I) section is followed by one designated as "Strategies for achieving goals" (Section II). This chapter identifies these items as objectives. In addition, the plan as provided does not include details about the assignment of staff to the tasks or the costs of the plan.

Arizona Opera Education Long-Range Plans 2000–2005

Arizona Opera Education Mission:
To provide innovative, engaging and imaginative music and theater experiences to encourage people of all cultural heritages, ages and abilities to explore fully the rich world of opera.

Arizona Arts Standards:
1) Creating Art—Students know and apply the arts disciplines, techniques and processes to communicate in original or interpretive work.

2) Art in Context—Students demonstrate how interrelated conditions (social, economic, political, time and place) influence and give meaning to the development and reception of thought, ideas and concepts in the arts.

3) Art as Inquiry—Students demonstrate how the arts reveal universal concepts and themes. Students reflect upon and assess the characteristics and merits of their work and the work of others.
   I. Goals for Arizona Opera Education and Outreach department
       A. Offer educational and outreach programs primarily designed to build new audiences reflective of Arizona's cultural and economic diversity
       B. Maintain fiscal responsibility within the education department
       C. Offer engaging opera education programs to K–12 school audiences that enhance and encourage their exploration of opera
       D. Provide resources and professional development opportunities for Arizona educators
       E. Create new and expand existing opera education programs that meet the Arizona Arts Standards (listed above) for students K–12
       F. Create new and expand existing opera education programs for adults
       G. Implement and coordinate apprenticeships and internships to build new artistic and administrative opportunities for young professionals
       H. Produce second stage opera for youth including multicultural repertoire chosen to reflect the diversity of Arizona
       I. Expand the education program to include a full-time education manager in the Phoenix office
   II. Strategies for achieving goals
       A.1. Continue elementary school touring program featuring a condensed opera throughout Arizona including urban and rural areas
          2. Hire a diverse group of young professional singers to perform the in-school tour
          3. Continue adult lecture series in accessible locations in both Phoenix and Tucson
          4. Continue inexpensive opportunities for students to attend dress rehearsals and Look-in programs
       B.1. Continue to create appropriate budgets that reflect current program needs while maintaining fiscal responsibility to the overall company budget
          2. During seasons 2000/01 through 2003/04, maintain current programs with little to no

expansion to accommodate overall company budget

C.1. Continue with Opera Look-in program that focuses on behind-the-scenes of creating opera, theater craft and production responsibilities

2. Continue collaborations with Arizona school districts featuring the Music! Words! Opera! curriculum in which children can explore the possibilities of opera by creating their own original opera

3. Continue to produce the Opera Briefs in-school tour and provide free performances to schools throughout Arizona including urban and rural locations

D.1. Provide 5-day workshop for Arizona educators featuring the Music! Words! Opera! curriculum

2. Provide opportunities for educators to bring students to opera rehearsals, productions and behind-the-scenes programs at little to no cost

3. Provide study guides for teachers to explore each mainstage production with students

4. Meet with Arizona educators to determine their needs and determine what type of resources Arizona Opera can provide them and their students

E.1. Current K–12 programs that meet existing Arizona Arts Standards:

a) Dress rehearsals—*Art in Context* (describing various musical styles; demonstrating appropriate audience behavior; identify by genre or style examples of music from historical periods and cultures; explain personal preference for a specific musical work, using appropriate terminology; describe characteristics of various musical genres and cultures; identify characteristics of an exemplary performance)

b) Opera Look-in—*Art in Context* (identify and describe the roles of musicians in various musical settings and cultures, compare the roles of musicians according to the various functions and the conditions under which music is performed, identify the roles and responsibilities of various music professions)

c) Music! Words! Opera!
Creating Art (show respect for personal work and the work of others; perform independent instrumental parts while other students sing or play contrasting parts; identify form, tension and release, and balance in music from listening to examples; create/arrange short songs and instrumental pieces within specified guidelines, using a variety of sound sources; sing/perform accurately and with good breath control, tone quality, posture and technique; compose

short pieces within specific guidelines, demonstrating how the elements of music are used to achieve unity and variety, tension and release, and balance; use a variety of traditional and non-traditional sound sources and electronic media when composing and arranging)

Art in Context (describe characteristics that make music suitable for each setting; discuss diverse functions which music serves)

Art as Inquiry (analyze how music is used to reflect particular moods and feelings; demonstrate a story utilizing the elements of music; create a story utilizing the elements of music)

  d) Opera Briefs in-school tour

Creating Art (show respect for personal work and the work of others; listen to musical examples with sustained attention and self-discipline; analyze the qualities that differentiate one instrument or voice from another)

Art in Context (identify music which creates changes in mood through listening examples; demonstrate audience behavior appropriate for the context and style of music performed; explain personal preference for a specific musical work, using appropriate terminology; identify characteristics of various musical genres and styles)

Art as Inquiry (express personal reactions to music through media such as movement, words, painting and sculpture; use appropriate terminology to describe and explain music; explain personal preferences for specific musical works and styles; describe criteria for evaluating performances and compositions; list constructs of performance; outline which constructs occurred in a given performance; evaluate a given performance based upon the constructs criteria)

F.1. Continue providing free lectures in Phoenix and Tucson at accessible locations

  2. Hire lecturers with extensive opera knowledge and/or knowledge of production elements

  3. Create new series featuring characters/ composers discussing opera

G.1. Coordinate apprenticeships and internships with each department within Arizona Opera

  2. Compile departmental needs and coordinate with available applicants

  3. Continue to work with artistic department to create a foundation for a Young Artists Studio

H.1. Work with community groups to produce operas reflecting Arizona's diverse community. These works would include Spanish *zarzuelas* (operettas performed in Spanish), *Brundibar* (an opera written for the children in the Terezin concentration camp), *Papagayo* (a puppet opera based on a children's book set in the jungles of South America) and other similar works

2. Have performances in appropriate and accessible locations for children and parents to attend

I.1. Hire full-time education manager in the Phoenix office in July 2004

SOURCE: Arizona Opera Company, June 2002. Used with permission.

Questions

1. How would you evaluate the clarity and intent of the mission statement contained in the plan?

2. Does the plan support the mission statement? Give examples of the connection between the stated mission and the plan.

References

1. Harold R. McAlindon, *Management Magic* (Lombard, IL: Great Quotations, 1989).
2. John R. Schermerhorn, *Management for Productivity* (New York: John Wiley & Sons, 1986), p. 100.
3. http://www.actorsguildoflexington.org/, Actors' Guild of Lexington, June 2002.
4. http://www.guthrietheater.org/, Guthrie Theater, June 2002.
5. http://www.sdco.org, San Diego Chamber Orchestra, June 2002.
6. http://www.alliancetheatre.org/atc_about_mission.html, Alliance Theatre Co., June 2002.
7. http://www.mfa.org/mission%5Fstatement.htm, Museum of Fine Arts, Boston, June 2002.
8. http://atlantaballet.com/fastfacts.htm, Atlanta Ballet, June 2002.
9. http://www.sfsymphony.org, San Francisco Symphony, June 2002.
10. Schermerhorn, *Management for Productivity*, p. 105.
11. Schermerhorn, *Management for Productivity*, p. 114.
12. Nello McDaniel and George Thorn, *Toward a New Arts Order* (New York: ARTS Action Issues, 1993), p. 44.
13. Richard Farson, *Management of the Absurd* (New York: Touchstone, 1996), p. 122.
14. Henry Mintzberg, *The Rise and Fall of Strategic Planning* (New York: The Free Press, Simon & Schuster, 1994), p. 32.
15. Arthur Bloch, *The Complete Murphy's Law* (Los Angeles: Price Stern Sloan, Inc., 1990), p. 52.
16. Schermerhorn, *Management for Productivity*, p. 64.
17. Ibid., p. 65.
18. Ibid., p. 76.
19. Ibid., p. 77.
20. Ibid., p. 79.
21. Ibid., p. 80.

22. Robert W. Crawford, "The Overall Structure and Process of Planning," in *No Quick Fix (Planning),* ed. F. B. Vogel (New York: FEDAPT, 1985), p. 14.
23. Ibid., p. 14.

Additional Resources

The following sources were also used in writing this chapter.

Kathryn M. Bartol and David C. Martin. *Management,* 3rd ed. Boston: Irwin, McGraw-Hill, 1998.

Arthur G. Bedeian. *Management.* New York: Dryden Press, 1986.

John M. Bryson. *Strategic Planning for Public and Nonprofit Organizations,* Rev. ed. San Francisco: Jossey-Bass, 1995.

James H. Donnelly, Jr., James L. Gibson, and John M. Ivancevich. *Fundamentals of Management,* 8th ed. Homewood, IL: BPI/Irwin, 1992.

Richard Farson. *Management of the Absurd.* New York: Touchstone Books, 1996.

Henry Mintzberg *The Rise and Fall of Strategic Planning* New York: The Free Press, 1994.

6
□ □ □ □ □

Fundamentals of Organizing and Organizational Design

The art of organization is not to create organizations but to multiply our effectiveness.
Rob Reiner, *Improving the Economy, Efficiency, and Effectiveness of Not-for-Profits*

Whether we like it not, we spend the greater part of our lives in organizations. Our contact with organizations may start with a day care center, then move to a series of educational institutions, then on to a place of work, and finally, we may live out retirement in an elder care system. The family, which is also an example of an organizational unit, can be a powerful force in shaping how we interact with others. Our ability to relate to the numerous complex organizations in our society determines how successful we are in achieving our personal goals and objectives. The powerful myths of the individual going it alone in society are offset by the reality that we need the support of people to achieve maximum results. One person can make a difference, but many people working together can create permanent change.

In this chapter, we analyze many of the basic concepts pertaining to organizations and organizational design; then we apply these theories to arts. We also examine the importance of matching structure to the task at hand. Finally, we review the phenomenon of organizations as cultures.

The Management Function of Organizing

In the study of management, organizing usually follows planning as the second basic function.[1] If you are to implement effectively the strategic plans formulated in Chapter 5, "Planning and Decision Making," you need a way to organize your resources to realize your goals and objectives. And, as the epigraph for this chapter points out, we need to stay focused on organizing to produce effective organizations.

A good starting point is to return to our earlier definition of an *organization* as "a collection of people in a division of labor working together to achieve a common purpose."[2] The term *organizing* was defined as "a process of dividing work into manageable components and coordinating results to serve a specific purpose."[3] We previously defined a *manager* as a person in an organization who is responsible for the work performance of one or more people, and we defined *management* as a process of planning, organizing, leading, and controlling.

Four Benefits of Organizing

No matter what project or production you plan to undertake, four benefits can be derived from organizing:[4]

1. Making clear who is supposed to do what.
2. Establishing who is in charge of whom.
3. Defining the channels of communication.
4. Applying the resources to defined objectives.

It is part of the arts manager's job as an organizer to decide how to divide the workload into manageable tasks, assign people to get these tasks done, give them the resources they need, and coordinate the entire effort to meet the planning objectives.[5]

Organizing for the Arts

The task of organizing to achieve results should always be the arts manager's objective. It is the underlying assumption of this text that an effective arts manager is functioning in a collaborative and cooperative relationship with the artist. People outside the arts sometimes erroneously assume that artists and arts organizations, by their very nature, are less structured than other organizations or that they function best in a disorganized setting. Nothing could be further from the truth.

Although there are different ways to approach the process of putting on an exhibition or presenting a theater, dance, opera, or concert performance, each art form shares an inherent organizational structure that bests suits its function. Each art form typically faces the pressure of being ready for an audience by a specific date and time. For example, theater is rooted in developing a performance based on many hours of text study, blocking and line rehearsals, technical and dress rehearsals, and eventually opening night. The organizational support required to prepare, rehearse, design, produce, and find an audience for the play need not be discovered each time a new show is put before the public. There are standard ways of pulling together a production. When the support system is in place and functioning correctly, it is almost invisible. However, when something goes wrong with this system, it becomes the hot topic of discussion.

As we will see in this chapter, there are various ways to go about organizing any enterprise. It is not an issue of a right or wrong way. As previously noted, organizational design and organizing should be aimed at achieving the desired results. Before exploring the structural details of various arts organizations, let us take a look at the overall concept of the organization as an open system.

Organizational Design Approaches

Management theory approaches organizational design by using concepts such as mechanistic versus organic organizations, the relationship to external environments, and the degree of bureaucracy within an organization.[6] The mixture of these concepts may be outlined in a model of an open system. Figure 6-1 depicts how an organization transforms inputs to outputs. Within the overall environment, a constant feedback loop exists back to the input stage. For example, if the output is exhibitions and the stated mission is education, you will want to monitor the

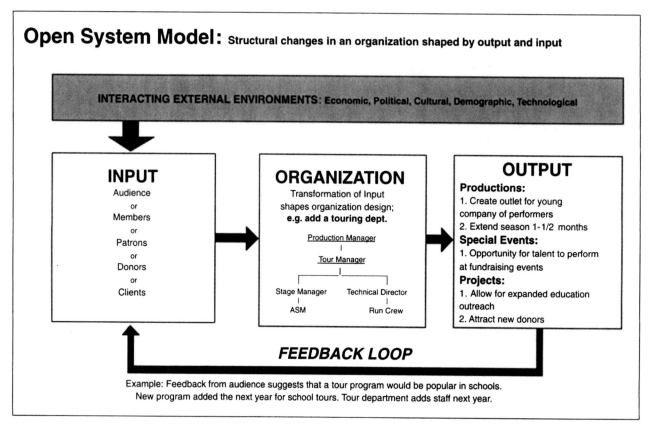

Figure 6-1   Organizations as Open Systems

input from the people using your product to see if you are fulfilling your mission. You would want to design the organization so that it had the ability to respond to the input from the public. This may translate into a department that gathers survey data, tabulates the results, and publishes reports informing management of how effectively the mission is being met.

Organic and Mechanistic Organizational Design

Arts organizations tend to be found at the organic end of the continuum of mechanistic versus organic organizational structure. The distinguishing features of an *organic organization* are a less centralized structure, fewer detailed rules and regulations, often ambiguous divisions of labor, wide spans of control or multiple job titles, and more informal and personal forms of coordination. A *mechanistic organization* tends to have a great deal of centralization, many rules, very precise divisions of labor, narrow spans of control, and formal and impersonal coordination procedures.[7] Of course, organizations vary in degree when it comes to classifying them on this continuum. Some arts organizations may adopt aspects of a mechanistic organization. The size and complexity of the operation usually dictate these attributes. For example, the Metropolitan Opera is more likely to adopt aspects of a mechanistic organization than would a smaller organization like the Opera Theatre of St. Louis. Why? The size and scale of the operation play a role in determining the placement of an organization along this continuum.

Bureaucracy

When an organization adopts a mechanistic organizational structure, we often refer to it as a bureaucracy. Ideally, a bureaucratic organization has clear lines of authority, well-trained staff assigned to their areas of specialization, and a systematic application of rules and regulations in a fair and impersonal manner.[8] This form of organization, originally found in governments administered by bureaus or civil servants, was created to overcome the excesses of nepotistic control of social infrastructures. Today, we tend not to associate bureaucracy with democratic principles. Instead, we have very negative perceptions of bureaucracy. Anecdotes abound regarding bureaucratic structures bringing out the worst in an organization. We have all seen a rigid and unwieldy organization where, like a black hole in space, things are sucked in and never seen again. Governmental agencies are often cited as prime examples of bureaucracy at its most entrenched. However, James Q. Wilson's insightful book, *Bureaucracy: What Government Agencies Do and Why They Do It*, argues that bureaucracies are not black boxes into which input is impersonally converted to output, but rather changing complex cultures.[9] Wilson also argues that the perceived mission of and the people within the government bureaucracies are significant forces in shaping interactions with the society at large.

Modern views of bureaucratic structure suggest that it would be best to adopt a contingency approach in organizational design in the arts. In other words, the organization adopts only the amount of bureaucratic structure necessary to accomplish its objectives. Does this mean that an arts organization needs to have some bureaucratic structures? Yes, to some degree. For example, an arts organization must establish ticket refund, crediting, and billing policies and procedures. It needs a consistent structure that handles most, if not all, transactions in the same manner. You cannot operate a box office with every employee setting his or her own rules or procedures for routine tasks. The patron who comes to the ticket office to request a refund or exchange should be given fast and efficient service. Staff members should not have to consult one another on the proper procedure.

Another area in which arts organizations need a great deal of structure is the payroll department. Employees may complain about the bureaucracy, but because the payroll department must interface with local, state, and federal agencies, there is no choice in the matter. Because of the complexity of state payroll and IRS regulations you cannot make it up as you go along.

The idea of a flexible framework of policies, rules, and regulations makes a great deal of sense for an arts organization when it comes to adopting bureaucratic structure. As we have just seen, different areas within the organization need more rigid structure than others. The box office and payroll both need a clearly defined framework with rules, regulations, and policies. However, a resident scene designer in a regional theater will not find a highly structured framework very helpful if he or she has to fill out a purchase requisition every time she wants a new pencil. Likewise, a curator at a museum should be expending his or her creative effort on activities that will enhance the public's enjoyment and understanding of an exhibition rather than be mired in restrictive paper shuffling within the organization.

Probably the most useful tool for an arts manager to use in managing the degree of bureaucracy in the organization is *testing*, that is, walking through the procedures that are in place. The manager may discover policies, procedures, or rules that are confusing, contradictory, or nonessential to the mission of the organization.

Organizational Structure and Charts

Let us delve into a more detailed examination of how to structure an arts organization. When we talk about *organizational structure*, we are referring to the "formal system of working relationships among people and the tasks they must do to meet the defined objectives."[10] These relationships and tasks are usually shown in an *organizational chart*, which is "an arrangement of work positions in an organization."[11]

In the business or arts world, adherence to the organizational chart must be tempered with a healthy dose of reality. It is important to establish the organizational chart to help clarify how things work and whom to contact about getting something done. The organizational chart should help, not hinder, operations. If an organization finds itself unable to accomplish its objectives because the organizational structure frustrates action, it is time to reexamine how it is organized.

A typical organizational chart should clearly show six key elements about the organization: divisions of work, types of work, working relationships, departments or work groups, levels of management, and lines of communication.[12]

Divisions of Work Each box on an organizational chart represents a work area. Each area should designate an individual or group assigned to complete the organization's objectives. Figures 6-2, 6-3, 6-4, and 6-5 show divisions of work in a hypothetical regional theater, symphony, and dance company, and a small art museum. Under each division are specific work areas assigned to complete the task. For example, in Figure 6-2 the production manager is responsible for the production area. The technical director is assigned the specific task of completing the scenery. The technical director in turn has designated staff supporting the work area: the scene shop manager and the construction crew. Figure 6-3 shows seven major department areas supervised by an executive director, while the art museum in Figure 6-5 is divided into three major areas: administration, collections, and exhibitions, programs, and development.

Type of Work Performed The title you use for the work area (e.g., finance, marketing and public relation, development, as shown in Figure 6-3) helps describe the kind of work the person or group will do. Care should be taken to avoid obscure work area titles. Vague or misleading titles often indicate that an organization is carrying staff positions that serve marginal functions.

Working Relationships The organizational chart shows who reports to whom in the company. The solid line in Figure 6-2 between the production manager and the technical director indicates a supervisor-subordinate relationship. The production manager and the sales, marketing, and publicity director are on the same level, and they report to either the producing artistic director or the managing director.

Departments or Work Groups The grouping of job titles under a work group or area should be communicated by your organizational chart. A performing arts organization may be large enough to warrant

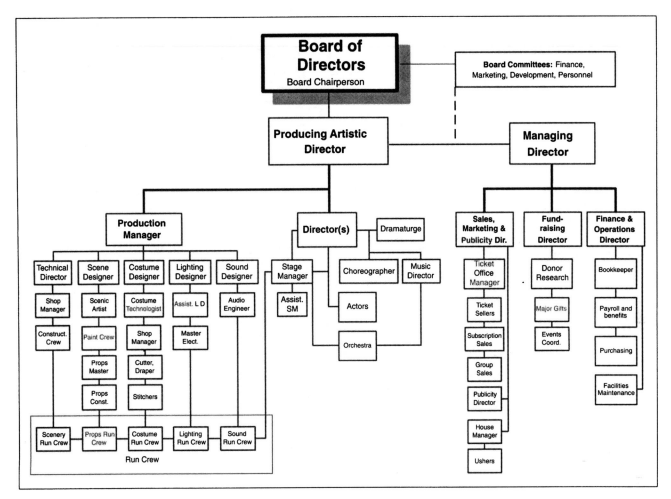

Figure 6-2   Theater Company Organizational Chart

separate departments for work areas. For example, Figure 6-5 shows the grouping of the curators under a chief curator of Collections, while the associate director responsible for Exhibitions, Programs, and Development has four workgroups with a supervisor for each.

In Figure 6-2 the box office might include all single and subscription sales. Group sales and telemarketing might also be included in this department. It is not unusual in a small operation to find one person heading up four or five different subdepartments. As an organization grows, the creation of separate departments usually follows.

The Levels of Management   The organizational chart should act like a map in depicting all management levels (upper, middle, and lower). In the organizational charts the upper levels for the theater, symphony, dance company, and museum are represented, respectively, by the producing artistic director and the managing director, the executive director and the music director, the artistic director and the general manager, and the museum director. In the theater organization (Figure 6-2) the production manager and the technical director could be identified as middle management, and the shop manager as lower-level management. This hierarchy theoretically reflects how information flows and work objectives are carried out in the organization. For example, one would

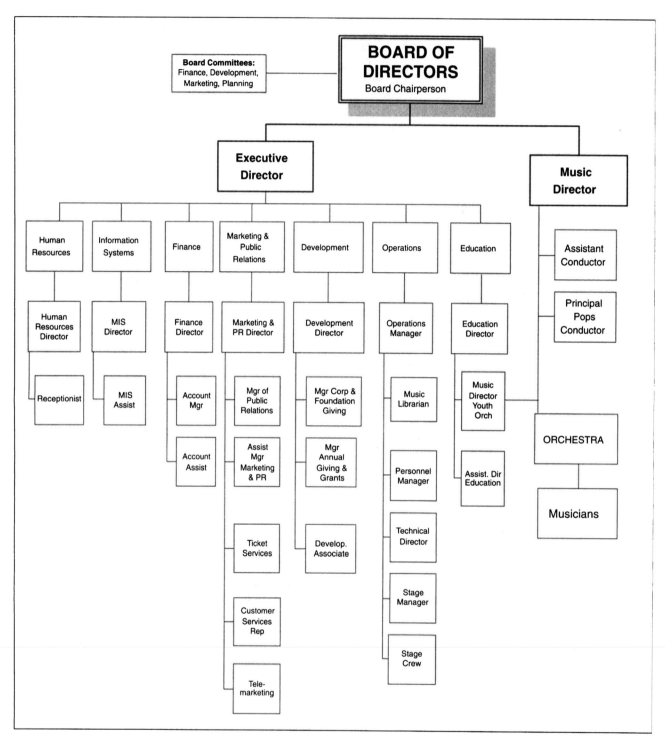

Figure 6-3   Symphony Orchestra Organizational Chart

expect the marketing/PR director to be the person passing along the information about the shows to the press and ticket office staff in the theater organization. In the symphony orchestra (Figure 6-3), the stage manager and technical director are listed under the operations area managed by the operations manager who in turn reports to the executive director.

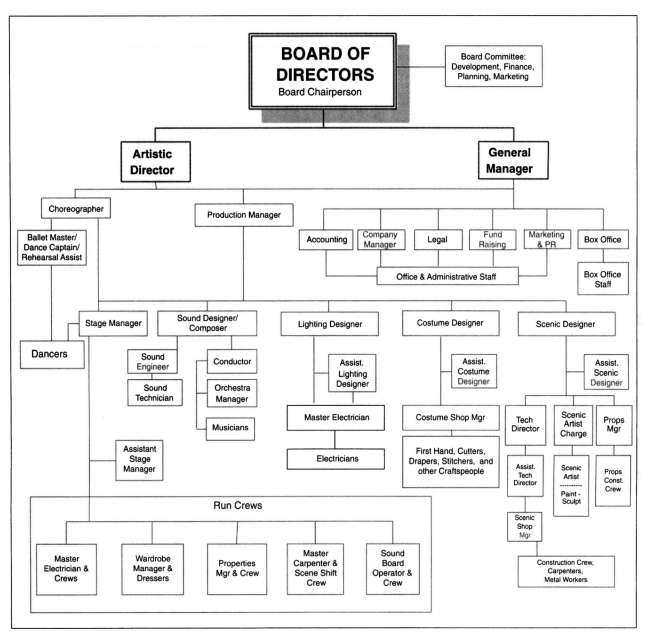

Figure 6-4 Dance Company Organizational Chart

As an organization grows, the layers of management also tend to grow. When an arts organization first begins to operate, each level is minimally staffed and each person fulfills several major job functions. For example, if you call the artistic director of a new dance company, the phone will probably be answered by a lower level administrative assistant who will connect you to the director. This administrative assistant probably provides support for most, if not all, of the artistic and management staff. Now let us assume our dance company is successful and expands its operation. It adds an associate artistic director, establishes a central receptionist to take all calls, and hires an assistant to the artistic director. Your call will now be taken by a receptionist, who in turn transfers you to the assistant to the artistic director, who then connects you to the associate artistic director. The associate artistic director

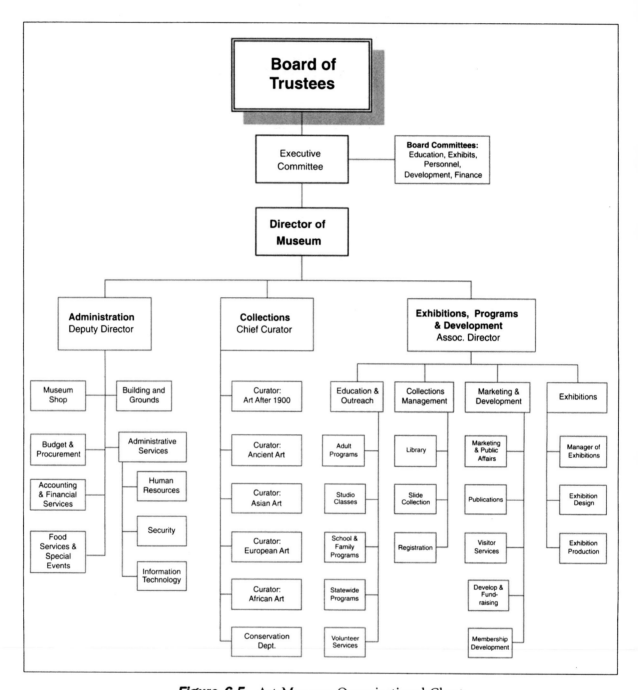

Figure 6-5 Art Museum Organizational Chart

screens the call to see if you really need to speak to the artistic director. By the way, when this type of scenario actually exists, it might be time to reexamine how many levels of management the organization really needs.

Lines of Communication   Finally, the organizational chart should represent the lines of communication throughout the hierarchy. For example, in a theater organization the scene shop manager tells the technical director that he will have to go over budget to complete the set as designed. The technical director informs the production manager of the situation. The production manager informs the artistic director, who in turn communicates to the managing director. In theory, the upper managers decide what they want to do, and that decision is passed back down through the hierarchy. The phrase "in theory" is not used to be facetious, but to remind the reader that the way things are supposed to work and the way they actually work in an organization do not always match up. This is partly due to the shadow or informal structures that develop as people work together over time.

Informal Structure

Every organization has an informal organizational structure. Good managers remain aware of this underlying framework and use it to their advantage. At the same time, they must discern when this informal structure is damaging the organization and hindering the achievement of its overall objectives.

One of the reasons why an informal structure exists is to fill in the gaps in the formal structure. Interactions in an organization involve people, and that translates into a complexity and a subtlety no chart can capture. Inventive employees will always find a way to get things done in an organization with or without using the formal structure. For example, suppose that the scene shop manager wants a new table saw, but the technical director has refused to act on the request for months. At a cast party, the shop manager casually lets the production manager know that the shop could speed up the set construction process if only it had that new saw. If the crafty shop manager uses this informal communication system properly, she may end up with a new saw before the technical director knows what has happened. This will also enhance the shop manager's status with the shop staff because of her ability to get what is needed despite the system. In so doing, the shop manager may unwittingly send a message to the staff that it is all right to bypass your supervisor to get things done.

Problems Inherent in the Informal System   This example points out some of the problems with the informal structure. One major fault is that the informal structure diverts efforts from the important objectives of the organization. This shadow organization may be more concerned with personal status. Another difficulty with the informal organization is its resistance to change. You may define new objectives and marshal your resources to put a new procedure in place, but if the informal organization rallies around the "old way," your efforts may be in vain.

As in the example of the table saw, an alternative communication system usually accompanies an informal structure. One key element of this informal system is the rumor-spreading mechanism. Arts organizations are no more or no less prone to rumor spreading than other businesses. The rumor mill is usually a prime source of informal communication in any organization. Good managers will determine how the informal communication system works in their organizations in order to track what employees are really saying about the workplace and their jobs. From time to time, it can be useful to feed information into the rumor mill. For example, you might let it leak that upper management is not happy with the lax compliance with the new no-smoking policy. If carefully leaked, the rumor might create greater adherence to the new rule if staff members think there will be consequences if they continue their current behavior.

Structure from an Arts Manager's Perspective

General Considerations

The complexity of the organizational structure should be directly related to the size and scope of the operation. It is a good practice to keep the structure to a minimum. If an arts organization's mission is to further its art and serve the public, creating elaborate organizational charts may be diverting time and energy. To help keep organizational design in perspective, consider the five elements that are often listed as influences on the final design: strategy, people, size, technology, and environment.[13] Of these five influences, strategy, people, and size have the most direct applications to the arts.

Strategy The organizational structure needs to support the organization's overall strategy. For example, if you are starting a new regional opera company, your objective might be to build a subscription base as quickly as possible. Your strategy in building that base might be to select your season around well-known titles with famous guest artists. Your organizational design would therefore stress more staff to take care of the artists and to carry out the organization's marketing, public relations, and ticket sales activities. To maximize resources, your strategy would also include keeping your operating costs as low as possible. One way to do that would be to rent all of the sets and costumes for the season. You would therefore need only a relatively small production department and no resident design staff.

A few years later, you might expand your audience development strategy by adding a community outreach program. Now your objective is to hire a tour director and a small staff to promote and support bringing opera scenes into schools. You might consider reorganizing another area within your existing organization to save on the expense of adding staff. Either way, you must make changes in the organization's design.

One of the reasons why new programs of activity sometimes suffer in an organization is that no one has thought about what is going to be done by whom. Without careful thought about job design, an organization can quickly overload an employee with too many tasks.

People The most important element in any organization is the people who work within the overall structure. Realistically, there must be flexibility between the structure and the people in an arts organization. The military is a prime example of a rigid organizational structure designed to mold its "employees" to the specific jobs at hand. A strict hierarchy and adherence to numerous rules and regulations are all focused toward a set of specific objectives. People usually do not join the staff of an arts organization because they want a rigid and highly controlled work environment. In fact, people who work in arts organizations are often highly self-motivated and vigorously resist regimentation.

Care must be taken when applying organizational theory to real organizations. In an arts organization, for example, the degree of structure varies with the type of job. For example, the director of a museum would probably be wise to allow for a high degree of creative independence among the department heads of the curatorial staff. The security guards, on the other hand, would have a rigid work schedule with limited independence to set their hours.

Size When an arts organization is first established, there may be no more than three or four people doing all of the jobs in the organization. The artistic director may direct the operas, write the brochure copy, hire all of the singers and the artistic staff, and do all of the fundraising. As the organization grows—a board of directors is added, staff specialists are hired to do the marketing, scheduling, advertising, and so on—the simple organizational chart and lines of communication suddenly become much more complicated. In management theory, the organization would be said to be moving from an "agency form" to a "functional department form."[14] An *agency organization* refers to a structure in which everyone reports to one boss, and this boss provides all of the coordination. Each staff member is in effect an extension of the boss. When an arts organization decides to hire a marketing director, it may be because the artistic director can no longer supervise all of these activities. In this scenario, a new department with a specific function and the support staff to do the marketing would be established. Problems and conflicts will arise if the artistic director attempts to give direct orders to the staff of the marketing director instead of going through the new structure.

Technology and Environment The other elements that influence organizational design are technology and environment. When speaking of the influence of technology in the business world, it is easier to see how new systems and methods can affect how products are produced. There is usually a direct connection between how an organization is structured and how technology may help it become more productive. For example, a large company may add a whole department to do nothing but assess new technologies and advise about their application to that business. Arts organizations, on the other hand, have used new technologies in office and information management and, in limited ways, applied new approaches to the technical production aspects of their operations. However, the technological changes do not radically transform what the arts organization does or how it goes about preparing or delivering its product. The addition of staff in such areas as computer support is probably the most obvious change found in many arts organizations.

External Environments The political and legal environments may legislate new laws that affect hiring or training in the organization. For example, there were virtually no affirmative action or health and safety programs in arts organizations 30 years ago. Today, there are probably staff members designated to administer and monitor these areas of activities in the organization. In addition, the ever-increasing complexity of tax laws and compliance with proliferating local, state, and federal regulations has no doubt added to the workload of the finance and accounting departments of many arts organizations.

Departmentalization

To *departmentalize*, or to set up departments in an organization, simply means "grouping people and activities together under the supervision of a manager."[15] Departments may be structured in three ways: by function, by division, and by matrix.

Function Most arts organizations use a structure defined by functional departments. It makes sense to group people by the specialized functions they perform within the organization. Figures 6-2 to 6-5 show how various managers supervise the functional departments within the organization. For example, the symphony (Figure 6-3) has a marketing and public relations area with a director, a PR manager, an assistant manager, and various related support areas such as telemarketing and patrons services.

Divisions Departments can be organized around a product or a territory. An example on a small scale is a major arts center that not only hosts touring productions but also produces its own shows, runs a gift shop and an art gallery, and operates a restaurant. An organization may decide to establish a divisional structure that keeps booking, production, exhibition, and food services separate. The logic behind this choice is that each of these activities involves very different operating conditions with specialized supervision and staff needs. The division in charge of production might include a marketing person to supervise the subscription series for the regular events. The division in charge of touring might employ another person to market the shows to other arts centers and producers. Both employees are marketing specialists, but they market their products from very different perspectives.

Another divisional structure is by territory. A dance company decides to pursue a strategy of dual-city operations. One of the first steps would be to establish an organizational structure to staff two different geographical sites. There would need to be some staff duplication. You cannot expect the city A marketing staff to do the marketing for city B without local staff designated for each campaign.

Matrix The most complex structure is a matrix organizational structure. The matrix is created by overlaying the departmental and functional organizations in a traditional vertical and horizontal pattern. The matrix system was created in the late 1950s by the cofounder of TRW Inc., Simon Ramo.[16] The department structure proved to be inadequate when TRW tried to manage several technologically complex projects for the defense industry. His scheme was to use a department structure for important activities like research and development (R&D) and place the department under the control of a department head. However, within the R&D department were smaller groups of people working on different projects under the supervision of a project manager. The vertical matrix in the structure is thus the department head working with the various R&D groups. The horizontal matrix consists of the individual project managers working with the separate R&D groups.

In an arts organization, a matrix structure often evolves, although no one sits down and actually plans a change to this type of structure. At its most basic level the matrix structure in an arts organization means an employee may have two or more bosses, depending on the project. For example, suppose that a museum is organized around a department structure. The six departments are responsible for various sections of the collection, and there are other departments for marketing, fundraising, operations, maintenance, accounting, and payroll.

The museum's centennial is coming up in three years. A staff member is designated as the director of the centennial project. If this project director is to achieve the objective of creating a successful celebration of all the things the museum has done in the last 100 years, a matrix structure must be created. The project director will require that each department head designate a person to be the centennial coordinator for that department. In addition to their regular duties, the marketing staff will also have to work on this special project with the project manager. The project manager, in effect, becomes their temporary supervisor.

Arts organizations often find themselves involved in special projects. However, without recognition of the need to shift to a matrix organizational structure, trouble may occur. For example, if the staff required to make a special project work are not hired, the project coordinator will have to work horizontally through the organizational structure. She will discover that the overworked staff in the various departments do not have time to give to the project, or worse, the staff will find the time at the expense of their regular responsibilities, and the effectiveness of the entire organization will suffer.

There are other examples of the matrix organizational structure in arts organizations (see Figure 6-6). There is a matrix working relationship between a resident design staff and the guest directors or choreographers that may come into a regional arts organization. The staff are hired by the organization and may work within separate departments. When a guest director or choreographer arrives, this staff now have a new "boss" specifically for a particular show. A good production manager will recognize this matrix structure and establish the needed lines of communication to keep all of these overlapping projects on track.

Coordination

A principal concept in organizing any enterprise is coordination. Coordination can be divided into vertical and horizontal components. The first area of concern, *vertical coordination*, is defined as "the process of using a hierarchy of authority to integrate the activities of various departments and projects within an organization."[17] *Vertical coordination* is split into four areas: chain of command, span of control, delegation, and centralization–decentralization. Each of these has applications to arts groups. *Horizontal coordination* simply refers to the process of integrating activities across the organization. Many arts organizations use this structure to promote interdepartmental cooperation.

Vertical Coordination
Chain of Command   Classic management theory, as exemplified by Fayol's Fourteen Principles (see Chapter 3), states that "there should be a clear and unbroken chain of command linking every person in the organization with successively higher levels of authority."[18] This is known as the *scalar principle*. The military is a good example of a thoroughgoing application of such a chain of command. Common sense should tell you that problems will develop in an organization that lacks clear authority and clear lines of communication. On the other hand, not all situations allow for a clear "unbroken chain of command" within an organization. A small arts organization may hire an administrative assistant to work for several people and departments. On paper, the job description says that the "administrative assistant is supervised by the managing director." However, as the organization grows, the assistant is asked to complete work for the artistic director, the new marketing director, the newly formed fundraising department, and others.

Unless the staff member is extremely good at time management and setting priorities, work may become backed up or simply not get done. Too many people have authority to ask the administrative assistant to work for them. Ironically, what often happens is that in order to survive in the job, the administrative assistant becomes the person

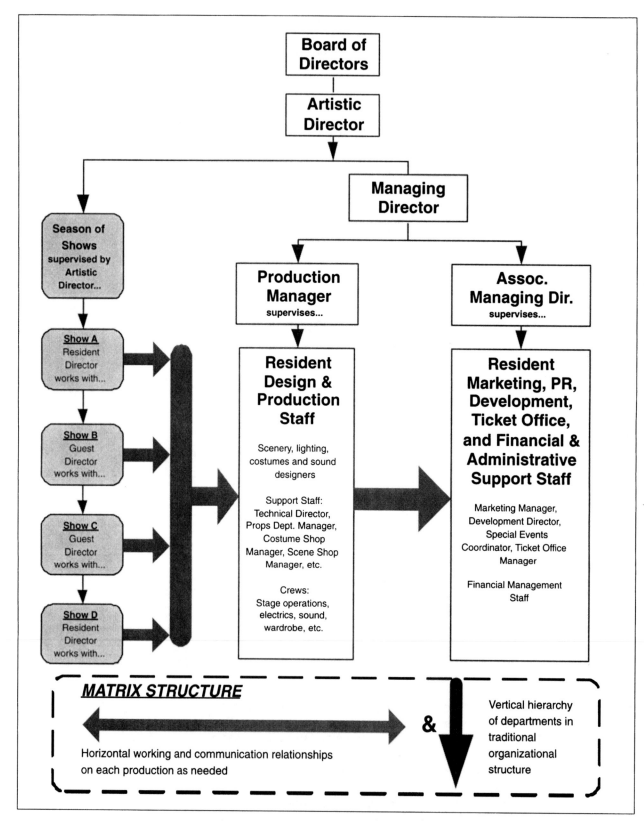

Figure 6-6 Simplified Matrix Organizational Chart for a Theater Company

determining what work is done for who and when. The administrative assistant becomes a de facto manager of the supervisors. This phenomenon is often seen in academic departments in colleges and universities. The "department secretary" often has many faculty and staff requesting administrative support. In order to cope with the workload the assistant determines when work gets done through self-management. The administrative assistant often becomes the "boss" of the department since he actually determines what work will get accomplished.

Span of Control   The span of control describes how many people report to one person. There are no fixed rules about how much or how little span of control one person should have in an organization. The factors often cited in determining this are "(1) Similarity of functions supervised, (2) physical proximity of functions supervised, (3) complexity of functions supervised and (4) the required coordination among functions supervised."[19]

Let us look at span of control in an arts setting. If the marketing director is asked to take over the supervision of the fundraising and ticket service operation, there is a reasonable match between functional areas and a limited span of control. However, if the marketing director tries to take over the management of the acting company—becomes, in effect, the company manager—there may be problems. The needs of the acting company are not similar to the needs of the marketing department. It is also possible to start to exceed the marketing director's expertise. The marketing director could possibly supervise the company manager—the person responsible for seeing to all of the needs of the acting company. However, the marketing director may not have enough understanding of the job to know if it is being done properly.

An example of physical proximity in span of control occurs when the production manager is asked to supervise the activities in performance spaces in three different locations in the city. The production manager soon discovers that it is impossible to be in three places at once. Three staff assistants are needed, one for each theater.

Similarly, if the functional areas become complex, as in the data-management system for an organization, you may need to reduce the span of control. The staff member in the accounting area, who became the "systems administrator" in the finance department by virtue of her knowledge, can no longer keep control of the expanded computer systems used in the marketing department, the box office, and fundraising. Either someone must be hired to coordinate the organization's computer needs, or the accounting work of the existing staff member must be reduced.

Delegation   As a manager, you must decide how much day-to-day work you should do yourself and how much should be assigned to others. *Delegation* is "a distribution of work to others."[20] The process involves three steps: assigning duties, granting authority, and establishing an obligation. When you assign duties, you must have a solid understanding of the work to be done, and you must spend time analyzing what you expect the employee to do. Problems sometimes arise with the second step: granting authority. If the delegation process is to be effective, you must give up some of your authority and transfer it to the employee. If you do not grant that authority, it is difficult to establish an obligation on the part of the employee to assume the responsibility. For example, suppose that you delegate the responsibility of providing daily sales summaries for the organization to your ticket office manager, but you go down to the office the next day and run the numbers yourself. The ticket office manager will wonder what happened to this delegated responsibility if you duplicate her work. She will assume that you do not trust her work. A key principle to remember is that the "authority should equal the responsibility when you delegate work."[21] If you give a staff member responsibility for a budget but then take away the authority to expend the funds, you have undermined the delegation process.

Unfortunately, no area creates more bad feelings in an organization than delegation. Overprotective managers tend to create employees who are bored with their jobs and not particularly committed to meeting the organization's objectives. Because they have not been given any real responsibility, they develop the attitude that is expressed in the phrase, "Don't ask me; I just work here." Meanwhile, the whole organization suffers because the manager is spending time doing work that would be more effectively done by others.

Centralization–Decentralization   This last area of vertical coordination simply refers to how the organization will concentrate or disperse authority. Colleges or universities are often cited as examples of decentralized organizations. The individual departments (history, government, physics, and so on) often have autonomy over personnel and course offerings. They report to a central authority—that is, the dean—but the faculty members of the department exercise a great deal of control over their own day-to-day activities. On the other hand, a large corporation may have a rigidly organized authority structure in which only designated managers have the authority to make decisions.

In an arts organization, the degree of centralization or decentralization depends on the functional area. For example, the process of running a subscription or membership campaign requires a centralized authority structure. One cannot have several people making key decisions about the campaign autonomously. To control the look and language of the campaign, one person must make the final decisions. In other areas, it may be more efficient to decentralize the authority. For example, the production manager delegates the purchasing of production supplies (lumber, fabric, steel, paint, and so on) to the technical director. The technical director then delegates the purchasing to the individual department heads.

Horizontal Coordination

Horizontal coordination is a key function in the matrix organizational structure. In the business world, the function of horizontal coordination is most often identified with such areas as personnel and accounting. All of the departments in the organization use the personnel department as a resource for hiring, firing, and evaluating employees. Payroll is a good example of another department that has a horizontal relationship to a vertical structure. Everyone in the organization is affected by the payroll department. Organizations could not function effectively if every department handled its own payroll.

In an arts organization, similar personnel and payroll functions may cut across departmental lines. As already noted, the project orientation of many arts organizations creates the need for horizontal coordination. A successful production, concert, or exhibition often requires that different departments cooperate and communicate over an extended period of time. For example, a stage manager must be able to coordinate with what is called *functional authority*. This authority allows the stage manager to cut across the formal chain of command. When a problem backstage needs to be solved instantly, the stage manager can issue orders that bypass the traditional crew head hierarchy.

When an event is presented, horizontal coordination is typically shown through the formation of a production team. The heavy emphasis on team management as an innovative approach to solving problems in the business world over the last 20 years is, in fact, standard operating procedure in the arts. Without effective horizontal coordination a theater, dance, or concert event or an exhibition opening suffers.

Organizational Growth

Organizations seem to have a way of growing beyond anyone's original expectations. As one sage wit once noted, "The number of people in any working group tends to increase regardless of the amount of work to be done."[22] Almost constant attention must be paid to the proliferation of staff with each new cycle of strategic planning. As new plans are implemented, the workload seems to increase, so new staff members are hired, and more levels of management are put into place. The production manager now has three production assistants. The secretary is now the director of office operations and has three administrative assistants working under her. This growth carries with it increased costs to the organization. The cycle of overloading the current staff, hiring new staff to help reduce the overload, overloading the budget, laying off the new staff, thus overloading the original staff, and so on, can be avoided if the manager retains control of the planning function.

One of the key elements of planning is keeping accurate records of where you have been. Tracking the growth of a department over a period of time can be a helpful way to monitor growth. In my comparisons of staff growth in arts organizations over the last 20 years, I found that increases of 25 to 125 percent were not uncommon. This is all the more significant since many of these organizations were only doing 5 to 10 percent more programming.

Managers must think of the design of the organization as a creative challenge and not a burden. As we have seen, the manager's job is to anticipate and solve problems. Lack of attention to problems with organizational design can lead to fundamental flaws in the operation of the enterprise, and these flaws could lead to the demise of the organization.

Corporate Culture and the Arts

Theory versus Reality in Organizations

In the last 30 years, management experts have found that organizations behave in ways that the theories cannot always explain. As you would expect, no theory of organizational design can take into account all of the variables that affect businesses. One of the more interesting approaches to analyzing how organizations behave may be found in Terrence Deal and Allen Kennedy's *Corporate Cultures: The Rites and Rituals of Corporate Life*.[23] The basic premise of the book is that organizations are social systems, and these social systems are based on the shared values, beliefs, myths, rituals, language, and behavioral patterns of the employees. All of these factors are carried on from year to year over the life of the organization. A manager may find comfort in the structure, policies, and procedures of the company, but in reality, these things are not necessarily why people choose to work in the organization. Deal and Kennedy list five elements in the corporate culture: (1) the business environment, (2) values, (3) heroes, (4) rites and rituals, and (5) the cultural network. As you will see, there are several points at which this study of corporate for-profit organizations intersects with the arts world.

Application to the Arts

Because many arts organizations are going through the transition from a strong founder-director orientation to a system with professional staff and volunteer board management, it is worthwhile to take a brief look at the cultural aspects of an organization. It is also important to gain insights into the rites and rituals that may affect your ability to function effectively within the formal and informal structure of an organization. Let us look briefly at each element of the corporate culture and examine how arts managers may benefit from a keen awareness of this often-overlooked aspect of organizational life.

Five Elements of Corporate Culture

Business Environment   As we have seen, organizations function in relation to various political, educational, technological, cultural, and economic environments. Deal and Kennedy found that "to succeed in the marketplace, each company must carry out certain kinds of activities very well. . . . This business environment is the single greatest influence in shaping a corporate culture."[24]

The authors identify four types of organizational cultures. As with all classification systems, creative combinations of some or all of the types may exist in complex organizations. Deal and Kennedy note that companies in highly competitive markets tend to develop approaches that stress a *work hard–play hard culture* to keep the sales force motivated. Companies like McDonald's, Xerox, and Mary Kay Cosmetics are cited as examples. Other cultures present the *tough-guy* or *macho culture*, which includes people in high-risk businesses who get quick feedback on their decisions. Such businesses include construction, advertising, and entertainment. The *bet-your-company culture* functions in the world of high risk and slow feedback. Large oil companies and the aircraft industry are examples of companies that must wait a long time before their decisions pay off. Finally, there is the *process culture*, a low-risk, slow-feedback business world. Government, heavily regulated industries like utilities, and financial service organizations tend to have this type of culture. The very low level of feedback "forces employees to focus on how they do something, not what they do."[25]

Arts organizations may take on some combination of these cultures, depending on the circumstances. For example, a newly formed dance company may have a very driven leader who creates an ongoing culture of risk-taking. As the organization establishes itself—a board of directors is formed; foundation, corporate, and public grants are found—another culture with a more process-oriented approach may evolve. The organization shifts from operating on the edge to focusing on a more stable and long-term perspective. As a matter of fact, there is an inherent conflict between the risk-taking and process cultures. This may explain why many arts organizations go through a great deal of personnel turmoil between artistic directors and boards. For example, a conservative board may want to move the organization in a different direction than the adventurous artistic director wants. Employees within the arts organization become caught in the conflict. A strong artistic director, creating a culture in the organization that stresses taking risks, will want to be surrounded with like-minded people.

Values   The values of the organization define the criteria for employee success and tell the employee what is important to the organization. These values are usually communicated through a corporate slogan (e.g., Ford Motors' "Quality is job one" and General Electric's "Quality is our most important product") or through glossy annual reports. Arts organizations usually produce annual reports, and the comments by the artistic director or chair of the board illustrate the values stressed by the leadership. For example, a 1989–1990 annual report by the American Repertory Theatre in Cambridge, Massachusetts, places a high value on "the presentation of challenging and innovative works."[26]

Although it is important to communicate values to the public, it is more important that the employees of the organization know how their work is guided by these values. A strong culture will reinforce the organization's values at every opportunity. This is not easy in a complex arts organization. For example, the artistic director may not direct every production in a season. Guest directors or conductors may bring into the organization values that are at odds with the organization's leadership. This requires that the staff constantly adapt to changing values. The entire strength of the organization's culture can be eroded if the problem is ignored. On the other hand, contrasting cultures could be used to advantage by deliberately creating the value, "We stress diversity."

Strong artistic leadership should bring with it a strong culture with clear values to which everyone in the organization can subscribe. Suppose you have the situation where a cutting-edge dance company, led by a true experimenter, tries working with a managing director who thinks the sun rises and sets on nineteenth-century story ballets. The result will most probably be a major conflict of cultures and values. The staff will notice these differences in obvious and subtle ways, and the overall enterprise will be hampered by such extreme contrasts.

Heroes   The expression of the organization's culture can most often be found in the person filling the key leadership role in the corporation or arts organization. For example, Steven Jobs was rehired by the Apple board and became a hero-rescuer when Apple Computer ran into leadership problems in the 1990s. His picture began appearing on the cover of magazines with each new product roll-out to help further enhance Apple's iconoclastic image. On the other hand, many companies use commercials and advertisements that depict employees articulating their commitment to the company and its products. Ford Motor Company ran ads for years that placed workers at the center of the message about the heroes behind the company's success.

Arts organizations, especially founder-directed groups, look to the artistic director, music director, and so on, to set the tone for the organization. This person should be a role model who can articulate the mission and values of the organization. A strong leader sets the standards for performance, motivates employees, and helps to carry on the history of the organization. Unfortunately, the true hero-leader is a rare creature. A hero-leader need not necessarily be loved by all of the employees, but he or she certainly is respected.

Arts organizations often experience a great deal of dislocation when a powerful founder or leader leaves the organization. The impact of the death of Robert Joffrey was felt for years by the Joffrey Ballet. George Szell's death had a similar impact on the Cleveland Orchestra. Choreographer Martha Graham's death created a series of problems for her company, not the least of which was the ownership of the dance works she created. The departure of Rudolf Bing from the Metropolitan Opera in 1972 created a significant change in the corporate culture of that organization.

Rites and Rituals   Just as the larger culture in a society has various rites and rituals to assimilate its people, organizations have routines and patterns of behavior that they expect their employees to follow. These may be yearly ceremonies or daily activities, but in either case, the objective is to show employees how to behave. In an organization with a strong culture, the message about what is expected of employees is clearly communicated. The way things get done is usually the first contact an employee has with the culture of an organization. The employee's initial orientation sets out the norms of behavior and performance. If carefully orchestrated, Deal and Kennedy point out, organizations will develop symbolic actions to help reinforce the values and beliefs of the company. They cite a number of social and management rituals that organizations adopt to surround employees with the organization, such as company recognition awards, clinics, and newsletters.

In the arts, rites and rituals extend throughout various organizations. The mere act of giving a public performance or putting on an exhibition connects the organization to the culture at large. Hundreds of different ways of doing things become established routine within the organization. Rehearsal and production schedules, performer warm-ups, backstage behavior, exhibition installation, and recognition of individual excellence all help to shape the culture of the organization. Each art form has its own sets of rites and rituals in addition to those associated with the individual company. Dancers, actors, singers, musicians, directors, designers, technicians, and craftspeople all have ways of doing things that feel comfortable and make sense to them. In fact, these rites and rituals are often so ingrained that people are not aware of them until conflicting cultures are introduced. A company of actors accustomed to working in a general pattern with a resident director may have trouble adapting to a guest director who brings very different values and approaches to the rehearsal process. Or a guest conductor may not be aware that the resident conductor's style of working and communicating with the musicians is radically different from theirs. Being aware of these rites and rituals and carefully channeling them can help build a strong and positive culture in an arts organization. On the other hand, ignoring cultural clashes of rites and rituals can lead to a breakdown of the spirit of an entire group of artists.

The Cultural Network   The last element that Deal and Kennedy discuss is the internal communication system, which acts as a network to circulate the values of the corporate culture. As noted before, organizations have both formal and informal structures. The "hidden hierarchy" in an organization's culture includes the "storytellers," "spies," "priests," and others who create the overall environment in the organization.[27] The authors accurately identify various characters who play roles in the culture. For example, the storytellers are good at putting incidents in the organization into a reality that others can understand. Storytellers usually add to and embellish the event, and, as you would expect, the good

FYI—A Book of Interest

The Addictive Organization, by Anne Wilson Schaef and Diane Fassel, explains "Why we overwork, cover up, pick up the pieces, please the boss and perpetuate sick organizations."

In this chapter, we have been examining the theory and practice of organizational design. Once an organization is in operation, it is important to constantly evaluate its "health." Organizations, like people, can become ill with a variety of "diseases." One of the more interesting management and psychology books to be published on the subject of organizational illness is *The Addictive Organization.* The authors take the perspective that organizations and individuals exhibit addictive behaviors that lead to their own self-destruction. Schaef and Fassel first identify the addictive system and the terms and characteristic behavior of people in the addictive system. Then they look at the four major forms of addiction in organizations. They wrap up their study with a look at the recovery process and the long-term implications of addictive organizations.

Arts organizations suffer from the same pattern of addictive behavior as large corporations. At the heart of the matter is what is best described as the addictive tendency in humans. Research points to the possibility that humans, by their genetic composition, are susceptible to addictive attachments to a variety of substances. When this research is coupled with a larger culture that stresses and rewards certain types of addictive behavior, there is an unhealthy situation. It is not an exaggeration to say that some people "work themselves to death." Arts organizations are often built on a cultural value system that stresses a willingness to sacrifice yourself for the good of the art form: You will work long hours for very little pay in often hazardous conditions and say you "love it!"

With the understanding that it can sometimes be misleading to quote out of context, here are two quotes from the section on "The Organization as the Addictive Substance" in *The Addictive Organization.*

Organizations function as the addictive substance in the lives of many people. We recognize that for many people, the workplace, the job, and the organization were the central foci of their lives. Because the organization was so primary in their lives, because they were totally preoccupied with it, they began to lose touch with other aspects of their lives and gradually gave up what they knew, felt and believed. (p. 119)

The organization becomes the addictive substance for its employees when the employees become hooked on the promise of the mission and choose not to look at how the system is really operating. The organization becomes an addictive substance when its actions are excused because it has a lofty mission. We have found an inverse correlation between the loftiness of the mission and the congruence between stated and unstated goals. (p. 123)

SOURCE: Anne Wilson Schaef and Diane Fassel, *The Addictive Organization* (San Francisco: Harper and Row, 1990).

---

ones develop an audience of rapt listeners. Storytellers can help provide a sense of history and perspective for new employees. They can also be conduits for passing along the myths and rituals of the organization. The organization's priests take on the role of confessors, arbitrators of moral dilemmas, and symbols of the mature and serious view of the organization. Spies function as they do in the general society. They look beyond the surface to what is going on behind the scenes. As the authors point out, "Truly effective spies never say a bad word about anybody and are thus much loved as well as much needed. . . . Sharp spies keep their fingers on the pulse of the organization."[28]

Because the cultural network does not appear in the organizational chart or in the memos or published reports, managers must learn to tap into the network to stay on top of what employees are thinking and feeling about the organization. Deal and Kennedy recommend that managers stay in contact with the storytellers and priests, in particular.

In an arts organization, it is particularly important to remain plugged into the cultural network. The ability to manage and shape this network can be especially important when an arts group finds itself in financial trouble and people begin to fear for their jobs. In addition, as arts organizations attempt to reach out to diversify their audiences and their staffs, entire new cultural perspectives will enter into the mix. For example, employees from different cultural and ethnic backgrounds will bring values and beliefs that may initially conflict with the prevailing culture of the organization. Managers need to be sensitive to the ethical issues of trying to reprogram staff to following the company culture at the expense of their belief system. It is important that everyone be aware of and support the organization's goals and objectives. However, care must be taken not to create an organization with such a rigid corporate culture that it forces people into uncomfortable circumstances.

Corporate Cultures and the Real World

When you start a new job, you are brought into an organization's cultural system. It may be a very strong culture that stresses maximum performance at all times, or it may be a very relaxed culture that stresses slow and steady progress. No matter where the culture fits along this continuum, it will exist. The sooner you recognize it, the sooner you can adapt to it as needed. For example, if you go to work for a marketing director in an arts organization that prides itself on huge leaps each season in its subscriber base, you better be ready to adopt the attitudes and beliefs that go along with the job, or you will find yourself outside the system and eventually out of a job. On the other hand, once you have established yourself as a manager in the organization and have come to know the culture, you can begin to alter it to better achieve the overall goals and objectives established in your strategic plans. Remember, the culture of an organization is not static. It adapts to changes in the internal and external forces that affect the organization.

Summary

Organizations are collections of people in a division of labor who work together for a common purpose. Organizing makes clear what everyone is to do, who is in charge, the channels of communication, and resource allocation. Managers should organize for results. Organizational structure and charts provide an operational map. All organizations have informal structures, which managers should monitor. Organizations can be designed to use functional, divisional, or matrix structures, or a combination of these. Organizations use vertical and horizontal structures and coordination to operate effectively. They may take on organic or mechanistic structures, depending on what they do. All organizations have social systems that define a distinctive culture. Strong leadership helps define the culture. Organizational design is affected by the culture and social systems.

Key Terms and Concepts

Organization
Organizing

Organizational structure
Mechanistic versus organic organizations
Organizational chart
Division of work
Informal organizational structure
Agency form of management
Functional department management
Departmentalization
Organization by division
Organization by matrix
Vertical coordination
Chain of command, or the scalar principle
Span of control
Delegation
Centralization versus decentralization
Horizontal coordination
Open system model of organizational design
Bureaucracy
Corporate cultures

Questions

1. What are the formal and informal organizational structures of the theater, dance, music, or art department at your college or university? Do these structures effectively support the mission of the department? Explain. How would you reorganize the department to make it more effectively support the mission of the university?

2. Can you cite examples of breakdowns in the vertical or horizontal coordination on a project or production with which you were recently involved? How would you improve the coordination systems to minimize these problems in the future?

3. Based on your own work experience, identify as many of the values, behavior patterns, language, rites, and rituals that formed the corporate culture of the organization.

Case Study

The following excerpt from a 1991 article in the *Chronicle of Philanthropy* provides a good example of how the concepts from Chapters 5 and 6 can be put to use. You may also assume that further changes in the Kennedy Center's organization structure have taken place since this was published; consult the website for the Kennedy Center at http://kennedy-center.org/about/welcome.html.

An Arts Institution's Management Overhaul

Plagued by a persistent deficit, Washington's Kennedy Center turns to techniques used by for-profit companies.
Vince Stehle

WASHINGTON—The John F. Kennedy Center for the Performing Arts here is trying to raise its standards of performance, from backstage to the board room.

After a year-long review, the Center is making changes in its fund-raising and marketing departments, as well as in other administrative offices, to bring the performance of its management team into line with the quality of its presentations on stage—and to erase a persistent multimillion-dollar deficit.

While many non-profits engage in strategic planning to improve their operations, the Kennedy Center's effort is unusual because of the depth of financial analysis it entailed and because it is based largely on techniques used by for-profit businesses.

The review prompted numerous changes in various departments and has led to more cooperation between divisions to make the center more efficient as a whole. . . .

James D. Wolfensohn, the respected New York investment banker who took over as the Kennedy Center's chairman and chief executive officer 18 months ago, has restructured the senior management team at the institution, delegating day-to-day control to a new official, the chief operating officer.

Many of the changes at the Kennedy Center were suggested by Cannon Devane Associates, a management-consulting firm in Washington. The management-review process began over a year ago, in June, when Mr. Wolfensohn, who works part-time as chairman, accepted an offer from Martin Cannon, the president of the firm, who volunteered to sort out the center's management systems on a pro bono basis. The two men had worked together as advisers in the sale of a major hotel chain.

In analyzing the center's management, says Mr. Cannon, he found that many of the same questions facing for-profit business companies applied to non-profit organizations.

"The reassuring message is that there are capabilities that have been largely devoted to the management of the for-profit business sector that are very relevant to the center's business operations," says Mr. Cannon. "And they should not feel embarrassed to call upon those capabilities. Successful businesses do it all the time. . . ."

[The Process]

After several months of analyzing the center's finances and management practices, [Mr. Cannon] says, the management study revealed numerous untapped sources of revenue, including greater potential income from the box office and private fund-raising efforts.

The consultants then began gathering information, including financial data from all the center's departments, data about competing local performing-arts institutions, and demographic information about the Washington metropolitan area. Some of the findings demonstrated that the Kennedy Center had some serious troubles:

- During the late 1980s, more than a third of the center's subscribers had failed to renew their subscriptions, and single-ticket sales had fallen sharply . . .
- Private donations . . . remained virtually flat from 1985 to 1990, while the costs of raising funds jumped from 13 percent to 18 percent of contributions.

In addition to the vast array of facts and figures, the consultants solicited the opinions of any staff member who wanted to be interviewed. Given the understanding that all interviews would be confidential, over 100 members of the 186-member staff agreed to talk to the consultants. . . .

Taking all the evidence together, Mr. Cannon presented two scenarios. In one, the center could continue business as usual, increasing its annual operating deficit from $3.9 million in 1990 to $6.3 million in 1993. In the other, Mr. Cannon showed how, by cutting costs and increasing revenues, the center could actually realize a $9.2 million surplus by 1993.

Cannon Devane projected that, among other things, administrative overhead costs and production costs could be trimmed by about $1.3 million, in part by establishing a single procedure for negotiating contracts that would cover the Kennedy Center employees and outside producers alike. . . .

[Implementation]

Despite the importance of a healthy balance sheet, most people at the Kennedy Center said they believed that financial considerations must be tailored to the center's mission statement, and not the reverse. So, before committing to the new regime, senior staff members created a new "vision" statement for the center. The statement says the center will "embody, stimulate, and transmit the values of freedom, creativity, expression, and joy inherent in the performing arts" and it will present high-quality, diverse performances and try to attract a wide audience.

Once the new mission statement was adopted, each department began drawing up new plans, setting goals and priorities consistent with the statement. Those plans are still under review by the new chief operating officer, Lawrence J. Wilker, former president and chief operating officer of the Playhouse Square Foundation in Cleveland. Even though Mr. Wilker hasn't made final decisions about the changes that will be made, some new programs and policies have already begun. . . .

New Fund-Raising Efforts Begun

Festivals
The Center sponsored a "Texas Festival," which was the first Kennedy Center festival to focus on the arts of a single state. The event, which included performances by the Houston Ballet, the Texas Boys Choir, and the Dallas Symphony Orchestra, as well as a popular music program known as the Roadhouse Cafe, helped raise $2.4 million in contributions from Corporations, foundations, and individuals, which more than paid for the additional costs associated with the festival.

New Policy for Board Members
The Center's Board of Trustees agreed to form a fund-raising committee and approved a resolution suggesting, but not

requiring, that all trustees either give, or obtain from others, commitments each year to give $100,000, payable over three years.

Giving Clubs
Two new giving clubs for donors have been set up: the "100 Club," for companies that give at least $100,000 over three years, and "The Trustees' Circle," for individual donors who do the same. The club has attracted 61 members so far.

The center's marketing department has adopted new policies and programs designed to attract new subscribers and, in some cases, to assist fund-raisers. For example, last season the marketing department designed a deeply discounted subscription package—three concerts at half price—at the request of the development department. . . .

Another of the management review's findings involved the high cost of attracting new subscribers. . . . The expense of promoting the institution to new customers prompted the management consultants to suggest that subscribing should be made easier, and that complaints be dealt with long before a customer became disillusioned.

A Window into What Didn't Work
In response, the center has made numerous changes to make it easier for subscribers to exchange tickets and make sure that patrons will have no difficulty finding their way to the six different theaters in the complex or getting something to eat in a hurry before performances.

Still, it's difficult for the administrative staff, most of whom work during the day, to know what's happening in the evening, when most of the center's performances take place.

"We'd get in the office, and the first phone call at 10 o'clock was from an irate patron, and that was your window into what didn't work the night before," says Geraldine Ottremba, director of government relations. "The obvious solution is to train people to solve problems as they happen."

In addition, she says, when customers now call to complain, the call is not passed around, "in what we affectionately called 'Kennedy Center roulette.'" Instead, all complaints are now routed to a central customer-service office. "Now you have a fairly accurate picture of what your complaint level is, and you have people who are trained to make reparations, whose goal is to recover that patron immediately, and not let them off the phone until they are satisfied. . . ."

SOURCE: Vince Stehle, "An Arts Institution's Management Overhaul," *Chronicle of Philanthropy* (September 24, 1991). Copyright © 1991, *Chronicle of Philanthropy.* Used with permission.

Questions

1. Summarize the main changes made in the Kennedy Center's management structure, as noted in the article.

2. Based on the information in the article, how would you characterize the management structure of the center? For example, is it divisional or a matrix?

3. What changes in the corporate culture of the center are implied in the reorganization plans?

References

1. John R. Schermerhorn, Jr., *Management for Productivity*, 2nd ed. (New York: John Wiley & Sons, 1986), p. 20.
2. Ibid., p. 161.
3. Ibid., p. 161.
4. Ibid., p. 162.
5. Ibid., p. 163.
6. Ibid., p. 190.
7. Ibid., p. 191.
8. Ibid., p. 188.
9. James Q. Wilson, *Bureaucracy: What Government Agencies Do and Why They Do It* (New York: Basic Books, 1989).
10. Schermerhorn, *Management for Productivity*, p. 163.
11. Ibid., p. 164.
12. Ibid., p. 164.
13. Schermerhorn, *Management for Productivity*, p. 167.
14. Arthur G. Bedeian, *Management* (New York: Dryden Press, 1986), p. 258.
15. Schermerhorn, *Management for Productivity*, p. 169.
16. Bedeian, *Management*, p. 265.
17. Schermerhorn, *Management for Productivity*, p. 173.
18. Ibid., p. 174.
19. Ibid., p. 174.
20. Ibid., p. 176.
21. Ibid., p. 177.
22. Arthur Bloch, *The Complete Murphy's Law* (Los Angeles: Price-Stern-Sloan, 1990), p. 62.
23. Terrence E. Deal and Allen A. Kennedy, *Corporate Cultures: The Rites and Rituals of Corporate Life* (Reading, MA: Addison-Wesley, 1982).
24. Ibid., pp. 13, 14.
25. Ibid., p. 119.
26. Barbara W. Grossman, *Annual Report 1989–90 of the American Repertory Theatre*, p. 2.
27. Deal and Kennedy, *Corporate Cultures*, p. 85.
28. Ibid., p. 94.

7 Staffing the Organization

□ □ □ □ □

Attracting, hiring, and ultimately retaining productive employees are obvious needs if firms are to achieve organizational excellence. While the level of rewards may have a direct impact on the number of individuals wanting to work in an organization, it is of the utmost importance that the right people apply.
Edward E. Lawler III, *Rewarding Excellence:*
Pay Strategies for the New Economy

The last two chapters covered the areas of planning and organizational design. We saw how the mission of an organization becomes the foundation on which the strategic and operational plans are built. Specific goals and objectives are then established. The plans also indicate how human and financial resources are to be used to meet the organization's goals and objectives. The organizing process is designed to move plans from an idea to a reality. The manager designs the organization to fulfill the plans. The structure of the organization, the lines of communication, and the combinations of vertical, horizontal, and matrix relationships are established among the departments and projects. Departments and other subunits are created to support the plan effectively.

The next stage in the process of creating an organization is staffing it. The human resources required to fulfill the mission and to support the strategic and operational plans of the organization become the key to the success or failure of the enterprise. The organization's strategic and operational plans must also provide staffing objectives. Descriptions of jobs and the complex working relationships among employees must be carefully factored into the organization.

Arts organizations face numerous challenges when it comes to staffing their organizations. As the epigraph to this chapter notes, having the right people is a key to organizational success. Unfortunately, the arts and not-for-profit job marketplace does not always provide the level of compensation many people are seeking, especially in the managerial or administrative area. The lack of competitive compensation can make finding the right person problematic.

An arts manager must also be aware of the laws regulating employment and must be versed in the art of negotiation. Several unions may represent employee groups throughout the organization, and they may have different contract periods. The task of finding the right people for the jobs, keeping them, and developing them is a never-ending process.

The Staffing Process

Any organization wants to fill its jobs with the best people available. Finding the most talented, qualified, and motivated people to work with you is much harder than it sounds. To make the overall system clear, we break the staffing process into six basic parts: planning, recruiting, selecting, orienting, training, and replacing.[1] We also look at how this process varies across the fields of theater, dance, opera, music, and museums. Figure 7-1 provides an overview of the entire human resource management system. As you would expect, there are variations among and within various art forms.

In the business world, the somewhat imposing-sounding phrase *human resources planning* simply translates into analyzing your staffing needs and then identifying the various activities you need to make the organization function effectively. In many large corporations, a manager identifies specific staffing needs to determine where the staffing resources are required. The manager then works with the human resources or personnel department to find the required staff. Because most arts organizations do not have human resources departments, it becomes all the more important for the manager to have an excellent grasp of the rules and regulations controlling the hiring and firing of employees. Mistakes in these areas can be very costly. More and more organizations face lawsuits because of badly handled personnel decisions. Given the often informal circumstances surrounding the hiring of many people in the arts, it is surprising that there are not more lawsuits. Let us take a look at the steps involved in planning to hire the people needed to make a performance or exhibition possible.

Job Analysis

Everyone would agree that an arts organization wants to hire the most talented artists. However, how are you going to judge the quality of your artists? What will be the screening process that insures you have the best your organization can afford? Your organization may have larger goals about the composition of the total staff for the organization. Do you have a commitment to diversity in the workplace? How will you insure that minority applicants apply for the openings you advertise? Will your workplace accommodate individuals with disabilities? Whatever the circumstances, the planning phase requires that you review five key areas for all of the jobs in the organization: work activities, work tools, job context, standards, and personnel qualifications.

Work Activities What is to be done? A performing arts organization will obviously need actors, singers, dancers, or musicians. Plans for the season often dictate the range of performer needs the organization will have. A dance company regularly performing *The Nutcracker* needs the correct mix of dancers to reach a desired level of quality. Acting companies seek to cast their shows with actors of the right age range if they are going to achieve a level of believability in various roles. An opera company must hire singers with the vocal talents necessary to perform the specific repertory. A season with Wagnerian opera requires different types of singers than a season with an Offenbach operetta. When considering the design staffing for a season, a producer works from the assumption that some designers are better than others at doing specific kinds of shows. Likewise, an organization considers how to market a

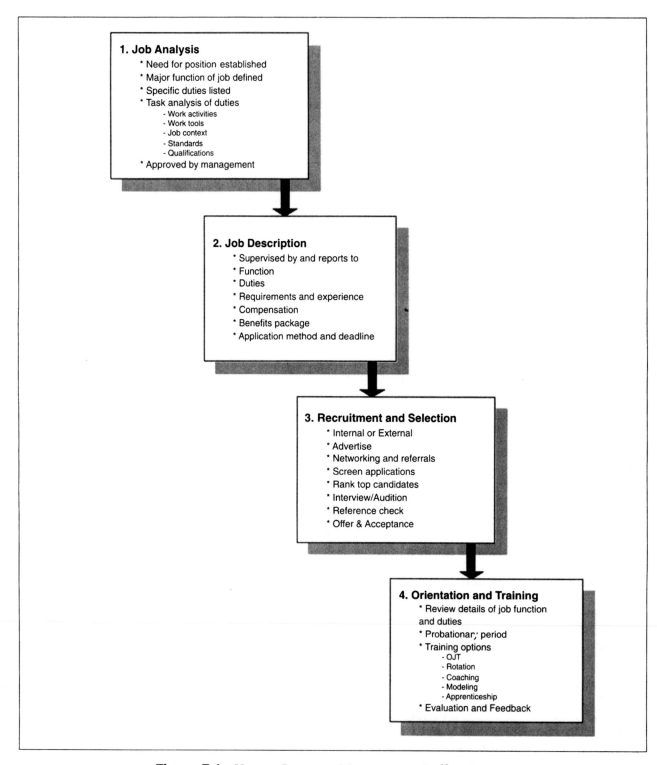

1. Job Analysis
* Need for position established
* Major function of job defined
* Specific duties listed
* Task analysis of duties
    - Work activities
    - Work tools
    - Job context
    - Standards
    - Qualifications
* Approved by management

2. Job Description
* Supervised by and reports to
* Function
* Duties
* Requirements and experience
* Compensation
* Benefits package
* Application method and deadline

3. Recruitment and Selection
* Internal or External
* Advertise
* Networking and referrals
* Screen applications
* Rank top candidates
* Interview/Audition
* Reference check
* Offer & Acceptance

4. Orientation and Training
* Review details of job function and duties
* Probationary period
* Training options
    - OJT
    - Rotation
    - Coaching
    - Modeling
    - Apprenticeship
* Evaluation and Feedback

Figure 7-1   Human Resource Management Staffing Process

season and wants a staff person fully capable of meeting the demands of promoting the season.

Based on your organization's design (as illustrated in Chapter 6, "Fundamentals of Organizing and Organizational Design"), you should be able to create a clear distribution for the rest of the staff you need.

In arts organizations, where staff resources are usually very limited, it is critical that the manager carefully analyzes how to combine the work activities to get the most productivity from each person.

Work Tools   Some employees need specific tools to do their jobs. For example, a regional ballet company that decides to set up its own scenery and costume shop will need thousands of dollars for equipment and space rental. An organization that hires a marketing director had better be ready to provide the computer equipment and software needed to do the job.

Job Context   Each employee has an overall context in which he or she functions. Performers have a set rehearsal and performance schedule; office personnel work within a daily schedule; and all employees work within an overall package that includes contracts, compensation, and benefits.

Standards   The manager of an organization must set clear standards for work output and quality. The manager of an arts organization may have various degrees of control, depending on contracts and agreements. The music director of the symphony and possibly a select group from the ensemble may be responsible for maintaining the performance standards at the highest level. On the other hand, complex negotiated agreements may limit the actions that the management may take to dismiss a musician who is not performing up to that standard.

Personnel Qualifications   The level of education and experience required for each position may vary widely in an organization. The process used to select performers requires different personnel qualifications than those used to hire ticket office salespeople.

One obvious problem that arts organizations face in hiring support staff with the right qualifications is the funding available for salaries. The low (or no) pay often associated with working for an arts organization leads to the practice of hiring or relying on unemployed artists to fill staff positions. A passion for the arts may lead artists to decide that working for an arts organization, even if it isn't in their specific talent area, is better than no job. But some artists are better than others when it comes to fulfilling the specialized staff functions in an arts organization. As in all industries, one doesn't always find the most qualified person filling a job. The net effect of this hiring practice is that the arts organization may find itself not being able to achieve its goals and objectives because the staff do not have the skills required to do the job.

Job Description
From this analysis of the basic requirements for the work to be done, the manager is able to create a job description for the new position. The description, which is usually distributed to the labor market, usually covers six areas: general description, responsibilities, specific duties, requirements for employment, compensation, and application method.[2]

The "Sample Job Description" shows how a staff opening might be worded. A shortened version of this description normally appears in a newspaper or job placement listing service. Let us look briefly at each section of this description.

General Description   The opening paragraph describes who is looking for what position and for what length of employment. The opening also clarifies to whom the employee reports and by whom the employee is supervised. Regardless of the exact wording chosen, these basic ingredients can be used in any job description.

Responsibilities   The next section of the description lists the employee's general responsibilities in the job. This example clarifies the scope of the job, the types of shows done, and the departments producing the events.

Specific Duties   Here you have the opportunity to list the tasks you expect the employee to carry out on a regular basis. In the example, the duties are ranked in order of frequency. Items 1, 2, and 3 are daily and weekly tasks, and items 4 through 7 occur on a monthly or semiannual basis. You can extrapolate this section to almost any job in the organization. The wording will be different, but performers, shop staff, ushers, museum guards, curators, and so on, all have lists of specific duties.

Requirements for Employment   The education, experience, and specific knowledge, skills, and abilities required are listed in this section. The *KSAs*, as they are often called, are important indicators for you in the screening process. Do the applicants have the knowledge of the area you are trying to fill? Do they have proven skills in specific tasks you need done? Do they have the general abilities to succeed in the job as defined? You can further clarify your KSAs by indicating which are required and which are desired. You may require applicants to have skills in specific software applications, but desire that they speak a second language. This specification does not mean that the employee must have these skills. In fact, he or she may bring unanticipated skills to the job that will benefit your organization.

Compensation   There are differing opinions about what to list for salary information. In some cases, unions may require that the salary be stated in the advertisement. In other cases, you may use a range to suggest some latitude in the salary to be offered. For example, "in the mid-20s" may mean as little as $23,000 to as much as $27,000. Other listings will simply say "compensation commensurate with experience." This lack of salary information could create budget problems for a manager when it comes time to negotiate a salary offer. For example, you would waste time by talking to an applicant who is making $40,000 when all you can offer is $30,000. One way to cover this contingency is to be sure that you clearly state the experience level required for the job in the requirements section. If you require an MFA (Master of Fine Arts) or equivalent experience, the applicant may take that to mean at least three years of work. This equivalent experience idea is based on the fact that most MFA programs require three years to earn the degree. In the end, you may save yourself and the applicant a great deal of confusion if you are clear about the compensation levels at the beginning.

Benefits   The term *full benefits* usually means the following:

- Health insurance
- Life insurance

- Disability insurance
- Retirement benefits

The benefits package an arts organization can offer is a budget decision in many cases. The costs of benefits can run as much as 30 percent of an employee's salary. In addition, many arts organizations expect employees to pay a portion of the health insurance. The employee's share may be as high as 50%.

Application Method   The final section of the job description explains what is required for the application, when the application is due, and to whom it should be sent. This section of the description is the appropriate place to state your concerns about seeking applications from special constituencies. You also want to include your participation in an equal-opportunity employment process.

The Overall Matrix of Jobs
In the initial stages of forming an organization, a great deal of time must be spent analyzing the minimum number of people required to operate

Sample Job Description

The Harper Performing Arts Center invites applications for the position of Ticket Service Manager. This is a full-time, 12-month, administrative staff position supervised by and reporting to the Managing Director.

Responsibilities
The incumbent will have general responsibility for the sales and accounting of individual tickets and subscriptions for productions produced by the Performing Arts Center. The Ticket Service Manager will perform the following duties:

1. Provide daily operation of a ticket service in a courteous and efficient manner through telephone sales, exchanges, and reservations. In addition, he or she will process mail-order, E-mail, and voice-mail message sales orders.
2. Using a computerized ticketing system, account for daily income and issue timely sales and deposit reports. In cooperation with other staff members, maintain a ledger file of revenue from cash sales, credit card charges, money orders, and open accounts.
3. Provide general information in response to inquiries about the Performing Arts Center and various performing arts events.
4. Update information on the Ticket Service website on a regular basis.
5. Train and supervise a staff of three and volunteer assistants in customer relations, subscription and single ticket sales, and general box office procedures.
6. Assist with marketing projects as needed and specifically with the following: (1) manage the ticket service and supervise the concession operations the night of performances; (2) train and supervise a house manager and ushers.
7. Assist with the maintenance and development of mailing lists for arts events.
8. Provide statistical reports on sales, subscriptions, and attendance at arts events during the year.
9. Perform other related duties as required.

Requirements
Three or more years of experience in box office management and sales required. A proven track record of positive interactions with customers and staff required. Other desired qualifications include a performing arts background, excellent computer skills, and familiarity with office equipment.

Compensation
Salary commensurate with experience (or you could say the starting salary is in the upper $20s). Full benefits package available.

Applications
Send cover letter, current résumé, and three letters of reference to the Human Resources Dept., Harper Performing Arts Center. EOE/AA.

the enterprise. This task is best done by identifying the key functions the organization must perform in order to present its programming. For example, if you present concerts of chamber music, a series of major activities have to be done if you want to sell tickets for a performance on a specific night in a specific place. As you begin to get a clearer picture of the overall scope of the jobs required to make the organization function, your job descriptions should reflect how you are going to achieve your objectives. The number of full-time and part-time employees and how they all relate to the performance season or exhibition schedule becomes the foundation of your operating budget. When salary and benefits often account for up to 80 percent of an organization's budget, it is critical that the manager keep the overall picture of the staffing as clear as possible. This overview makes the planning process easier. For example, when it comes time to initiate a new program or project, being able to look at the overall organizational structure can prove helpful. Being able to see where you can make adjustments and predicting the possible impact of staffing changes should make the planning process less difficult.

Constraints on Staffing

The costs related to staffing a position play a key part in the constraints placed on managers. For example, if you hire an administrative assistant for $20,000, your first-year costs must also include another $8,000 for benefits and taxes. If you consider a $28,000 staff position over a five-year period, assuming an inflation rate of 3 percent, your salary and benefits cost for this position will be in excess of $32,000 by the fifth year. Over five years, you will have paid out more than $153,000 in salary and benefits. This cost does not include equipment or extra training the employee may require. Assuming you are able to justify the expense for the staff addition, you must still face the ever-increasing complexity of laws and regulations that control hiring in the United States.

Government Regulations   Arts organizations are not necessarily exempted from the rules and regulations on hiring. The Equal Employment Opportunity Commission (EEOC) rules generally apply to all private and public organizations that employ 15 or more people. In addition, some state laws supplement various federal laws. In Chapter 4, "Arts Organizations in a Changing World," we discussed the impact of the political and legal environment on arts organizations. Here are examples of some of the major pieces of federal legislation that affect the hiring process:

- The Title VII Civil Rights Act (1964) and the Equal Employment Opportunity Act (1972) prohibit employment discrimination based on race, color, religion, sex, or national origin.
- The Equal Pay Act (1963) prohibits wage discrimination based on sex. The law requires equal pay for equal work regardless of sex.
- The Age Discrimination Act (1967; amended 1973) protects people from 40 to 70 years old against discriminatory hiring.
- The Rehabilitation Act (1973) provides for affirmative action programs for hiring, placing, and advancing people with disabilities.
- The Mandatory Retirement Act; Employment Retirement Income Security Act (1974) was designed to prohibit mandatory

retirement before age 70. The law also provides for some pension rights for employees.

- The Privacy Act (1974) gives employees the right to examine letters of reference in their personnel files.
- The Pregnancy Discrimination Act (1978) requires pregnancy and maternity to be treated as a legal disability.
- The Immigration Reform and Control Act of 1986 requires employers to check the identities and work authorization papers of all employees.
- The Americans with Disabilities Act (1990) requires businesses and public services to open up jobs and facilities to disabled people.
- The Older Workers Benefit Protection Act (1990) prohibits age discrimination in employee benefits.
- The Civil Rights Act of 1991 strengthens Title VII of the 1964 Civil Rights Act, granting the opportunity for compensatory damages and clarifying the obligations of employers and employees in unintentional discrimination cases.
- The Family and Medical Leave Act (1993) allows up to 12 weeks of unpaid leave during a year for the birth or adoption of a child, family health needs, or the employee's own health needs.

Organized Labor An organization required to employ people working under a union contract must adopt rules and policies for employment that fulfill specific legal procedures agreed to by the union and the management. Although union membership has been dropping steadily since 1956,[3] a variety of unions represent various employment groups in the arts and entertainment industries. Unions represent artists and craftspeople such as actors, singers, musicians, writers, directors, choreographers, and technicians. In addition, specific contracts with unions like the Teamsters (who may control the loading and unloading of trucks at the performance space) might be required in larger metropolitan areas.

The human resource function of an arts organization must take into account the myriad rules and regulations that typically accompany a union contract. We discuss this area later in this chapter under "Unions and the Arts."

Recruitment

Depending on the situation, you may face many or few choices in filling a staff position. The range involves the limits placed on the overall contractual relationship between the employees and the employer. If you need an extra electrician for a lighting setup in a union theater, the local sends over whomever it has. If, on the other hand, you need to fill the position of head electrician for the theater complex, you take steps similar to filling a salaried staff opening. The three steps in recruiting for a standard staff position are advertising the opening, screening possible candidates, and critically evaluating possible candidates for a list of finalists.

Internal As you may know, many jobs are filled before anyone hears about the openings. The internal recruitment process is common in companies that have a promote-from-within policy. For example, if you are hired as the assistant to the marketing director for the museum and you are aware that the promotion policy favors internal candidates, you may have an additional motivation to do your best work. In fact, many organizations lose good employees because there is no room for advancement within the organization.

External   Many arts organizations use a dual policy of internal and external recruitment. As organizations seek to create more multicultural staffs, active external recruitment has become a regular procedure. When doing external recruiting, there are various avenues to pursue, depending on what you seek. Some organizations may arrange auditions just to build files of possible performers for the future. Specialized publications like *ArtSEARCH*[4] can be used to seek out executive and administrative staff, designers, technicians, and craftspeople. Trade newspapers covering the arts may be found in some of the larger cities. General publication newspapers may also be used. Mailings to universities and colleagues can generate applications. Finally, a professional recruitment service can be hired to find candidates for higher level positions. Although "head-hunter" services may be an extra expense, they may also generate the most likely candidates for executive level positions, such as museum director or artistic director. A designated subcommittee of the board may also carry out searches for executive-level personnel.

Recruitment Philosophy   There are two fairly common philosophies about recruiting.[5] One approach assumes a traditional "selling" of the organization, and the other takes the "realistic," or real-time, approach. In the selling approach, you stress the most positive features of the job and the work environment. Essentially, you try to present an upbeat picture of the organization. The real-time approach tries to depict accurately what day-to-day life is like in the organization. You try to present an objective view of the work situation and are not shy about answering questions about the less positive aspects of working in the organization. Organizations often blend these two approaches in their recruitment campaigns, but the tendency is to sell the organization. After all, who wants to paint a picture that might scare off the applicants? People involved in the recruitment process have been known to use the realistic approach to discourage candidates that they perceive as not being "right" for the company. Obviously, care must be taken when selling the organization in the recruitment process. If an interviewer frames the wrong picture of the organization, an applicant could be very unhappy once he or she gets the job.

Recruitment Difficulties   Arts and other nonprofit organizations have complex personnel needs like any other business. Arts organizations hire people for vastly different jobs in meeting their objectives. Recruiting a soprano for an opera, hiring a marketing director, filling an administrative assistant position, or negotiating a union contract with the musicians or stagehands requires different priorities and strategies. Staff recruiting for salaried positions is often difficult because many arts organizations do not offer competitive pay rates. Artists, on the other hand, often negotiate contracts through their agents that exceed union scale minimums. Employees who work for wages that are negotiated by union representation often receive pay at rates comparable to those of private industry. This difference may lead to pay disparities that have a negative impact on recruitment strategies.

Trying to attract quality candidates to staff positions with no advancement possibilities, low salary, minimal (if any) benefits, and an overwhelming workload is a difficult task. It is not surprising that there is a high turnover rate in lower-level staff positions. Ironically, the people in these positions often do the basic work that keeps the organization going, such as payroll taxes, ticket office sales, or shop work. Competent, skilled administrative staff members are needed to ensure that the organization complies with all of the federal, state, and local laws pertaining to collecting and reporting taxes. Your ticket office can help build a positive relationship with the community. Without skilled help in your shops shows will not be of a high enough quality. Some of the lowest paid positions in an arts organization typically fall into these categories.

Selection Process

Auditions Different selection processes are used for different employee groups. The performers may all be selected by audition, depending on how the schedule is organized. For example, most resident theater companies now hold auditions in New York and a few other selected cities at various times during the year. Very few theater companies have actors in residence for a full season. Ballet companies, on the other hand, have yearly auditions for a resident group of dancers. Smaller dance companies try to provide at least 26-week contracts for their dancers. Lead dancers for special performances in the repertory may be contracted as the need arises. The larger regional opera companies, which have lengthy seasons, tend to audition resident choruses, dancers, and musicians and to hire the principal singers and conductors on a show-by-show basis. Smaller regional opera companies often work with a minimal staff and contract for all singers, dancers, and musicians on a show-by-show basis. Larger orchestras usually have a blind audition process in which the musician plays behind a screen so the judgment about their musicianship is based on their sound. The competition for places in the major orchestras is very stiff. Regional and smaller orchestras also have some type of audition process. However, the limited performance schedule may mean the players hold other full-time jobs as music teachers in schools and universities.

The audition process requires a great deal of data management. Records, which may include photos, lists of special skills, and so on, must be organized so that they can be easily retrieved. An audition space with a piano, tape player, dressing room, and warmup areas must be secured. If union contracts are in force, restrictions may apply to a variety of actions taken by management. For example, the Actor's Equity Association (AEA) contract with League of Resident Theaters (LORT) contains dozens of stipulations about auditions.[5]

Ultimately, the organization's survival depends on its ability to select the right talent for the positions available. Since the performer is the product that the audience "purchases," it is critical that the artistic management establish criteria that match the company's desired quality level. A poor casting choice or a weak player can bring down the overall quality of the artistic product.

Traditional Application Process The typical pattern for filling many staff positions in an arts organization follows these six steps: formal application, screening, interviewing, testing, reference check, and hiring.[6] Let's take a brief look at each stage.

In the News

American Theatre magazine sponsored a debate entitled "On Cultural Power" in January 1997 at the Town Hall in New York City. Robert Brustein, artistic director for the American Repertory Theatre, and playwright August Wilson met to carry on a dialogue about issues of race, casting, funding, multiculturalism, and arts and society. The issues raised have implications for arts managers trying to address programming and staffing that reflect the diversity of the audiences and the workforce. As reported by Stephen Nunns, the spirited discussion, which was punctuated by heckling, touched on subjects such as ebonics, color-blind casting, and questions about the validity of Black History Month as a way to effectively serve African-American audiences. The discussion raised questions such as "Is the classic American image of the 'melting pot' a thing of the past? Is the country metamorphosing from a democracy to a 'meritocracy'? What does the future hold for (in Brustein's words) 'the only hyphenated nation on earth'?"

SOURCE: "Wilson, Brustein and the Press," *American Theatre* (March 1997), pp. 17–19. *American Theatre* is published by the Theatre Communications Group.

Formal Application   Standard forms are used to take applications for job openings. Arts organizations often invite applications and request a cover letter, a résumé, and three or four references. In some cases, organizations actively seek out specific individuals and ask them to apply for the opening. The advantage of the application form becomes clear when you begin reviewing the candidates for the job. By using a similar format for gathering data, it may be easier to see which candidates have the qualifications you seek. When no formal application form exists, the person responsible for reviewing the files must develop a checklist of qualifications and requirements for the job. This checklist should be easily gathered from the job description you wrote.

Screening   The next step requires narrowing the list of applicants by eliminating those who do not match your search criteria. Further fine-tuning of the applicant pool usually reveals a short list of qualified candidates for the job. This work may be done by an individual or by a committee. For example, if the board is trying to hire a new artistic director, a search committee will be established and chaired by one of the board members. The screening process may become a very difficult stage in the hiring process because of strife within the organization. The search committee may be divided about the kind of person being sought, or the committee may arrive at a set of finalists that the rest of the board finds unacceptable. Needless to say, a significant number of variables can add to the complexity of the screening process.

Interviewing   The interview is equivalent to the audition for a staff position. If the search is being conducted by a staff member (not a search committee), the usual procedure is to interview several of the top candidates and to schedule second interviews for the best candidates. The committee approach may involve interviews with the top two or three candidates over a day or two by a wide range of people. Because the costs of conducting staff searches can run into the thousands of dollars, it is important to take the time to narrow the list of finalists before beginning the interview process. When pressed, some of the finalists may withdraw their candidacy, leaving you to fall back on other candidates on the list.

During the scheduled interviews, care must be taken to deal fairly with the candidates. Questions about age, marital status, family, national origin, handicaps, or religion are not legal. The same questions should be asked of each candidate, and they may be structured in such a way that you can legally discover whether the prospective employee can meet your work schedule, can communicate and write effectively, and can perform the specific tasks you require. Requesting writing samples, reviewing a detailed production schedule, or testing may help you assess the potential employee's ability to do the job.

Prospective employees should not leave the interview process with the impression that you were engaged in discriminatory activities. Your organization may have to answer to a lawsuit if you do not manage your interview process carefully.

Testing, Reference Check, and Hiring   The decision to hire the candidate who is best suited for the job sometimes rests on intangible emotional responses. After you evaluate and compare the composite skills of the people most likely to fill the staffing needs of the organization, you may still be left with a high degree of uncertainty. Further background checks and additional on-site interviews may help. Ultimately, a degree of chance is always involved in hiring.

Many large corporations use detailed screening tests for applicants in an attempt to narrow down the variables involved in hiring. Psychological, medical, or specific skills tests are often administered in large companies. Because of the high cost of hiring the wrong employee, corporations are not shy about spending several thousand dollars to hire the right person. On the other hand, the company's needs must be balanced against the individual's right to privacy.

Arts organizations must work with very limited recruitment budgets. High staff turnover creates an even greater burden on the budget because too much time is spent seeking replacements for people who quit. Few arts organizations have the time to conduct an extensive background check on a prospective employee. As a result, the organization may find itself on a hiring treadmill.

Legal issues also enter into the hiring process. If you narrow your candidates down to two or three finalists, the potential for sending misleading signals to the candidates is very high. You will need sufficient documentation to stand up in court about why you did not hire candidate B or C—should your decision be challenged. When you make any hiring decision, you face some risk that the rejected finalists will take legal action. This potential outcome may sound pessimistic, but more organizations face lawsuits over hiring practices each year.

Orientation and Training

The fourth stage in the process begins once the hiring has been completed. There are countless variations on employee orientation. Some organizations have fixed probationary periods (three or six months) in which very specific activities are planned to acquaint the employee with the organization. In other cases, a new person is hired and told to direct any questions to a specific individual or mentor.

The most important element in the orientation process is the socialization of the new employee into the organization. New employees are often anxious about their new jobs. They want questions to be answered and clarifications made about where they fit into the entire operation. The informal interactions new employees encounter will help shape their perceptions of the entire organization. To avoid problems later, it is best to schedule a review of the overall policies with new employees near the end of their probationary period. It is also important to note the date that you reviewed all of the relevant material with the new employee. You may later incur a problem with an employee who claims to have never been told about a specific policy. It may prove helpful to document when you reviewed a specific problem area with the employee.

Training and Development   In corporate America, millions of dollars are spent each year on employee training and development. Many employers need to train their workers in such basic areas as reading, writing, and simple mathematics. Due to their limited resources, arts organizations do not have such training programs. Training usually takes place only after costly errors have been made by a new employee. Although employee training is recognized as a real cost to organizations, few take into account the financial impact of not having a training program.

Hiring Tip

A saying is often heard in the personnel field: "Hire the person who best fits the job, not necessarily the best qualified." This statement implies that you need not force yourself to hire the person with the most qualifications. Remember, the key factor in attaining the maximum productivity from a staff member is finding someone who matches the overall job environment. The person you hire must be compatible with the corporate culture of the organization. In some cases, hiring the most-qualified (or overqualified) person can lead to problems.

On-the-Job Training　Most arts organizations use some variation of on-the-job training (OJT). The formal approach includes very specific work abilities that are tested by the supervisor at specific time intervals. The less formal approach usually includes quick demonstration sessions, after which the new employee is expected to get on with the task at hand. More rigorous OJT structures include some combination of job rotation, coaching, apprenticeships, and modeling.

Job Rotation and Cross-Training　In this system, employees move around to different areas to receive training in specific activities. This training is helpful when an employee later has to fill in for someone who may be out of the office. Organizations also often engage in cross-training their staff. The idea is to always have two people who can accomplish a set of tasks in the event that someone is out of the office or leaves for another job. For example, having only one person who processes subscription orders could prove harmful to an organization dependent on daily sales revenue.

Coaching　With coaching, as the term implies, a new employee receives very specific help with a skill related to the job. For example, an experienced stagehand may guide a new crew member through the operation of a follow spot. The stagehand watches the employee's performance and offers suggestions on improving his or her technique as he or she runs the spot.

Apprenticeships　The apprentice system is used extensively for training in the arts. Ideally, the apprentice works alongside a more experienced employee. If the system is really to function effectively, apprentices should be given specific tasks that allow them to assume substantial responsibility.

Modeling　In modeling, a new employee watches the performance of the supervisor or trainer. Personal demonstrations of what is expected help form a consistent presentation of the organization. This technique is especially important for employees who come into contact with the public. For example, people who sell subscriptions or museum memberships are involved in performance-related skills. They must be able to act out the script with which they have been provided to make the correct sales presentation. Watching and listening to a more experienced staff member go through the "scene" is a useful way to train a person.

Replacement and Firing

There may be a number of reasons to replace an employee. You may have made a selection error that resulted in a poor match between the individual and the organization, or the person you hired may have outgrown the job. You may move someone to a new job and create a vacancy due to reorganization. The person you hired may have violated the rules and procedures of the organization, leaving you no choice but to fire him or her. You may experience a slowdown or a budget cut that requires you to lay someone off, or an employee may develop an illness and be unable to work for an extended period. You may need to replace someone due to a retirement, military service, or death, or the employee may quit.

Firing No part of the staffing process is more troubling than firing an employee. Obviously, care must be taken when firing someone because of the legal ramifications. A poorly handled employee termination can cost an organization millions of dollars. *Wrongful-discharge* suits, as they are called, are becoming more common in the not-for-profit sector. Assessing the risks of firing an employee has led to better evaluation and documentation procedures. Verbal and written warnings must usually precede a termination. Although a union contract may stipulate very precise steps that must be taken, it should not be assumed that it is impossible to fire a union employee. Clauses that provide for the rights of management usually address this issue. On the other hand, many people work with no contracts whatsoever. Most arts organizations hire staff under what is called *employment-at-will*. Simply stated, you can be fired at any time with no or limited notice, but you may also quit with the same limited notice. If you have provided some indication to an employee that his or her job performance is not satisfactory, and you are operating in an employment-at-will environment, firing is best done swiftly. Typically, when someone resigns the notification period is 14 to 30 days. However, employment-at-will means that you may be fired at 9:00 A.M. and be told to clear your office by noon.

Some upper-level management staff have very detailed contracts developed by their lawyers and the organization's legal advisers. Precise language is often used to cover all aspects of compensation, evaluation, retirement, and termination.

Volunteers in the Arts

In addition to the paid staff, volunteers may constitute a significant portion of the workforce in an arts organization. There is a long history of volunteerism in a variety of nonprofit organizations in America and, in fact, the IRS provides the opportunity for a tax deduction for volunteers who assist nonprofit organizations.

The management of the volunteers is often a separate functional work area in the organization. The staff volunteer coordinator serves the important role of managing a resource that may save the organization thousands of dollars in staff salaries. However, the time and energy required to recruit, train, supervise, and evaluate volunteers can be considerable. Volunteers also have a different relationship to the organization and therefore must be evaluated with criteria that are relevant. Most active volunteers come to the organization with a commitment that is refreshing. In other cases the volunteer may possess special skills the organization can use in areas such as advertising, marketing, legal, or accounting.

To effectively operate the usually understaffed arts organization, volunteers will no doubt be needed in many areas. They can help realize the mission of the organization and help fulfill its goals and objectives by covering key areas where staff resources are limited. However, for the volunteers to be effective, as much attention must be paid to their job descriptions, recruitment, and training as for paid staff.

One obvious consideration in the use of volunteers is the risk factor. Management must assess the risk of using volunteers based on the work to be done. For example, it would probably be unwise to use a volunteer accountant or bookkeeper to manage the day-to-day financial activity of the organization. On the other hand, volunteers could be effective in seeking renewals by calling lapsed subscribers or members.

In the News—High Court Extends Job-Bias Scope

WASHINGTON—The U.S. Supreme Court gave new legal protection Tuesday to workers who say their ex-bosses wrote bad references or took other vengeful action against them for filing discrimination claims.

In expanding the scope of federal civil-rights law, the justices handed a unanimous victory to Charles Robinson, a black man who was fired by Shell Oil Co. in 1991 after 11 years as a sales representative.

He filed a racial-bias charge with the U.S. Equal Employment Opportunity Commission. Four months after he was fired, and while his EEOC complaint was still awaiting action, Shell sent an unfavorable recommendation about him to a prospective employer, Metropolitan Life Insurance Co. Robinson did not get the job.

Maureen Mahoney, a Washington lawyer who represents employers, said she now expects employers to refuse to provide references or to require that employees surrender their right to sue in exchange for references.

The decision is expected to also help older people who have been fired, because the Age Discrimination in Employment Acts contains similar retaliation provisions.

SOURCE: "High Court Extends Job-Bias Scope," Knight-Ridder Washington Bureau (February 19, 1997). Copyright © Knight-Ridder, 1997. Used with permission.

Their personal commitment to the organization may make them ideal salespeople. Assisting with specific group projects such as stuffing envelopes for a big renewal campaign can be a good affiliation building experience. Many organizations have guilds that sponsor annual fundraising events. The social element of the volunteer's participation in the organization can be a very positive way to strengthen ties to the organization. Ultimately, a well-managed arts organization needs a volunteer staffing system that is an integral part of the overall operating plan.

The volunteer staffing system also has its disadvantages. For example, it is difficult to manage volunteers in the same manner as staff since they are not being paid. The working relationship between volunteers and staff may become strained, as can any working relationship. However, in this case, if your volunteer is also a major donor to the organization, how do you say that his or her "job" performance is not adequate? Philip Kotler and Joanne Scheff, in their book *Standing Room Only*, point out that organizations often do not anticipate full output from their volunteers:

> One manager of a large volunteer force has developed what he calls his "rule of thirds." One-third of his volunteer workforce works avidly with very little direction and encouragement. One-third will work only with considerable motivation and are only effective with careful supervision. And one-third will not work at all under any circumstances. . . .[7]

Regardless of how productive your volunteers may be, there is enormous benefit to a well-managed volunteer system. Since the model of so many arts organizations includes a volunteer board of directors and general volunteers working with a paid staff, the necessity of developing and maintaining a healthy organization requires a staffing plan that allows for and uses volunteers.

The Board of Directors

As seen in Chapter 6, "Fundamentals of Organizing and Organizational Design," one of the distinctive elements of many arts organizations is the board of directors. This group represents a very potent element in the overall personnel mix of a typical not-for-profit arts organization. The dynamic between the executive leadership, staff, and volunteer board can be challenging for even the most experienced arts manager.

The board–staff working relationship will be discussed in more detail in Chapter 8, "Fundamentals of Leadership and Group Dynamics." The process of putting together a functional and productive board of directors follows many of the same guidelines used for staffing the organization. The general scope and responsibilities of the board are usually defined in the bylaws of the organization. A typical board of directors includes a core executive committee usually composed of key people in areas such as finance, marketing, and fundraising, as well as the secretary, vice chair, and chair of the board. The general board members usually have committee assignments as part of their responsibility.

An effective board should make use of the same tools used to organize the staff. Creating position descriptions, establishing clear functions and purposes for committees, and defining a system for evaluating the "job" performance of volunteers is critical to the long-term success of the organization. However, while the executive leadership of staff has

Volunteer Contracts?

It may be helpful to develop a contract form to use with your volunteers. Some of the obvious advantages of a contract are clear expectations about the work schedule, responsibilities, and duties and what support you will be providing to cover the expenses incurred by the volunteers. One good source for an example of such a contract may be found in Emily Kittle Morrison's book *Leadership Skills: Developing Volunteers for Organization Success*. This 1994 publication by Fisher Books offers some excellent guidance on selecting volunteers for service in the organization, as well as listing comprehensive criteria for selecting board membership.

control over the scope of the staff duties and their job performance, the same cannot be said of the board. It is up to the board leadership to establish the benchmarks for performance that determine if a volunteer remains on the board.

Ideally, an organization has a board and board leadership that is fully functioning and meeting the responsibilities set down in the bylaws and in the board policies, ethics, and procedures manual. In practice the effectiveness of not-for-profit boards (or for-profit boards, for that matter) runs along a continuum from highly effective to ineffective. Having clear job descriptions and leadership committed to professionally operating the board will make the manager's job significantly easier.

Unions and the Arts

Some of the unions involved in the arts are Actor's Equity Association (AEA) for actors and stage managers, American Federation of Musicians (AFM), American Guild of Musical Artists (AGMA), American Guild of Variety Artists (AGVA), American Federation of Television and Radio Artists (AFTRA) for performers, United Scenic Artists (USA) for scenery, costume, and lighting designers, and International Alliance of Theatrical Stage Employees (IATSE), and Motion Picture Machine Operators of the United States and Canada representing stagehands.

The opportunity to review actual contracts is now possible by going to the websites for many of these unions. For example, you may look at the detailed contract with AGMA and several opera companies. Many of these contracts include pay rates and per diem information as well as detailed explanations of working conditions and work rules. The Actor's Equity Association (AEA) website includes downloadable files for the many different contracts used with theaters.

Large arts organizations like the Metropolitan Opera in New York City must negotiate with multiple unions. The Met management must negotiate contracts with everyone from the musicians to the people who hang the posters in the marquees. Museums located in the larger cities must also work with unions who represent employees from many different groups, such as security guards.

Definition and Purpose

The classic definition of a trade union is a "continuous association of wage-earners for the purpose of maintaining or improving the conditions of their working lives."[8] Unions arose to fight the exploitation of employees, which was, more often than not, the norm. Although it might be argued that the unionization of the arts has created a division between salaried artists and employees who are paid a wage, the reality is that unions are here to stay.

The union's primary responsibility to the workers is to derive benefits from the working relationship with the employer through a written contract. This contract is carefully negotiated by individuals elected by union members to represent them and designated representatives from management. The life of the contract is generally limited to two or three years. Although there are thousands of variations on the terms in a contract, the six key areas are:

1. Compensation and benefits: pay increases and extent of benefits.

Board of Directors Responsibilities and Duties

What exactly are the responsibilities and duties of a board of directors? In a not-for-profit arts organization this group constitutes the legally empowered group that has the ultimate responsibility and financial responsibility for the corporation.

Typically, this group is empowered to serve a public purpose (see Chapter 2, "The Evolution of Arts Organizations and Arts Management"—see Legal Status and Financial Statements) and is sanctioned by the laws of the state in which the organization operates. At a bare minimum, a board must file annual reports with the state, and it is the entity that hires the executive director or other staff leadership to run the arts organization on a day-to-day basis. The general duties of a board includes:

- Hire, evaluate, and replace, if necessary, the executive leader.
- Provide oversight of the staff and generally make sure the management of the organization is doing what it should to fulfill the mission.
- Approve the annual budget.
- Accept and approve the annual financial report.
- Help raise funds to support the organization as it fulfills its mission.
- Set and monitor policies that provide guidance to the board and staff on how the organization will operate.

Sample Wording from a Contract

The following is from the Actor's Equity Association (AEA) contract with the League of American Theatres and Producers for the time period of June 26, 2000 to June 27, 2004:

7. Billing
(A) House Boards
   (1) The names of all Actors employed in the production shall be listed on the house boards in the front of the theatre in letters no less than one-half (1/2) inch in height. Such house board shall be entitled "The Company." Stage Managers, (and) Understudies and Swings* may be listed separately.
   (a) The Producer agrees, in instances where there is no house board outside the theatre, to place one prominently inside the lobby.
   (b) At least one such house board with names in alphabetical order shall be displayed so as to be clearly visible to the public at all times.
   (2) Should the Producer fail to comply with this clause (A) prior to the first performance, on the day following the giving of written notice, by the Actor or Equity, the Producer shall pay the Actor whose name is omitted, one-eighth (1/8) of the contractual salary for each performance that the violation continues to exist.

*A *swing* is a performer who covers roles in the chorus of a musical.

SOURCE: "Agreement and Rules Governing Employment Under the Production Contract," *Actor's Equity Association*, 2000, p. 18. For more information about AEA, go to http://www.actorsequity.org/home.html.

FYI—Actor Salaries

Based on the AEA contract with the League of American Theatres and Producers the minimum* salaries for actors and stage managers in many Broadway theaters effective June 30, 2003 are:

Actor: $1,354 per week, 8 shows per week
Stage Manager:
   (Musical) $2,225 per week, 8 shows per week
   (Dramatic) $1,913 per week, 8 shows per week
Assistant Stage Manager:
   (Musical) $1,760 per week, 8 shows per week
   (Dramatic) $1,563 per week, 8 shows per week

*Many performers, stage managers, and designers negotiate salaries above the minimum.

SOURCE: "Agreement and Rules Governing Employment Under the Production Contract," *Actor's Equity Association*, 2000, p. 94. For more information about AEA, go to http://www.actorsequity.org/home.html.

2. Job specifications: what exact duties will be proscribed for the employee?
3. Grievance procedures: in the event labor or management has a grievance, how will it be resolved?
4. Work rules: start and stop times, overtime, breaks.
5. Seniority rules: often affects internal promotions and sets criteria.
6. Working conditions: health and safety, equipment provided, training.

Disputes

The agency most often involved in labor and management disputes is the National Labor Relations Board (NLRB). This organization investigates unfair labor practices by employers and unions. A NLRB representative listens to both sides of a dispute and renders a decision aimed at resolving the conflict. If either party is unhappy with the ruling, the court system is the next step. The high cost of litigation motivates both sides to try to reach an out-of-court agreement.

Many companies are now making use of mediation services to avoid a prolonged NLRB process or the courts. Specialized firms now offer this service on a contract basis, thereby helping companies keep their legal costs down. However, since the results of these mediations are final, employees do not necessarily do as well as they would if they went to court. In fact, some critics have noted that since the company hires the mediation firm, there is a tendency to seek out firms that side with management more than labor.

Because the corporate culture of many nonprofit arts organizations stresses "giving to the cause," nonunion staff tend to focus on horror stories about union abuses. The most common complaint is

FYI—Designer's Contract

In 2002, Local 829 of IATSE (formerly USA-829) was able to negotiate with the League of Resident Theatres (LORT) that a category identified as "Tony Eligible" should be added to the contract. Before that time the contract covered LORT theatres D to A.* In addition, sound designers were added to the contract. Here are the published contract minimum rates for the 2002–2005 agreement:

Contract	Scene Design	Costume	Lighting	Sound
Tony Eligible	$8,746	$8,746	$8,213	$6,750
A	$6,300	$6,300	$4,700	$3,760
B+	$5,150	$5,150	$4,000	$3,200
B	$4,200	$4,200	$3,325	$2,660
C-1	$3,150	$3,150	$2,400	$1,920
C-2	$2,450	$2,450	$2,000	$1,600
D	-------------------------------Individual Negotiation-------------------------------			

*D to A LORT classifications are determined by weekly box office sales. A is the highest ticket sales range.

SOURCE: Union Local 829 website: http://www.frontpage.shadow.net/usa829fl/.

In the News—Press Release (April 22, 2002)

Denver Box Office Employees Vote for Union Security

A successful vote was taken of box office employees at the Denver Center for the Performing Arts (DCPA) for a union security clause, it was announced by International President Thomas C. Short. The IATSE recently organized box office employees at the Center, and the election was held in compliance with Colorado Labor Law mandating an "All Union Election and Referendum."

The affirmative vote resulted from the successful completion of negotiations for a contract covering the box office employees who recently elected for IATSE representation in the Union's organizing efforts.

The "All Union Election and Referendum" is a part of Colorado Labor Law and requires that prior to the imposition of a union security clause in any contract, 75% of the bargaining unit employees must approve such a clause by secret ballot.

The Colorado Department of Labor and Employment supervised the balloting of the box office employees on April 16 and 17, 2002. Box office employees voted 43 in favor and 2 opposed to the question. This will now allow the union to require that all bargaining unit employees share the same financial obligations to the union.

SOURCE: IATSE website: http://www.iatse.lm.com/prdcpa.html.

featherbedding, or creating jobs that are not really essential to the project. The unions are often blamed for creating a very high overhead for professional productions. However, since the union's mandate is to achieve the best wages and working conditions for its membership, equally compelling arguments for the number of employees working an event can be made. From the union's perspective, having the correct number of workers at the event could be an important safety issue. This is especially true if the event has dangerous scenery changes or special effects or complex costume changes. The producer's goal is, of course, to keep the number of staff as low as safely possible, since over the run of a show one extra person will add thousands of dollars to the cost of a show.

In the News

Labor disputes usually are a result of a negotiation process that fails to satisfy the union's initial demand. Management typically brings to the bargaining table less than labor is willing to accept. The result can be a work stoppage. For example, on September 22, 1996, the Atlanta Symphony Orchestra went on strike for 10 weeks. They had played for a month without a contract. In December they signed a four-year agreement that provided an 8 percent increase over the life of the contract, a minimum salary of $62,500, and 95 tenured positions with the orchestra. The orchestra members wanted a greater say in tenure review, tour planning, and "revolving seating for string players."[9] Out West, the San Francisco Symphony Orchestra went on strike on December 4, 1996, to force a contract settlement. The negotiations had started in March of 1996 and the then-current contract expired November 23, 1996. The musicians were seeking a 5.5 percent increase to bring their minimum salary to $78,520. They also were seeking a reduction in their performance schedule because of the high rate of repetitive stress injuries.

In both cases the work stoppage had a detrimental effect on the orchestra's finances. However, the unions did make some progress in meeting their demands. The issues of repetitive stress injuries and health insurance coverage continue to be subjects in other orchestra contracts around the country.

SOURCE: Allan Kozinn, "San Francisco Symphony Goes on Strike," *New York Times* (December 6, 1996), Section B, p. 8.

The 1980s saw a major shift in the way in which the business community dealt with unions. Led by President Ronald Reagan's dissolution of the air traffic controller's union, company after company simply let unions call strikes and then went out and hired replacement workers. Management became much bolder in demanding concessions from the unions. Unions continued to fight a losing battle in the 1990s as more companies shifted work overseas. Well-paid union workers were seen by many companies as a liability, not an asset, in a competitive world economy. The cost of labor in the United States was simply too high, so many companies took the work elsewhere. Congress passed legislation requiring advance notice of plant closings, but this law had little effect on the trend.

For companies that stayed in America the strategy became to work in a more cooperative association with labor. Many union contracts began to include differential pay scales for new hires, reduced benefits, early retirement buyouts, and a modification of restrictive work rules. Many of these changes trickled down into negotiations between arts organizations, performing arts centers, producers, and the unions. These changes were not met with enthusiasm, and suspicion about the motives of management remained high.

Unfortunately, an attitude of "us versus them" is still very much a part of the day-to-day relationship of labor and management. The negotiation process often tends to set up a win-lose mentality that can lead to internal strife. To a large extent, the corporate culture of the arts organization can play a big part in forming the overall attitude about employees and the perceived value of their contribution to the organization's goals and objectives. If the organization's values express the attitude "We are here to do quality work as creatively and efficiently as possible, and we appreciate and reward people who have these work ethics," the odds are that the relations with the union will be fairly positive. However, if management's attitude is, "You can't trust them, they always goof off, and they are slow to get work done," a work environment filled with suspicion and mistrust is reinforced. The union members and their leadership will be more likely to respond favorably if the culture of the organization is cooperative, not confrontational. However, if the union members, from the stagehand to the first violinist, feel that management is out to get them, the entire artistic product may suffer. Cultivating good labor-management relationships in an arts organization must be a high priority from the board president on down.

Maintaining and Developing the Staff

If an organization is to be successful over the long run, it must have a dedicated and experienced staff. The only way to build such a staff is to monitor the work environment constantly. A good manager should be aware of the staff's changing needs. The degree of intervention exercised by the manager depends on whether problems have arisen that require correction.

The psychological atmosphere of the workplace changes almost every day. One of the most important parts of the manager's job is staying attuned to the mood of the workplace. You can employ several strategies to help you stay in touch with your employees. Organizations must develop ongoing systems to assess regularly the concerns of employees in the workplace. Annual or ongoing evaluations, scheduled project assessments, production meetings, informal lunch or dinner meetings, and awards for outstanding performance or achievement all form a menu of choices that an organization must have available. (See "Performance Appraisal Systems" in Chapter 9, "Organizational Controls and Budgets.")

Career Management

If an organization places a high value on employee retention, a career management system must be established. Employees need to believe that they are learning and growing in their jobs. Some of the ways to help employees develop a long-term commitment to the organization is to offer support for additional training, provide leaves of absence for outside study, and solicit employee input about job and work expectations. Obviously, there are limits to the amount of career enrichment available for every level within an organization, but the creative application of these ideas can help promote an organizational culture that places a high value on people. For example, it would be a mistake to assume that someone functioning as a receptionist is only capable of answering the phone and directing inquiries. It is true that this job is not a staff position with a great deal of potential for career development. However, by carefully designing the job to provide additional duties, such as assisting with gala event planning or conducting donor research, you may be able to make the job more challenging for an employee.

The "Right Staff"

The importance of staffing the organization cannot be stressed enough. All of the neat and tidy organizational charts, beautifully detailed strategic plans, forceful mission statements, and carefully designed marketing and fundraising campaigns will be of no use without the people to make it all happen. To function effectively as an organization you must have the personnel with the skills and dedication suited to the mission. As you will see in the next chapter, the success or failure of an organization is directly related to the effectiveness of its leadership. Finding the right people for the jobs you have and building a team of productive staff members is one of the most difficult tasks a manager faces. In situation after situation, the failure to assemble the right combination of people on the workforce leads to the failure of organizations to achieve their aims. A symphony with a brilliant conductor is only as good as the musicians in the orchestra. The finest collection in a museum will fail to live up to its potential without an effective curatorial staff. A dynamic choreographer or director needs equally dynamic dancers, actors, or singers to grab the audience's interest and support.

Summary

The staffing process can be broken down into four major steps: job analysis, job description, recruitment and selection, and orientation and training. The process of analysis assumes that you are staffing the organization to realize strategic and operational objectives. Job design helps integrate the staffing plan with specific job responsibilities and duties. Organizations must function within the laws that affect hiring personnel. Union contracts and stipulations are a fact of life in the arts. Arts managers must be well versed in negotiating contracts and structuring their organizations to work effectively with unions. The two

Personnel Odds and Ends

As this story demonstrates, employee problems can be manifested in various ways.

News of the Weird
Chuck Shepard

In May, Los Angeles Philharmonic bassist Barry Lieberman was suspended without pay for assaulting colleague Jack Cousin as they were leaving the stage after a performance. Lieberman alleged that, because of an ongoing dispute, he was justified in shoving his bass into the back of Cousin's legs to trip him as they were filing off the stage.

SOURCE: Chuck Shepard, "News of the Weird," *Cleveland Plain Dealer* (January 6, 1991). Copyright © 1991 by the *Cleveland Plain Dealer.*

Employee Manual

Listed below is the Table of Contents from a typical employee manual for an organization. This sample is used by USITT (U.S. Institute for Theatre Technology) for the operation of a six-person office. Whenever you have four or more people in an office, it is a good idea to develop a manual to answer typical employee questions or clarify important policy issues decided by the board of directors. The section on hiring is printed in full to give the reader an idea of the kind of issues that need to be covered in a manual of this type.

General Information
I-A Equal Opportunity
I-B Hiring Procedures [detailed]
1. Selection of candidates for all positions follows USITT Equal Opportunity policies.
2. USITT provides an opportunity for employees to take initiative toward their career development and to enhance their possibilities for advancement within USITT. Current employees are considered for filling a vacant position prior to hiring from the outside based on their qualifications and work history.
3. Qualifications matching existing position descriptions provide the basis

for initial screening of applications.
4. Verification of employment information provided by the applicant is part of candidate selection. Generally, the only information to be verified from prior employers is the following, unless the applicant agrees, in deference to the applicant's privacy:
   a. Dates of employment
   b. Positions held and duties for each
5. Applicants must be advised that this information will be verified. Verified information shall be documented and maintained in the successful candidates' personnel files.
6. New employees must confirm their acceptance for employment within three business days after being offered a position. At that point, new employees complete all pre-employment forms, benefit applications, and enrollment forms; and are provided basic information regarding pay policy, leave policy, benefits, and working hours.
7. Each new employee shall receive a complete

copy of the current Employee Manual prior to beginning work.

I-C Employment Classifications
I-D Performance Review
II-A Workday and Payroll
II-B Overtime Compensation
II-C Meal Break and Rest Period
II-D Compensatory Time
II-E Flextime
III-A Insurance
III-B Retirement Annuity Program
III-C Vacation/Personal Leave
III-D Holidays
III-E Personal Time Off
III-F Leave of Absence
III-G Compassionate Leave
III-H Jury Duty
IV-A Employee Incurred Expenses and Reimbursement
IV-B Conferences and Meetings
IV-C Professional Memberships
V-A Sexual Harassment
V-B Substance Abuse
V-C Smoking
V-D Grievances
Appendix: Position Descriptions

major recruitment methods are internal and external recruitment. Recruitment options include auditions and traditional application and screening processes. When interviewing candidates for jobs, managers must carefully follow legal guidelines. The hiring and orientation of new staff can be assisted through formal procedures to ensure that consistent information is presented. Job training and long-term staff development are a key component in building an experienced and productive staff. Firing and replacing staff can be legally risky if handled improperly.

Key Terms and Concepts

Human resources planning
Job description
KSAs
Job matrix
Equal Employment Opportunity Commission (EEOC)
On-the-job training (OJT)
Wrongful discharge
Employment-at-will
National Labor Relations Board (NLRB)

Questions

1. Based on your own employment experiences, give an example of how the job requirements differed from the official job description. Relate the problems or benefits of the situation.

2. Discuss the pros and cons of unions in the arts. Make a case for each side of the argument.

3. Write a job description for a position in an arts organization using the outline provided in the "Sample Job Description."

4. Have you ever gone through a formal job orientation? Was it an effective tool for bringing you into the work environment?

References

1. John R. Schermerhorn, Jr., *Management for Productivity*, 2nd ed. (New York: John Wiley & Sons, 1986), p. 241.
2. Ibid., p. 243.
3. Howard M. Wachtel, *Labor and the Economy*, 2nd ed. (New York: Harcourt Brace Jovanovich, 1988), p. 373.
4. *ArtSEARCH* is published by the Theater Development Fund, New York, New York. Yearly subscriptions are available.
5. Actor's Equity Association, *Agreement and Rules Governing Employment in Resident Theatres.* Effective February 26, 1996; terminates February 26, 1999.
6. Schermerhorn, *Management for Productivity*, p. 249.
7. Philip Kotler and Joanne Scheff, *Standing Room Only* (Boston: Harvard University Press, 1997), p. 427.
8. Sidney Webb and Beatrice Webb, *The History of Trade Unionism* (London: Longmans, Green and Co., 1894), p. 1.
9. Allan Kozinn, "Symphony Strike Is Settled," *New York Times* (December 5, 1996), p. B-1.

Additional Resources

Many textbooks cover the field of personnel management in depth. A quick check of business books in a university bookstore should turn up at least an undergraduate-level book in this area. Three excellent sources for more information about personnel issues may be found in the following books.

Michael Carrell, Frank Kuzmits, and Norbert Elbert. *Personnel: Human Resource Management*, 3rd ed. Columbus, OH: Merrill, 1989. This text was used in developing this chapter.

Stephen Langley. *Theatre Management and Production in America*. New York: Drama Book Publishers, 1990. Chapter 4 provides much information on personnel for all levels of theater.

Thomas Wolf. *Managing a Nonprofit Organization*. Englewood Cliffs, N.J.: Prentice-Hall, 1990. Chapters 3 and 4 provide clear information about putting together a workforce and establishing personnel policies.

A good resource for your own use as an employee in an organization may be found in the Nolo Press book entitled *Your Rights in the Workplace* by Barbara Kate Repa, 1996.

Fundamentals of Leadership and Group Dynamics

When people described to us their personal-best leadership experiences, they told of times when they imagined an exciting, highly attractive future for their organization. They had visions and dreams of what could be.

James M. Kouzes and Barry Z. Posner,
The Leadership Challenge

We are now ready to examine the complex areas of leadership, the management communication process, and group dynamics in arts organizations. In this chapter we discuss the use of power in leadership and briefly review trait, behavioral, contingency, and situational approaches to leadership. We take a look at what motivates people, as well as the key factors required to successfully work with and lead groups. Lastly, we review the important issues related to communication in the workplace. Figure 8-2 is a graphic representation of the main topic areas of this chapter. To gain more expertise in the area, I also suggest you explore the list of books at the end of this chapter.

Up to this point, we have created an organization, given it an overall structural framework, established strategies and plans to realize its mission, and begun staffing the enterprise with the best people we can find. Before we move into the specific operational areas of finance, budgeting, scheduling, marketing, and fundraising, we need to finish building the organization's interpersonal structure. Every day, arts organizations face the changing dynamics of people working together. With sensitive and adaptive leadership, the organization will go far. As you will see in this chapter, developing an organization with effective leadership is a continually challenging process.

Leadership Fundamentals

The subject of leadership is explored in numerous books each year. If you stop by your local bookstore and go to the section on business books, you will find dozens of titles on this topic. The search for the best way to develop leadership skills and how to use those skills to create an organization that flourishes is a popular topic in today's business literature.

As you see from the epigraph to this chapter, one element of leadership is inspiring a vision of what could be. In order for that to happen the person in the leadership role must first be able to influence others. Simply put, *leadership* is the manager's use of power to influence the behavior of others.[1] *Power*, as we will use the term, is defined as the ability to get someone else to do something you want done. The effective use of power in a leadership situation is also influenced by respect for the person who is doing the leading. Someone may have power over you, but you may have little respect for that person. This ultimately does not make for an effective leadership situation.

In all of our discussions of leadership, keep in mind that leadership success is a necessary, but not the sole, condition for managerial success. It is also important to remember that although a good manager should be a good leader, a good leader is not necessarily a good manager. People have ranges of skills, some of which are more developed than others. For example, someone identified as an excellent leader may not be particularly good at planning and organizing. Some managers may be wonderfully organized with detailed plans but lacking in leadership abilities. Let us look at the two basic leadership modes: formal and informal.

Formal and Informal Leadership Modes

Formal leadership is leadership by a manager who has been granted the formal authority or right to command.[2] The director of the play, the conductor of the orchestra, and the chair of the board of directors have been given formal authority by the organization to act on behalf of the organization. *Informal leadership* exists when a person without authority is able to influence the behavior of others.[3] Often informal leadership grows out of specific situations where an individual steps in and takes over. For example, suppose that an inexperienced student stage manager is unable to control the cast. A cast member with some stage managing experience steps in and starts giving orders. Because other students have respect for her, they listen to this informal leader and ignore the formal leader.

Theory X and Theory Y Approaches to People

Before we examine the details of various leadership theories, consider again a topic we touched on in Chapter 3, "Evolution of Management." Douglas McGregor argued that Theory X and Theory Y represented the contrasting fundamental beliefs that managers have about the people who work for and with them. A Theory X manager assumes that people dislike work, lack ambition, are irresponsible, resist change, and prefer to be led rather than to lead. A Theory Y manager works with people from the opposite perspective; he or she assumes that people like to work, are willing to accept responsibility, are capable of self-direction and self-control, and can be imaginative, ingenious, and creative.[4] McGregor's theory raises the issue of the self-fulfilling prophecy. This psychological term applied to the management of people simply means people will perform in their jobs at the level you establish for them. In other words, if you treat your staff, cast, and crew like idiots, they will tend to fulfill your expectations.

This topic of self-fulfilling prophecies, for example, is fundamental to the underlying attitude a manager has about the people he or she works with and supervises. The psychology of the workplace is usually very complex. If you assume a leadership position without having developed an overview about the people you work with, you will probably run into a series of personnel problems that will limit your effectiveness.

Before you can develop your leadership skills, you must seriously evaluate your attitudes about work and people. In many arts organizations, both X and Y attitudes operate. Needless to say, these conflicting approaches usually lead to varying degrees of employee satisfaction. In addition, some arts organizations function with leadership that borders on the tyrannical, while other organizations appear to be without leaders. As we saw in Chapter 6, "Fundamentals of Organizing and Organizational Design," the corporate culture of an arts organization is established and reinforced by its leadership.

Power: A Leadership Resource

The word *power* often has negative connotations. Yet without power, it would be impossible to operate most organizations. As we defined it, power is the ability to get someone to do what you want. However, in most arts organizations (or any organization), you have only as much power as your coworkers are willing to give you.

We begin our investigation of leadership power by posing three questions:

1. What sources of power are available to the manager?
2. What are the limits to the manager's power?
3. What guidelines exist for acquiring and using power?

Sources of Power

Two sources of power are available to the manager: *position power* and *personal power*.[5] The first comes with the job you occupy, and the second is directly attributable to you.

Position Power   As we saw in Chapter 6, the organizational design process should establish the working relationship between and among employees in the organization. No matter how little vertical or hierarchical structure exists in the organization, managers are given power by their designated positions. For example, a production manager has more power than a technical director, a technical director has more power than a stage carpenter, and so forth. Management texts identify three types of position power: reward, coercive, and legitimate.

Reward power is the capability to offer something of value as a means of controlling others.[6] For example, a position may carry with it the power to grant raises, promotions, special assignments, or special recognition.

Coercive power is defined as the ability to punish or withhold positive outcomes as a way of controlling others.[7] For example, if you have ever received a verbal reprimand or a demotion or been fired from a job, you have been subjected to coercive power. Control over the work schedule may be used as a form of coercive power. (Scheduling could also be used as a reward power in some cases.)

Legitimate power is the ability to control others by virtue of the rights of the office.[8] It is asserted in the phrase, "I am the boss, and therefore you must do what I ask."

Personal Power   Along with the position you hold, you bring your unique attributes and talents to the situation.[9] The two types of personal power are expert power and reference power.

Expert power is simply the ability to control others because of your specialized knowledge.[10] This could include special technical information or experience that others in the organization do not possess. For example, a stage manager with production experience may have expert power when it comes to planning a scenery shift on stage. This would allow the stage manager to exercise more power in a production meeting when alternative ways of doing a set shift are being discussed.

Reference power is derived from a more personal level of interaction with employees. Reference power is the ability to control others because of their desire to identify personally with the power source.[11] This use of power is often found among strong founder-directors of arts organizations. Their charismatic personality and forceful approach to managing the organization are used as a way of controlling others.

It is fairly easy to apply the five types of power—reward, coercive, legitimate, personal, and reference—to such familiar roles as conductor, director, production manager, technical director, stage manager, or choreographer. Each of these leadership positions requires the use of some combination of these powers. You have probably realized that some individuals are better than others at using the power they have been given.

Limits to Power

Now that we have looked at the sources of power, let us examine some of the limits of power. In the organizational setting of the arts, the power to control others is more often a potential than an absolute.

Dance Leadership in the News

This excerpt from a December 2001 article in the *New York Times* points out the problems inherent in a strong founder-director not establishing a clear successor.

Dance: Who Owns a Dance? It Depends on the Maker

. . . The protracted battle involves Ron Protas, the sole heir to whom Graham willed her considerable stable of ballets, and the Martha Graham Center of Contemporary Dance, which wants the right to dance and teach her works. Last August Judge Miriam Cedarbaum in United States District Court in Manhattan denied Mr. Protas an injunction barring the Graham Center (including the Martha Graham Dance Company) from using the choreographer's name, which he had trade-marked. But a larger issue remains to be settled: will the very company that Ms. Graham founded be able to license and dance her ballets again?

Even Clytemnestra, one of Graham's signature alter egos, settled her score with the gods in a mere three acts. So what went so terribly wrong? The plaintiffs claim that the Graham Center is trying to usurp copyrighted property, while the defendants say Mr. Protas is using a nonprofit organization to profiteer. Graham, who choreographed the bulk of her works as vehicles for her own formidable talent, may have subconsciously wished to take her work with her to the grave. But what seems clear is that she did not carefully assess the repercussions her choices would provoke.

The case has shoved a litany of issues about the ownership of dance property to center stage. As a result, some choreographers have begun to consider the future of their works through copyrighting and estate planning.

"There is a tremendous disconnect between the dance world and the legal world, due to a lack of information," said Dale Cendali, the lead counsel for the Graham Center. "A lot of dance companies and other arts institutions have not thought through all the issues of successorship and the legal implications and done all the advance planning they could have done."

SOURCE: Joseph Carman, "Dance: Who Owns a Dance? It Depends on the Maker," *New York Times* (December 23, 2001).

Although history provides many sad examples of individuals abusing the power they have had over others, there are limits to power. In arts organizations several different groups of employees work to support the organization's stated goals and objectives. Within each employee group, differing degrees of power are exercised. The union stage crew has a different relationship to the power structure of the organization than the senior staff has. However, whatever the differences may be within each work group, there are limits to how effectively power can be used to control work output.

Acceptance Theory   As noted in Chapter 3, "Evolution of Management," Chester Barnard's 1938 book entitled *The Functions of the Executive* articulated what is known as *acceptance theory*. Simply stated, power is only realized when others respond as desired—that is, when they accept the directive.[12] Acceptance theory states that people are most likely to accept orders or requests when one or more of these four conditions are met:

1. They truly understand the directive.
2. They feel capable of carrying out the directive.
3. They believe that the directive is in the best interests of the organization.
4. They believe that the directive is consistent with their personal values.

Zone of Indifference   Another part of Barnard's leadership theory focuses on what is called the employee's *zone of indifference*. This theory states that power in organizations is limited to the range of requests and directives that people consider appropriate to their basic employment or the psychological contracts they make with the organization.[13] A directive that falls within the zone of indifference tends to be accepted and followed automatically. For example, if a marketing research assistant in a museum is asked to check the membership list for zip code distribution in comparison to census data reports, he would not react negatively. However, if his supervisor asks him to pick up her dry cleaning on the way to work, the odds are good that the supervisor has crossed the zone of indifference. The assistant will react by saying, "That is an inappropriate request to make." He may still pick up the dry cleaning, but resentment and negative feelings about the supervisor will no doubt affect the employee's attitude and work behavior.

Both of these theories can be easily applied to an arts organizational setting. Trying to ignore these theories may make the leadership role very difficult. Put yourself in the position of a cast member, intern, or crew member, and think about how the acceptance theory may affect your interaction with your supervisor.

Guidelines for Using Power

Consider using the guidelines that follow when you find yourself exercising formal or informal power. These very practical applications of Barnard's acceptance theory are summarized from an article by John R. Kotter in the *Harvard Business Review*.[14]

1. Don't deny your formal authority. It is acceptable to act like the boss if you keep your perspective and remember that you are dependent on the goodwill and cooperation of the people who work for you.

2. Don't be afraid to create a sense of obligation. Doing a few favors or clearing the path so that employees can get their jobs done will help establish their obligation to follow your direction.
3. Create a feeling of dependence. Although care must be taken not to create a negative dependence (employees can't make a decision without you), it can be helpful to establish a situation in which people depend on your help to make their job easier. This will make it easier to gain their cooperation later.
4. Build and believe in expertise. A few solid examples of your having accomplished something will help build a belief by others in your expertise. No one likes working for know-nothing bosses who do not seem qualified to hold the positions they do. (Many good examples of negative employee behavior in such situations may be found in the Dilbert cartoon series.)
5. Allow others the opportunity to identify with you as a person. When you create an environment in which the people you work with know and respect you as a person, they are more likely to follow your direction and supervision.

Approaches to the Study of Leadership

Management researchers have developed several theories that attempt to predict why some people are better leaders than others. The first studies of leadership examined the personal traits and psychological characteristics of people in leadership roles.

Trait Approaches to Leadership

The earliest research was based on the assumption that a person with particular traits has leadership potential. The idea was to establish an inventory of traits and to match them to people. This early research focused on physical and psychological attributes. However, there proved to be a limited correlation between these traits and leadership. Recent studies have shown, however, that the specific traits of intelligence, dominance, aggressiveness, and decisiveness do tend to be associated with people identified as leaders.[15] However, the focus on traits is still secondary to most research on leadership. The actual behavior of leaders is the current focus.

Behavioral Approaches to Leadership

Other researchers have tried to formulate a leadership model by studying recurring patterns of behavior by people in leadership positions. This research has focused on the leader's orientation toward tasks and people. Leaders who were highly concerned about the tasks to be done exhibited certain behaviors: planning and defining the work to be done, making clear assignments of task responsibility, setting work standards, and following up on task completion, and monitoring. The people-oriented leaders tended to emphasize other behaviors: developing social rapport with employees, respecting the feelings of others, and developing a work environment of mutual trust. These styles of leadership are diagrammed in Figure 8-1. A practical application of this matrix is the relationship between a stage director and the cast. Consider your own experience, and try to place an arts leader you have worked with somewhere within this matrix.

Four Leadership Styles

More concerned about people than tasks

Examples:
   * Director spends long hours working with actors and falls behind on the rehearsal schedule.
   * Development director works so closely with donors that he/she does not have time to complete weekly donor research reports.

Concerned about people and tasks

Examples:
   * Marketing Director works with staff on large mailing project and leads lively discussions and provides refreshments.
   * Technical Director takes time to train crew on difficult scene shifts and explains how crew can remain safe during rehearsals and performance.

Low concern for tasks and people

Examples:
   * Conductor gives a half-hearted effort on a concert that they wished they had never agreed to do. Gives little correction to orchestra.
   * Long-term shop manager is invested in his new sailing hobby. Supervising construction and crew is of little personal interest.

More concerned about tasks than people

Examples:
   * Lighting designer stays late after rehearsal to get cues set. Disregards crew complaints as "whining."
   * Choreographer insists section of new work must be redone after long day of classes and rehearsals by dancers.

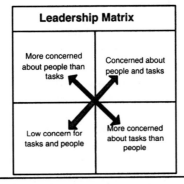

Leadership Matrix

More concerned about people than tasks	Concerned about people and tasks
Low concern for tasks and people	More concerned about tasks than people

Different leadership situations require applying task and people concerns in varying intensities.

Figure 8-1   Four Leadership Styles

Contingency and Situational Approaches to Leadership

Circumstances in the workplace change, and these changes may require different leadership approaches. Researchers questioned the idea that any one particular leadership style is effective in all situations. Out of their studies came *contingency* or *situational leadership theories*. The source for these theories is Fred E. Fielder's 1967 book *A Theory*

Arts Leadership in the News

Media reporting on the comings and goings of artistic leadership is typically without the informed perspective of the employees or managers who actually work with the person in the leadership position.

In a recent article about a change in leadership at the Royal Shakespeare Company the leadership behavior of one artistic director seemed to be called into question. Adrian Noble announced his resignation from the job of artistic director on April 25, 2002, after 11 years as head of the world-famous acting company. Mr. Nobel had "come under strong criticism in recent months,"

according to a *New York Times* article by Alan Riding, for his plan to demolish the 1930s Royal Shakespeare Theatre and replace it with a $145 million facility.

The article offered a mixed perspective on the leadership of Mr. Noble. The *Times* noted, "In announcing his decision 'to seek out new artistic challenges' next year, Mr. Noble said the broad lines of the company's renewal program were now in place. In a statement praising Mr. Noble's 'outstanding contribution,' Lord Alexander, the chairman of the company also said, 'We look forward to building on' Mr. Noble's ideas."

Two other issues regarding leadership behavior were also brought up in the article: "Mr. Noble . . . has also been criticized for taking time off to direct a new West End production of the musical 'Chitty Chitty Bang Bang'," and "By the late 1990s . . . he was coming under criticism for no longer drawing top-ranking actors and directors to the company's Mainstage. . . ." The article reveals that because arts leadership is very public, it therefore falls under a lot of scrutiny.

SOURCE: Alan Riding, *New York Times*, "Artistic Director Leaving Royal Shakespeare" (April 25, 2002), p. B-1.

---

of Leadership Effectiveness.[16] Fielder's study indicated that leaders differ in how oriented they are to tasks and people. Some situations require more focus on tasks and some toward people. (See Figure 8-2.) Here are two examples of contingency leadership required in a typical arts setting.

A membership manager for a museum must coordinate a renewal and new members drive each year. Once it is planned, the entire operation is very task-oriented and specific. The leadership requirements in this situation would be directed toward ensuring that employees were being accurate in completing routine tasks. At the same time, because this project requires repetitive work on the part of the staff, the manager's challenge is to keep people motivated and productive. Therefore, the manager might structure the day with frequent breaks or some other form of stress relief for the staff.

After finishing the big renewal campaign, the membership manager has been appointed to chair an ad hoc committee to study and improve management and employee relations. Different leadership skills will be required. The goal is defined, but the specific tasks are not indicated. Other committee members will be volunteers, and the manager will have little direct control over them. This situation requires strong group leadership skills. The manager must also develop clear objectives for all phases of the study. Deadlines will have to be set, objectives defined, and committee procedures established.

Another leadership theory aligned with the situational approach is called the *normative leadership model.* This model, from Victor Vroom and Phillip Yetton, bases its approach on the idea that a leader acts from either an autocratic, consultative, or group decision-making style.[17] As an autocratic leader you either solve the problem or make the decision yourself with the available information or after consulting a subordinate. If you engage in consultative leadership behavior you may gather ideas

Overview of leadership and motivation theory and group dynamics

LEADERSHIP THEORIES

Trait Approach
Acts and looks like a leader
- Intelligence
- Dominance
- Aggressiveness

Behavior Approach
Recurring behavior
- Task oriented
- Sets standards
- Rapport with people

Contingency and Situational Approaches

Fielder: Type of work situation dictates leadership style - Focus on tasks and people

Vroom, Yetten: Normative Leadership Model
Leader makes decisions
- Autocratically
- In consultation
- In groups

Hersey, Blanchard: Situational Leadership: depending on the task leader either tells, sells, participates, or delegates

House, Mitchell: Path-Goal Theory: Leader is directive, supportive, participative or achievement oriented

Bass: Transaction and Transformational Leader: Motivates people to perform tasks or inspires people to go beyond circumstances

THEORIES OF MOTIVATION

Need Theory
* Maslow: Hierarchy of 5 needs
* Alderfer: ERG - 3 levels of need
* Herzberg, Syndermann: Two-Factor Theory - Motivators or Hygiene (dissatisfiers)
* McClelland: Acquired needs of achievement, affiliation, and power

Cognitive Theory
* Adams: Equity Theory, Inequity is a motivator
* Vroom: Expectancy Theory, motivation from the belief appropriate rewards will result

Reinforcement Theory
* Skinner: Operant Conditioning, control behavior by manipulating consequences - ABC
* Bandura: Social Learning Theory, continuous interaction of behavior, environments and personal factors

GROUP DYNAMICS

Formal Groups
* Command: manager supervises work groups
* Task: a production team
* Interest: health and safety
* Committee: standing and ad hoc and by functional areas (finance)

Group Development & Behavior
* Stages: forming, storming, norming, performing, adjourning
* Dysfunctions: Groupthink, also disruptive behavior by individuals such as aggressiveness, special pleading, withdrawing, etc.

Effective Group Management
* Task Activities: initiating, information transfer, summarizing, elaborating
* Maintenance Activities: gatekeeping, following along, harmonizing, reducing tensions

A good leader will draw on all these approaches to effectively manage organizations and people

Figure 8-2 Leading and Managing

from your subordinates individually or in groups, and then make the decision yourself. Or if the situation warrants, you may decide that a group approach to solving the problem works best, in which case you accept and implement the group decision.

Yet another model was developed by Paul Hersey and Ken Blanchard: It is "based on the premise that leaders need to alter their behaviors depending on one major situational factor—the readiness of followers.[18] *Situational leadership theory* focuses on two leader behaviors: *task* and *relationship*. The task behavior refers to how much the leader tells people what, how, when, where, and who is to do something. Relationship behavior describes the communication processes used by the leader: listening and facilitating.[19] This model is based on the assumption that, depending on the task and the employee's readiness, the leader may need to use some combination of telling, selling, participating, or delegating to accomplish a task. For example, telling may be used as the leadership approach if the employee is "unable or also unwilling or too insecure to take responsibility for a given task."[20] A ticket office manager would be wise to use this approach when training a new employee to process a credit card phone order. Given the fact that errors may be costly, this type of leadership is appropriate. On the other hand, this same manager would probably want to use a participating style when establishing the work schedule during a particularly heavy part of the season. Working with employees and gaining their investment in developing a schedule in which the work load is perceived as being equally distributed will probably have a positive effect.

Management researchers Robert J. House and Terence R. Mitchell developed the *Path-Goal Theory* as another major approach to the study of situational leadership. This approach focuses on how leaders affect the "way subordinates perceive work goals and possible paths to reach work and personal goals."[21] The situational behaviors of the leader include *directive*, *supportive*, *participative*, and *achievement-oriented*. The leader needs to assess which combination of their four behaviors will work best depending on the subordinates' current situation and the anticipated end result. The challenge in this leadership model is that the leader must understand that what worked in one situation may not work in another. For example, using a directive approach to explain to an intern the process for putting labels on season brochures when, in fact, they have already done this task before, can only lead to the intern thinking "this person must really think I am dumb." In this case, the directive approach places a barrier for the intern whose goal may be to be recognized as someone employable by the organization, not a lowly intern.

Transactional and Transformational Leadership

Leadership expert Bernard M. Bass distinguished between the *transactional leader*, people who motivate people to perform tasks and achieve stated objectives, and the *transformational leader*, someone who motivates and inspires people to go beyond their normal work behavior.[22] In Bass's model, managers are people who "do things right" over and over, while a leader is someone who innovates, inspires, and changes by getting people to the "do the right things."[23] A good leader should be able to perform both leadership behaviors. The leader's analysis of the situation should help clarify how much of each approach to apply. For example, an opera director communicating her concept for a production of *The Magic Flute* could outline for the design team her ideas in a more directive or transformational leadership approach. She might begin by being very directive and talk about when the show must be completed, where she sees it being set in time and place, and how it should look. Or, she could take a more transformational approach by focusing on larger philosophical issues of the piece and discuss what the music evokes in each of the designers' imaginations. In other words, she could work from a more transformational style by using a participative process to inspire the group to move beyond a standard vision of a work of art.

Applications to the Arts

Management theory tries to be scientific about creating "experiments" and "controls" in an attempt to "test" the theories. In reading the literature, it becomes apparent that no one theory can explain why some people are dynamic, productive leaders and others are not. There is no single test you can take and pass that identifies you as a good leader. As you have seen from the myriad theories we have touched on, a great deal of individual effort must be taken by an arts manager to identify and cultivate leadership skills that are appropriate to the situation and that can inspire people to do better.

In an arts organization, keeping the creative spirit alive is a full-time job for a manager. It is extraordinarily easy to become bogged down in the day-to-day operation of the organization. For example, leadership directed at trying to run an arts organization "just like any other business" could be a formula for disaster. Although it is true that an arts organization must function in a businesslike way, arts managers must address the larger issues of the relationship of their organization to the larger society and culture. For example, authors like Warren Bennis (see "Additional Resources" at the end of this chapter) point out that the trend to two- and three-part leadership—distributed leadership—of organizations only tends to dilute the effectiveness of each leader. Instead of leadership, the result is more bureaucracy.[24] Instead of looking to the future, managers spend their time dealing with the routine of supporting the bureaucracy.

Future Leadership?

As more arts organizations move away from the founder-director leadership structure, the trend seems to be toward adopting the multiple-manager leadership model. The older, intuitive leaders with great charismatic appeal seem to be fading from the scene. Corporate structures and distributed leadership may be the only way that arts organizations can gain the required fundraising credibility in the community, but it seems doubtful that this is a formula for artistic leadership that goes beyond a safe, conventional approach. (See the Case Study in Chapter 6.) There are many examples of upstart arts organizations founded in the 1970s that are now cornerstones in regional arts consortiums. Obviously, artistic leadership need not succumb to conventionality just because it is accepted in the community. However, since so much funding for the operation of arts organizations comes from ticket sales and local fundraising, there is a point at which controversial leadership becomes a detriment to the organization.

Arts managers will eventually find themselves solving critical problems and making big decisions through groups—which is the very nature of the contemporary organization. It might be considered a type of "art by committee." The trend toward the committee-style management of arts organizations may prove irreversible. If this is the

Arts Leadership in the News

A recent wire service story high-lights a leadership situation that came to an unhappy ending. In this case, the leadership behavior of a symphony conductor was seen as problematic by some of the musicians. The article does not contain the perspective of the conductor, which would no doubt have offered a different point of view.

Canada's Symphony Director Resigns

The music director of Canada's leading symphony orchestra resigned after complaints from musicians became public. The Quebec Musicians Guild said Montreal Symphony Orchestra director Charles Dutoit had developed an abusive and arbitrary rehearsal style and had started dismissal proceedings against two musicians for what other players considered to be personal reasons. Dutoit could not be reached Friday for comment. His resignation was announced Wednesday. Dutoit had led the orchestra since 1977. The Montreal Symphony Orchestra won two Grammys under Dutoit's tutelage while producing more than 75 recordings under the Decca/London label, garnering some 40 national and inter-national awards.

SOURCE: *Tallahassee Democrat* (Sunday, April 14, 2002), p. 17A.

case, a leader with great skill as a transformational leader and negotia-tor will be required. Moving boards of directors, staff, and patrons to new frontiers and to new challenges takes consummate skill that is all too often rare.

Motivation and the Arts Work Setting

No discussion of leadership would be complete without examining the area of individual and group motivation and the communication process. To lead effectively, you must understand basic concepts about what motivates individuals to make them want to work and create. At the same time, most of the activity that occurs in an arts organization revolves around groups. As we have seen, organizations are divided into work groups that should match the operational and planning ob-jectives that the organization has established. Creating, maintaining, and keeping these work groups productive is one of the manager's major leadership responsibilities. To work with individuals and groups, you must communicate your expectations and objectives, and the people you work with must effectively communicate their progress and problems to you.

Let us look at the area of motivation first. The people who make up a large portion of an arts organization are usually highly self-motivated. The discipline and motivation required to become a singer, dancer, actor, designer, or musician are not universally found in society. Ideally, professional performers need not be told to learn their lines, practice the music, or rehearse the movements. However, we do not live in an ideal world. People respond in often unpredictable ways to various challenges they face in work and in life. Therefore, even the most gifted and motivated may benefit from carefully structured com-munications that help them achieve their goals.

Theories of Motivation

Management texts usually devote large sections to the subject of moti-vation. Motivation theories and applications arise from research in psy-chology. These applications are directed toward the workplace and making workers more productive. Researchers have identified four broad theory areas: need, cognitive, reinforcement, and social learning. *Need theories* "argue that we behave the way we do because of internal needs we are attempting to fulfill."[25] *Cognitive theories* attempt to isolate the thinking patterns we use in deciding whether or not to behave in a cer-tain way."[26] *Reinforcement theory* "relies heavily on the *law of effect*, which states that behaviors having pleasant or positive consequences are more likely to be repeated and behaviors having unpleasant or negative con-sequences are less likely to be repeated."[27] Lastly, *social learning theory* "argues that learning occurs through the continuous interaction of our behaviors, various personal factors, and environmental forces.[28] (See Figure 8-2.)

Need Theories

Abraham H. Maslow's 1954 book *Motivation and Personality*[29] created a foundation on which business psychologists have built. Maslow pro-posed that human beings have five levels of needs arranged in a hierar-chy of importance. These fell into lower-order needs (physiology, safety, and society) and higher-order needs (esteem and self-actualization).

The system is based on the assumption that only unmet needs act as motivators. The other key principle is that these needs are arranged in a strict hierarchy. The implication is that an individual can move to the next level only after satisfying the needs in the next lower level.

Maslow's theory has been embraced by much of the business world, but that doesn't mean that it can explain all facets of human behavior. Cultural differences, the reality that strict hierarchy doesn't always describe how people behave in a work environment, and the fact that people's needs change over time were not easily accommodated by Maslow's theory.

Researcher Clayton Alderfer proposed an alternative to Maslow's hierarchy known as *ERG Theory*. His approach took the five need levels and compressed them to three: Existence, Relatedness, and Growth. Existence needs cover things such as food, water, shelter, and work-related desires such as pay, benefits, and the actual working conditions. Relatedness needs encompass things such as relationships with friends and families, work groups, and professional associations. Our desires to be accepted by others and to have some control over our lives also fall under this classification. Growth needs cover things such as creativity and innovation. Alderfer argues that we could be concerned with more than one level at a time and that if we are continually frustrated from reaching a level such as growth, we may cease to be concerned about that need. This concept was expressed in what he called the *frustration-regression principle.*[30]

In an arts organization, providing a job in a comfortable work environment (physiological need) that does not endanger health (safety need), has a degree of group stability (social needs), recognizes good performance (esteem need), and provides opportunities for creativity (self-actualization need) should not be an impossible task. However, if employees fear for their lives whenever they go out on the stage because the overhead stage rigging system is dangerous, their safety and physiological needs are not being met.

Two-Factor Theory   Frederick Herzberg and B. Syndermann's 1959 book *The Motivation to Work*[31] became the cornerstone for another need theory of motivation. This study focused on what the authors called the *two-factor theory* of motivation. The *hygiene factors* were items that seemed to make individuals dissatisfied with their jobs. For example, people may become less motivated if they think their pay, benefits, company policies, or the working conditions are not as they perceive they should be. *Motivators* were identified as things such as achievement, responsibility, the work itself, recognition, growth, and personal achievement.

The limited scope of the study on which the two-factor theory is based (only about 200 engineers and accountants) invalidates the theory for some critics. For example, by only studying professionals, Herzberg and Syndermann do not address the fact that hygiene and motivational factors might differ for hourly employees. In other words, the staff members in the marketing department of a performing arts center will probably have different perceptions about motivators than the stagehands who unload the trucks at the loading dock.

However, the limited nature of the study does not invalidate the two-factor concept. Managers may obviously adjust the range of hygiene and motivational factors for particular work groups. For example, most employees like recognition. Prominently displayed "employee-of-the-month" plaques with photographs and accompanying praise for some accomplishment can boost morale. Unfortunately, the two-factor theory doesn't provide much guidance on how the motivational factors can be translated into measurable increases in productivity.

Acquired-Needs Theory   The last needs-related motivational theory is a product of psychologist David C. McClelland's research. His studies focused on three needs: achievement, affiliation, and power.[32] The need for achievement, in McClelland's view, was a "desire to accomplish challenging tasks and achieve a standard of excellence in one's work."[33] Affiliation was seen as "the desire to maintain warm, friendly relationships with others,"[34] and power was "the desire to influence and control one's environment."[35] He further broke power down to *personal power* and *institutional power*.[36] Some individuals enjoy using power over others, and others are able to work in organizational settings to express their power needs. McClelland developed the Thematic Apperception Test as a measurement tool to assess the degree to which individuals were motivated by these varying needs. In this theory one could posit that an individual with a strong need for affiliation would probably not be successful in a high-level leadership position because his or her primary motivation would interfere with the requirements of exercising power and control over people and organizations. A good director, conductor, and choreographer will probably exhibit strong needs to achieve. Their success in different institutional settings will depend to some degree on how strong their needs for power and affiliation are. For example, high-powered and driven guest artists brought into an academic environment may find that they lack the affiliation needs required to successfully relate to students and to carry on positive work relationships with others.

Cognitive Theories

We now turn to two of the cognitive theories of motivation. Essentially, these theories look at how people think about their jobs and their work. The theories attempt to isolate the patterns of thought people use in deciding which behaviors to choose. It is assumed that people find their own sources of motivation and dissatisfaction in the workplace.

Equity Theory   The equity theory of motivation is based on J. Stacy Adams' work in the 1960s.[37] The theory states that *a perceived inequity functions as a motivator*. When employees believe that they are not being treated equitably, they are motivated to try to change the source of the perceived inequity. Employees perceive inequities whenever they feel that they are not rewarded for their work at the same level as someone else who works equally hard. To resolve the equity conflicts, Adams predicts that employees will change how much work they do, try to get their salary increased, rationalize the inequity, or quit.[38]

Equity issues most often arise with highly separated work groups. For example, an arts organization might have union stage employees with a high school education who receive $20 per hour for their labor, and a marketing assistant with a master's degree who receives the equivalent of $8.50 per hour. Based on a forty-hour workweek, the stagehand could gross $41,600 a year while the marketing person might earn $17,680. It will not take long for the research assistant to pick up on these wage differences, thanks to the informal communication system in most organizations. According to Adams' equity theory, the research assistant will probably create some rationalization to minimize the inequity, or she will quit. If she approaches the head of the marketing area for a pay increase and is told that the budget is too tight, she may go back to work, but she will probably temporarily reduce her work output. The inequity will not go away. In fact, the problem may grow as the unhappy employee lets other employees know that they are receiving a lot less money for their hard work than others in the organization. The employees may also say to themselves, "If that's all you think I'm worth, then that's all the work you are going to get from me." The net result is dissatisfied employees with low motivation levels and less work output. Of course, our marketing assistant may also have long-term goals that are based on the assumption that a job that pays $8.50 an hour is not a reflection of her true skill and, in the short-term, she can accommodate the inequity.

This issue of pay equity is a hot topic in the business world. Lobbying groups for the business community are hard at work in Washington, trying to control the growth of the concept of comparable worth. If the marketing assistant is doing work of similar value to the organization as the stagehand, why isn't she paid the same rate? Should the organization pay equally for equal work?

Arts managers would do well to read up on equity theory. They must anticipate these issues and formulate some strategies to help employees. The employee's perspective is important here. For example, when it is time for contract negotiation with union employees, typically nonunion employees will start talking about wage inequities. Managers might explain that the stagehands often do not work year-round, so they do not make as much as imagined. In fact, they may make less on average per year than salaried employees.

Expectancy Theory Another motivation theory often cited in management textbooks is the *expectancy theory*. Simply stated, Victor Vroom's theory postulates that people will be motivated to work if they expect that they will be adequately rewarded for their effort.[39] The expectancy theory has three major components: effort, performance, and outcome.

The first component is *effort-performance expectancy*.[40] The employee may ask how probable it is that he or she can actually perform at the required level. If you are given a task such as updating a 20,000-name mailing list in two days, or building an entire set of stage platforms without any assistance in three days, your expectancy will be zero. On the other hand, your expectancy will probably be higher if you are given six weeks for the mailing list and three weeks for the construction project.

Next we assess the *performance-outcome expectancy*, or the belief that "our successful performance will lead to certain outcomes."[41] If you are told that you will receive an extra vacation day if you finish the mailing list or the construction project early, you must decide whether the value of the reward is worth the extra effort. In this example, since the value of your performance expectancy is so low ("I can't do all that work in that short a time!"), the outcome expectancy of getting a day off is equally low. Outcome is affected by the types of rewards the employee perceives are available. Vroom identifies *extrinsic rewards* as things such as a day off, a bonus or merit pay, awards, and promotions. *Intrinsic rewards* include things such as feelings of achievement, being challenged, or being given the opportunity to grow.[42]

The last component in Vroom's motivation theory is *valence*, or our assessment of the anticipated value of the various outcomes or rewards.[43] The motivational strength of rewards for the work effort is determined by the value we assign to these rewards. If, for example, you have not had a day off in weeks, that promised day may be a strong motivator despite the low expectancy that you can complete the task.

For the arts manager this theory suggests that you need to be aware of the performance-outcome expectancy when you are planning projects and creating tasks to accomplish. For example, suppose you assign four people to the mailing list project and you divide the task into four parts, 5,000 names each. You give an equal pay bonus to all four employees, even though only two of the four actually did the work on time. Have you not sent a mixed signal about your performance-outcome expectancy to the two employees who actually did the work on time? In this case the motivational strength of the pay bonus is weakened for the high-achieving employees by the fact that the underachievers were paid the same.

Probably the most important element of this theory centers on the extrinsic and intrinsic rewards system you establish in your arts organization. The limited budget resources will probably curtail the use of monetary rewards as a motivator. A good source for ideas for nonmonetary rewards may be found in Bob Nelson's book *1001 Ways to Reward Employees*.[44] He offers a comprehensive list of informal and formal awards as well as awards for specific achievement and activity awards.

Does this theory of motivation offer any help to arts managers? Yes. For example, you can influence expectancy by establishing a general attitude in your work group that the work is important and does make a difference. You can also hire and train people in the work group who are willing to accept the attitude you desire. You can influence preferences by developing an ongoing system of listening to employees' needs and guiding them toward results.[45]

Never underestimate the power of perception, and never assume that the people who work for you have the same values and assign the same priority to the work to be done. Your effectiveness in the leadership role is dependent on your ability to motivate the people with whom you work. Understanding what motives them, what they perceive as a reward, and what they value in the workplace is a key element to your success.

Reinforcement Theory

The third area of motivation falls under the broad heading of reinforcement theory. The motivational theories just described approach behavior from the perspective of how people perceive the value of work, how they satisfy needs, or how they try to resolve inequities. Reinforcement theory focuses on the behavior or the output of the person and does not concern itself with what may be behind the behavior. The use of positive and negative reinforcement is the motivating force that managers use in their leadership roles. As a manager you cannot possibly know the psychological issues all of your employees bring to work with them. Your job is not to be their psychologist but their supervisor or leader. Reinforcement theory requires observing behavior and modifying it to support the mission of the organization. Let us take a quick look at this topic. (See Figure 8-2.)

Organizational Behavior Modification *Organizational behavior modification (OBM)* is an approach that uses the principles of B. F. Skinner's research on human behavior.[46] *Operant conditioning*, a key element in the research, assumes that you can control behavior by manipulating its consequences. By using positive and negative reinforcement, you can increase desired behaviors or eliminate undesired behaviors. Another key concept in the system is the *law of contingent reinforcement*, which states that for a reward to have maximum impact, it must be delivered only if the desired behavior is exhibited. Equally important is the *law of immediate reinforcement*, which states that the quicker the delivery of the reward after the desired behavior, the greater the reinforcement value. This theory is often summarized as *ABC* or *antecedent, behavior, consequence*.[47] The antecedent is what precedes the actual behavior, and the consequence is the result of the behavior. For example, a policy about lateness to rehearsals establishes an antecedent, showing up on time would be the desired behavior, and the consequence is starting on time. If a performer is late (the behavior) and there is no consequence (a fine?), reinforcement theory predicts that this person will continue to engage in this behavior. You may modify the behavior if you enforce a consequence that causes the person to change the behavior.

Does behaviorist theory have a place in an arts organization's leadership system? Yes, if carefully applied. Something as subtle as nodding occasionally during a meeting as your assistant makes a presentation about a new marketing plan can have a positive reinforcing effect. As an example of behavior modification through *negative reinforcement*, suppose that you always make a point of saying, "I thought we had a no-smoking rule on stage in this theater" whenever you find the crew head smoking. Then one day you see that the employee isn't smoking, and you walk by without saying anything. You stop nagging the employee when he stops the undesired behavior. Negative reinforcement, by the way, is not necessarily the best way to approach behavior modification. Unfortunately, for most of their lives, people hear only about the behaviors that they are not supposed to engage in. In some organizations, negative reinforcement is the main operating mode. It is often summarized by employees who say, "The only time I get noticed around here is when I do something wrong."

As an approach to organizational leadership, behavior modification has been criticized because it focuses solely on extrinsic reinforcers. The complex reasons behind a particular behavior pattern are of little interest to the leader who relies on behavior modification. Critics argue that self-motivated artists, who are independent and creative, will laugh at attempts to influence their behavior through simplistic, positive-reinforcement techniques. However, praise is a powerful leadership tool, and as a positive reinforcer, most people do not seem upset when it is used sincerely.

An aware arts manager who carefully and thoughtfully uses some components of operant conditioning usually can't go wrong. A director, choreographer, or manager of any type will usually get better results with positive reinforcement than with negative reinforcement. Berating and belittling people usually instills hostility and resentment among employees or volunteers. Managers who believe that the only way to get top performance from their employees or volunteers is through terror tactics are sadly out of touch with reality.

Social Learning Theory   The second and final motivational theory we will discuss is based on integrating cognitive and reinforcement theory. Albert Bandura's *social learning theory* posits that "learning occurs through the continuous interaction of our behaviors, various personal factors, and environmental forces.[48] The learning that in turn affects our behavior includes three cognitive processes: *symbolic processes, vicarious learning,* and *self-control.*[49] Let's look at how this theory may be applied in motivating employees.

The *symbolic processes* include how we use verbal and imagined symbols to process and store experiences in words and images. We also use *self-efficacy* to imagine and project goals and outcomes that we desire.[50] We would be motivated, for example, if we imagine the outcome of our completion of the labeling or platform construction project as leading to more significant or weighty tasks or a promotion.

Social learning theory also includes the concept that "*vicarious learning,* or observational learning is our ability to learn new behaviors and/or assess their probable consequences by observing others."[51] For example, as a new employee, you observe a particular staff member who seems to be respected and rewarded for the way he does his job. You in turn model your behavior along the lines of this person and find reinforcement and rewards for doing so.

Lastly, we engage in forms of *self-control* in the workplace. We control our behavior and provide for our own self-rewards.[52] You may congratulate yourself for completing a project ahead of schedule by going out to dinner or simply giving yourself a break. In other words, social learning theory recognizes self-reinforcement as part of a behavioral response that motivates people.

In an arts organization the social learning theory can be applied as a motivational tool by establishing clear and visible rewards for learning and developing new skills. Encouraging and rewarding employees who acquire new skills or who provide models for interns should have a positive outcome. Establishing and supporting a corporate culture of learning makes a great deal of sense in a workplace that tends to attract highly educated people in the first place.

Theory Integration

Figure 8-2 summarizes the various theories about leadership, motivation, and group dynamics discussed in this chapter. The manager's objective is to be as effective as possible in getting people in the organization to achieve the results that support the organization's goals and objectives. It isn't by chance or through the efforts of one person that an organization reaches and exceeds its goals. The motivational theories are tools to be used by the manager. Within an arts organization, some employee groups are motivated by extrinsic rewards, others by how they perceive their role and status, and still others by the need to achieve some degree of self-actualization. It will take time and experimentation to find the best mix of motivators in any work situation. The investment of time by the leadership of an arts organization in establishing a coherent and effective motivational system will help maintain a positive work environment. The fact that so many organizations, arts and business, operate with motivationally and psychologically dysfunctional cultures speaks directly to the lack of training in working with people by the leadership and managers. It is safe to say that employees, no matter how highly educated or self-motivated, are not maintenance-free entities.

Group Dynamics

A fact of organizational life is that leaders must work effectively with many different groups. Whether the group is formal or informal, when you put several people together, a collective behavior pattern emerges that is usually different from an individual acting singly. Therefore, a leader should understand group dynamics, which is the actual behavioral output exhibited when the various standing groups interact on a daily basis within an organization. Arts organizations are made up of several groups: a cast, corps de ballet, ensemble, crew, board of directors, committees, subcommittees, task force, and so on. The effective leadership of all of these various groups can result in a dynamic, creative organization that has a positive impact on the community. By the same token, ineffective group leadership can result in low-quality events and productions, poor use of resources, high turnover of staff and board members, labor problems, and marginal community support. Let us look at some of the basic terms and concepts of group management and leadership. (See Figure 8-2.)

Group Management Activities and Forms

A *group* is a collection of people who regularly interact with one another in the pursuit of one or more common objectives.[53] A *formal group* is created by the formal authority structure within an organization to transform inputs into product or service outputs.[54] For example, a theater company sets up a formal group (e.g., a cast) by deciding to do a play and present it to the public. A board of directors creates a formal group when it selects a personnel search committee to find a new museum director. Organizations may establish permanent work groups to carry on specific operational activities. For example, the production staff in an opera company or the curatorial staff in a museum may meet regularly as a group to make plans, assign work, and evaluate progress. Temporary groups, such as a personnel search committee, may be established to accomplish a particular task. The group is disbanded after it completes the job.

An *informal group* is "one that emerges in an organization without any designated purpose."[55] These informal groups can satisfy employee needs for socialization, security, and identification.[56] Informal groups can also help people get their jobs done by establishing a network within an organization. For example, a production manager in an arts organization may establish a formal working relationship with the crew heads through regular staff meetings. However, various informal groups may form within the crews that can help or hinder the overall operation, such as a group (usually with an informal leader) centered on the belief that the production manager is incompetent. This informal group may try to influence others in the formal work group about the manager's incompetence. Soon, the production manager finds that things are not getting done or are being done in the way that the informal group decides is best. Direct intervention by the formal leader of the group may be the only way to disrupt the influence of the informal group.

Types of Groups   Various types of groups are formed in organizations, including command, task, interest, and committee groups.[57]

Command groups are established in an organizational chart by defining the working relationship between supervisors and subordinates. In Chapter 6, the Theater Company Organizational Chart

FYI

Running meetings and working with groups will be very much a part of your job as an arts manager. Here are two excellent books to consider for your management library to help you lead meetings and work with groups in the decision-making process.

Meetings: Do's, Don'ts and Donuts: The Complete Handbook for Successful Meetings, by Sharon M. Lippincott (Pittsburgh, Penn.: Lighthouse Point Press, 1994).

The Facilitator's Guide to Participatory Decision-Making, by Sam Kaner with Lenny Lind, Catherine Todi, Sarah Fisk, and Duane Berger (British Columbia, Canada: New Society Publishers, 2001).

(Figure 6-2) depicts the command group relationship between the managing director and the marketing, finance, and fundraising directors.

Task groups are groups of employees who work together to complete a project or job. A major portion of the activity in arts organizations is accomplished by task groups. Figure 6-6 in Chapter 6 depicts that "Show A" is a task group.

Interest groups form when employees unite around a particular issue. The members of this group could be from different work groups who are brought together to resolve a short-term problem. For example, when a symphony orchestra announces that, due to a shortfall in fundraising, all medical benefits for the regular staff will cease, an interest group forms to deal specifically with this issue.

Finally, we have the *committee*, which has been humorously defined as "the only life form with twelve stomachs and no brain."[58] The seasoned manager in an organization might see the operations of a committee falling under Old and Kahn's law: "The efficiency of a committee meeting is inversely proportional to the number of participants and the time spent on deliberations."[59] A more formal definition of a committee is "a group of two or more people created to perform a specific task."[60] Organizations establish standing committees to fulfill ongoing needs (e.g., a finance committee) or ad hoc committees to fulfill specific needs (e.g., the search committee). Numerous books offer suggestions for making committees function effectively in organizations. Such issues as committee composition, size, clarity of purpose, and ability to bring resources to bear on a problem are covered in a variety of texts and business books. The disadvantages of compromised decisions, long deliberation periods, and expense are often cited in the literature. However, committees do tend to proliferate in organizations. Care must be taken to avoid using the committee approach to avoid taking individual responsibility for decisions.

Stages of Group Development   The study of groups shows that when a new group is formed, it typically undergoes five stages: forming, storming, performing, and total adjourning.[61]

In the *forming stage*, the group tries to establish its purpose, define its operational rules, establish the identity of members of the group and what they have to offer, and define how people will interact with each other.

The *storming stage* may be very emotional or relatively calm, depending on the personalities of the group members. For example, an ad hoc committee to examine employee benefits that is made up of staff and hourly workers could experience substantial personal style differences that take some time to work out. It could take several heated discussions to move everyone to a common agenda.

The *norming stage* is characterized by building group cohesiveness, developing consensus, and clarifying roles. It is typically at this stage that the group leader will emerge. Constructive ways of handling disagreement will be found, and group discussions will allow differences to be expressed. Group members will feel more confident about their specific responsibilities and will help keep the group focused on the problems that must be solved.

As a group reaches the *performing stage* it begins to actively address its purpose. If the group leader is able to effectively engage everyone, the entire group should be contributing to the committee's work. Unfortunately, many groups do not reach this stage. More often than not there are a few members of the committee who actually work and a few who are marginal. The group still performs, just not as effectively as it could if everyone were contributing.

In the final stage, *adjourning*, the committee wraps up its work and disbands. The search committee completes its job and no longer needs to meet.

A group such as a cast of a play will go through some variation of this process as it moves from auditions to rehearsals. Other ensemble efforts share similar patterns of development. When a committee is formed by the board of directors, patterns similar to those noted take place. An arts manager must watch vigilantly for committees that become dysfunctional. For example, some committees never achieve norming and performing. The committee output is often slow in coming or is marked by minority reports by differing subgroups that form within the larger committee.

Group Norms and Cohesiveness   *Group norms* is a familiar phrase related to leading and managing groups. Norms are the rules that guide group behavior.[62] The leader of a group must establish behavior norms ("One person talking at a time, please") as well as performance norms ("We must finish deliberations and report to the board by March 1").

At the same time, a leader must develop cohesiveness among the group if it is to be effective. *Cohesiveness*, in this case, refers to the degree of motivation of members to stay in the group. For example, a running crew for a production is a task-specific group that often requires a high degree of cohesiveness. You can use specific circumstances, such as having to do a complex scene change in a limited time, as a way of building cohesiveness among a group. For example, if the performance norm is to complete the scene change in one minute, the group may be challenged to beat that norm and do the shift in 45 seconds. When this new norm is established, the group usually feels some sense of collective accomplishment, which is a way of building cohesiveness.

Successfully managing groups in an arts organization requires careful thought about establishing norms, performance expectations, and building cohesiveness. In arts organizations, group performance extends from the board through the construction shops. Let's look now at some of the problems that can arise with groups.

Dysfunctional Group Activities

One of the well-noted problems with groups that are too cohesive has been termed *groupthink*. In an article in 1971, Irving Janis defined the groupthink phenomenon as "a tendency for highly cohesive groups to lose their critical evaluative abilities."[63] Unless a member of the committee or work group is designated as the devil's advocate, there is the danger that groupthink will establish itself in an organization. The peer pressure to appear to agree is enormous. A group leader should make it a point to have conflicting points of view aired before the group.

Some of the symptoms of groupthink are rationalizing data that contradict the expectation; self-censorship by group members; and creating an illusion of unanimity by stopping the discussion of a topic prematurely. As an example of groupthink, imagine a design-development discussion that includes a director, the designers, and key technical staff. The production manager, who is running the meeting, knows that the

Arts Leadership in the News

John Rockwell's article "Bravos in the Hall, Booing Backstage" offers some insights about the risks involved in leading and managing a group such as a symphony orchestra. Valery Gergiev is credited with being a brilliant and inspiring conductor, especially of Russian music. However, the spotlight can be intense on an international conductor, as the article points out: "As with any career ascent so brilliant, a virulent backlash has become apparent of late. For years, administrators have groused that Mr. Gergiev's superhuman workload has made for sudden cancellations, breathless arrivals at the last minute (or occasionally later), and a generally helter-skelter atmosphere." These and other criticisms aside, Mr. Rockwell goes on to say, "I would argue that many musicians and critics are suspicious of charisma. Like the young Leonard Bernstein . . . Mr. Gergiev seems to annoy people because he operates outside expectations." Rockwell points out a leadership behavior not unknown in the arts—being charismatic and exceeding expectations. At the same time, a conductor needs to be able to exercise a degree of transformational leadership if the concert performance is to be a truly memorable event for the audience. Mr. Gergiev may not be the best at managing his time, but his leadership at the podium seems to be well respected.

SOURCE: John Rockwell, "Bravos in the Hall, Booing Backstage," Part 2, *New York Times* (March 24, 2002), p. 8.

proposed set design is too big and expensive to produce, but the designer and director do not want to hear that. In fact, the director has said on several occasions, "Don't tell me what you can't do, tell me what you can do." The technical director has tried to tell everyone that this design is more than the shop can handle. Every time the technical director tries to bring up the subject of time, money, and personnel constraints, the production manager cuts off the conversation. The schedule dictates that construction start immediately. The group "decision" is really nothing more than a groupthink trap. The technical director knows it can't be done, but goes along with the group decision anyway. The shop proceeds to construct the set as designed. Later, when the show is over budget and behind schedule, the technical director may be asked, "Why didn't you say something before we started building the set?"

Strategies for Making Groups More Effective

There are many predictable common problems that occur when people get together to function as a group. An aware leader must act immediately to stop these dysfunctional activities from disrupting the group. Here are some behaviors you may find disrupting a meeting:[64]

- *Aggressiveness*—One or more members of the group uses an aggressive tone of voice to dominate the discussion. "Well that's a stupid idea. I think we should do this."
- *Blocking*—Committee members who go off on tangents or bring unrelated personal experiences in to the meeting can sidetrack discussion. For example, a season selection committee is trying to pick programming and one member chimes in with, "I remember several years ago when we performed a piece by Philip Glass, people walked out of the concert."
- *Self-confessing*—Sometimes committee members interject their personal non-group feeling into a meeting. In a budget planning discussion a committee member chimes in with, "I am uncomfortable with this investment plan, and it just seems to me we should be rethinking this whole approach."
- *Competing*—Some committee members think they must have the final idea on how something should be done. After a lengthy discussion about a change in the season schedule and as the group starts to approach consensus, a committee member offers, "Yes, well, that's all well and good, but I think my idea is best, and in fact, this current idea lacks merit."
- *Seeking sympathy*—Some committee members feel compelled to share their ideas for purposes that do not advance the agenda. For example, a ticket office manager uses the meeting as a chance to whine about how out of date his computers are. "If the budget committee would only pay attention to my pleas, this equipment is so slow and I just can't do my job with this junk."
- *Special pleading*—Our ticket office manager above not only seeks sympathy, but is also providing an example of someone trying to get a special need or pet project addressed by the committee.
- *Horsing around*—Some members of the committee may find that clowning, joking, or mimicking someone is enjoyable. While a little humor is always useful to move a group along, these types of behaviors are usually disruptive.

- *Seeking recognition*—On occasion you may have a committee member who feels it is necessary to propose extreme ideas or to try to dominate discussion. "I think we should do away with the concerts in the park. It is too hot outside, and I don't like sitting on the ground."
- *Withdrawing*—When a committee member becomes passive, doesn't engage in discussions, daydreams, doodles, or starts whispering to others, he or she is disrupting the meeting by withdrawing or acting preoccupied.

To counteract some of these behavioral problems in a meeting it would be wise to build in some simple behavior patterns as norms from the very beginning. The first set of behavior patterns falls under the heading of *task activities*, and the second group is called *maintenance activities*. Both support a set of healthy group interactions.

Edgar H. Schein, in his book *Organizational Psychology*, lists these *task activities* as:

1. Initiating: Setting agendas, giving ideas, defining problems, and suggesting solutions.
2. Giving and seeking information: Offering information directly related to the problem, asking others for ideas, and seeking facts.
3. Summarizing: Restating the highlights of the discussion can help keep everyone on track.
4. Elaborating: Clarifying ideas by citing relevant examples can help keep the group working effectively.

The *maintenance activities* include the following:

1. Gatekeeping: Allowing various members of the group to talk. Sometimes one person will try to dominate the discussion and direct the group to his or her opinion by monopolizing the discussion.
2. Following: Going along with the group and agreeing to try out an idea.
3. Harmonizing: When appropriate, reconciling differences and promoting compromise can help keep the group going.
4. Reducing tensions: Using humor as an antidote when the situation becomes emotional. This can help shift the energy of the group long enough to put the conflict in perspective.[65]

Application to Working with the Board of Directors Leaders in arts organizations will find people engaging in combinations of these behaviors on a regular basis. Someone in the role of executive director or managing director would do well to actively engage in the strategies suggested by Schein to head off problems in the board and staff working relationship. Keeping board committees and subcommittees productive is hard work.

The dynamic between a board and the staff can also be very fragile. Given the unfortunate tendency of human beings to misunderstand or misinterpret the motives of others, an arts manager and leader must work very closely with the board president to address group dynamics problems when they arise. A smoothly run meeting is part of the "art" of being a leader. Sensing when a group is getting off track and bringing the discussion back to the issue at hand without being heavy-handed about it is a highly prized skill. Realizing that there are very practical methods you may use to keep a group on task and productive will help further the mission and goals of the organization.

Distributed Leadership

For any organization to function effectively as a group, there must be a healthy interchange among its members. Arts organizations, especially performing arts organizations, spend a lot of time engaged in group activities. The management of these various group efforts calls for the recognition of the concept of *distributed leadership*. Simply put, it means that the group members share the leadership responsibility. As a member of a committee, a work group, or a cast, you share a responsibility to keep the group from becoming dysfunctional. Leaders who point out effective strategies and dangerous behaviors have the best chance of bringing distributed leadership to life for the group. As noted earlier, distributed leadership can create another layer of management and can add more bureaucracy in an arts organization. However, if all members of the group adopt the attitude that being a leader means making decisions, the organization does not have to become mired in inaction.

Communication Basics and Effective Leadership

Underlying the entire area of leadership is the assumption that good communication and listening skills are used daily. Success as a leader directly relates to your ability to send, receive, interpret, monitor, and disseminate information. However, because the process of communication is so simple and at the same time so complex and subtle, we often overlook the obvious when we hunt for the source of a problem. The consequences of miscommunication—ranging from the simple "go" on a cue by the stage manager to the complex report by the director of finance to the board—can be devastating: a missed special effects cue may be life-threatening to a performer, and a misunderstood financial report may lead to bankruptcy for the enterprise. Almost all organizations say, "We have a communication problem around here." Whether this is true or not is irrelevant. If the phrase is repeated often enough, the perception that a communication problem exists will be created.

We next examine some of the basic terms and definitions in communications, and then explore some strategies to minimize the problems.

The Communication Process

We use the following definitions as a starting point:

> *Communication* is the creation of meaning through the use of signals and symbols. Furthermore, meaning is defined as the perception that takes place when we formulate the relationship between two statements or images. Lastly, signals and symbols are key components in a message. Signals mean the messages which a communicator feels are beaming from a source, and they suggest very limited but concise meanings. Symbols suggest broader and more complex meanings assigned to the verbal and nonverbal language of the communicators.[66]

Suppose that a museum director walks into work on Monday morning, scowls at everyone, goes into the office, and slams the door. This nonverbal symbolic behavior communicates a wealth of information to the office staff. People in the office speak more quietly and become anxious—"What's wrong?" Or imagine that the director of a play watches a scene and says to the cast in a monotone, "Very good." The message is mixed. The verbal tone communicating a half-hearted endorsement contradicts the meaning of the words: "Very good" might mean, "You did fine, but I really was not impressed."

As you can see from these examples, the communication process carries many nuances that have different meanings to people. Figure 8-3 depicts a simplified overview of the communication process. Let's briefly review what takes place in a typical interchange between two people.

The communication process includes a sender, who encodes and delivers a message through a communication channel, and a receiver, who decodes the message and perceives a meaning. The sender receives some feedback or an acknowledgment that the message has been received. At the same time, the communication channel is directly affected by noise that interferes with the message. Noise, in this case, means anything that disrupts the message or the feedback.

Perception

For the communication process to be effective, both the sender and the receiver should be aware of four key elements that modify the perception of the communication by each party. These four elements are stereotypes, the halo effect, selective perception, and projection.[67]

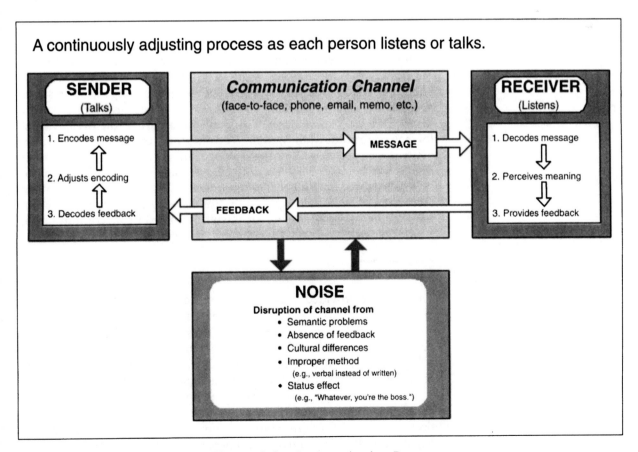

Figure 8-3 Communication Process

Stereotypes   When you speak of "dumb dancers," "techie types," or "musicians!" you are communicating in *stereotypes*. When you refer to the board of directors as the "board," you are implying that they are all of one mind, stereotyping individual members as if they all acted and thought the same way. If you are to become a credible leader, you must drop stereotypical thinking patterns and change your thinking.

Halo Effect   The *halo effect* is the perception of an individual based on one strong attribute. For example, a person who shows up late for a rehearsal or a meeting more than once will suddenly be known throughout the organization for "always being late." The halo effect can also be used positively. For example, a recent report on the long-term funding prospects for the organization may make a staff member a star just in time for the annual board meeting when, in fact, this individual has been coasting all year and does not deserve the praise.

Selective Perception   *Selective perception* refers to noticing only those incidents or behaviors that reinforce what you already strongly believe about a situation or a person. You may choose not to see problems that particular employees are having because it is inconsistent with your perception of them.

Projection   When you project, you assign your personal attributes to someone else. The classic example of *projection* is when you assume that everyone who works for you shares your attitudes and beliefs about their job and the organization.

Formal and Informal Communication

Within an arts organization, formal and informal networks exist to communicate with and among employees. Managers must give constant attention to how well both systems are serving the organization's communication needs. Memos, E-mail, small group meetings, forums, newsletters, and annual meetings make up a part of the organization's formal communication system. The informal communication system exists at every level in the organization. Phone conversations, waiting in line to use the copy machine, coffee breaks, and rehearsal breaks may all be touch points for informal communication. The informal system may seem impossible to manage, but by simply recognizing its existence and monitoring the information (or misinformation) being communicated, a manager can creatively intervene when required.

Conclusion

This chapter provided background on one of the most important areas in operating an arts organization. One question remains, "What makes a good leader?" As you have seen, it takes a great deal of hard work to be an effective leader. Having a vision of where you want to go, and being skilled in such areas as communication, interpersonal relations, observation, and situation analysis are equally important.

In fact, being a leader means playing a role to some degree. Some people are very comfortable performing on a stage, making a presentation in front of a group, arguing a point, or carrying on an intensive negotiation. People you work with perceive your performance as a leader in much the same way that an audience perceives a performer and develops an impression of a character during the course of the show. A complex combination of body language, tone of voice, and ultimately the conviction with which you deliver your lines forms your coworkers' overall perception of and opinion about your leadership. If you are unsure and do not act committed to the idea or project, it will be hard to convince your "audience" that you have the leadership needed to see something through to the end.

Is there a lack of good leadership in many organizations? Sadly, yes. Coping with ineffective leadership is the topic of Muriel Solomon's *Working with Difficult People*.[68] Chapters such as "When Your Boss Is Belligerent," "When Your Boss Is Arrogant," and "When Your Boss Is Exploitative" depict real-world examples of less than effective leadership in the workplace.

Good management and good leadership do exist. Although there are few studies of arts organizations, authors like Tom Peters (*In Search of Excellence*) are reporting on companies that meet their goals and keep their people happy and productive. For arts organizations, with their never-ending struggle against limited resources, it is especially critical for the leadership to recognize and reward the hard work and sacrifices of its employees.

Summary

Leadership is the use of power to influence the behavior of others. Power means getting others to do what you want. Formal leadership is granted to a manager by the organization. Informal leadership arises from special situations. A manager can draw on position power and personal power. Power is limited by acceptance theory and the zone of indifference.

Leadership theories have developed from trait studies that tried to identify leadership qualities by evaluating personal attributes. Behavioral theories are based on the study of a leader's attitudes about tasks and people. Contingency and situational theories work from the concept that leadership approaches must be adjusted based on the particular situation. Transactional leaders work to motivate people to perform tasks and achieve objectives and transformational leaders work to inspire people to exceed their capabilities.

An effective leader must understand the four main motivation theories and how they apply in the workplace. Need theories argue that we behave the way we do because of internal needs we are trying to fulfill. Maslow, Alderfer, the two-factor theory, and McClelland's acquired-needs theory all offer variations on the concept that we seek to meet needs such as recognition, self-esteem, responsibility, and growth, and to become self-actualized. Various factors such as working conditions, pay benefits, and polices may act to reduce motivation. Cognitive theories are based on isolating and studying the thought processes used to select work behavior, the idea being that people find their own sources of motivation in the workplace. Adams' equity theory argues that people use perceived inequities to motivate them to action. Vroom's expectancy theory states that we work most effectively when we believe the effort we put in will produce a desired outcome; if the probability of success is believed to be low, then we are less motivated to attempt the task or project. Reinforcement theory assumes that through operant conditioning and controlling rewards people are motivated to repeat behaviors that are productive to them and the organization. Lastly, social learning theory integrates cognitive and reinforcement theories to create a model in which the continuous interaction of the behaviors of processing words and images, vicarious learning, and self-control motivates a person to action. Real-life situations require that managers recognize that different work groups are motivated by different things. Theory integration is a possible model.

Managers must lead and effectively work with groups. Both formal and informal groups are a part of every organization. Group dynamics include understanding what happens when people are brought together to achieve certain objectives. Norms of behavior and cohesiveness are key elements of group development. Like people, groups can become dysfunctional over time. Groupthink is one symptom of ineffective group management.

An effective leader understands and uses the communication process between people and among groups. Elements of the process include the sender, the receiver, the channel, and the effects of noise on communication.

Key Terms and Concepts

Leadership and power
Formal and informal leadership
Theory X and Theory Y
Position power: reward power, coercive power, legitimate power
Personal power: expert power, reference power
Acceptance theory
Zone of indifference
Approaches to leadership: trait, behavioral, contingency and situational, transactional and transformational
Motivation and theories of motivation
Need theories: hierarchy of needs (Maslow), ERG (Alderfer), two-factor theory (Herzberg and Syndermann), acquired-need (McClelland)
Cognitive theories: equity theory (Adams), expectancy theory (Vroom),
Reinforcement theory: organizational behavior modification (OBM), ABC
Social learning theory
Group dynamics: formal and informal groups; command, task, interest, and committee groups; group development stages; group norms and cohesiveness; groupthink
Distributed leadership
Communication process: stereotypes, halo effect, selective perception, projection

Questions

1. The use of power is a key component in leadership. Discuss examples from your work experience in which power was used effectively or ineffectively.

2. What are some additional examples of acceptance theory and the zone of indifference in the psychological contract people have in an arts organization?

3. Can trait theory be effectively applied in evaluating arts leadership? Explain.

4. A directive or autocratic leadership style is often exhibited in an arts setting. Is it possible to have a strong artistic vision for a project and a participative leadership style? Explain.

5. Cite examples in which situational leadership worked or failed in an arts setting.

6. Analyze a recent motivation problem you encountered in your work or educational setting. What steps would you have taken to motivate the individual or group involved?

7. Can you cite a recent example from your own experience of a dysfunctional group? How would you have solved the problem knowing what you do now about group behavior?

Cooper-Hewitt Shake-up and Layoffs Reverberate
Celestine Bohlen

Case Study

When he first arrived at the Cooper-Hewitt National Design Museum just over a year ago, Paul W. Thompson sent out clear signals that the country's preeminent museum of design—part of the Smithsonian Institution—badly needed a makeover. And that was before the events of Sept. 11 prompted museums all over New York to tighten their belts.

Finally, two weeks ago, Mr. Thompson summoned his staff and announced that he was abolishing four positions, including the registrar and two of four top curatorial jobs at a museum noted for its rich collections of wall coverings, textiles and decorative arts.

But in fact the loss of senior people at the museum on Fifth Avenue and East 91st Street has been much greater than announced. Over recent months, more than a dozen administrators, curators, researchers and part-time consultants have left the Cooper-Hewitt, fleeing an atmosphere described by a former employee as "draining" and by another as "total misery."

"It is very sad because there is an enormous institutional memory that has walked out the door, or is walking out the door," said Linda Dunne, the former deputy director who left in April to become the chief administrative officer at the American Folk Art Museum.

Mr. Thompson, 42, a Briton whose last job was director of the Design Museum in London, insists that the changes are part of a grand plan to wake up a museum that had gone dormant over the last five years or so and bring it into the edgy world of 21st-century design. The plan hinges on the appointment, now pending, of a new chief curator, who will oversee all four curatorial departments, which are responsible for the collections of textiles, drawings and prints, wall coverings and applied arts.

"There is a lot of change, a new beginning, and that is always going to be difficult," he said in an interview in his starkly white office in what was once Andrew Carnegie's Fifth Avenue mansion. "Some people find it very tough, and some are enthusiastic about being part of the new Cooper-Hewitt."

One impetus for the layoffs was payroll cuts ordered by the Smithsonian in Washington as a result of a drop in tourism at its national museums after Sept. 11. The Cooper-Hewitt's attendance figures have remained steady, if small, at a monthly average of 12,000, and the museum did get an emergency $750,000 grant this spring from the Andrew W. Mellon Foundation.

But to the fury of many of its employees, that was not enough to protect three longstanding employees—Cordelia Rose, the registrar who had worked at the museum for more than 20 years and kept track of items in the collection, and two top curators, Marilyn Symmes, an 11-year veteran who managed the drawings and prints collection, and Deborah Shinn, curator of applied arts with 14 years of experience there.

Several current and former employees, speaking on condition of anonymity, faulted Mr. Thompson for not consulting curators about his plans, even as he was publicly promising to spotlight the permanent collection of more than 250,000 objects. "If he is so interested in having the collection shine, then why is he firing curators?" one former curatorial employee asked. "The point is he was reorganizing people's jobs without ever having talked to them."

Mr. Thompson noted that many of the changes simply bring the Cooper-Hewitt in line with standard museum practice, in particular putting a top curator in a senior management position. "There was an anomalous situation at the Cooper-Hewitt," he said. "It was only for weird historical reasons that curators were not curating the shows."

In some ways the uproar at the Cooper-Hewitt has a familiar ring. It is not the first time that a new director, charged with shaking up a venerable arts institution, causes an outcry as soon as people's jobs are put on the line. But some employees strongly dispute the notion that their objections are prompted by a knee-jerk resistance to change.

"I would support any kind of thoughtful cost-cutting measure because I know what is going on in the world," said Jeff McCartney, a former licensing consultant to the Smithsonian, whose contract at the Cooper-Hewitt ended this spring. "But what has happened here is the almost wholesale termination of the curatorial expertise that resides at the museum. Even though it is only a handful of positions, it is significant, because they only have a handful of positions." Of 131 employees, 41 work with the collections, and of these roughly a dozen are curatorial staff, staff members say.

"The whole thing about change is bogus," a former staff member said. "The museum was ready for change. I for one was very excited about new things happening. I hated to go, but I had no confidence that we weren't all going to be mulched."

The elimination of top curatorial positions has sparked anxiety in other parts of the sprawling Smithsonian Institution, whose chief executive, Lawrence Small, has alarmed professional staff with his tilt toward a commercial approach and willingness to accommodate donors.

"With every curatorial position you lose, you lose generations of knowledge and expertise," said Helena Wright, a curator at the Smithsonian's Museum of American History, who noted that concern about the situation at the Cooper-Hewitt was expressed last week at the council of the Smithsonian Congress of Scholars, a curatorial association.

Some staff members in New York have noted that Mr. Thompson's style and vocabulary are an echo of Mr. Small's approach. Museum professionals bristle at words like "line managers" or "middle management" to describe people whose jobs might include overseeing a collection of rare hand-painted wallpaper.

The key question will be how the museum looks in another year or two, when Mr. Thompson's changes have taken effect. "I am positive about the museum's future, about a future that uses the gallery as an arena to draw in the public," said Donald Albrecht, who is an exhibition curator at the Cooper-Hewitt, "but the burden on the new chief curator will be very significant."

Mr. Thompson has said that the new chief curator will be a "world-class scholar who is as comfortable with digital as with Regency," who can merge the museum's strong historical collection with a more contemporary sense of what is "hot."

Mr. Thompson plans to open a permanent gallery on the museum's first floor to show off a permanent collection that, he noted, had been strangely overlooked in recent years. That new gallery—plus the creation of a new gallery for digital art in the basement—are the core of a $3.2 million reconstruction plan to be completed in 2003. Also scheduled for 2003 are a series of new exhibitions, including the new permanent collection gallery to be curated by Mr. Thompson himself and two other shows by guest curators including the fashion designer Hussein Chalayan.

Mr. Thompson noted that his mandate from the museum's board of trustees (recently expanded by 8 new members, to 22), is to make changes at an institution that in his words had not seen change in 15 years. That mandate, he said, may even extend to the name itself.

"That debate has been circling around the institution," Mr. Thompson said. "You have to admit the name is long, and a bit of a tongue twister."

"The name may or may not change, but the thing is that the brand should change," he added. "This institution needs to be revivified, and to use that horrible phrase, we need to leverage the brand."

SOURCE: Celestine Bohlen, "Cooper-Hewitt Shake-up and Layoffs Reverberate," *New York Times* (June 25, 2002). Copyright © 2002 by The New York Times Company. Reprinted with permission.

Questions

1. How would you describe Thompson's leadership style?

2. The article points out dissatisfaction about how much the staff was consulted in the process of making change at the Cooper-Hewitt. If you were in charge of this organization, how would you approach making changes?

3. Identify at least two communication problems that arose in this controversy. What could have been done to address the concerns raised about Mr. Thompson's "style and vocabulary"?

4. How should a board of directors fit into this type of change process?

References

1. John R. Schermerhorn, Jr., *Management for Productivity*, 2nd ed. (New York: John Wiley & Sons, 1986), p. 275.
2. Ibid., p. 276.
3. Ibid., p. 276.
4. Ibid., p. 46.
5. Ibid., p. 279.
6. Ibid., p. 279.
7. Ibid., p. 279.
8. Ibid., p. 279.
9. Ibid., p. 280.
10. Ibid., p. 280.
11. Ibid., p. 280.
12. Chester Barnard, *The Functions of the Executive* (Cambridge, MA: Harvard University Press, 1938), pp. 165–166.
13. Schermerhorn, *Management for Productivity*, pp. 280–281.
14. John R. Kotter, "Acquiring and Using Power," *Harvard Business Review* 55 (July–August 1977), pp. 130–132.
15. Kathryn M. Bartol and David C. Martin, *Management*, 3rd edition (Boston: Irwin McGraw-Hill, 1998), p. 417.
16. Fred E. Fielder, *A Theory of Leadership Effectiveness* (New York: McGraw-Hill, 1967).
17. Victor H. Vroom and Phillip W. Yetton, *Leadership and Decision Making* (Pittsburgh: University of Pittsburgh Press, 1973).
18. Bartol and Martin, *Management*, p. 429.
19. Ibid., p. 429.
20. Ibid., p. 430.
21. Ibid., p. 431.
22. Ibid., p. 434.
23. Ibid., p. 434.
24. Warren Bennis, *Why Leaders Can't Lead* (San Francisco: Jossey Bass, 1989).
25. Bartol and Martin, *Management*, p. 385.
26. Ibid., p. 392.
27. Ibid., p. 400.
28. Ibid., p. 405.
29. Abraham H. Maslow, *Motivation and Personality* (New York: Harper and Row, 1954).
30. Bartol and Martin, *Management*, p. 388.
31. Frederick Herzberg and B. Syndermann, *The Motivation to Work* (New York: John Wiley & Sons, 1959).
32. Bartol and Martin, *Management*, p. 389.
33. Ibid., p. 390.
34. Ibid., p. 390.
35. Ibid., p. 391.

36. Ibid., p. 391.
37. J. Adams Stacy, "Toward an Understanding of Inequity," *Journal of Abnormal Psychology* 67 (1963), pp. 422–436.
38. Schermerhorn, *Management for Productivity*, pp. 338–340.
39. Victor Vroom, *Work and Motivation* (New York: John Wiley & Sons, 1964).
40. Bartol and Martin, *Management*, p. 392.
41. Ibid., p. 393.
42. Ibid., p. 393.
43. Ibid., p. 394.
44. Bob Nelson, *1001 Ways to Reward Employees* (New York: Workman Publishing, 1994).
45. James H. Donnelly, James L. Gibson, and John M. Ivancevich, *Fundamentals of Management*, 7th ed. (Homewood, IL: BPI-Irwin, 1990), pp. 313–316.
46. B. F. Skinner, *Science and Human Behavior* (New York: Macmillan, 1953); B. F. Skinner, *Contingencies of Reinforcement* (New York: Appleton-Century-Crofts, 1969).
47. John N. Marr and Richard T. Roessler, *Supervision and Management* (Fayetteville, Ark.: University of Arkansas Press, 1994), pp. 9–12.
48. Bartol and Martin, *Management*, p. 405.
49. Ibid., p. 405.
50. Ibid., p. 405.
51. Ibid., p. 405.
52. Ibid., p. 406.
53. Schermerhorn, *Management for Productivity*, p. 359.
54. Ibid., p. 359.
55. Ibid., p. 361.
56. Ibid., p. 361.
57. Donnelly, Gibson, and Ivancevich, *Fundamentals of Management*, pp. 346–347.
58. Arthur Bloch, *The Complete Murphy's Law* (Los Angeles: Price-Stern-Sloan, 1990), p. 48.
59. Ibid., p. 71.
60. Arthur G. Bedeian, *Management* (New York: Dryden Press, 1986), p. 508.
61. Bartol and Martin, *Management*, p. 490.
62. Schermerhorn, *Management for Productivity*, pp. 370–371.
63. Ibid., p. 374.
64. J. William Pfeiffer and John E. Jones, eds., *Annual Handbook for Group Facilitators* (San Diego: Pfeiffer and Co., 1976).
65. Edgar H. Schein, *Organizational Psychology*, 2nd ed. (Englewood Cliffs, NJ: Prentice-Hall, 1970), p. 81.
66. John J. Makay and Ronald C. Fetzer, *Business Communication Skills: Principles and Practice*, 2nd ed. (Englewood Cliffs, N.J.: Prentice-Hall, 1984), pp. 5–6.
67. Schermerhorn, *Management for Productivity*, pp. 310–315.
68. Muriel Solomon, *Working with Difficult People* (Englewood Cliffs, NJ: Prentice-Hall, 2002).

Additional Resources

Judith M. Bardwick. *Danger in the Comfort Zone*. New York: American Management Association, 1995.

Robert C. Benfari. *Understanding and Changing Your Management Style.* San Francisco: Jossey-Bass Inc., 1999.

Warren Bennis. *Why Leaders Can't Lead.* San Francisco: Jossey-Bass Inc., 1997.

Kenneth H. Blanchard, Paul Hersey, and Dewey E. Johnson. *Management of Organizational Behavior,* 8th ed. Englewood Cliffs, NJ: Prentice Hall, 2001.

Phillip L. Hunsaker and Anthony J. Alessandra. *The Art of Managing People.* New York: Touchstone Books, Simon and Schuster, Inc., 1986.

James M. Kouzes and Barry Z. Posner, *The Leadership Challenge,* 3rd ed. San Francisco: Jossey-Bass Inc., 2002.

Marilyn Loden. *Feminine Leadership.* New York: New York Times Books, 1985.

Henry Mintzberg. "The Manager's Job: Folklore and Fact." *Harvard Business Review* (July–August 1975).

Emily Kittle Morrison. *Leadership Skills: Developing Volunteers for Organizational Success.* Tucson, AZ: Fisher Books, 1994.

Noel M. Tichy and Mary Anne Devanna. *The Transformational Leader.* New York: John Wiley & Sons, 1986.

Abraham Zaleznik. *The Managerial Mystique: Restoring Leadership in Business.* New York: Harper and Row, 1989.

Organizational Controls and Budgets

Before we move on to the topics of finance, economics, marketing, and fundraising, we need to examine the areas of controls, management information systems, and budgets. We have seen how planning helps set the organization's direction and allocate its resources. We have studied the organizing process to see how best to bring together people and resources. Our discussion of the leadership part of the process focused on directing people in the utilization of resources. We now look at control, the part of the management process that ensures that the right things happen, in the right way, and at the right time.[1] We will also study how organizations need to establish internal communication systems and budgets as part of the overall control system in an organization.

In an arts organization, the word *control* carries connotations that often make people uncomfortable. People generally do not like to think of themselves as being controlled by others. At the same time, however, they are not comfortable in situations that could be described as being "out of control." If an arts manager is to lead an organization successfully, systems of control must be in place and must function effectively. Far too often we hear of the results of a faulty control process in an arts organization, particularly as it pertains to budget. A budget is both a spending plan and a control. When you read an article about a dance company that ran up an unanticipated deficit of $200,000 in one season, you have to ask yourself how this could happen. The assumption is that the budgetary and financial control systems must have broken down. After all, a $200,000 deficit does not just appear in a budget report one day.

Control as a Management Function

We will use the term *control* to mean "a process of monitoring performance and taking action when needed to ensure that the desired results are achieved."[2] The elements that enter into this process and affect how well the system works are uncertainty, complexity, human limitations, and the degree of centralization in the organization.

As noted in Chapter 5, "Planning and Decision Making," uncertainty exists in all planning. Every organization must plan for uncertainty, and the control system must take this into account. One useful way of accommodating uncertainty is to evaluate regularly the progress being made in meeting the defined objectives. This becomes a control point at which you may make adjustments in the activities being performed.

Issues related to complexity are sometimes more elusive. Over time, organizations grow and become more diverse. The controls required to monitor activity in an organization often lag behind growth. For example, if you shift from processing all of your ticket and subscription revenue through your own box office to a new performing arts center, your old control for tracking revenue will probably be inadequate for the new system. At the same time, you are still going to need accurate, up-to-date reports. New processes and procedures will be put in place and the level of complexity will most likely increase.

All control systems must take into account human limitations. Errors will be made. An incorrect amount will be entered in the computer, an order form will be misplaced, a costume or set piece will be constructed incorrectly, or a purchase order or invoice will be lost. The control system must recognize that these things will happen. For example, the accuracy of the cash accounting could be enhanced if two different people counted ticket sales before depositing funds in the bank.

The basic design of your organization may require different control processes because of the degree of centralization or decentralization. If you operate a decentralized organization, authority will normally be delegated to more people in middle- and lower-level management positions. Control systems that ensure accountability will be required. For example, if the scenery construction shop is five miles from the administrative offices, you do not want to make a staff member drive over to the office every time a purchase order is needed. Instead, you will probably delegate the authority to approve purchases up to a designated amount to a staff member at the shop. Then on a weekly basis purchase orders and invoices can be reviewed by a member of the accounting staff.

Elements of the Control Process

There are four elements of the control process: *establishing performance objectives, measuring results, comparing the actual outcome with the objectives*, and *implementing corrective procedures.*[3] Figure 9-1 is a diagram of this process using an example of a missed sales target.

The first area to examine in the control system is the *performance objectives*. What were the expectations about how much, how good, how expensive, or how timely the work being performed was? How many membership or subscription orders do you want to process in a day, in a week, in a month, in a year? How many costumes were supposed to be built in a two-week period? How far along should the painting of the set be after two weeks?

The second step in the control process is to *measure and compare* what was achieved. How much did sales increase? How long did it take to build the scenery or make the costumes? In order for the measurement system to work you must have the mechanisms in place to track the data and compare it to previous years.

The third step requires an *assessment of what caused the difference* between your objective and the actual results. Was there a lack of resources, poorly trained staff, high turnover, or weak management? Were the fabrics ordered on time? Were the fabric patterns made in time? Was the gel ordered soon enough?

The fourth step culminates in taking *action to correct the problem*. Assuming that your control system is providing feedback in a timely manner, you may increase staff, institute new training programs, or replace the manager leading the work group. In the production example, you may need to intervene immediately if a deadline has been missed.

The control system extends into areas that may not be as easily quantified. For example, what is the appropriate output standard for the rehearsal process of a play, opera, dance, or concert, or for the preparation of an exhibition or special event? Assuming that all of these events have a deadline for an "opening night," the person in the leadership role (director, choreographer, and others) must make it clear through the schedule what will be expected during the preparation stage for the event. However, if no one monitors the process, the control system breaks down. For example, if the artistic director is directing a play and spends the first five weeks of a six-week rehearsal period on the first act, who is left in a control position to take corrective action? The stage manager may point out that the play is behind schedule, but if the person in charge of the whole operation does not stick to the schedule as written, there isn't much to be done.

For many arts organizations, there may be no solution to an ineffective or dysfunctional control system. For example, the manager in a position of authority may hold others to the established output standard while personally ignoring it. The net result is an organization in a constant state of panic about getting an event ready for opening.

This is a circumstance where strong board leadership could influence the control systems. For example, the board president and the personnel committee could mandate that a different working relationship between an artistic director and a managing director be established. The board would have to grant the managing director authority to monitor the schedule and take corrective action when required. Under this scheme, the managing director would point out at the appropriate times that the published rehearsal schedule is not being followed. He or she would request adjustments in the schedule be made, and it is hoped, the show gets back on schedule.

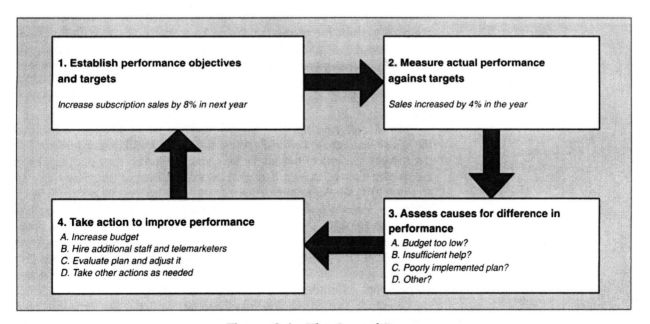

Figure 9-1 The Control Process

In the real world, of course, it is much harder to get people to accept intervention in their projects. It is often the case in arts organizations that people occupy multiple positions of control. The artistic director may be very effective at setting the output standards for a guest director and others in the organization yet react violently to being criticized for falling behind schedule. Ultimately, the ability of the organization to effectively realize its mission depends on how well the control systems function.

Another component of the control process is to set *input standards*. The process involves evaluating the effort that goes into a task. One way to evaluate the work is to look at how well the person used the available resources. For example, a staff member might ask for two extra helpers to complete the subscription orders within the six weeks allotted for the task. If the orders actually take nine weeks to complete and, halfway through the schedule, two more people had to be hired, the supervisor might wonder about the staff member's ability to estimate the resources needed to complete a project.

Once you establish objectives for output, you face the issue of *measuring performance*. In some cases, a manager can define clearly the quantitative measures and communicate them to the employees. For example, a manager expects at least 25 subscription orders to be processed each day. The actual number of orders filled in one day gives the manager a specific piece of information. A lower output would lead to an investigation of the work process, and it may be found that by changing the order in which the work is completed, the average number of orders filled daily exceeds 25.

Since many areas in an arts organization deal with specialized craft work and custom construction techniques, it is much harder to make accurate projections about the performance level of a staff member. Suppose that eight chairs must be built for a dining room scene in a play or opera. The shop supervisor asks the properties master how long it will take to build the chairs, and they agree on five days as the output standard. At the end of that period, only three chairs have been completed. The shop supervisor notes that the expected output level was not met and intercedes to change the input standard. Two extra people are assigned to assist the properties master to complete the remaining chairs.

The previous examples demonstrate how a manager will compare the actual performance with the standards and make adjustments to correct any problems. The success of any of the projects cited in these examples depends on active and involved management of the control process.

In an arts setting, the critical work of all of the creative artists must also undergo a similarly active interaction with management. For performers, the roles they act or sing and the music they play represent a complex mix of talent, ego, and ensemble interaction. How do you set standards, evaluate performance, and take corrective action when a performer does not measure up to expectations? One tool at your disposal is to develop the ability to tactfully communicate that the problem exists, suggest alternatives, and ultimately, if the work does not meet the expected standards, replace the performer. Circumstances may prevent taking such direct action, however. For example, a union contract may prevent or hinder abrupt changes in casting.

In some situations, you may have no recourse. For example, suppose that the scene designer you hired to do the sets for your opening production misses the deadline for submitting the plans. Your shop staff cannot start building the set, and the entire construction process begins behind schedule. Your only recourse would be to refuse to hire that designer for your next show. By the time you confront the problem of failing to meet an output standard, it is too late to take much corrective action.

Management by Exception

One way of creating a control system is to establish a *management by exception* (MBE) process within the organization.[4] Essentially, the MBE process (shown in Figure 9-2) works as a part of the comparative element outlined in the control system. Once you establish clear performance standards and communicate them throughout the organization, you focus your energies on the exceptions to the norm. In this approach, you spend time on the less-than-standard performance. However, you can boost morale and productivity if your management team recognizes and rewards people who meet or exceed the standards.

For MBE to work, internal control must be at a high level in the organization. High standards for performance must be central to

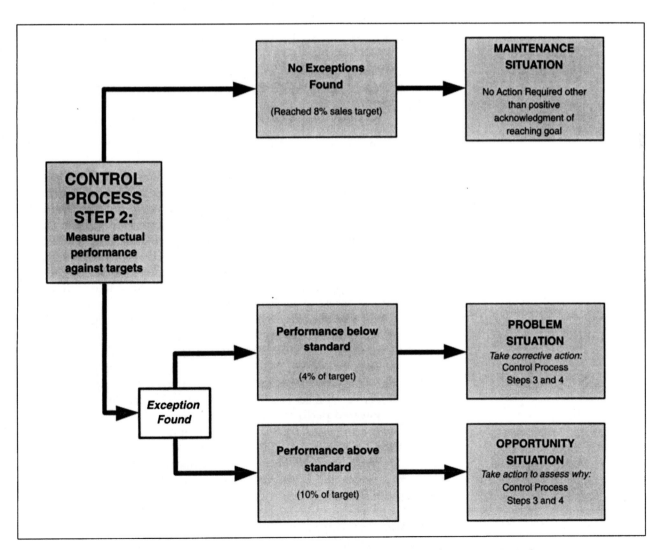

Figure 9-2 Management by Exception—Control System at Work

the culture and value system of the organization. From this strong culture should come attitudes among your staff that support them in setting high goals for their own work output. An arts manager who approaches the staff from McGregor's Theory Y perspective, as noted in Chapters 3 and 8, will assume that staff members want to do a good job. Of course, if clear standards are not communicated to employees, you cannot expect even the most highly self-motivated people to meet your expectations.

Another element in the MBE process is a system of external controls. Every organization needs some ongoing policies and procedures to guide work behavior and to state expected standards clearly. When the organization sets these standards (smoking policy, break periods, vacations, sick days, and so forth), it frees the manager from expending energy on routine expectations. The manager need only be concerned with the exceptions to the external controls.

Management by Objectives

In the late 1960s, the concept of *management by objectives* (MBO) began to be applied widely in the business world. Simply put, MBO is an integrated planning and control system that involves a formal agreement between a supervisor and subordinate concerning:[5]

1. Employee's performance objectives for a specific period of time;
2. Plan(s) to be used to accomplish the objectives;
3. Agreed upon standards for measuring the work accomplished; and
4. Procedures for reviewing results.

When properly applied, MBO is integrated into the overall strategic plan for the organization. For example, if one of an organization's goals is to increase the level of donations from corporations, and the objective is to increase corporate giving by 10 percent this year, then the development staff can specifically develop quantitative objectives for the year. Specific methods would be developed to meet the objectives (phone, mail, and direct contact campaigns), and standards of achievement would be set for each employee (each staff member is given a specific dollar amount as the goal for a specific time period). During regular meetings, the employee and the supervisor would evaluate the employee's progress in meeting the objective.

As you can see, the MBO process can take a lot of time. When you begin to account for all of the time spent drawing up objectives, meeting regularly to review and revise objectives, and documenting the MBO of each employee, you can begin to see one problem with this approach—it is very time-consuming. You may also encounter problems if the objectives you set are too easily reached. In a sense, you begin to establish lowered performance expectations.

In an arts organization, different employee groups have different time frames in their work. As a system, MBO does not make much sense for performers. Elements of MBO may make sense in administrative and production areas in the organization, provided that the time and commitment to support the extensive demands of MBO really exist.

Performance Appraisal Systems

When an arts organization grows big enough to keep a staff employed on a year-round basis, a *performance appraisal system* will have to be established. Performance appraisal simply means formally evaluating work performance and providing feedback so that performance adjustments can be made.[6] Performance appraisal is part of the overall control system for the organization. If the system is working well, it should provide employees with constructive feedback about their strengths, and areas for improvement and concrete suggestions for developing their potential. The objective of the appraisal system should be to benefit the employee and the supervisors and to help the organization reach its goals.

Appraisal Methods   The business of evaluating people should be tailored to the organization's overall design and structure. The people who work in arts organizations would probably be put off by the various numerical rating scales devised by business specialists. For example, there is dubious value in giving an employee a rating of 7 on a scale of 1 to 10. However, a rating of "unsatisfactory" on a behavioral scale in a specific job area ("relates well to others") might draw more attention.

Arts organizations find the *critical incident appraisal* technique to be more acceptable for monitoring job performance. The supervisor keeps a running log of positive and negative work performance over a given time period and reviews it with the employee at specific intervals. Arts organizations also could use a *free-form narrative* to evaluate employees. This essay format usually notes overall job performance, specific accomplishments, strengths, and weaknesses.

Timely Feedback   The annual evaluation is a key part of an organization's overall control system, but it does not provide feedback on work performance on a day-to-day basis. An effective control system must give employees regular feedback about their work output. Some organizations tend not to comment about the good work someone is doing until the annual evaluation. The net result is that the employee spends a year working in a vacuum. Even worse, a serious problem in an employee's work habits will be left unattended for a year.

A good manager realizes that each employee has a different need for feedback. Some people need constant monitoring, and others are happy when left alone. An appraisal system must be flexible enough to accommodate a range of employee needs.

One additional point to consider: even organizations with a seasonal workforce or interns can benefit from developing a system for giving feedback about job performance. From a management point of view, it can be problematic if seasonal employees are not performing up to the expected standards. Tight timetables or production schedules may not allow for replacing someone quickly. Therefore, having a system in place that allows for immediately identifying employees who are having problems meeting the work standards can be a significant asset. Correcting problems and helping an employee or intern get back on track will be less stressful for all parties.

Summary of Control Systems
The control process extends into all areas of an organization. The planning, organizing, and leading functions of management interact with the control systems in a way that should provide an effectively managed organization.

As noted earlier in this chapter, the word *control* is a source of discomfort to many people. How can you have a dynamic, creative arts organization and still have effective control systems? The two elements do not need to cancel each other out.

In an arts organization there will ideally always be an element of creative chaos. The creation of an evening of theater, dance, opera, or music, or the creation and installation of an exhibit, will develop a life of its own. Your plans may be in place, but then circumstances dictate sudden changes in your course of action. The whole process may be very messy. The artistic process could very well be filled with conflict, tension, and passion. It has been my experience that no two events will ever come together in exactly the same way, and therefore one must be careful to not overcontrol a production or a project. Being an adaptable manager is a requirement for survival and effective monitoring in an arts organization.

What, then, is an effective way to establish a control system in the arts environment? One simple approach is to recognize that producing art is not the same as producing large quantities of a product or rendering a service. The unique event being presented needs a set of mutually agreed upon rules, regulations, and guidelines specific to that project. Recognizing that the event may interface with an ongoing organizational structure, the challenge to the arts manager is to find a way to create bridges between the inherent bureaucracy of organizations and the typically more free-form artistic projects.

For example, the financial and accounting aspects of the organization require a great deal of control. Rules, regulations, and laws must be obeyed. You can increase compliance with the rules by making them clear and simple to follow. If, to purchase three yards of fabric for a costume, a staff member must fill out six forms in triplicate and have them signed by two different people, the odds are good that people will do whatever they can to avoid using the "correct" procedures. In this example, the organization would benefit from a different control system for its purchasing procedures.

Management Information Systems

Let us now look at a key supporting system that makes organizational control work effectively. A *management information system* (MIS) is formally defined as "a mechanism designed to collect, combine, compare, analyze, and disseminate data in the form of information."[7] For an arts organization, a well-designed MIS should serve as an almost invisible element. The design, implementation, and maintenance of the MIS may not be particularly exciting to people working in the arts. In fact, many organizations never establish a formal MIS; one evolves. The evolution of the MIS often comes from the crisis management style exercised by many organizations.

For example, it is the middle of summer before you discover subscription sales revenue is down 15 percent and your cash flow has all been spent to meet creditors' bills and last month's payroll. This has never been this big a problem before. What has happened? In this case, maybe the MIS, as it existed, simply did not get financial information about sales and accounts to you quickly enough. The MIS currently in place may also be too informal. Suppose that you are planning a major tour in which your ballet company will perform in five large cities. Two days before the tour starts, you are informed by the management in the first city that only 35 percent of the house has been sold. Whenever you asked about how sales were going, you were told, "Orders are coming in at a steady pace." Because you were led to believe that the sponsor would easily be able to sell 60 percent of capacity, based on previous dance company performances, you signed a contract based on a percentage of the house, not a guaranteed fee. In this example, the lack of hard data delivered in a timely manner could very well mean bankruptcy for the dance company.

Both of these examples demonstrate the importance of a good MIS. A key function of the MIS is to help arts managers make decisions. To make a decision implies you have a choice. To exercise choice means that you select from alternative plans of action. The choices you have may become increasingly limited as time passes. In the case of a subscription campaign, you have to make the sale before the season opens. If you learn early enough that sales are down, you can implement planned courses of action to increase sales. If you learn too late about the shortfall in revenue, all you can do is plan for an operating deficit. Let's examine how to establish an effective MIS so that many of these problems can be avoided.

Data and Information

When we defined an MIS, we used the terms *data* and *information*. Each of these terms implies a great deal about the MIS. With the advent of the personal computer, the term *data* has found its way into our daily vocabulary. Data typically comes to us in the form of facts and figures, which we then process to form a meaningful conclusion. We disseminate this conclusion to others in a regular pattern of information within the organization. For example, the actual number of subscriptions sold and the revenue collected each day at the box office represent raw data that we process and disseminate to those who need the information.

Data and information are not neutral terms. Because people process data, certain biases may affect this part of the process. For example, 25 subscriptions sold in one day may seem like a basic piece of data. You might ask how this number compares to the number sold at this time last year or how the number compares to projections of expected sales to date. If, on the other hand, the box office manager only took in revenue from 18 sales and the other 7 sales were phone calls from people who said they would be renewing, the data collected implies something quite different. The ticket office manager may have been telling you what he thought you wanted to hear because he wanted to present as optimistic a sales picture as possible. The point is that the MIS you have in place is meaningless if individuals manipulate the data to present misleading information.

Management Information Systems in the Arts

In Figure 9-3, a partial MIS is shown for an arts organization. Ideally, the system would be set up so data and information can be shared. A small arts organization does not require a supercomputer to function as its central databank. Although computerization would certainly assist the management decision-making process, simply walking from department to department to gather information is a far less costly alternative. For example, daily reports from the stage manager and technical director to the production manager support the design and production information system. Reports made in weekly staff meetings by the production manager to the managing director complete the cycle of data gathering and distribution.

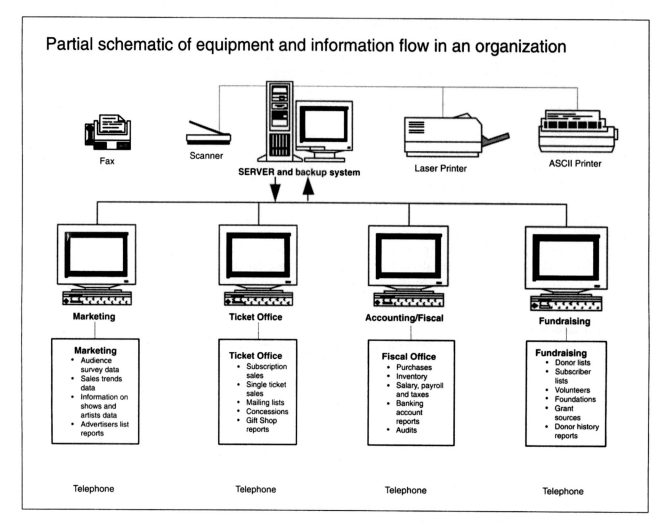

Figure 9-3   Management Information System (MIS)

Most arts organizations start with a small staff of two or three people. The MIS exists as informal communication among people who are often part of a well-established social unit. The group may have morning meetings to review the day's activities, and this meeting becomes the core of the MIS. One person may deal with accounting, finances, and logistics, while someone else covers marketing and fundraising. A personnel system isn't even needed. As the organization grows, more staff members are added, and specialization and departmentalization occur.

Organizational design has a direct impact on the MIS. For example, the MIS of a regional theater company with three theaters in different locations in the city must take into account the potential problems of decentralization. How will these remote locations operate in relation to the accounting department? How will accounting know about purchases unless the MIS includes the accounting department in the ordering stage? If the information system is required to keep track of and control funds expended, it cannot record purchases based on invoices that may come 15 to 30 days after an item has been purchased.

Computers and the Management Information System

Computers and management information systems seem to have been made for each other. The computer's ability to store large amounts of data and distribute it through networks within an organization has had a major impact on the business world. The ability to gather, store, and manipulate data is now very cost-effective. The smallest arts organization usually has at least one computer to do the bookkeeping or to manage a mailing list. In fact, many arts organizations now designate an MIS position in the organization structure (e.g., "MIS Director" in Figure 6-3). Whatever the scale of operation, careful planning is required if the maximum benefit of computerization is to be realized. The cost of purchasing computer hardware has dropped significantly, which has been of great benefit to resource-starved arts organizations. However, the cost to upgrade software and train staff to make the best use of the software can be problematic for arts groups with minimal budget support.

An Effective Management Information System

The purpose of any MIS is to facilitate the accomplishment of the organization's objectives through improved problem solving and decision making. In shaping and revising an MIS, three factors must be taken into account: There are uncontrollable, partially controllable, and fully controllable factors that determine how effective the MIS will be.[8]

Uncontrollable Factors   Some factors, such as organizational structure and the organization's relationship to its external environments, are beyond the control of the MIS. For example, in a highly decentralized organization in which subgroups have a great deal of autonomy, it may prove difficult to implement an MIS effectively. A regional theater, opera, dance company, or museum may have administrative offices in one location, rehearse in two or three different spaces, build sets and props in yet another locale, and perform in two different venues during the year. A museum may have multiple locations in a community or specialized local exhibitions. This structure would make it more challenging to set up an MIS linked by computers. Yet the flow of information would be possible by using a well-designed website and various data transmission formats, such as facsimile machines and modems hooked up to remote computers that report back to the administrative offices. A computer that functions as a server in the central office may be installed to help manage the data flow and act as a place to share files. However, the resources needed to pay for all of this may limit the overall system.

An unstable internal or external business environment also has an effect on the MIS. For example, suppose that you are trying to track audience response by collecting data from your mailings. Between the first and second mailings, a fiscal crisis forces the organization to drop two shows from the season. How will you collect meaningful data about the effectiveness of a second mailing if the season package keeps changing?

Many small arts organizations simply do not have the financial resources or expertise to install computer networks. The uncontrollable factor in this case may be that there are five personal computers in the organization, all use different software, and all are isolated from each other. The fundraising staff member uses one type of software to track the donors, and the box office uses a different software to collect sales and subscription information. Data isn't shared and information transfer is limited.

Partially Controllable Factors   It is possible to gain some short-range control over a poorly structured MIS by bringing available resources to bear on the problem. In the previous example, for instance, a managing director might be able to intercede and make sure that the different computer systems use common software. Data files could then be copied from one machine to another, and information could be shared over what is called a *shoe leather network*. For this to succeed, people in the organization must understand the importance of creating a data gathering and information dissemination system.

Fully Controllable Factors   The MIS that has fully controllable factors is supported and encouraged by the organization and its management. In this ideal world, a staff member would be designated to oversee the data and information system. This would be a senior staff position with support staff to assist with system maintenance. The MIS would be fully integrated into the overall organizational operation.

Integrated computer systems and ongoing operating procedures would support regular data gathering and storage. For example, an effective MIS would allow a marketing staff member to track subscription sales by type of purchaser over the previous five years by accessing a database of subscriber files. When a staff member in the press office needs to look up information about a singer who was in an opera produced by the company three years ago, the information would be available in a database of artist biographies.

Common Mistakes

Care must be taken to avoid some common mistakes in establishing an MIS. As noted earlier, many arts organizations evolve and grow without paying much attention to the MIS. Much time is often wasted hunting down information that should be readily available. However, trying to force an MIS on an organization that is not yet ready for it can damage the credibility of the system. Even when the MIS is accepted, there are still pitfalls to avoid. Here are four problems with bringing a management information system into operation.[9]

1. More information is not always better. The issue here is quality, not quantity. Data that is translated into too much information may turn out to be more of a hindrance than a help. It does not take a great deal of effort to overwhelm people with too much information.
2. Do not assume that people need all the information they want. When designing an MIS for an organization, it is important to review with the various staff members exactly what information they need to be more productive. People tend to request more information than they will possibly have time to process and synthesize.
3. Despite receiving more information, decision making might not improve. Information does not translate into more effective management. In some cases, too much information may result in decision paralysis for some managers.
4. Don't assume that computers can solve all of your information management problems. Arts organizations, which are often resource poor, have benefited greatly from the continuing decrease in cost and increase in power of computer systems. The greatest benefits come when a well-designed soft-

ware system is carefully integrated with a clear vision of the organization's information management needs. However, organizations tend to forget that time is needed to train people to use a computer-based MIS effectively. A poorly designed and managed MIS will probably be abandoned by the users, and everyone will return to the old procedures.

Management Information System Summary

If you ask a staff member in an arts organization how well the MIS is working you might get a puzzled look. If, on the other hand, you ask him or her whether the monthly account statements that detail the expenses of the department are informative, the staff person will probably say yes. In this case, the MIS appears to be working.

The way information and data flow in an organization can be critical to its long-term strength. For example, Figure 9-4 depicts a typical decision-support system that most arts groups have in place. Whether they refer to it as the MIS or not, the way information is distributed and then analyzed is instrumental in helping the board and the staff plan for the future.

The effectiveness of an MIS in an arts organization often boils down to integrating the existing systems shown in Figure 9-4 that produce data and information. The accounting reports of expenses, bills, and payroll, the box office reports of sales, and the fundraising reports of donor amounts may simply need to be pulled together in an overview for the staff and board. Probably the most effective way to quickly pull together an MIS is to ask some very basic questions about what information the organization and the staff need on a daily, weekly, monthly, quarterly, and annual basis. A chart that lists the data, reports, and so on, needed for each time frame can become the foundation for a very simple and effective MIS.

The Future

Arts organizations have only begun to tap into the potential of computers as an organizational support and MIS tool. The current application of computers in arts organizations has focused on automating manual procedures. This has resulted in productivity gains in isolated parts of the organization. It may now take minutes to gather the information that used to require days. As computer networks become more common and computer processing speed increases, the arts manager of the future will need to be creative in extending the effectiveness of the automated MIS beyond record keeping and data management. The new technology is creating systems that will allow the multimedia use of computers. For example, designers, directors, and data managers will be able to update designs, visualize a staging, or manipulate data many times faster than ever imagined. Many arts organizations are using their website to post information for external as well as internal use.

Budgets and the Control System

In this final section on control systems we look at the important area of budgeting. Budget control and management can very quickly become the major focus of an arts manager's job. Being able to project revenue accurately and to monitor and control expenses is an extremely valuable set of skills to possess. The very survival of an arts organization often

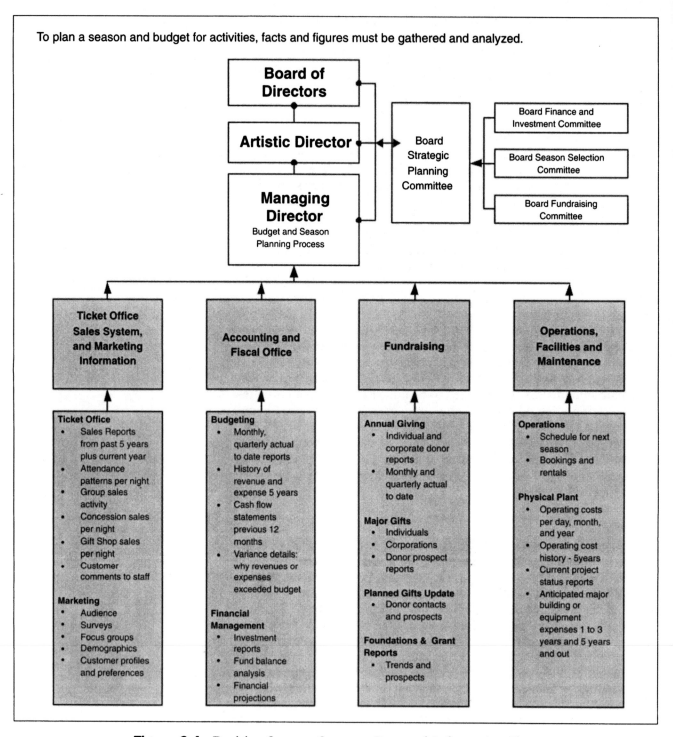

To plan a season and budget for activities, facts and figures must be gathered and analyzed.

Board of Directors

Artistic Director

Managing Director
Budget and Season Planning Process

Board Strategic Planning Committee

Board Finance and Investment Committee

Board Season Selection Committee

Board Fundraising Committee

Ticket Office Sales System, and Marketing Information

Accounting and Fiscal Office

Fundraising

Operations, Facilities and Maintenance

Ticket Office
- Sales Reports from past 5 years plus current year
- Attendance patterns per night
- Group sales activity
- Concession sales per night
- Gift Shop sales per night
- Customer comments to staff

Marketing
- Audience
- Surveys
- Focus groups
- Demographics
- Customer profiles and preferences

Budgeting
- Monthly, quarterly actual to date reports
- History of revenue and expense 5 years
- Cash flow statements previous 12 months
- Variance details: why revenues or expenses exceeded budget

Financial Management
- Investment reports
- Fund balance analysis
- Financial projections

Annual Giving
- Individual and corporate donor reports
- Monthly and quarterly actual to date

Major Gifts
- Individuals
- Corporations
- Donor prospect reports

Planned Gifts Update
- Donor contacts and prospects

Foundations & Grant Reports
- Trends and prospects

Operations
- Schedule for next season
- Bookings and rentals

Physical Plant
- Operating costs per day, month, and year
- Operating cost history - 5years
- Current project status reports
- Anticipated major building or equipment expenses 1 to 3 years and 5 years and out

Figure 9-4   Decision Support System—Data and Information Flow

depends on being able to keep current with income and expenses. This is especially important for arts organizations with limited cash reserves. As a control center, budgeting is a key element in the overall MIS of the organization.

What exactly is a budget? One common definition of a *budget* is "a quantitative and financial expression of a plan."[10] A budget therefore represents an allocation of resources in support of the activities of the organization. If the control process is to be effective, the person supervising the use of the funds must be held responsible for the budget. Depending on the organization's culture, the budget development and implementation process may range from highly structured and formal to informal and casual. Formal budgeting implies a proposal and review process before budget changes are approved. Depending on the structure of the organization, proposing and making changes in the budget could involve very precise procedures. See Figure 9-5 for an overview of a budget development process.

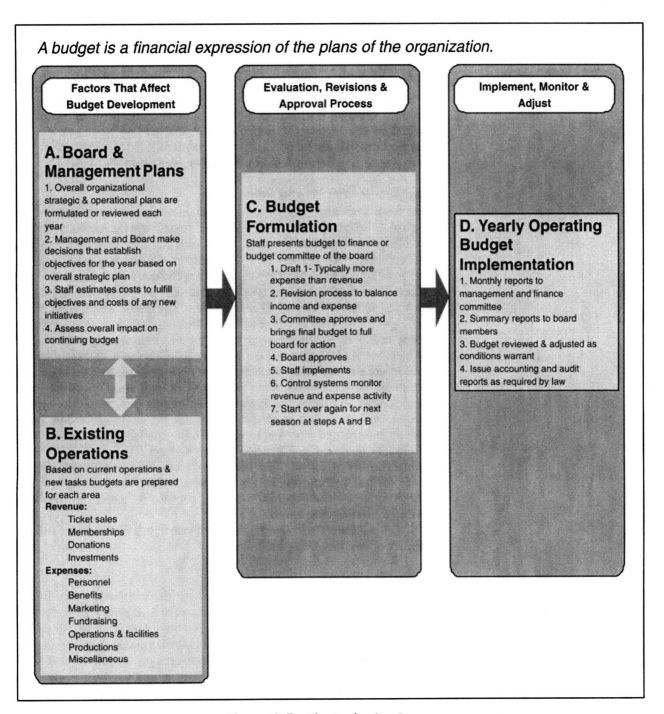

Figure 9-5 The Budgeting Process

Budgetary Centers

Before an arts organization begins the process of trying to fulfill the mission it has set for itself, a budget must be prepared. Even the smallest organization will need to look at two key centers: revenue and expenses. The *revenue centers* include income from the sale of tickets or memberships, donations, grants, concessions, program advertising, rentals, and merchandise. *Expense centers* generally follow the organizational structure that has been established. These two components form the overall operating budget of the organization.

Budgets as Preliminary Controls

A budget is a preliminary control because it establishes the resources allocated to achieve the objectives outlined in the operational plans for the organization. An opera company that allocates one-third of its production budget to one show of a five-show season is making a statement of artistic priority. The monthly budget reports should give the production manager a clear sense of whether the resources allocated for each show are being used as projected. A budget functions as a preliminary control when the production manager tells the designers that they have a specific amount for sets, costumes, and so forth.

Budgets as Top Secret Documents

One would assume that if the budget is such a central part of the control and operational systems of arts organizations, having a copy of the budget available to the staff would be a fairly common occurrence. Sadly, this is often not the case. The culture of many organizations creates barriers for staff attempting to gather budget information. It is not uncommon in arts organizations to find that very few people actually have access to current budget information. The result is that most of the staff operate without any true sense of the budgetary impact of decisions being made or plans being contemplated. The secrecy with which budgets are treated more often than not inhibits the exchange of information about the financial status of the organization. The attitude contained in the expression that "the Board doesn't need to know about that" is often at the root of many of the financial problems arts organizations encounter. It is more often than not the case that budget information is kept and not shared. By the time the budget information is widely distributed it is often too late to address the financial problems facing the organization. The more open the information exchange is about the budgets and the current financial state of the organization, the better equipped the organization is to respond as a team to whatever financial crisis it may be facing.

Let us now review some of the basic types of budgets and the process of creating budgets.

Types of Budgets

In a *fixed budget*, allocations are based on the estimated costs from a fixed base of resources. For example, the salary budget is set for the year, and resources are allocated to cover that expense. Typically the fixed budget becomes the base budget for the work area and is increased or decreased on an incremental basis according to activities and plans proposed each year. For example, some organizations work from incremental increases approved by the board based on the overall consumer price inflation rate. A budget may therefore be increased a fixed amount of 3 percent, assuming that was the inflation rate.

A *flexible budget* assumes that activity levels will influence resource use. The organization may have a fixed overall budget, but will have a range of revenue or expense projections based on the level of activity. For example, a museum's payroll budget may respond to increased traffic flows due to programming. If the museum has a big exhibit that brings in a larger than average number of paid admissions (increased revenue), it may also have to hire two additional part-time guards to control the crowds (increased expense).

A *zero-based budget* is a planning and objective-setting tool used by some arts organizations. At the end of a fiscal cycle all budget lines are zeroed out. Revenues and expenses must be projected and justified in relation to the plans and objectives for the whole organization for the coming year. No budget line amount carries over from the previous year. Compared to the fixed budget with its yearly incremental increases, the zero-based budget can be an effective tool to help keep an organization from creating budgets filled with underutilized line items.

An *operating budget*, as already noted, is normally a yearly budget created to carry out the organization's operational plans. This budget is typically structured with a revenue or income section, an expenses section, and an indication of the running balance or deficit in the overall budget.

A *project budget* (sometimes called an *opportunity budget*) is typically associated with an event that has a start and end time and isn't repeated on an annual basis. A fundraising event, a gala, a benefit concert, or a special production may have a budget specifically set aside for this event. Both revenue and expenses may be kept track of separately from the regular operating budgets. Since arts organizations often do special projects, it can be easier to identify and account for the revenue and expense activity if the budget is kept separate from the normal day-to-day operating budget.

A *capital budget* is typically used for a large-scale or one-time equipment or facility expense. Adding a new wing on a building, replacing the seats in the theater, or buying new equipment that will most likely have a useful life of more than a year are often identified as capital expenses. Organizations usually set a dollar amount for capital expenses and classify items below that amount as regular operating expenses. Setting a threshold such as purchases of $5,000 or above may be appropriate. The amount used will vary from organization to organization.

The Budgetary Process
As depicted in Figure 9-5, the budgeting process usually begins with a projection of the organization's various sources of revenue. In arts organizations, revenue comes from a variety of sources. The organization's MIS should be able to provide detailed reports of all revenue from the previous year or years. The evaluation of the previous revenue distributions and the comparison with the budget projections for the coming year are the next step. Care must be taken when projecting revenue. A few too many optimistic revenue projections could lead to a midseason budget crisis.

The same type of activity takes place in the organization's various expense centers. Comparing the current year's expense patterns and evaluating the project and programming plans for the next year must be done in the context of the overall revenue for the organization.

FYI—Budgeting Information Resources

Two excellent resources on budgeting formation and process are published under the Jossey-Bass Nonprofit and Public Management Series:

The Budget-Building Book for Nonprofits, by Murray Dropkin and Bill LaTouche (San Francisco: Jossey-Bass, 1998).

The Cash Flow Management Book for Nonprofits, by Murray Dropkin and Allyson Hayden (San Francisco: Jossey-Bass, 2001).

The next stage in the process compares and adjusts budgets based on expected revenue. If, after subtracting revenue, expenses still exceed the available resources, a series of revisions are made in the expense budgets.

Arts organizations sometimes find themselves adjusting revenue projections to match expenses. This is a dangerous method of budgeting that usually leads to chronic financial trouble for the organization. For example, unrealistic projections of fundraising or subscription sales revenue may result in a balanced budget to present to the finance committee of the board, but such budget practices are nothing short of fraud.

Budget Reality

A manager in an organization soon discovers that the control process in budgeting extends into anticipating behavior patterns by staff members. Staff members can become very territorial about budgets. Some people overestimate needs, while others try to make the budget allocation process a competition for resources within the organization. (One tool for controlling this problem is to work with zero-based budgets.) Very few staff members will loudly proclaim, "I don't need this much. Here, take back some of my budget."

Budget Controls

Trying to control a budget can be a full-time activity. Theoretically, the organizational MIS will provide the manager with the required information about revenue and expenses. For budget control to be effective, the manager must have this information as quickly as possible each month. Without computers, this work becomes more time-consuming, but it is not impossible. Simple year-to-date percentage expectations for revenue and expenses can give a manager some element of control over a budget. For example, at the end of a specific period of time, a specific percentage of the budget should have been expended. The manager's efforts can then be focused on variances from the expected distributions.

Another key element in the budget control process involves the authorization procedures for expending funds. A system of review and approval must exist if the organization is to control its budget effectively. The "In the News" excerpt pertaining to students embezzling funds provides a good example of why budget approvals are an important control in an arts organization.

Finally, the manager must recognize and develop strategies for dealing with the political nature of budgets. Organizational politics play a role in the budget control process. Staff members try to obtain as many resources as possible for their work areas. The information that a manager receives may have been filtered by department heads to distort the true budgetary condition of a subunit within the organization.

Budgets in Detail

Budgets usually cover what is commonly called a *fiscal year* (FY), which can be any designated 12-month period of expense and revenue activity. Most financial planners suggest that organizations set their fiscal year around the programmatic profile of the organization. The IRS tax year, for example, is January 1 to December 31. However, a performing arts group with an eight-month season of October to May would prob-

In the News

An article in the *New York Times* (February 7, 2002) points up why financial checks and balances are a critical part of any control system in an organization. Two students were accused of embezzling $100,000 from the Hasty Pudding Theatrical club at Harvard University. The two were accused of transferring funds from the club's credit cards to their personal bank accounts. The funds were allegedly used to support a drug habit of one of the students and for stereo equipment and vacations. The two students were the coproducers of the Hasty Pudding Theatricals the year before. The financial discrepancy was found by another student producer for the event. The group's bank account balance was $40,000 to $50,000 less than the financial reports indicated.

SOURCE: Pam Belluck, "Two Harvard Students Accused of Embezzling from Theater Club," *New York Times* (February 7, 2002), p. A-14.

ably find that a fiscal year of July 1 to June 30 better fits their programming and expense patterns.

The summary budget usually works well for smaller operations with a limited number of account lines. Figure 9-6 shows part of a proposed budget for a small theater group. This budget is simplified for the purposes of this presentation format. There might be many more actual expense lines than are shown. In addition, this budget does not show benefits costs (health insurance, retirement, etc.).

In a typical fiscal year, the income and expense lines form the most active part of the budget. The budget does not reveal whether the organization is financially healthy. It simply tells what is expected in revenue and what is planned in expenses. In this example the theater company has a current year budget that is designed to produce a $40,500 surplus of income over expenses. The budget planning for next year anticipates an even larger surplus, $75,000. As you review this budget you will see that certain planning expectations are funded. For example, the company plans to increase its marketing expenses by 20.3 percent, slightly more than the 18.7 percent expected rise in subscription sales. This would indicate some major effort will be undertaken to increase the number of subscribers.

The budget shown in Figure 9-7 goes into more depth. Account numbers are assigned to the individual line items in the budget. This is a typical component of a budget control system. The account numbering system helps identify the type of transaction that took place, and the system can be further broken down into account subcodes to provide as much detail as possible. For example, under the marketing budget (3,000), there is a line item for a season program (3,007) and for telemarketing (3,008 and 3,009).

Figure 9-7 also shows in each line the expenses incurred to date and the percentage of the budget expended. This information is very important to the person responsible for issuing budget reports. For example, the marketing area has used 94.8 percent of its budget to date (see Subtotal Marketing Expenses to Date). The information in the revenue lines shows that the theater company has completed 11 months of the season and is at 97.3 percent of its revenue budget (see Total Ticket Sales). Thus, the marketing department has kept its budget on track in relationship to the season. However, a closer look shows that certain expense lines exceeded budget. For example, general advertising (3,003), printing (3,006), and photography have all gone over budget. In these examples the amount of the overage is shown as a positive balance. In line 3,005 (Broadcast Advertising), for example, the underage is shown as $2,000 in the Balance column. The marketing director would need to assess why and determine whether adjustments in next year's budget are called for in those lines.

Another way to organize a budget is along project or department lines. A project budget distributes revenue and expense centers across the organization. Figure 9-8 shows one way the theater company could express its budget by using this approach. In this example, the account titles are distributed across five major operational areas: Regular Season, Touring, Educational Outreach, Building Fund, and Special Events. This budget format gives much more information about how the organization plans to distribute its income and expenses. For example, it is possible to see that the educational outreach activities are generating more expense than revenue. The variance section of the report at the bottom of the page shows a deficit of $120,700 in the outreach program. In

Summary Budget—Theater Company

INCOME	Current Year Budget	Proposed Budget Next Fiscal Year	$ Change	% Change
Subscription Ticket Sales	817,000	970,000	153,000	18.7%
Single Ticket Sales	602,000	600,000	(2,000)	-0.3%
Group Sales	56,000	60,000	4,000	7.1%
SUBTOTAL Sales	**1,475,000**	**1,630,000**	**155,000**	**10.5%**
Advertising	77,000	85,000	8,000	10.4%
Concessions	56,000	65,000	9,000	16.1%
Gift Shop Income	15,000	14,000	(1,000)	-6.7%
Interest	16,000	23,000	7,000	43.8%
Costume & Scenery Rentals	3,500	2,500	(1,000)	-28.6%
Space/Equipment Rentals	7,000	5,000	(2,000)	-28.6%
Education	5,200	8,000	2,800	53.8%
Miscellaneous	6,500	5,000	(1,500)	-23.1%
Surcharges on Ticket Sales	17,000	18,000	1,000	5.9%
SUBTOTAL Other Income	**203,200**	**225,500**	**22,300**	**11.0%**
TOTAL EARNED INCOME	**1,678,200**	**1,855,500**	**177,300**	**10.6%**
DONATED INCOME	Current Budget	Proposed	$ Change	% Change
Individuals	250,000	300,000	50,000	20.0%
Corporations	100,000	125,000	25,000	25.0%
Foundations	100,000	125,000	25,000	25.0%
Co-producers	75,000	100,000	25,000	33.3%
Special Events	205,000	250,000	45,000	22.0%
Matching Contributions	250,000	300,000	50,000	20.0%
TOTAL DONATED INCOME	**980,000**	**1,200,000**	**220,000**	**22.4%**
GOVERNMENT FUNDING	Current Budget	Proposed	$ Change	% Change
State Grants	48,000	45,000	(3,000)	-6.3%
City/County Grants	94,000	100,000	6,000	6.4%
Federal Grants	0	0	0	
TOTAL GOVT FUNDING	**142,000**	**145,000**	**3,000**	**2.1%**
TOTAL INCOME	**2,800,200**	**3,200,500**	**400,300**	**14.3%**
EXPENSES	Current Budget	Proposed	$ Change	% Change
Artistic Salaries/Fees/Expenses	872,045	1,060,000	187,955	21.6%
Technical Salaries/Fees/Expenses	615,907	665,000	49,093	8.0%
Production Cost	139,669	150,000	10,331	7.4%
Administrative Salaries/Fees/Expenses	152,409	160,000	7,591	5.0%
Marketing Salaries and Expenses	542,522	652,500	109,978	20.3%
Development Salaries and Expenses	162,942	192,500	29,558	18.1%
Special Events & Receptions	128,000	88,000	(40,000)	-31.3%
Concessions	35,858	40,000	4,142	11.6%
Gift Shop Expenses	6,435	6,500	65	1.0%
Occupancy (Utilities, phones, etc.)	70,352	75,000	4,648	6.6%
Contingency	33,561	36,000	2,439	7.3%
TOTAL EXPENSES	**2,759,700**	**3,125,500**	**365,800**	**13.3%**
VARIANCE - Surplus OR (Deficit)	**40,500**	**75,000**	**34,500**	

Figure 9-6 Summary Budget—Theater Company

Detailed Budget—Theater Company

SAMPLE INCOME ACCOUNT LINES   Assumes 11 months into FY

Acct Num	Account Title	Budget	To Date	Balance	Percent
300	Subscription Sales	817,000	775,000	(42,000)	94.9%
321	Single Tickets - Show 1	85,000	84,000	(1,000)	98.8%
322	Single Tickets - Show 2	85,000	82,500	(2,500)	97.1%
323	Single Tickets - Show 3	148,000	152,000	4,000	102.7%
324	Single Tickets - Show 4	85,000	79,000	(6,000)	92.9%
325	Single Tickets - Show 5	85,000	87,000	2,000	102.4%
326	Single Tickets - Show 6	114,000	116,000	2,000	101.8%
	SUBTOTAL Single Tickets	602,000	600,500	(1,500)	99.8%
421	Group Sales - Show 1	8,000	7,700	(300)	96.3%
422	Group Sales - Show 2	7,200	6,800	(400)	94.4%
423	Group Sales - Show 3	22,000	24,000	2,000	109.1%
424	Group Sales - Show 4	5,800	6,000	200	103.4%
425	Group Sales - Show 5	5,000	7,200	2,200	144.0%
426	Group Sales - Show 6	8,000	8,500	500	106.3%
	SUBTOTAL Group Sales	56,000	60,200	4,200	107.5%
	TOTAL TICKET SALES	1,475,000	1,435,700	(39,300)	97.3%

SAMPLE EXPENSE ACCOUNT LINES

Acct Num	Account Title	Budget	To Date	Balance	Percent
3000	**MARKETING**				
3001	Salaries	221,000	202,000	(19,000)	91.4%
3002	Payroll Taxes	20,322	18,600	(1,722)	91.5%
3003	General Advertising	7,000	7,400	400	105.7%
3004	Newspaper Advertising	50,000	47,000	(3,000)	94.0%
3005	Broadcast Advertising	32,000	30,000	(2,000)	93.8%
3006	General Printing	30,000	32,000	2,000	106.7%
3007	Season Program Printing	53,700	52,223	(1,477)	97.2%
3008	Telemarketing Expenses	6,325	6,500	175	102.8%
3009	Telemarketing Commissions	50,025	48,000	(2,025)	96.0%
3010	Displays and Signage	6,000	6,200	200	103.3%
3011	Photography	13,000	15,000	2,000	115.4%
3012	Postage & Distribution	12,000	11,950	(50)	99.6%
3013	Distribution of Brochures	1,800	1,500	(300)	83.3%
3014	Program Ad Sales Commission	15,000	14,000	(1,000)	93.3%
3015	Group Sales	15,000	14,000	(1,000)	93.3%
3016	Hotel Commissions	3,000	2,800	(200)	93.3%
3017	Dues/Subscriptions/Clippings	2,000	1,850	(150)	92.5%
3018	Materials and Supplies	3,500	2,900	(600)	82.9%
3019	Miscellaneous	850	250	(600)	29.4%
	SUBTOTAL MARKETING	542,522	514,173	(28,349)	94.8%

Figure 9-7 Detailed Budget—Theater Company

Budget Distribution—Project Basis   Current Year

INCOME	Regular Season	Touring	Educational Outreach	Building Fund	Special Events	TOTAL
Subscription Ticket Sales	653,500	163,500	0	0	0	817,000
Single Ticket Sales	481,600	120,400	0	0	0	602,000
Group Sales	36,400	11,200	8,400	0	0	56,000
Advertising	61,600	15,400	0	0	0	77,000
Concessions	47,600	8,400	0	0	0	56,000
Gift Shop Income	12,000	3,000	0	0	0	15,000
Interest	12,800	3,200	0	0	0	16,000
Costume & Scenery Rentals	3,500	0	0	0	0	3,500
Space/Equipment Rentals	7,000	0	0	0	0	7,000
Education	0	0	5,200	0	0	5,200
Miscellaneous	6,500	0	0	0	0	6,500
Surcharges on Ticket Sales	12,000	0	0	0	5,000	17,000
SUBTOTAL	1,334,500	325,100	13,600	0	5,000	1,678,200
DONATIONS & GOVT FUNDING						
Individuals	100,000	0	0	50,000	100,000	250,000
Corporations	45,000	25,000	25,000	5,000	0	100,000
Foundations	40,000	10,000	40,000	10,000	0	100,000
Co-producers	45,000	15,000	15,000	0	0	75,000
Special Events	0	0	0	0	205,000	205,000
Matching Contributions	200,000	50,000		0	0	250,000
State Grants	0	25,000	23,000	0	0	48,000
City/County Grants	29,000	30,000	35,000	0	0	94,000
Federal Grants	0	0	0	0	0	-
SUBTOTAL	459,000	155,000	138,000	65,000	305,000	1,122,000
TOTAL	1,793,500	480,100	151,600	65,000	310,000	2,800,200

EXPENSE	Regular Season	Touring	Educational Outreach	Building Fund	Special Events	TOTAL
Artistic Salaries/Fees/Expenses	557,745	175,000	130,800	0	8,500	872,045
Technical Salaries/Fees/Expenses	389,407	125,000	95,000	0	6,500	615,907
Production Cost	96,669	28,000	15,000	0	0	139,669
Administrative Salaries/Fees/Expenses	84,059	30,500	15,000	7,600	15,250	152,409
Marketing Salaries and Expenses	425,000	102,000	10,000	0	5,522	542,522
Development Salaries and Expenses	72,942	10,000	5,000	10,000	65,000	162,942
Special Events & Receptions	9,000	0	0	12,000	107,000	128,000
Concessions	35,858	0	0	0	0	35,858
Gift Shop Expenses	3,735	1,200	0	0	1,500	6,435
Occupancy (Utilities, phones, etc.)	70,352	0	0	0	0	70,352
Contingency	25,061	3,500	1,500	0	3,500	33,561
TOTAL EXPENSES	1,769,828	475,200	272,300	29,600	212,772	2,759,700
VARIANCE - Surplus or (Deficit)	23,672	4,900	(120,700)	35,400	97,228	40,500

Figure 9-8 Budget Distribution—Project Basis

effect, the other activities of the organization are subsidizing this activity. Of course, this may be a management decision, and this deficit may have been anticipated.

The project budget is an excellent way to help with the fundraising needs of the organization. For example, the educational outreach area could make a case for an additional $120,700 to achieve its objectives. If the $120,700 could be raised from outside sources, funds could be shifted to help pay for other priority projects that the organization has established in its planning process.

Another useful element of the project budget is its ability to show the proposed distribution of resources across the entire organization. The salary lines for the artistic, technical, and administrative staff present a clear picture of how much of the budget has been allocated to support the educational outreach program.

From the Budget to Cash Flow
The budget shows the manager the planned revenues and expenses for the fiscal year. The budgeting process that took us to the point of preparing a detailed budget still does not tell us if we have enough resources to operate the organization during the year. To make the budget work, a cash flow projection must be developed. It will provide a detailed look at the budget before the organization begins to spend money.

Cash Flow Projections   It is possible to anticipate periods during the fiscal year when the organization may not have enough cash to pay its bills. Figure 9-9 shows the theater company's budget distributed over the current fiscal year that begins in July and ends in June. Performances will take place October through April. The touring activity is scheduled for December and April.

In this example, the variance line of the cash flow statement shows that the company will spend more than it makes in sales and donations for five months out of the year. The actual cash flow projections at the bottom of the page show that four months of the year the company will have a cash flow deficit (February, March, April, May). However, by carefully planning the use of cash reserves, the company should be able to make it through the year.

In this example, if the company starts the year with $154,800 in income in July and $50,085 in expenses, it will have $104,715 left at the end of the month. The balance remains positive until February (see Balance row under Cash Flow Projections). In this month the theater is short $72,913 at the end of the month. We would describe the organization as "running in the red." It carries that deficit into March. Income exceeds expenses in March, but the theater is carrying a projected deficit of $30,367. The good news is that by June the company has a balance that is positive, or "in the black."

It is easy to see from this simple example how an arts organization can get into financial difficulty. Even though the company is projecting ending the season with a $80,940 surplus (see Reserves in the Total column), there might be four months of the season where the cash flow is negative. The financial manager for the theater company would of course take action to prevent this. Funds from reserves could be deposited into the account so it would not be overdrawn. If reserves did not exist in the organization, the possibility of a short-term bank loan might be explored.

Often an arts organization will not have sufficient reserves to cope with receiving money at times that may not coincide with when it

Cash Flow Projections—Theater Company

INCOME	July	Aug	Sept	Oct	Nov	Dec	Jan	Feb	Mar	Apr	May	June	TOTAL
Subs Ticket	100,000	175,000	150,000	25,000	0	0	0	0	42,000	75,000	125,000	125,000	817,000
Single Ticket	0	0	7,000	50,000	125,000	150,000	75,000	65,000	60,000	70,000	0	0	602,000
Group Sales	0	10,000	15,000	6,500	7,500	5,000	5,000	2,500	2,000	2,500	0	0	56,000
Advertising	25,000	22,000	22,000	0	0	0	0	0	0	0	1,000	7,000	77,000
Concessions	0	0	0	7,500	8,000	11,000	9,000	8,000	7,500	5,000	0	0	56,000
Gift Shop	0	0	0	1,500	2,500	3,500	2,000	2,000	1,500	2,000	0	0	15,000
Interest	1,300	1,500	1,700	1,200	1,200	1,450	1,400	1,200	1,200	1,300	1,350	1,200	16,000
Set/Cost Rental	0	0	0	0	0	0	3,500	0	0	0	0	0	3,500
Space Rentals	3,500	0	0	0	0	0	0	0	0	0	0	3,500	7,000
Education	0	0	0	0	0	2,500	0	0	0	0	2,700	0	5,200
Miscellaneous	0	0	0	0	0	0	0	0	0	0	3,500	3,000	6,500
Surcharge Tkts	0	0	0	2,100	2,500	2,600	2,500	2,500	2,500	2,300	0	0	17,000
Individuals	8,500	9,500	10,000	10,000	25,000	35,000	30,000	30,000	35,000	30,000	15,000	12,000	250,000
Corporations	6,500	7,000	7,500	9,000	15,000	20,000	15,000	8,000	6,500	3,500	1,000	1,000	100,000
Foundations	0	0	25,000	0	0	25,000	0	0	25,000	0	0	25,000	100,000
Co-producers	10,000	10,000	20,000	0	0	30,000	0	0	5,000	0	0	0	75,000
Special Events	0	0	0	0	0	0	45,000	55,000	100,000	5,000	0	0	205,000
Matching	0	0	0	100,000	0	10,000	100,000	40,000	0	0	0	0	250,000
State Grants	0	0	0	24,000	0	0	0	0	24,000	0	0	0	48,000
Grants	0	0	31,000	0	0	31,000	0	0	0	32,000	0	0	94,000
Federal Grants	0	0	0	0	0	0	0	0	0	0	0	0	-
INCOME	154,800	235,000	289,200	236,800	186,700	327,050	288,400	214,200	312,200	228,600	149,550	177,700	2,800,200

EXPENSES	July	Aug	Sept	Oct	Nov	Dec	Jan	Feb	Mar	Apr	May	June	TOTAL
Artistic Staff	0	0	87,045	110,000	110,000	125,000	110,000	110,000	110,000	110,000	0	0	872,045
Technical Staff	0	61,591	61,591	61,591	61,591	61,591	61,591	61,591	61,591	61,591	61,591	0	615,907
Production	0	38,000	25,000	15,000	10,000	10,000	10,000	10,000	10,000	10,000	1,699	0	139,699
Administrative	12,701	12,701	12,701	12,701	12,701	12,701	12,701	12,701	12,701	12,701	12,701	12,701	152,409
Marketing	18,022	24,500	35,000	100,000	60,000	50,000	5,000	50,000	50,000	50,000	75,000	25,000	542,522
Devel Sal & Exp	13,500	20,000	13,500	13,500	20,000	13,500	13,500	13,500	13,500	13,500	8,000	6,942	162,942
Special Events	0	0	0	0	1,500	1,500	25,000	97,000	1,500	1,500	0	0	128,000
Concessions	0	0	0	4,800	5,000	6,200	5,358	5,500	4,500	4,500	0	0	35,858
Gift Shop	0	3,500	0	0	0	2,935	0	0	0	0	0	0	6,435
Occupancy	5,863	5,863	5,863	5,863	5,863	5,863	5,863	5,863	5,863	5,863	5,863	5,863	70,352
Contingency	0	0	0	15,000	15,000	3,561	0	0	0	0	0	0	33,561
TOTAL EXP	50,085	166,154	240,699	338,454	301,654	292,850	249,012	366,154	269,654	269,654	164,853	50,505	2,759,730
VARIANCE	104,715	68,846	48,501	(101,654)	(114,954)	34,200	39,388	(151,954)	42,546	(41,054)	(15,303)	127,195	40,470

CASH FLOW PROJECTIONS													
RESERVES	0	104,715	173,560	222,061	120,407	5,453	39,653	79,041	(72,913)	(30,367)	(71,421)	(86,725)	$ 40,470
BALANCE	104,715	173,560	222,061	120,407	5,453	39,653	79,041	(72,913)	(30,367)	(71,421)	(86,725)	40,470	$ 80,940
	July	Aug	Sept	Oct	Nov	Dec	Jan	Feb	Mar	Apr	May	June	TOTAL

Comment: The company is projected to have an $80,940 cash balance at the end of the season.

Figure 9-9 Cash Flow Projections—Theater Company

needs to spend money. Once an arts organization begins to find itself in a cycle of borrowing to make up cash flow and paying very high short-term interest rates, the erosion of the fiscal foundation of the organization begins. It may take two or three years, but overestimating revenue in combination with overspending and poor cash flow management will eventually lead to a deficit that could bankrupt the organization.

We cover financial management strategies in more detail in Chapter 10, "Economics and Financial Management." As you will see, the business of running an arts organization is much the same as running any small business. You must make more than you spend. The best way to know if the organization is following this simple rule is to have a good budget reporting system in place. A budget is the key tool to help the manager and the staff stay well informed about the current financial status of the organization.

Summary

Control is the process of monitoring performance and making adjustments as required to meet planned objectives. Uncertainty affects all planning. The degree of complexity, human limitations, and centralization also influence how effective an organization's control system will be.

Output and input standards must be clearly established. Measurement standards must be in place so that a manager can compare what was done with what was expected. A control system requires that there be mechanisms in place for correcting work that does not meet the standard. Management by exception (MBE) allows a manager to focus attention on variances in expected performance. Management by objectives (MBO) encourages the integration of planning objectives and work objectives.

Performance appraisal systems are formal methods for providing feedback to employees on a regular basis. Numerical rating scales, behavioral rating scales, critical incident method, and free-form narratives are techniques used to appraise work output.

Effective control systems depend on data and information gathered from the organization's management information system (MIS). The MIS extends into all areas of the organization and is influenced by factors related to the controllability of the information flow through the organization. The organizational design might promote or hinder the effectiveness of the MIS. Some of the possible shortcomings in an MIS include providing too much data, providing irrelevant data, or assuming that computerizing operations will improve the MIS.

Budget control systems are a critical component of an organization. Controlling the distribution of resources and monitoring how effectively the resources are used is a full-time job. Organizations must identify revenue and expense centers and project monetary activity accordingly. A budget can function as a preliminary control on a project by defining the limits on the available resources. Budgets can be fixed, flexible, or zero-based and cover a short- or long-term period. Budget controls concentrate on the timely monitoring of revenue and expenses for all areas of an organization. Budgets may be formatted in a variety of ways to explain how resources are being used. Summary, detailed, project, or cash flow budgets may be used in various combinations to provide the information needed to make decisions about the programming for an arts organization.

Key Terms and Concepts

Organizational control system
Output and input standards
Internal and external controls
Management by exception (MBE)
Management by objectives (MBO)
Performance appraisal system
Management information system (MIS)
Budgets
Fixed and flexible budgets
Zero-based budgets
Short- and long-term budgets
Budgetary process
Budget control system
Summary budget
Detailed budget
Project budget
Cash flow projections

Questions

1. What is the relationship of control to the manager's other functions?

2. What are the four steps in the control process? Give a specific example of the control process in an arts setting.

3. Describe the typical steps involved in applying the management by exception process. As a system, how does MBE affect an organization's planning process?

4. From your personal experience, describe a situation in which the control system for an organization did or did not work well. Offer suggestions for appropriate improvements, if applicable.

5. What are the four main appraisal methods used in a control system? Briefly evaluate some of the things you have accomplished in the last year.

6. Define the term *management information system*.

7. What will be some of the future applications of MIS computers in the arts?

8. How is a budget part of the control system?

9. What are the five types of budgets? Which type or types would be most effective in supporting an arts organization?

10. Outline the budget process.

Case Study

The following article points out problems with an organization's control system. You should be able to find numerous flaws in the system used to keep staff activities in check.

Radio Station Officials Got Free Cruises

Officials with a college's public radio and television station have received tens of thousands of dollars worth of free ocean cruises through fundraising promotions of questionable value to the station.

Last year, the station manager and his wife were sent on an all-expenses-paid cruise to China, Korea, and Japan by a travel agency that had a promotional contract with the stations—a contract that the station manager signed. Records show the travel agency also paid $2,700 toward a cruise package for one of the radio station program directors.

A glossy, full-color promotional brochure sent to 33,000 of the station's donors described the 18-day excursion as a once-in-a-lifetime opportunity and boasted of the ship's excellent chefs and fine dining. Ports of call included Shanghai, Hong Kong, Pusan, and Nagasaki, with three nights in Peking.

Although the cruise was heavily promoted as a fund-raiser to benefit the area's only public broadcast outlets—with $200 from every cruise package sold being donated to the stations—the chief benefit appears to have been to station officials.

The cruise packages given to the station manager, his wife, and the program director were worth a total of $11,000 to $15,000. The cruise line sold more than $125,000 worth of cruise tickets through the station and received thousands of dollars worth of free advertising.

The stations, meanwhile, received a $4,800 "contribution" from the cruise line and an additional $7,250 from auctioning off two cruise packages donated by the cruise line for the station's annual membership drive. The 24 people who bought the cruises received a $200 tax write-off per person.

The station manager said that he and his wife were asked by the travel agency to host the trip because the agency thought that having them do so would sell more cruises.

The station manager, his wife, and the program director, who have been on most of the cruises that the station has sponsored, were listed in the station's promotional brochures as the hosts of the cruise.

A special assistant to the president of the college and legal counsel to the college said that he approved the idea of the station manager taking his wife along and said that the manager asked his permission before doing so.

As manager of a college-owned station, the station manager is a public employee, the legal counsel said. State law prohibits public employees from using their official position "to secure anything of value" for themselves that they would not ordinarily receive in the performance of their official duties.

The station manager said that the official duties that required him to go on the cruise were "being the head of the station and having the expertise in the East."

The station's marketing director said that the station had done only one cost-benefit analysis of the cruise promotions since they began in the early 1990s, and those records showed that the promotion cost more than it raised.

According to documents provided by the station, the previous year's cruise promotion brought in a $6,800 "contribution" from the cruise line and $9,500 from a donated cruise that was auctioned off.

But to get that money, it cost the station $20,941 for such things as providing 71 free 30-second ads on the FM radio station, numerous television spots for the cruise, additional air fare for the auction winners, staff salaries, and full-page ads in the station magazine.

The travel agent, who began arranging the cruises for the station three years ago, said that the station manager complained during the negotiations for last year's China trip that the station wasn't getting enough out of these promotions.

During the negotiations, records show, the cruise line initially offered to pay most of the costs of the station manager's wife's cruise, which was described in a letter the travel agent wrote to the station as "a favor" from the cruise line, but that created "an additional expense (for the station) that is difficult to explain."

In the end, the station paid for part of the program director's cruise, and the station manager's wife's entire cruise.

The travel agent said it was routine for cruise lines to provide free trips in an effort to entice groups to sell cruise packages.

"It's the carrot they hold out. Everyone wants a free cruise," she said.

The marketing director said that the station is no longer receiving free cruises for station personnel because the college's Alumni Association is now cosponsoring the promotion. She said that the cruise line now handling the arrangements simply donates one cruise for the annual fundraising auction.

According to the marketing director, the station decided last year that the cruise promotions were taking up too much of station personnel's time and were not producing enough revenue.

SOURCE: The information in this case study was developed from an article by Gary Webb that was published in the *Cleveland Plain Dealer* in 1988.

Questions

1. Was there a conflict of interest when the station manager signed a contract that gave him free cruises?

2. The case study alleges that the station manager and his wife used station funds to cover their personal expenses. If you were on the board of directors for the station, how would you handle this issue?

3. The legal counsel said that the station manager sought permission before accepting the cruise, and the station manager claimed that his travel was part of his job responsibilities. Was there a violation of the control mechanism implied in the regulations prohibiting state employees from accepting gifts?

4. If the cost-benefit analysis indicated that the station was taking a loss on the cruise promotions, why do you think they continued to offer them for four years?

5. What kinds of controls should have been in place to prevent the station from entering into such a costly promotional campaign?

References

1. John R. Schermerhorn, Jr., *Management for Productivity*, 2nd ed. (New York: John Wiley & Sons, 1986), p. 397.
2. Ibid., p. 397.
3. Ibid., pp. 398–399.
4. Ibid., p. 400.
5. Ibid., pp. 414–416.
6. Ibid., pp. 404–405.
7. Arthur G. Bedeian, *Management* (New York: Dryden Press, CBS College Publishing, 1986), p. 588.
8. Schermerhorn, *Management for Productivity*, p. 447.
9. Ibid., pp. 449–450.
10. Ibid., p. 428.

10

□ □ □ □ □

Economics and Financial Management

Yet no matter how highly we may value them, art and culture are produced by individuals and institutions working within the general economy, and therefore cannot escape the constraints of the material world.

James Heilbrun and Charles M. Gray,
The Economics of Art and Culture

One of the objectives of this chapter is to help you gain an understanding of the impact of the economy on arts organizations. We also will review some basic concepts in economics, financial management, and accounting as applied to the arts. This chapter is not intended as a substitute for courses in economics, finance, or accounting. Basic course work in these subjects will be invaluable to your career in arts management. Skills and knowledge about managing the basic business affairs of an arts organization can help keep everyone focused on the mission. Without sufficient financial resources your mission statement will be just that—a statement. To put your mission into action you will need cash and credit just like any other business.

The economy has a direct effect on artists and arts organizations every day in the United States. Staying aware of the economic environment allows arts managers the opportunity to prepare plans of action designed to ensure the survival of the organization. Here are some basic questions related to the economy:

1. Will there be a downturn or an upturn in the economy?
2. Will people have more or less disposable income?
3. How will inflation affect operating costs?
4. How will changes in interest rates affect the budget and the organization's investments?

Ultimately, the answers to these and many other questions remain uncertain because the economic information that a manager needs to make decisions is often contradictory. One report says that the economy is headed for recession, and another says that the growth economy will continue for another year. A mixture of good judgment, diverse sources of information, and a healthy dose of skepticism are necessary ingredients for an arts manager.

The Economic Problems and Issues Facing the Arts

A limited number of studies have been done and a few books have been written about the arts and economics. One book that is required

222

reading for all arts managers is William J. Baumol and William G. Bowen's landmark study, *Performing Arts: The Economic Dilemma,*[1] published in 1966. The book was the first detailed analysis of the economic conditions of the arts in the United States. A much newer source for information about the economy and the arts is James Heilbrun and Charles M. Gray's *The Economics of Art and Culture*, published in 2001. This book provides a comprehensive and updated view on the microeconomics of the arts and public policy in America. Other writers have also explored the relationship of the arts and economics.

The Cultural Boom from an Economic Perspective

During the mid-1960s there was much talk of a "cultural boom" in America. Attendance at arts events was up, the number of performing arts groups was increasing yearly, and regional performing arts centers were being built everywhere. Baumol and Bowen found that, although there was indeed a lot of activity, the actual growth of the arts in relation to all other factors of the economy was very modest. By adjusting and correcting the data for inflation, population increases, and income growth, they found very little change between 1929 and 1963.

Heilburn and Gray's more recent data came to a more positive conclusion. They noted, "Many of the indicators of real arts activity showed rates of increase during the 1970s that exceeded the growth in real income."[2] They go on to indicate, "The performing arts were gaining faster than the economy as a whole during the 1970s and 1980s."[3] The key measure Heilbrun and Gray examined was spending on the arts as a function of disposable personal income (DPI). "After reaching a level of less than 7 cents per $100 of DPI in the mid-1970s, consumer spending on the performing arts rose to 9.1 cents per $100 in 1980 and 13.4 cents in 1990."[4]

Trend Shift in the 1980s

Heilbrun and Gray go on to note that toward the end of the 1980s the number of performances and performing arts organizations began to decline. The DPI increase in spending on the arts noted in the late 1980s and early 1990s therefore seems to be due in part to the price increases for admissions and tickets.[5]

The Arts Audience

Before Baumol and Bowen's study, there was very little statistical data available about who was attending various theater, dance, opera, and concert performances in the United States. The authors used detailed audience surveys to gather data on income levels, education, age, gender, and preferences. They found that the "common man" was fairly uncommon among those who attended live professional performances. Audiences were predominantly white-collar with high levels of education and income. Forty-five percent of the audience members were between 35 and 60 years of age. Their research led them to estimate that in 1966 about 4 percent of the U.S. population over 18 years of age attended some professional arts event. Taken at today's population levels, that would translate to around 12 million people.

Heilbrun and Gray's book updates Baumol and Bowen's study with the assistance of various NEA surveys done in the 1980s. (Note: The NEA website contains many statistical reports about current attendance patterns.) For example, one recent survey comparison pointed out that 93 percent watched television and 63 percent attended movies, while only 24.5 percent attended musicals, 15.6 percent classical music concerts, 15.8 percent theater, 5.8 percent ballet, and 4.7 percent attended opera.[6] They found similar results when profiling the participation rates at music concerts, theater, and art museums. Income also pays a major role in arts participation. For example, participation at the lower income levels for classical music was 6.8 percent. The highest level of incomes recorded participation rates at 35 percent. The same sort of gap seemed to exist for theater (8.2 percent lower income versus 31.9 percent highest income) and for museum attendance (18.8 percent lowest versus 59.6 percent highest).[7]

In the almost 40 years since Baumol and Bowen's study, not a great deal has changed when it comes to audience composition. The audience for "high culture" events such as opera, theater, dance, and museum exhibits continues to be a defined segment of the population. One trend commented on in *The Economics of Art and Culture* that is of particular concern to arts managers is that, as a percentage, the baby boom generation does not seem to attend arts events to the degree the older pre-WWII generation did. For more details on this trend, please see *Age and Arts Participation*, Research Division Report #34, National Endowment for the Arts, 1996.

An often repeated claim in the arts community is that there is a higher attendance at arts events than at sporting events. However, when the millions who watch sports on television are taken into account, it would probably be reasonable to assume that more people, representing a greater cross-section of the population, would consider themselves to be sports, not arts, fans. In fact, the economic values of our society are clearly expressed in such things as the salaries now paid to some athletes. To put this in perspective, consider the fact that a sports star's salary in some cases could be higher than the entire operating budget of a regional orchestra, opera, ballet, or theater company.

The Productivity Issue

Baumol and Bowen's detailed economic study uncovered data that supports the conclusion that the financial difficulties arts groups were experiencing would probably only worsen over time. The basis for their finding was directly related to how the entire economic system has seen slow but steady growth in productivity. In theory, new technologies and processes of production increase the quantity of work output for each employee, that is, worker productivity increases over time. This, in turn, should reduce the cost per unit for production and increase profits. To stay ahead of *inflation*, which is the constant increase in the price levels of everything, a business must find ways to more productively use the labor force and any other inputs needed to produce the product or service. Without productivity gains, the producer would have to raise the price higher and higher to cover the increasing input costs. If other companies that make a similar product are able to increase productivity, the prices they charge could be kept lower. This would cause consumers to buy the less costly product and would eventually put the less productive company out of business.

Baumol and Bowen applied this theory to arts organizations and found the basis for the gap between their income and their expenses. The authors argued that the technology of presenting an arts event was subject to limited increases in productivity. The time it takes to rehearse and perform a play, opera, dance, or symphony was not subject to increases in productivity. In addition, the supply of the product was limited. A live performance can only be repeated a certain number of times in a day.

The application of technology to almost all phases of American business has also helped increase productivity. Technology in the offices or production areas of arts organizations has helped make people more productive. However, no amount of technology will have a significant impact on shortening the time spent on rehearsing a scene or repeating a musical passage until it is perfect. The final product will take about the same amount of time to present. The result is that gains in productivity realized by computerizing the arts organization's office will be offset by increasing costs to present the basic product.

From that conclusion, and from the income-expense gap data collected over a 15-year period, Baumol and Bowen predicted that arts productivity would actually decline over time as other segments of the economy became more productive. The long-term effect of this is an ever-increasing income gap. They predicted that without regularly increasing donations, the income gap would continue to increase even with increasing ticket prices. They projected cost increases caused by inflation coupled with limited productivity and higher labor costs would further increase the income gap for the arts. In most cases, salaries and the costs of benefits, utilities, supplies, and so forth, are increasing each year. Therefore, unless ticket prices are increased, more performances are scheduled, or more funds are raised, arts organizations will be facing an ever-increasing income gap. Any arts group that attempts to ignore the implications of the income gap in its strategic planning, marketing, or fundraising efforts will eventually find itself going broke. However, there was some good news to report by Heilbrun and Gray. They made the important finding that increased revenue from higher ticket and admission prices had mitigated the severity of the productivity issue and the projected income versus expense gap.

What do Baumol and Bowen's and Heilbrun and Gray's studies lead us to conclude thus far? The optimist might conclude that the economic system has worked well enough to get us to the point where a substantial number of arts organizations are operating in a wider geographical distribution than ever before. On the other hand, a pessimist might conclude that arts organizations have expanded too much in relation to the real market demand for their products. As a result of this overexpansion, there may be too many arts groups chasing too few dollars.

One could argue that our culture is expressed in part through its artistic creations and activity. Society will continue to invest its resources in the arts because enough people want and need what the arts provide. The satisfaction gained from creating and consuming the arts ensure their place in the overall economic system. However, if the system is to work for the benefit of everyone, the artists and the arts organizations must take an active role in shaping public policy about the place of the arts in society.

Basic Economic Principles Applied to the Arts

Arts managers need to understand some very basic principles of economics when contemplating how best to support and sustain an organization in today's business world. What we call "economics" is at its most basic level a study of how people use the financial resources they

In the News—*The Producers*

In October 2001 an article appeared in the *New York Times* noting that the Broadway show *The Producers* was selling 50 tickets a night for $480 each. Demand was so high at the time that selling 50 tickets a night at that rate was not difficult. The article pointed out that ticket scalpers were selling tickets for $742.50 online. This premium seating idea was actually part of a trend that started in the 1980s when special seating sections with very high prices became common at sports arenas and ballparks. Setting higher prices for a better seating location is of course common in the performing arts. However, a $480 ticket price was a first for a Broadway show.

SOURCE: Jesse McKinley, "For the Asking, a $480 Seat," *New York Times* (October 26, 2001), p. A-1.

possess. How do they use the money they have? After paying for the basics such as food, housing, and clothing, what do people "buy" that isn't essential to survival?

As an arts manager you are especially interested in how consumers behave with these discretionary monies relative to your "products." Buying tickets to a show or an admission to a museum, or becoming a subscriber, member, or donor, is something consumers have the choice to do. They may decide to buy something else to achieve whatever entertainment needs they have.

There is stiff competition directed at influencing which arts and entertainment products people use. It is important for an arts manager to develop an understanding of the demand for their arts product relative to the supply, how much people are willing to spend on consuming it, and what the long-term potential is for support through donations or gifts from their supporters.

Another economic issue to consider is that for any business to sustain itself in our economy it must bring in as much or more income than it spends to deliver its goods (things) or services (e.g., the experience of attending a show). If you are in the for-profit business of providing an entertainment experience such as a Broadway show, then you must charge enough for the tickets to pay all the costs of doing the show day after day. You must also eventually pay back the investors a profit for the risk they took with their money in the first place. For example, in the early twenty-first century, tickets for Broadway shows often cost in excess of $80 to $100 per seat. In some cases, the price may be even higher (see "In the News—*The Producers*"). The incentive for the investor in these for-profit entertainment ventures is that maybe someday they will make back their investment plus a profit.

The other core concept to remember is that our economic system also supports activities that do not necessarily pay for themselves through sales. Government is a sector of the economy, for example, that is not driven solely by the profit motive. Some of the basic services provided by government are not designed to generate a profit. They exist as a benefit for us all. Police and fire protection in your community tend not to be operated for a profit, but rather from a motive of providing us with security and peace of mind.

The sector of the economy that many nonprofit arts organizations operate in is also driven, to a large extent, by this motive of providing benefit to society. Government sanctions a special status to nongovernmental agencies to provide goods and services that the profit sector cannot efficiently deliver. Over the last century the nonprofit sector became the main force behind the delivery of the fine and performing arts in America. Why? The economist might say that this is due in part to a *market failure*. This simply means that the supply and demand for the fine and performing arts are not in balance, and some intervention is needed in this market to ensure its continuance. (A *market* is defined as a designated interaction of buyers and sellers for a product or service.)

The profit sector, with the exception of Broadway shows, is not in the "business" of delivering the fine and performing arts to its market due to the simple fact that it cannot make a profit doing so. To address this failure of the marketplace the nonprofit tax-exempt organizations arose to solve this economic problem. Although this is a complex subject, the central idea is that the combination of the revenue from discounted admission or membership fees (or ticket prices) plus the resources raised through government support and donations of money and volunteer time cover operating costs for an arts service that the normal market cannot sustain.

The Economics of Making More than You Spend
From an economic perspective many arts organizations operate in a marketplace in which they cannot make enough money to sustain themselves from the revenues collected from admissions to performances or exhibitions. In other words, arts organizations often deliberately underprice their product with the rationale that they are making it more widely available to the community. The motive is often stated that nonprofit arts groups are in "business" to deliver their experience to the greatest number of people by keeping the price as low as possible.

The common understanding is that in exchange for doing these performances or exhibitions, the government will grant an exemption from paying taxes on the income from sales, and it will allow organizations to solicit funds from individuals, foundations, and corporations. In addition, any surplus revenue above operating expenses will be used to support the mission of the organization and not individual "shareholders," or in this case, the board members. Governments also agree to allow people who wish to donate money to the organization to accomplish these good things, the ability to deduct from their personal income taxes a percentage of their donation.

Economic Impact of the Arts
One key area that arts managers have stressed to their communities in the last few years is the positive economic impact of the organization. Arts organizations expend funds; pay salaries, wages, taxes, and benefits; and purchase goods and services in the community. They also help stimulate the local economy through the multiplier effect of money. The *multiplier effect* describes a process whereby money expended for one purpose (paying a salary) has an impact beyond that single use. For example, the salary paid to a staff member is used to buy groceries, make a rent payment, as well as pay for other goods and services in the community. The "In the News" articles provide ample support for this concept.

The impact of the basic operation of the arts organization extends into other areas of the community. As noted, the salaries paid to staff members are used to pay for goods and services. The money is also then used by the property owner, bank, or store to purchase things or to make loans. In effect, the money that the arts organization puts into the local economy ripples throughout the region. In addition, when consumers buy tickets and make the journey to the performance, they may pay for a baby-sitter, gas for the car, a meal at a restaurant, parking, and a purchase at the arts center's gift shop. The $40 paid for the ticket may generate four or five times that amount in other goods and services.

Organizational Impact
Several additional economic terms and concepts relate to how an organization operates in the total economic environment. For example, calculating the impact of such things as total fixed costs, total variable costs, average fixed and average variable costs, and marginal costs helps the organization with financial and operational planning. The ideas related to the law of diminishing returns, long-term operational costs, and economies of scale have some application to the arts. Let us take a brief look at some of these economic theories and laws.

In the News—Economic Impact

In the summer of 2002 the Americans for the Arts released a comprehensive report on the economic impact of not-for-profit arts organizations.

Arts and Economic Prosperity
Arts and Economic Prosperity: The Economic Impact of Nonprofit Arts Organizations and Their Audiences, released on June 10, 2002, reveals that America's nonprofit arts industry generates $134 billion in economic activity every year, including $24.4 billion in federal, state, and local tax revenues. The $134 billion total includes $53.2 billion in spending by arts organizations and $80.8 billion in event-related spending by arts audiences:

- The $53.2 billion represents a 45 percent increase (from $36.8 billion) since 1992, when Americans for the Arts last studied spending by arts organizations.
- The $80.8 billion in event-related spending by arts audiences reflects an average of $22.87 per person in spending for hotels, restaurants, parking, souvenirs, refreshments, or other similar costs—with non-local attendees spending nearly twice as much as local attendees ($38.05 compared to $21.75).

The $134 billion in total economic activity has a significant national impact, generating the following:

- 4.85 million full-time equivalent jobs
- $89.4 billion in household income
- $6.6 billion in local government tax revenues
- $7.3 billion in state government tax revenues
- $10.5 billion in federal income tax revenues

The most comprehensive economic impact study of the nonprofit arts industry ever conducted, it is based on surveys of 3,000 nonprofit arts organizations and more than 40,000 attendees at arts events in 91 cities in 33 states, plus the District of Columbia.

SOURCE: Americans for the Arts website: http://www.artsusa.org/EconomicImpact/.

Fixed, Variable, and Marginal Costs

All organizations must identify the fixed costs of operation to form the base operating budget. Total fixed costs (TFC) typically include expenses for such things as renting or leasing space, paying salaries, and repaying loans. These costs will not change whether you do 2 or 20 performances or if the museum is open to the public that day. Salaries for a core staff and the various benefits paid to them represent the largest fixed overhead cost of an arts organization.

When performers, designers, technicians, and other specialized staff are hired for a given production, project, or event (assuming a season of several shows or exhibitions), these expenses are usually added to the *total variable costs* (TVC). Materials purchased for the scenery and costumes, phone calls, blueprints, paint, and labor to produce the show are all part of the TVC. The *total cost* (TC) represents the total of the fixed and variable costs (TC = TFC + TVC).

Another key indicator of costs is the *marginal cost* (MC), which is defined as the cost of producing an additional quantity of the product. In the performing arts, the most obvious output increase would be the number of performances scheduled. For example, when you plan for an evening concert performance, you can estimate the total variable and fixed costs associated with that concert. The marginal cost of doing another performance that afternoon would probably be less than the marginal cost of scheduling another performance for the next day. One reason why the MC might be lower is that the rental of the performance space is based on a daily rate of eight hours. If you use the space for only four hours in the evening, you still pay for the time you do not

In the News

In June of 2002 the National Governors' Association also published a report on the economic impact of the arts. A small section of the Issue Brief is published below.

Direct Economic Impact of the Arts

Nationally, the nonprofit arts industry is a $36.8 billion business that supports 1.3 million full-time jobs. Governments also reap considerable economic benefits: $790 million in revenue at the local level, $1.2 billion at the state level, and $3.4 billion at the federal level. Economic impacts on individual states and regions include the following:

• The arts generated $849 million in revenue for Virginia businesses, provided 18,850 full- and part-time jobs, and produced $307 million in value-added income for Virginia's workforce and entrepreneurs.

• Total spending of $188 million by nonprofit arts organizations in Louisiana has provided nearly 2,500 full-time jobs and produced $4.8 million in state and local government revenues.

• Every dollar Michigan invests in the state's Council for Arts and Cultural Affairs results in $10 of in-state direct spending.

• Oregon is home to 441 nonprofit arts and cultural institutions that injected $100.2 million of direct spending in the state's economy in fiscal 2000. Oregon's nonprofit arts sector employed 3,623 individuals.

• The arts support more than 245,000 jobs throughout the six states of New England, 3.5 percent of the region's total job base, and more than the area's software or medical technologies industries. The arts industry exhibited a 14 percent growth over a four-year period, much higher than New England's overall economic growth of 8 percent.

Economically, the nonprofit arts sector has an important—if difficult to measure—symbiotic role with the commercial arts sector. According to the Policy Economics Group of KPMG Peat Marwick, the nonprofit sector acts as a research and development arm for many for-profit enterprises, such as television and film, design, advertising, media, publishing, recording, and emerging multimedia industries.

SOURCE: NGA Center for Best Practices, Issue Brief, "The Role of the Arts in Economic Development," June 25, 2002, 2. Used with permission. For more information link to: http://www.nga.org/center.

---

use the space. The matinee performance would not add to the variable costs of the hall.

On the other hand, your payroll and production costs would rise with the extra performance. These variable costs would offset the gains from the decreased hall rental and would allow the organization to gain firsthand experience with the *law of diminishing returns*. The law states that "as more and more of a variable factor of production, or input (e.g., labor) is used together with a fixed factor of production, beyond some point the additional, or marginal, output attributable to the variable factor begins to fall."[8] To put it simply, at some point the costs rise enough to reduce the marginal gain from scheduling the additional performance.

A similar scenario can be developed for an exhibition. Adding to the time an exhibit is opened may bring increased marginal costs and gains to the organization. The marginal costs for being opened more hours or to run the exhibit longer would need to be calculated to see if indeed the organization was reaping some benefit for the extra expenses.

Profit-making arts ventures must constantly watch all costs related to making, selling, distributing, and advertising the product as well as the marginal costs. Otherwise, there will be no money left to call a

Exercise—Doing the Math

Let us put these concepts of fixed, variable, and marginal costs into perspective. The first important point to consider is that for arts organizations most costs are fixed costs (FC). Over time, the organization develops a pattern of events that becomes predictable. You open your season in October and end it in May, or your exhibitions change every 16 or 18 weeks. Therefore, in many arts organizations the variable costs (VC) would only surface if you decided to extend the run of the show or the exhibition.

In Figure 10-1 is an example of a performing arts group charging $14 a ticket to an event in a 500-seat theater that sells an average of 70 percent of its seating capacity. After five performances the group begins to make more money than it costs to produce each performance of the event. If the group schedules 13 performances, it begins to make more money than the original investment of $25,000 in fixed costs and $500 in variable costs. Average costs (AC) go down significantly as the number of performances go up (AC = TC/Number of Performances).

NOTE: The numbers used in Figure 10-1 are fictitious and are not intended to depict any specific arts organization. In the "real world," the fixed costs (FC) would be made up of the materials and labor expenses required to produce the event. The variable costs (VC) in this example could be attributed to extra box office staff, house management staff, or run crew hired to work only the performances of the show. The assumption is that the actor and designer fees or salaries are part of the fixed costs.

profit. Nonprofit organizations may not try to generate revenue above costs for the owners or investors, but they must also carefully control fixed, variable, and marginal costs. In fact, a nonprofit organization may generate a surplus of revenue as part of its overall budget plan. To generate a surplus or to break even, the arts manager must draw on a great deal of skill in controlling costs, setting prices, and estimating demand. In other words, operating a nonprofit arts organization requires as much financial skill as do for-profit ventures.

Economies of Scale

Another issue related to overall cost is how economies of scale operate in an organization. The technical definition of *economies of scale* is "a decrease in the long-run average total costs (ATC) of production that occur when larger facilities are available for manufacturing a product."[9] These economies are achieved because the business is able to specialize production techniques, its labor force becomes more expert, volume discounts are available for materials used to produce the product, or the by-products of manufacturing reach a large enough quantity to become salable.

There are applications of economies of scale in aspects of the production process and in operating an arts organization. For example, instead of setting up and equipping its own scenery and costume production shop, an organization could develop a central production center used by all of the major arts organizations in the region. This production center could achieve cost savings from scale through construction techniques and bulk purchases as well as by covering shop personnel costs. By scheduling various construction projects and buying in quantity, several organizations may be able to achieve a large enough scale of operation to reduce overall costs.

Another example of economies of scale is a performing arts center with multiple spaces. The assumption is that it is less costly to run three theaters under one roof than three theaters under three roofs. However, *diseconomies of scale* can also affect such centralized operations if management is not careful to control growth as the organization matures. A diseconomy of scale might be achieved by having to hire extra people and buy extra tools to take on the increased scale of production. This would increase the average total costs to produce the sets in the central shop. The savings realized by the scale of the operation would be quickly negated.

Supply and Demand

Trying to identify the demand for a particular show or exhibition requires that a manager weigh numerous factors that influence the behavior of consumers. The well-known factors of supply and demand are directly translated into activities at the core of an arts group's financial planning. Let us begin by looking at the area of demand.

Law of Demand

The *law of demand* describes the relationship between the amount of a good or service that a buyer both desires and is able to purchase, and the price charged for the good or service. The lower the price charged for a good or service, the larger the quantity demanded. Conversely, the higher the price, the lower the quantity demanded. This law of demand is based on an important assumption: *only the price change affects the*

Output - # Perfs	Fixed Costs (FC)	Variable Costs (VC)	Total Costs (TC) = (FC)+(VC)	Avg Cost (AC) = (TC)/Output	(Assumes $14/tkt) Total Rev @70% cap of 500 seats	Profit or (Loss)
1	$ 25,000	$ 500	$25,500	$25,500	$ 4,900	$ (20,600)
2	$ 25,000	$ 750	$25,750	$12,875	$ 9,800	$ (15,950)
3	$ 25,000	$ 1,250	$26,250	$8,750	$ 14,700	$ (11,550)
4	$ 25,000	$ 2,000	$27,000	$6,750	$ 19,600	$ (7,400)
5	$ 25,000	$ 3,000	$28,000	$5,600	$ 24,500	$ (3,500)
6	$ 25,000	$ 4,250	$29,250	$4,875	$ 29,400	$ 150
7	$ 25,000	$ 5,750	$30,750	$4,393	$ 34,300	$ 3,550
8	$ 25,000	$ 6,500	$31,500	$3,938	$ 39,200	$ 7,700
9	$ 25,000	$ 7,500	$32,500	$3,611	$ 44,100	$ 11,600
10	$ 25,000	$ 8,800	$33,800	$3,380	$ 49,000	$ 15,200
11	$ 25,000	$ 10,000	$35,000	$3,182	$ 53,900	$ 18,900
12	$ 25,000	$ 11,500	$36,500	$3,042	$ 58,800	$ 22,300
13	$ 25,000	$ 13,000	$38,000	$2,923	$ 63,700	$ 25,700
14	$ 25,000	$ 14,500	$39,500	$2,821	$ 68,600	$ 29,100
15	$ 25,000	$ 14,500	$39,500	$2,633	$ 73,500	$ 34,000
16	$ 25,000	$ 14,500	$39,500	$2,469	$ 78,400	$ 38,900
17	$ 25,000	$ 14,500	$39,500	$2,324	$ 83,300	$ 43,800
18	$ 25,000	$ 14,500	$39,500	$2,194	$ 88,200	$ 48,700
19	$ 25,000	$ 14,500	$39,500	$2,079	$ 93,100	$ 53,600
20	$ 25,000	$ 14,500	$39,500	$1,975	$ 98,000	$ 58,500

Figure 10-1 Production Profit versus Loss

quantity demanded. Other factors that can influence the ticket buyer are called *demand determinants* and include such things as the prices of other goods and services, income levels, and individual tastes.

Price of Other Goods *Substitute goods or services* may cause a shift in the demand if their prices change. To understand how these factors work, suppose that another group is presenting a classical music concert featuring the same Mozart symphony on the same night in your community. Because the other group is charging $5 less per ticket, the demand for your concert might decline, meaning that the overall demand will go down. Likewise, if the other group is charging $5 more than your group, the demand for your concert may increase.

The demand will also change if a *complementary good* is introduced into the business interaction. A complementary good, which is defined as a good or service that is used jointly with the original good, can cause the demand to change depending on whether the price of a complementary good goes up or down. For example, if a large increase in parking fees occurs, some consumers may be discouraged from purchasing tickets.

Income Another factor that could affect demand is individual income. If income increases, the demand for normal goods and services will also increase. Conversely, if income levels decrease, the demand for normal goods and services will decrease. *Normal goods and services* are defined as those things that people want as their income increases. *Inferior goods or services* are defined as those things that people will choose when their income decreases. For example, if there is a significant drop in income levels due to an economic recession, people might choose less expensive forms of entertainment. Instead of buying a $300 season subscription or single tickets to the symphony or theater, people may shift their spending to a less expensive community orchestra or theater series. The community orchestra and theater may not perceive themselves as an "inferior good or service," but in economic theory, the definition fits.

Expectations Demand is affected by individual expectations about the overall economic situation. If consumers think that the price may go up for a good or service, they may make the purchase immediately. This expectation would increase demand. On the other hand, if consumers thought that the price was going to drop, they may delay making the purchase. If enough people share this expectation, overall demand would go down. An arts manager might take advantage of this phenomenon by stressing in a subscription renewal campaign that prices will go up next season but that subscribers who renew by a certain date can save money. This tactic would probably help increase the renewal rate and the demand for tickets.

Tastes Personal consumer tastes also cause demand to change. If a significant number of people shift their interests away from classical music toward bluegrass, the demand for one will go down while the other increases. An increase in demand also might result from a popular soloist being added to a concert performance.

Market Demand and the Arts
Do these concepts have any place in the day-to-day planning activities of an arts manager? They do when the principles are applied realistically. For example, a dance group with the mission of bringing postmodern dance to its community would be wise to start with the expectation that there will be limited demand for the product. Although the community may regularly support dance performances by the regional ballet company—indicating a market for the entertainment service of dance—there is no guarantee that this market will also support an experimental dance troupe. How can this organization affect demand for its concerts? Advertising is one way to affect the demand for a particular product within an overall market. However, reaching individual consumers with the message about a particular dance organization and being able to make a sale are two different matters. To understand the entire relationship of the arts organization to the economic environment, we must also look at the supply of the product or service.

Law of Supply
We have seen that there is a relationship between price and quantity demanded for a product or service. Now let us look at the supply side of the theory. The application of these concepts to the operation of an arts organization requires some explanation.

The relationship between the amount of a product and its price is at the center of the *law of supply*, which states that "suppliers will supply larger quantities of a good at higher prices than at lower prices."[10] For example, from a theoretical perspective, if you are the supplier of symphony orchestra performances and your players are all under contract, it is to your benefit to offer this service as many times as possible. Your incentive as a supplier is to offer this product at the highest price you think you can obtain in that market. However, since the product we offer in the arts has a fixed supply (e.g., a concert season of X number of performances), it is much more difficult to apply the law of supply to what we do. As in the case of demand, there are also other variables that affect the supply of arts events. These variables are called *supply determinants* and include the price of resources, the number of suppliers, and suppliers' expectations.

Price of Resources   If the price of resources used in creating the good or service rises or falls, the supply will change. The term *factors of production* is used to describe the "inputs of labor services, raw materials, and other resources" used to create the final product or service.[11] For suppliers, a drop in the factors of production translates into greater profits. Therefore, suppliers have the incentive to supply more because they can make more profit. Conversely, if the factors of production go up, suppliers have an incentive to supply less because their profit margin goes down. Hence, suppliers reduce output to bring production costs into line with the quantity supplied.

However, arts organizations usually have very limited control over the price of resources and even less control over the production costs. For example, a season is selected and the supply of concert performances is set with players paid a prearranged fee or salary. The arts manager has little or no ability to intercede by changing the program to reduce the number of players required for a concert.

In the case of arts organizations, we seldom see the behavior exhibited by the theoretical supplier of concert tickets. The law of supply, as applied to this example, does not translate into the ticket supplier reducing the quantity of performances supplied. The idea of creating a shortage of supply is usually not a problem. In fact, if costs increase, the typical concert ticket seller would simply pass the cost along to the consumer in the form of a price increase. The other alternative is to go into debt by not charging enough to cover the costs of production. Ironically, this is what many nonprofit arts organizations do.

Number of Suppliers   The entertainment industry, taken as a whole, generally has a great many suppliers at various prices. The supplier of classical music concerts might be able to increase prices if a great number of alternative forms of entertainment disappeared. On the other hand, if you have the only performance available of a specific work with a special performer, you may be able to raise the price despite the number of suppliers in the entertainment industry. A "star" entertainer is a limited supply product that allows the arts organization to typically increase its price. A star and a single performance become a supply situation that may motivate the supplier to increase the price. It is not unheard of for producers of a special show featuring a "star" to sell tickets at $500 per seat.

Suppliers' Expectations   When establishing the quantity to produce, suppliers consider many different factors. For example, the concert supplier expects that this will be the final performance before the famous soloist retires and thus increases the number of concert performances and the ticket price.

Supply, Demand, and Revenue Maximization

One of your goals as an arts manager is to maximize revenue from your limited number of events. You need to seriously consider how much to charge for the event based on what your community is willing to pay. Your first source of information for pricing can be found in the other arts groups in your community. A little time spent analyzing the "competition" before setting your prices can help you find the right combination of prices for your arts offering. You must also consider all the other entertainment offerings in your community in your pricing strategies, including theme parks, festivals, first-run films, and so forth.

In Figure 10-2 you will see that if you set your price too high ($50 per ticket) or too low ($10 per ticket) you run the risk of making less revenue. Although revenue maximization is not typically the stated purpose of nonprofit arts organizations, the fact remains that there are people in the community who are willing to pay $50 for the ticket and others who are willing to pay only $10. In the end, it makes little sense to charge too much or too little for an arts event. Therefore, it should be a priority to master the art and science of setting admission prices. In the example given in Figure 10-2, the optimum price to charge is $22 per ticket based on selling 600 tickets.

What happens if you sell 900 tickets at $22? Obviously, you generate $19,800 in revenue, which one assumes is a good thing. However,

Ticket Price	Estimated Demand with 900-Seat Capacity	Revenue	Comments
$50	200	$10,000	
$46	225	$10,350	
$42	250	$10,500	
$38	300	$11,400	
$34	350	$11,900	
$30	400	$12,000	
$26	500	$13,000	**Range where ticket prices and demand generate maximum revenue.**
$22	600	$13,200	
$18	700	$12,600	
$14	800	$11,200	
$10	900	$9,000	

Figure 10-2   Price and Revenue Matrix

based on our very rudimentary discussion of demand and supply, it would make more sense to provide $50 tickets to the audience members willing to pay $50 and $10 to the people interested in the less costly tickets.

Figure 10-3 shows how you can scale ticket prices to match the supply of tickets at certain prices with the demand for those tickets. This example illustrates differential pricing or *scaling the house* using a 900-seat venue. If you were producing an event that was relatively inexpensive, you might be able to charge $14 and $22. Based on your estimated demand you might be able to generate $13,400 in gross sales. On the other hand, this same 900-seat venue could produce almost three times more revenue by pricing your tickets with four levels. The assumption is that there are a number of people who will want to see the event and are willing to pay $50 to sit in a good location. There is also an assumption that a larger number of people are willing to pay only $34 to see the same artists. Similar price differentials are used in

Revenue maximization using principles of supply and demand
Assumes 900-seat capacity

Ticket Prices	Quantity to Sell (Supply)	Revenue If Sold	Comment
$50	100	$5,000	Pricing based on $4 increments and
$42	150	$6,300	placing a premium on location.
$38	300	$11,400	Assumes a demand for more & less
$34	350	$11,900	expensive seats for the event.
TOTAL	900	$34,600	

OR

Ticket Prices	Quantity to Sell (Supply)	Revenue If Sold	Comment
$46	200	$9,200	Pricing based on $4 difference in top
$38	300	$11,400	prices and $8 difference with the lowest
$30	400	$12,000	priced ticket.
TOTAL	900	$32,600	

OR

Ticket Prices	Quantity to Sell (Supply)	Revenue If Sold	Comment
$22	600	$13,200	Pricing based on $16 difference
$38	300	$11,400	between low and high price.
TOTAL	900	$24,600	

OR

Ticket Prices	Quantity to Sell (Supply)	Revenue If Sold	Comment
$14	800	$11,200	Pricing based on customers looking
$22	100	$2,200	for a bargain. Assumes event costs
TOTAL	900	$13,400	are low.

Figure 10-3 Scaling Ticket Prices

the arts by increasing admissions on the weekends or discounting the admission on weekdays. For example, a museum may charge less Tuesday through Friday and more on the weekends. Depending on your project goals or the cost to produce the event, either pricing approach may be appropriate.

The price scaling of the house may also become a demand-increasing tactic that could have long-term benefits to an organization trying to build an audience. Economists refer to this as the *income effect*. In other words, a price reduction gives people more money to spend. When faced with a choice of paying a minimum ticket price of $34 or $50 for the same event, most people would rather make their dollar go further.

Although this is a simplification of the entire ticket-pricing process, it is a reminder that fundamental concepts in economics are part of the arts manager's job. Most arts organizations base their prices on a complex mix of financial need and educated guesses about what the market will bear. Seldom, if ever, do arts organizations respond to demand issues. For example, if you price tickets at $20 for an event and you sell out in the first day, you obviously underpriced the tickets. You may think you have just had a big success, when in fact you have in one respect failed by underpricing your product. You may also be making the error of not supplying enough of the arts product to satisfy demand. Conversely, if you priced the tickets at $50 and sold only 100 of 900 after six weeks, you overpriced the event. Either pricing decision creates problems for the organization.

Summary of Basic Arts Economics

The basic economic principles and theories discussed thus far in this chapter have a clear application to the arts. The relationship of the organization to the macroeconomic environment (the whole economy) and the conditions in the microeconomic environment (the markets) in which the organization operates should affect planning. Understanding the supply and demand issues facing the organization is critical. Being able to predict and control fixed and variable costs and being able to predict marginal costs and gains can help keep the organization from falling into financial trouble. Finally, it is important for nonprofit organizations to accept that the income gap is a fact of life. Strict cost-control strategies and plans can be adopted to minimize the negative consequences of this underlying problem. Now let us move on to the important business of managing the funds you do generate from sales, donations, and grants.

Overview of Financial Management

We have seen thus far that to manage an arts organization successfully one must understand something about economics. The financial management of the arts organization is the practice of applying many of the principles of economics to the day-to-day operation of the organization. The financial management, budgeting, and accounting system in an arts organization is in a sense the bridge between the economic environment and the operating budget.

In *Managing a Nonprofit Organization*, Thomas Wolf notes, "financial management is, for many, one of the most forbidding aspects of the administration of nonprofit organizations."[12] This is due in part to phobias about anything related to quantitative thinking. When faced with reviewing a budget or balance sheet, board members may develop a glazed look in their eyes and suddenly lose the ability to reason. Even worse, they may approve budgets and accept financial statements without fully understanding the numbers. Unfortunately, comprehension usually comes to the board of directors when it is too late to correct a financial problem that has been staring them in the face for months.

In this section we first develop an overview of financial management in profit and nonprofit organizations and then move on to the financial management information system. We integrate the whole system into the balance sheet and statement of account activity. Lastly, we develop a basic structure for the business management of the arts organization.

In many arts organizations, the responsibility for financial records, budgets, payroll, and money management falls to a business manager who works under the supervision of a general manager or managing director. In a smaller organization, an office manager who also acts as an accountant or bookkeeper may do the business management and the processing and record keeping. This person reports to the artistic director and the chair of the board of directors. As we saw in Chapter 9, "Organizational Controls and Budgets," many arts organizations do not start with a management information system (MIS). Instead, a system evolves as the organization grows. The same is true for the financial management of the organization. If it is to be effective, a *financial management information system* (FMIS) must be a comprehensive investment, reporting, control, and processing system that helps managers realize the financial objectives of the organization. The financial management of the organization is one of the manager's most important responsibilities. The long-term health of the enterprise depends on the arts manager's vigilance in monitoring the revenue, expenses, and investments of the organization.

Nonprofit Financial Management

Because the primary objective of most nonprofit arts organizations is not focused on increasing the wealth of the owners or stockholders, the financial manager's job is somewhat different than in the profit sector. A nonprofit organization is still a business, however, and it must collect as much or more revenue than it expends, or it will go out of business.

The financial manager's job in a nonprofit organization is critical to planning and using the limited resources available. For example, if the artistic director wants to add another show to the season, do a world premiere, or take a production on tour, how will the organization pay for this activity? Understanding the cash flow, current debt load, assets, and so on, is the first step in analyzing what can and cannot be done.

A good financial manager maximizes the use of the available resources. For example, funds raised through ticket sales or donations should be invested to generate further revenue. If an organization collects $200,000 from subscription sales for next season's shows, that money should be invested in interest-earning accounts before it is needed for the new season's operating budget. A financial manager also actively seeks out ways to minimize costs for insurance (health and life) and to reduce other operating costs.

Financial Management Information System (FMIS)

In Chapter 9, "Organizational Controls and Budgets," we learned that the management information system is responsible for gathering data,

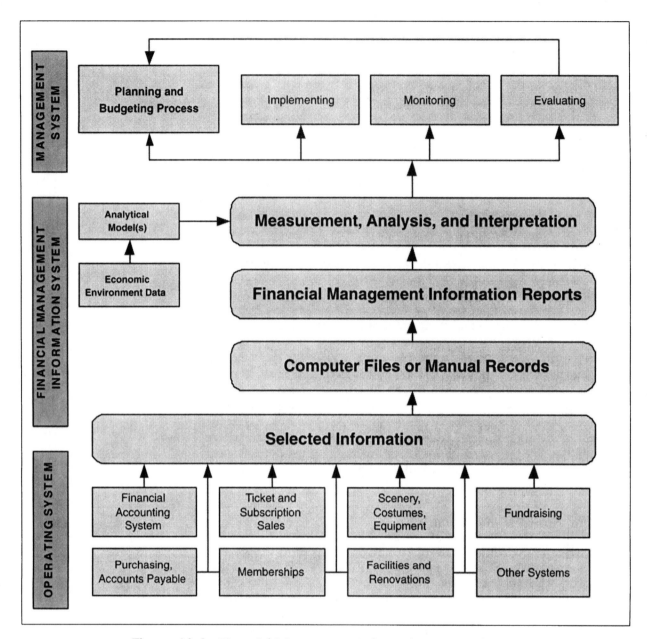

Figure 10-4   Financial Management Information System (FMIS)

Source: Frederick J. Turk and Robert P. Gallo, *Financial Management Strategies for Arts Organizations* (New York: American Council for the Arts, 1984). Copyright 1984 by the American Council for the Arts. Used with permission.

formulating information, and distributing it throughout the organization. The FMIS is a key part of the overall MIS. Figure 10-4 shows a schematic drawing of an FMIS.

The FMIS must ultimately provide the board of directors and management with accurate, timely, and relevant information based on the data that the system has gathered. Without this information, making decisions and planning will not work effectively. The questions are usually very simple: Did we spend more than we budgeted? Why? Did we raise less than we budgeted? Why? Did we increase or decrease our debt? Will we have sufficient resources to continue operating? Can we make the payroll?

If the system is working properly, the answers to these questions pose no problem for management. For the system to work properly, the operating system in Figure 10-4 must accurately gather the data needed to process the records. These data become the information used in reports and in the analysis of the current financial health of the organization. At the same time, the organization has specific legal responsibilities to report on its financial activities to various state and federal agencies. The FMIS must be capable of gathering and reporting this information if the organization is to retain its nonprofit legal status.

The FMIS serves two important purposes. It provides information about the fiscal health of the organization to people inside the organization, and it reports to external agencies, such as the IRS, and to granting agencies, such as the NEA and state and local arts councils.

Developing a Financial Management Information System

The financial management information system illustrated in Figure 10-4 requires that data from the operating system be transmitted to the records system. These data are then assembled in various reports used by the different departments in the operation. To report accurately on the fiscal activity of the organization, an accounting and record-keeping system must be in place. Figure 10-5 shows one version of an accounting system. In this case, the flow is from the top to the bottom of the page.

The personal computer and inexpensive accounting software have had a tremendous positive impact on arts organizations. Inexpensive systems are available to help small organizations quickly enter data and print reports. However, due to the nature of nonprofit businesses, different reporting formats are required when discussing how much the "business" is worth and how it is using its assets.

Accounting and Bookkeeping

Accounting is usually defined as identifying, collecting, analyzing, recording, and summarizing business transactions and their effects on a business. A *transaction*, which is a key element in this definition, is an exchange of property or services. *Bookkeeping* involves the clerical work of recording the transaction. In a sense, the accountant begins where the bookkeeper leaves off by summarizing and interpreting the records or books. In many cases, bookkeeping and accounting are done by the same person.

The Financial Accounting Standards Board (FASB) oversees the practices of the profession and regularly updates what is referred to as the generally accepted accounting principles (GAAP). Accounting has evolved its own specialized language to describe transaction activity. Let's look at a few key terms.

Cash-Based Accounting   A personal checking account is one example of a cash-based accounting system. You make a deposit, you write checks, and at the end of the month, you have a positive or negative balance. The major problem with the cash-based system is that it gives you no information about how much you are worth, how much you owe, or how much is owed by others to you. However, it is simple to keep this account, and many small organizations keep cash accounts to record their business activities.

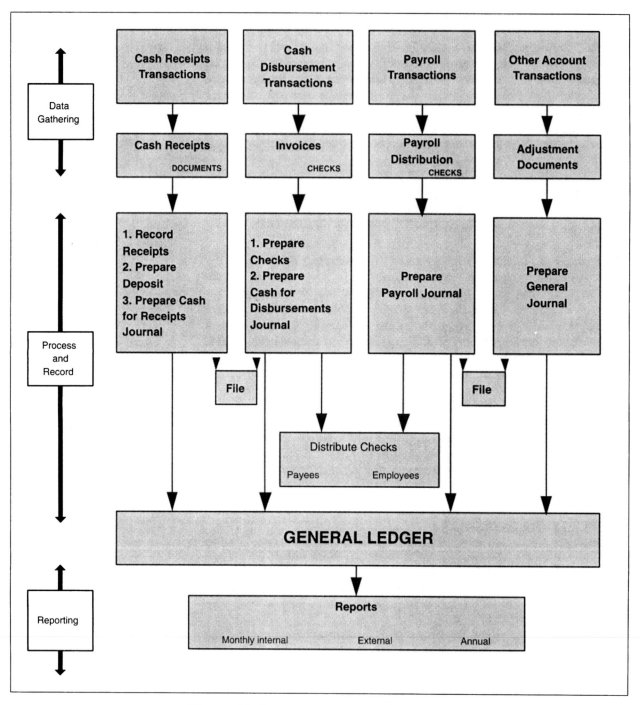

Figure 10-5 Accounting System Overview

Source: Frederick J. Turk and Robert P. Gallo, *Financial Management Strategies for Arts Organizations* (New York: American Council for the Arts, 1984). Copyright 1984 by the American Council for the Arts. Used with permission.

Accrual-Based Accounting   The accrual system recognizes expenses when they are incurred and income when it is committed. The primary advantage of this system is that it shows future commitments and how much money you owe. When you charge something to a credit card, for example, you are using an accrual system. You will have to make a future payment to an ongoing account in your name.

An organization typically opens charge accounts with several different local vendors. Office supplies, lumber, and paint are purchased with the understanding that the organization will pay for the materials when they are billed. For example, when $250 worth of office supplies are purchased from a local supplier, the $250 becomes a *payable*, and when the bill is paid, it becomes an *expense* item in the budget. A foundation grant for $5,000 awarded to the organization is called a *receivable*. When the check arrives and is deposited, it becomes *revenue*. The accounting system deducts the payables, adds the receivables, and arrives at the balance with which the organization will operate.

Fund-Based Accounting and Budgets   Because nonprofit organizations receive money in such forms of income as grants and gifts, the FASB has a special set of standards for nonprofit organizations to use to report the overall account activity. Fund accounting is a system of classifying resources into activities or projects so that each area can accurately report account activity during a fiscal year.

Frederick J. Turk and Robert P. Gallo note that "the fundamental principle in fund accounting is stewardship," and the "funds are accounted separately according to restrictions established by donors" or the board.[13] In Figure 9-8, for example, the theater company's activities related to the regular season, touring, education, and the building fund could all be established as fund accounts. Each account becomes a separate entity and may be designated as either a restricted or an unrestricted fund. A *restricted fund* is designed to control how the funds are used from a specific account. For example, if an organization has an endowment fund, the money received or expenses incurred will need special approval. In the project budget shown in Figure 9-8, the building fund could be a restricted account because gifts and expenses are intended for a specific purpose. In this example the theater company may decide to designate funds as "temporally restricted." This allows for the flexibility to use "restricted" funds to support other activities in the event of a financial emergency. The regular season fund, on the other hand, would be *unrestricted*, meaning that resources could be expended for a wide variety of organizational activities, as approved by the board. The revised financial accounting terminology used by the FASB now allows organizations to classify various fund accounts as restricted or unrestricted *net assets*. The term *net assets* is often used now in place of *fund balances* in financial statements.

The Accounting System Overview

To extract the information required for an effective FMIS, the accounting input must be as detailed as possible. Figure 10-5 shows how a typical system takes the input of cash receipts, invoices, payroll, and other documentation and processes the data to produce monthly external and annual reports.

When an organization establishes its accounting system, specific account numbers and designated subcodes are used to identify *liabilities* (money owed or funds committed) and *assets* (property or resources owned by the organization). When expenses are incurred, they are recorded as liabilities that reduce the organization's overall worth. When money is received in the form of revenues or gifts, it is classified as an asset that adds to the organization's overall worth.

The accounting system shown in Figure 10-5 identifies a data-gathering area where cash is received, checks are written (disbursement

Web Source for Financial Statements

An excellent source for financial information about arts organizations, including Form 990 tax reports on file for an arts organization, is www.Guidestar.com. This website presents this information in an easy to use format. When you arrive at the website, enter the arts organization name in the "Quick Search" box and select "Go." Typically, the search will bring up data with several options to select about financial information on the organization.

transactions), payroll is processed, and all other account activity takes place. A general ledger processes the four other journals (receipts, disbursements, payroll, and general journal) and allows reports to be assembled that provide the information required by management and the board.

Computers and software automate the bookkeeping to the point that the journal and ledgers are modules within the software. However, all accounting systems still generate a tremendous amount of paperwork. Check stubs, invoices, receipts, purchase orders, requisitions, credit card slips, and so forth, can quickly overwhelm an organization. Organizations are required to keep all of this documentation—it is sometimes called a *paper trail*—to complete an audit or a simple review by an outside accounting firm. Since most not-for-profit organizations file a Form 990 tax return with the IRS (required if you have an operating budget over $25,000) it is a good idea to review the categories of assets and liabilities used by the IRS when establishing your account system reports (IRS website: http://www.irs.gov/pub.irs-pdf/i990-e3.pdf). If nothing else, it will make it easier to transfer data when filing taxes each year.

Accounting Formula   The record-keeping system used in accounting is based on the simple formula that assets must equal the liabilities plus the net assets $(A = L + NE)$, and the net assets must equal the assets minus the liabilities $(NE = A - L)$. For example, an arts organization starts with $5,000 in cash. The accounting formula expresses this relationship as $5,000(A) = $0(L) + $5,000(NE)$. The assets total $5,000, and because no debts have been incurred, there is $0 in liabilities and $5,000 in net assets. (In the profit sector, the net asset would be called equity, and the formula would read $A = L + E$.)

The organization buys a computer system for $2,000 on credit. The business takes on a liability it must pay. The cash assets are reduced by $2,000 and the liabilities are increased by $2,000. To recalculate the net assets of the business, we apply the formula. In this case, we find a net asset balance of $3,000 by subtracting liabilities from assets $(NE = A - L)$.

Financial Statements

So far, we have been looking at accounting documentation from the FMIS that was designed for internal use by the staff and the board. These various budget reports do not tell us about the overall fiscal health of the organization. Does the organization have any money in the bank? How much does it owe in short or long-term debt? To locate this information, we need to review two standard reporting formats in the accounting system: the balance sheet and the statement of activity.

The example used in Figures 10-6 and 10-7 depicts a theater company that is in fairly good financial condition. As you will see, it has an excess of revenue over income and has funds to see it through some tough times.

Balance Sheet   The accounting profession typically refers to the balance sheet as a financial snapshot. This means that on the date the report was issued (usually June 30 or December 31), the balance sheet shows how much money the organization had and how much it was "worth" on that date.

The balance sheet shown in Figure 10-6 is an example of the $A = L + NE$ formula. The top half of the balance sheet details the current and

Balance Sheet as of June 30	**ASSETS = LIABILITIES + NET ASSETS**					
	Unrestricted Funds		**Temporally Restricted Funds**			
Assets	Operating Fund	Gala Fund	Building Fund	21st Century Fund	Current Year TOTAL	Last Year TOTAL
Cash	$70,812	$106,000	$100,000	$50,000	$326,812	$144,000
Accounts receivable	2,800	19,626	15,000	-	37,426	12,000
Shop equipment	25,000	0	0	0	25,000	22,000
less depreciation	(9,000)	0	0	0	(9,000)	(3,000)
Office equipment	25,000	0	0	0	25,000	20,000
less depreciation	(12,568)	0	0	0	(12,568)	(4,000)
Scenery & Costume inventory	35,000	0	0	0	35,000	40,000
TOTAL ASSETS	$137,044	$125,626	$115,000	$50,000	$427,670	$231,000
Liabilities						
Accounts payable	$47,299	$2,500	$0	$0	$49,799	$18,000
Accrued payroll and taxes	18,933	0	0	0	18,933	6,000
Bank notes payable	25,000	0	0	0	25,000	24,000
TOTAL LIABILITIES	$91,232	$2,500	$0	$0	$93,732	$48,000
Net Assets (Fund Balances)						
Unrestricted fund balances	$45,812	$123,126	$0	$0	$168,938	33,000
Temporally restricted fund balances	$0	$0	$115,000	$50,000	$165,000	150,000
TOTAL NET ASSETS	45,812	123,126	115,000	50,000	$333,938	$183,000
Total Liabilities & Net Assets	$137,044	$125,626	$115,000	$50,000	$427,670	$231,000

Figure 10-6 Theater Company Balance Sheet

previous years' total assets as of June 30. The bottom half of the sheet shows the organization's liabilities and net assets (fund balances). On this day, June 30 of the current fiscal year, the organization had $326,812 in cash, $37,426 in accounts receivable, and so forth. In comparison to the previous year ("Last Year TOTAL" in the far right column) the organization had $144,000 in cash and $12,000 in accounts receivable. The total assets for the current year were $427,670 and $231,000 the previous year. Therefore, the organization increased its assets in the current year.

The liabilities that the organization incurred also increased. The company has higher liability for the accounts it owes (accounts payable) and it owes $25,000 for a bank note (a loan) it took out during the year. The company has good news in its various net assets or fund balances accounts. All the funds (Operating, Gala, Building, and 21st Century) were positive at the end of the current year. Overall, the total net assets increased from $183,000 to $333,938.

Statement of Activity
The second of the financial reports is the statement of activity and changes in net assets. The example shown in Figure 10-7 makes it clear

As of June 30

Revenue	Unrestricted Funds		Temporally Restricted Funds		Current Year TOTAL	Last Year TOTAL
	Operating Fund	Gala Fund	Building Fund	21st Century Fund		
Ticket Sales	1,475,000	0	0	0	$1,475,000	$1,425,826
Other Income	198,200	5,000	0	0	$203,200	$198,522
Donations	567,000	305,000	65,000	43,000	$980,000	$895,636
Grants	142,000	0	0	0	$142,000	$125,000
Total Revenue	$ 2,382,200	$ 310,000	$ 65,000	$ 43,000	$2,800,200	$2,644,984
Expenses						
Staff Salaries	1,602,511	30,250	7,600	0	$1,640,361	$1,510,963
Productions	139,669	0	0	0	$139,669	$142,895
Marketing	537,000	5,522	0	0	$542,522	$535,892
Development	87,942	65,000	10,000	0	$162,942	$154,258
Special Events	9,000	107,000	12,000	0	$128,000	$135,259
Concessions	35,858	0	0	0	$35,858	$27,891
Gift Shop	4,935	1,500	0	0	$6,435	$7,259
Occupancy	70,352	0	0	0	$70,352	$64,895
Contingency	30,061	3,500	0	0	$33,561	$28,569
Total Expense	$ 2,517,328	$ 212,772	$ 29,600	0	$2,759,700	$2,607,881
Changes in Net Assets (Fund Balances)						
	-$135,128	$97,228	$35,400	$43,000	$40,500	$37,103
Net Assets - Beginning of Year						
	$80,940	$125,898	$79,600	$7,000	$293,438	$145,897
Board Designated Fund Transfers						
	100,000	(100,000)	0	0	$0	$0
Net Assets - End of Year						
	$45,812	$123,126	$115,000	$50,000	$333,938	$183,000

Figure 10-7 Statement of Activity and Changes in Net Assets—Theater Company

where the operating fund deficit came from and what changes took place in the net assets or fund balances. This sheet has a more direct connection to the budget and depicts the annual revenue and expenses for the organization. The breakdown of revenue and expenses allows the reader to see how the organization arrived at its financial condition at the end of its fiscal year and to compare these figures to the previous year.

The revenue section tells us how much money came in to the organization from various sources. In comparison to last year, the overall revenue rose by $155,216 (total of $2,800,200), and expenses increased by $151,819 (total of $2,759,700). Upon closer examination you can see that the operating fund ended the year with a $135,128 deficit. In other words, the expenses exceeded the revenues attributed to the operating fund. The other funds ended with a positive balance (expenses minus revenues, or "Changes in Net Assets"). The operating fund ended the year with a positive balance of $45,812 due to a transfer of $100,000 from the Gala Fund. Internal transfers of this type are typically done with the approval of the board and the accountants.

The overall good news for the theater company is that it ended the year with net assets of $333,938, up from $183,000 the previous year. Although the company does not have an endowment account, it has a building fund and what has been designated a 21st Century Fund. Both of the funds are modest (they total $165,000: $115,000 in the Building Fund and $50,000 in the 21st Century Fund), but they represent a little insurance for the organization. However, if a serious financial situation arose (a significant drop in single ticket and subscriptions sales), these fund balances would represent a small percentage of the overall operating budget.

Ratio Analysis   Ratio analysis is a quick way of examining the organization's balance sheet and statement of activity. For demonstration purposes two ratios have been selected. Figure 10-8 compares two key indicators of the theater company's fiscal health. In our example, the *ratio of expendable assets to total liabilities* has declined in the current season. Turk and Gallo recommend that organizations have at least a 1:1 ratio of assets to liabilities. The balance sheet for the theater company shows that assets exceed liabilities by a good margin in the current year (3.89:1 versus 3.25:1). In this example the increase in the ratio from 3.25 tells a manager and board member that they are doing well managing their liabilities. The example shows that liabilities increased from $48,000 the previous year to $93,732 this year. However, the cash on hand also increased significantly, and the manager and board maintained a healthy ratio of debt to assets.

The *ratio of expendable net assets* (fund balances) to total expenses for the current year is 0.121, up from 0.070 the year before. This ratio is a measure of how well the organization is doing at building its financial base. Turk and Gallo suggest that this ratio should be closer to 0.3:1. For the theater company to achieve that ratio it would have to increase its net assets to over $800,000 in relation to its expenses in the current year. In this case, the organization could do better building its cash reserves.

Problem Areas   If, as a member of the board of directors of the theater company you read the cash flow projections (Figure 9-9), balance sheet, and statement of activity, what would be your reaction? A board member might want to ask about the increasing accounts payable (Figure 10-6). The reports also show that operating expenses exceed revenue (Figure 10-7). The total net assets of the organization increased by $150,938 (Figure 10-8, $333,938 − $183,000 = $150,938), but the net assets are still a smaller ratio of expenses than is desirable.

The immediate problems facing the theater company include balancing the operating budget and better controlling its cash flow (see Figure 9-9). Continued overexpenditures in the operating fund will only erode the financial health of the organization. It will be very difficult to build an endowment if funds have to be constantly transferred to the operating fund to offset deficits. As a board member or a manager for this organization it is important to solve these problems, because in the long run the ability of the organization to attempt new programs or enhance existing operations will be hampered by these financial problems.

Investment

One of the most important responsibilities of a financial manager in a nonprofit arts organization is to work with the board of directors to

1. Ratio of Expendable Assets to Total Liabilities

Expendable Assets

Total Liabilities

Current Year			**Last Year**		
Cash	326,812		Cash	144,000	
Accts Receivable	37,426		Accts Receivable	12,000	
Assets $	364,238	= 3.89	Assets $	156,000	= 3.25
Liabilities $	93,732		Liabilities $	48,000	

Comment: In the current year the organization had fewer liabilities in relation to its assets. The ratio of expendable assets to total liabilities is therefore greater.

2. Ratio of Expendable Net Assets to Total Expenses

Expendable Net Assets

Total Expenses

Current Year			**Last Year**		
Net Assets	333,938	= 0.121	Net Assets	183,000	= 0.070
Expenses	2,759,700		Expenses	2,607,881	

Comment: In the current year the organization increased its net assets in a higher ratio to expenses than in the previous year.

Figure 10-8   Ratio Analysis—Theater Company

develop investment strategies that will help ensure the survival of the enterprise. The fiduciary responsibility, or trusteeship, of the organization's resources is the fundamental role of the board of directors. To exercise this fiduciary responsibility, the board must have accurate information about the assets and liabilities of the organization. At the same time, a finance committee should work with the financial manager to seek out ways to maximize the assets available. The management of the various fund balances of the organization must be monitored closely by the board.

In *Financial Management Strategies for Arts Organizations*, Turk and Gallo detail the best way to approach the asset management of the organization.[14] Their suggestions include developing a system for managing the cash available to the organization. Cash control can be realized through limiting access to cash accounts, timing the payment of bills, and closely monitoring the organization's accounts receivable. They recommend that the organization invest in a mix of short-term interest-earning instruments, such as certificates of deposits (CDs), Treasury bills (T bills), and money market funds. The objective of short-term investment is to maximize the interest-rate return while maintaining quick access to the funds should an emergency arise.

The board of directors also needs a long-term investment policy. One strategy is to take a conservative approach and invest in a variety of well-known stocks and bonds. Higher risk investments will usually provide greater returns, but board guidance is necessary to ensure that the financial manager invests the organization's assets safely.

Finally, Turk and Gallo urge managers to monitor the fixed assets of the organization, including inventories and expensive capital equipment and property. Maintaining sufficient insurance for equipment, inventories, and buildings helps minimize the financial risk to the organization if a disaster strikes.

Another approach that an organization might adopt would be to establish another business to supplement its cash flow. "In the News" describes several ventures undertaken by arts groups.

In the News

In the business world diversification can bring new revenues to the enterprise. This article points up how the financial planning for arts organizations could be affected by operating additional businesses.

Beyond the Box Office: Arts Groups Find New Ways to Generate Income
Vince Stehle

In recent years, leaders of nonprofit arts groups have heard a constant refrain from their supporters in the business and foundation worlds: Become more self-reliant by becoming more entrepreneurial.

For some groups that have answered the call, the experience has been profitable. But others have found that running a business is easier said than done. For them, the lure of big profits has led to wasted efforts, lost money, and disillusionment.

Some of the most successful ventures by arts groups have involved little more than an expansion of long-standing mercantile enterprises, such as museum stores, or branching out into areas that they know best—like the Portland Opera, which has been applying the ex-

pertise it gained in presenting classical opera to become the largest presenter of touring Broadway shows in Oregon. Last year, the opera earned more than $100,000 through such shows.

But several arts groups have created, bought, or even been given for-profit businesses that fall farther afield from their main pursuits.

In most cases, the arts groups hope that the money they earn from those business ventures will help them further their artistic missions. But many of the ventures have a second bottom line that is more difficult to measure: building audiences.

Even so, some in the nonprofit world worry that the distraction of running a business is too much for many nonprofit groups, and will cause traditional marketing and fund-raising activities to suffer.

"The most important thing is to make sure you are operating at capacity," says Cynthia Massarsky, president of CWM Marketing Group in Tenafly, N.J. For instance, before a theater group contemplates opening up a high-technology consulting firm, she says, it should make sure it is doing everything it can to sell all of its tickets.

[Examples of some of the ventures include:]

- In San Francisco, the profits of a cutting-edge information-technology company called the Content Group are used to underwrite experimental theater.
- In Seattle, a classical-music radio station is owned by an arts consortium. And Opera America, a Washington, D.C., association of opera organizations, recently bought a catalogue company that sells opera recordings and other merchandise, even though the group had never run a private business before.
- In New York, the nonprofit group Art Matters devoted a large amount of its human and financial resources to building a successful and critically acclaimed art catalogue—only to see its investment go down the drain after the group was unable to attract adequate funds to keep the enterprise going.

Summary of Financial Management

It is important to remember that the FMIS is a tool designed to help the organization fulfill its mission. Maximizing revenue, building the endowment, controlling cash flow, and conducting ratio analyses are important, but these activities should not be the organization's controlling force. The primary objective of the FMIS is to support the organization in achieving its mission and artistic goals. If the FMIS is working effectively, it should help, not hinder, goal achievement. It should also be remembered that the system is only as good as the people who use it. Inexperienced or poor management, not the FMIS, usually leads an organization into a financial crisis.

For example, if the artistic director insists that the only way to attain a high level of production quality is to build the costumes and sets in the company's own shops, it is the financial manager's responsibility to explain how much this will cost. If it can be done with the resources available in the short and long run and the board approves the idea, then it should be done. If the organization cannot afford to build its own costumes and sets, the financial manager has an obligation to say so. Unfortunately, this scenario is not always followed. Instead, either the manager cannot stand up to the artistic director, or the cost analysis is done without a real understanding of the organization's fixed and variable costs. When poor management is combined with a lack of understanding about the fiscal health of the organization, even the most sophisticated FMIS will not help.

Managing Finances and the Economic Dilemma

Without cash coming in, there is little chance that the show will go on or that the exhibit will open. The noble artists and staff can come to the rescue by working for free or for half pay once in a while, but in the long run, trying to operate an arts organization by using a crisis financial management technique will spell doom. Limited productivity and ever-increasing labor costs mean that all arts organizations must adapt a flexible plan to keep up with the income gap. For example, if we take our hypothetical theater company's budget for $2,800,200 and project the budget for five years with a 3 percent per year increase to allow for inflation, the budget will grow to $3,246,200. Finding the additional $446,000 in revenue to offset expenses will be daunting, especially if ticket prices are not raised each year. In reality, the cost increases that the company will face will probably exceed 3 percent per year. Salaries, artist fees, construction materials, rents, and so on, will all increase at rates that are very difficult to project accurately.

Without careful planning, the organization will be susceptible to this familiar cycle: a growing deficit leads to a budget crisis, followed by a high-visibility fundraising campaign and a last-minute rescue by a group of donors.

These realities make it all the more important for arts organizations to have at least a five-year plan that establishes expense and revenue projections. Longer-range plans make sense for organizations with very high fixed costs, such as museums. Changing economic conditions require that arts managers and board members revise the financial plans at least every year. In times of recession or when inflation rates begin to exceed 6 percent per year, organizations may need to revise the long-term plans every quarter.

Reserve Funds

The question of how much should be set aside for reserves is not easy to answer. As we have seen, most arts organizations operate with a very thin margin between the cash coming in and the expenses going out. As you will also see in Chapter 12, "Fundraising," donors prefer giving to financially healthy organizations. A donor does not want to see his or her money being used to support an organization that does not know how to manage its resources. However, since most arts organizations start out undercapitalized (i.e., with insufficient startup funds) the cycle of cash flow shortages usually plagues many arts groups. Controlling costs and not being overly optimistic about ticket sales still remain the best strategies for cash-poor organizations. However, also setting a goal to have "rainy day" funds—that will allow the organization to remain solvent if there were a 25 percent drop in revenue in two consecutive years—would be prudent. For example, the sample theater company used in this chapter should have about $1.4 million in net assets (unrestricted fund balances) to see it through two seasons of poor sales and weak fundraising.

Looking Ahead

In the next two chapters, we study various approaches to maximizing the financial resources needed to realize the organization's goals and objectives through marketing and fundraising. We will look at how the key areas of marketing and fundraising relate to the FMIS of the organization.

Questions

1. Summarize the key findings in the Baumol and Bowen study of the economics of the arts.

2. Give two examples of economies of scale that could be applied to an arts organization's daily operation.

3. List three reasons why an arts organization may not price the admission fees high enough to cover costs.

4. What are the key components of an FMIS?

5. What are the three major responsibilities of a financial manager in a for-profit business?

6. Why is it better for organizations to have unrestricted, rather than restricted, net assets?

7. What is the accounting formula, and what does it reveal about an organization's fiscal health?

8. Using the formula in Figure 10-8, solve for the ratio of expendable assets to total liabilities and expendable fund balances to total expense and explain whether the organization has a financial problem or not. The organization has $250,000 in expendable assets, $125,000 in total liabilities, $1.25 million in expendable net assets, and $225,000 in total expenses at the end of a fiscal year.

Creating a Financial Report

Case Study

In order to better understand how a financial report is developed please read the following description and respond to the five questions immediately following.

Dance Company Financial Report

The Wing and a Prayer Dance Company just finished its third season of operation. The company performs four weekends, distributed across one weekend each in October, December, February, and April. They perform from Thursday to Saturday in a 1,000-seat theater. The single ticket prices are $10 and $16, and the series subscription prices to the four weekends are $32 and $52. During this last season, 60 percent of the subscriptions were sold at $52. The single ticket revenue was distributed through sales of 55 percent for the $16 tickets and 45 percent for the $10 tickets.

Statement of Activity and Changes in Net Assets

Revenue   This year, the company was able to generate $99,950 in revenue. They sold $30,000 in single tickets and $39,855 in subscriptions. They received a grant from the state arts council for $10,000 and donations of $13,545. They raised $6,550 from a benefit dinner.

Expenses   The expenses for the year totaled $96,450. The total was distributed in the following manner: $25,500 for salaries and benefits, $30,000 for guest artist fees, $2,400 for the office, $6,450 for travel, $7,800 for marketing, $15,000 for productions, $1,800 for utilities, $6,500 in mortgage payments, and $1,000 for miscellaneous expenses.

Net Assets   They had net assets of $11,500 in their operating fund at the beginning of the year, and $1,500 in a restricted endowment fund.

Balance Sheet

Assets   According to the bookkeeper for the company, the year ended with $79,400 in total liabilities and net assets. The unrestricted assets were made up of the following: $13,800 in cash, $1,200 in accounts receivable, $2,500 in prepaid expenses (deposits they made), a $13,000 inventory of scenery and costumes. Their temporarily restricted assets included $1,500 in a restricted endowment fund, and $47,400 in a restricted account for land and a building.

Liabilities   The unrestricted liabilities were listed as $500 in accounts payable, $15,000 in a loan due to the bank, and the $23,000 in restricted liabilities was from balance due on the mortgage. The total liability was $38,500.

Questions

1. Prepare an annual financial report for the dance company, showing the information above in the standard form of a Balance Sheet and a Statement of Activity (Figures 10-6 and 10-7).
2. Based on the balance sheet you created, what is the change in the dance company's net assets? Did net assets increase or decrease this year?

3. Assuming that cash, accounts receivable, and prepaid expenses are totaled to make expendable assets, what is the ratio of assets to total liabilities? What does this figure tell you about the company's financial condition? (See Figure 10-8 for ratios.)

4. Based on a total of 12,000 seats (a 1,000-seat theater times four weekends times three performances per weekend), what was the average number of tickets sold per performance by the dance company?

5. What is the percentage of total income earned through sales versus the total amount from donations, grants, and other sources?

References

1. William J. Baumol and William G. Bowen, *Performing Arts: The Economic Dilemma* (Cambridge, MA: MIT Press, 1966).
2. James Heilbrun and Charles M. Gray, *The Economics of Art and Culture*, 2nd ed. (Cambridge, England: Cambridge University Press, 2001), p. 18.
3. Ibid., p. 20.
4. Ibid., p. 20.
5. Ibid., p. 21.
6. Ibid., p. 43.
7. Ibid., p. 47.
8. Roger N. Waud, *Economics*, 3rd ed. (New York: Harper and Row, 1986), p. 503.
9. Ibid., p. 514.
10. Ibid., p. 70.
11. Ibid., p. 72.
12. Thomas Wolf, *Managing a Nonprofit Organization* (Englewood Cliffs, N.J.: Prentice-Hall, 1990), p. 139.
13. Frederick J. Turk and Robert P. Gallo, *Financial Management Strategies for Arts Organizations* (New York: American Council for the Arts, 1984), p. 102.
14. Ibid., pp. 141–154.

11

□ □ □ □ □

Marketing and the Arts

In these troubled times, arts organizations everywhere must learn new ways to attract the resources they need to sustain their mission and quality. Arts organizations must improve their skills in increasing and broadening their audience base, improving accessibility to various art forms, and learning how to better meet the needs of specific audience segments and contributors.

Philip Kotler and Joanne Scheff, *Standing Room Only*

An arts manager must plan, organize, implement, and evaluate various marketing and fundraising strategies in an effort to maximize revenue to meet the organization's established objectives. There can be enormous satisfaction in seeing a full house, a packed museum, or the groundbreaking for the building made possible by the efforts of a well-designed marketing or fundraising campaign. However, we will also see that no amount of managerial brilliance or sophisticated marketing efforts will amount to much if the basic product does not meet the needs of the consumers for whom it is intended. It is important to remember that, like a management information system or a computer, marketing and fundraising are nothing more than tools. Marketing and fundraising cannot make a bad script good or a weak performance strong. At best, marketing and fundraising can help support a long-lasting relationship between the individual consumer and the organization. If properly managed, this relationship can evolve, and the consumer can grow from a single-ticket buyer to a subscriber or member and finally to an annual supporter. Unfortunately, this operational objective is much easier said than done.

In the United States today, it is almost impossible to avoid the efforts of someone trying to sell you something every day. We are bombarded with thousands of messages every week in the form of television commercials, newspaper and magazine advertisements, flyers and letters in the mail, junk E-mail, or phone calls from total strangers. Thousands of new consumer products are released in the market every year. Billions of dollars and millions of hours of labor are expended on product research, design, and distribution.

Promotional activities related to the profit sector of the entertainment industry relentlessly let us know that a new film is opening, a new book is coming out, the ice show is in town, or a new ride is starting at the theme park. The escalating mixture of media blitz, promotional hype, and advertising competitiveness used to get the consumer's attention does not leave a great deal of room for low-budget local arts organizations to make an impact. For example, it is not unusual for a movie studio to spend more money advertising one new film than a major arts organization has in its operating budget for an entire year. An article in the *New York Times Magazine* pointed out that the film industry "budgets $35 million on advertising [per film], and anywhere from $250,000 to $750,000 on trailers alone."[1]

As we have seen, the economic environment in which arts organizations must function requires constant effort to find the resources to survive from year to year. The need to retain and increase the number of subscribers, ticket buyers, members, or donors also places an enormous amount of pressure on the arts manager. Arts managers with expertise and a successful record of managing marketing and fundraising campaigns are very much in demand. However, because organizations depend so heavily on revenues generated from sales, a decline in income may cause once-successful managers to find themselves suddenly unemployed.

An Event in Search of an Audience

No matter how lofty the aesthetic aims of an organization, without the regular support of an audience, patrons, or members, there will not be enough money coming in to keep the enterprise alive. In other words, there must be enough demand for the product, or the enterprise will be out of business.

Before the advent of "marketing," arts organizations had a fairly standard set of activities that they undertook in an effort to create enough demand for a show or an exhibit. A press release announcing the upcoming event was sent to the local papers (a photo or two may have accompanied the release) and posters were put up wherever they were allowed. Flyers were sometimes distributed, a few very small advertisements were placed in the paper, and a low-cost brochure was mailed out to names on the mailing list. If the organization was lucky, a preview article might appear in the arts section of the local paper. Organizations with larger budgets placed bigger ads in the paper, and they sometimes ran a few radio or television commercials.

Many managers and board members wondered why, after the term *marketing* came into vogue, their arts organization continued to do the same things but spent twice as much money to get the same audience. What happened was that organizations were really not engaged in marketing. They were still trying to sell events in a scattershot method to an ill-defined public. As a result, they wasted a great deal of money trying to convince people to buy their product without really knowing to whom they were selling. Spending more on advertising, in this case, was wasted money and effort.

As we see in this chapter, real marketing requires that the organization adapt and change its fundamental perceptions about its relationship to consumers. Marketing requires the adoption of a customer-orientated perspective that is often unfortunately perceived as being incompatible with the fundamental mission of high-culture arts organizations. Selling, on the other hand, which is what most organizations do, means that the organization tries to get the consumer to buy the product because it believes the product is inherently good and would be beneficial to the consumer.

A Means to an End

No matter what term is applied to the energy and resources used to find, develop, and keep an audience or membership base, these activities are still only a means to an end. Philip Kotler and Joanne Scheff noted in their definitive text, *Standing Room Only*, that we must view marketing as "a *means* for achieving the organization's goals, and using marketing and being customer-centered should never be thought of as the goal in itself."[2]

Let us now look more closely at the definition of marketing and many of the key concepts inherent in this vital area of study.

Marketing Principles and Terms

A key part of any arts organization's strategic plan is how it plans to market itself. The marketing plan normally forms a major section in the foundation of an organization's strategic approach to its long-term growth. We will see how the term *marketing* is often used incorrectly to describe various promotional activities that organizations undertake.

The American Marketing Association's definition of marketing is "the process of planning and executing the conception, pricing, promotion and distribution of ideas, goods, and services to create exchanges that satisfy individual and organizational objectives."[3]

Needs and Wants

The marketer strives to achieve a match between human wants and needs and the products and services that can satisfy them. Theoretically, the better the match of wants and needs, the greater the satisfaction. Marketers define a *need* as "something lacking that is necessary for a person's physical, psychological, or social well-being."[4] Charles D. Schewe's textbook notes that food, shelter, and clothing are universal needs. Psychological needs (such as knowledge, achievement, and stability) and social needs (such as esteem, status, or power) are shaped by the overall value system of the culture.

A *want* is defined as "something that is lacking that is desirable or useful."[5] Wants are intrinsic to an individual's personality, experience, and culture. You may have a need for knowledge, but you want to pursue an idea from a specific book. You need to eat, but you want a particular brand of pizza.

When you have needs and wants to satisfy, two other marketing principles come into play: *functional satisfaction* and *psychological satisfaction*. When we purchase an item like a refrigerator, we achieve a functional satisfaction because of the tangible features of the product. When we purchase a car, we may satisfy a functional need, but a particular make and model may provide an intangible psychological satisfaction for recognition or esteem.

Obviously, functional satisfaction and psychological satisfaction are not neutral terms. Americans have attitudes about products that have been shaped by advertisements on television and radio and in print. Accordingly, the "goal of (the) marketers (is) to gain a competitive edge by providing greater satisfaction."[6] Unfortunately for many consumers, the idea that a fine arts event could provide a degree of satisfaction is foreign. In many cases, arts organizations do not even see their mission as providing satisfaction to customers. After all, in the minds of those inside an arts organization, a symphony concert is not a mass consumer product like soft drinks or toothpaste. However, the reality is that arts organizations function in a highly competitive entertainment market. Ultimately, if the symphony concert does not provide some degree of satisfaction to audience members, they will not continue to purchase the product.

Exchange Process and Utilities

Wants and needs are satisfied through the process of *exchange*, which occurs when "two or more individuals, groups, or organizations give to each other something of value in order to receive something of value. Each party must want to exchange, believe that what is received is more valuable than what is given up, and be able to communicate with the other parties."[7]

For example, suppose that you want to hear a piano recital, and the pianist wants to perform. You believe that the time you are spending listening to the artist and the money you give up for the ticket are worth the exchange. The pianist believes that the fee and the satisfaction derived from playing will be personally rewarding. The performance and the recognition of applause form the communication to complete the exchange process. Performers sometimes forget just how important this final communication really is for the audience. The level of satisfaction felt is greatly diminished when the performer walks off the stage without acknowledging the audience.

The exchange process depends on four utilities that marketers have identified as form, time, place, and possession. The utilities interact as part of the exchange process in ways that promote or hinder the final exchange or transaction.

The *form utility* simply means the "satisfaction a buyer receives from the physical characteristics of the product."[8] Attributes such as style, color, shape, and function affect the exchange. Arts organizations that have gift shops must be very sensitive to this utility because the customers usually have fairly sophisticated tastes, and filling the shop with cheap products will do more harm than good for the organization. Unique, high-quality items may provide the organization with a chance to build a strong bond with the discriminating buyer.

Except for the printed program, a performance does not offer any form utility. The live performance is, as we all know, an intangible event. However, the psychological satisfaction gained from the event can form a powerful bond between the audience and the organization. The memories that trigger emotional and intellectual responses in relation to a particular performance or exhibit can help build a lifelong relationship between the arts organization and the consumer.

The *time* and *place utilities*, which involve "being able to make the products or services available when and where the consumer wants them,"[9] have a direct impact on arts organizations. Arts organizations usually have little flexibility when it comes to time and place. The customer has the choice of either coming to the performance at a specific time and a specific place or not seeing it at all. Experimenting with different performance schedules or locations or different exhibit hours may offer arts organizations occasional opportunities to increase consumer access to their products. However, the live performing arts, by their very nature, will always be limited in their manipulation of the time and place utilities. The advent of television and home videotaping offers a way of partially overcoming the inherent limitations of the live performance. *Live from the Met* broadcasts, for example, have provided a way for opera to reach audiences that would never be able to attend a production in New York City. Art museums have experimented with different programming and exhibit schedules. (See "In the News—A Customer Orientation" later in this chapter.)

The *possession utility*, which refers to "the satisfaction derived from using or owning the product,"[10] has some application in the live performing arts. The tangible items offered by the organization can create a degree of consumer satisfaction in much the same way that the form utility did. For example, long-time subscribers often view the seats they regularly sit in as their possessions. For two or three hours on a given night, they do indeed possess those seats. Allowing subscribers to keep their seats each year can be a powerful tool for maximizing on the possession utility. It is also possible to reinforce the experience of having attended through the secondary means of selling souvenir programs or other related material.

As we have seen, the exchange process for consumers of arts products and services fits within the theoretical framework of basic marketing principles. As part of an arts organization's core strategic planning, it makes sense for the staff and the board to spend time asking very fundamental questions about exactly what they are offering to the public. For example, how does the organization's corporate structure and philosophy affect its relationship with its audience? Do its programs and activities satisfy the wants and needs of the audience? What mechanisms are in place to get feedback from the audiences about the organization's programming?

If the organization is to survive, it must be able to adapt to and plan for changing conditions in the marketplace. "*Strategic market planning* is a managerial process of developing and implementing a match between market opportunities (i.e., unsatisfied wants and needs) and the resources of the firm."[11] This process is not exclusive to the profit sector. One need only look at the necessary changes that nonprofit hospitals have made in the mix of services they offer in the last decade to see how essential organizational adaptability is.

Evolution of Modern Marketing

Marketing has moved through three eras in its evolution. It is important to note that although these phases represent a progression, many organizations still hold to attitudes and beliefs about their product or service that have not changed much in 75 years. As a result, there are no clean breaks in this evolutionary development.

The first era is tied to the production and manufacturing techniques that began with the industrial revolution in the eighteenth century.[12] The main emphasis up through the beginning of the twentieth century was on fulfilling the basic needs of consumers. Mass production techniques dictated an approach of making assumptions about what the consumer wanted and then manufacturing the product in the most cost-effective way. The theory was that consumers would buy whatever was manufactured.

During the second era, more attention was focused on sales of the mass-produced products. The rise of the salesperson as a dominant figure in a system of getting goods to consumers is a part of the American myth. The period after the Civil War was marked by economic growth and expansion. Masses of immigrants came to the United States, which also fueled rapid growth. Thousands of salespeople spread out over the country, trying to sell products to people whether they wanted them or not.

The marketing era, the third era, is an outgrowth of the diversification of consumer wants and needs that resulted from the demands of unprecedented growth in the economy after World War II. More companies began to pay attention to what consumers were saying about the available products. The idea of a consumer-driven economy meant that companies needed to consider their basic relationship with the consumer. The research and testing of products and the application of psychological theories about purchase behavior led to a greater emphasis on developing a long-term relationship with the consumer.

Modern Marketing

By the 1990s, the concepts of marketing had been applied in just about every segment of profit and nonprofit business in the United States, including the use of marketing as a tool for electing candidates to office. The use of computers to store massive amounts of information about consumer preferences and to provide almost instant feedback to companies about what is selling has revolutionized the marketing industry. The ability to track sales via *point-of-purchase systems* offers marketers immediate access to information about what people are buying. The ubiquitous bar code now gives the store and the suppliers up-to-the-minute sales information about what people are buying. The rise of the Internet in the 1990s expanded the reach of marketers through E-mail and websites. Online sales activity, including services such as Tickets.Com or Ticketmaster, has revolutionized the process of buying a ticket to an event, concert, or film.

The proliferation of products designed to satisfy consumer needs and wants has led to an explosion of specialty goods and services. A journey to the supermarket provides evidence of products designed to meet special health and nutritional concerns. In fact, the reality of global marketing has led companies to use satellite communications to monitor worldwide sales and to make adjustments in production much more rapidly.

Marketing and Entertainment

A news article entitled "Off the Street and Into the Audience: Tourists Help Pick Fall TV Schedule"[13] provided an accurate description of the degree to which the commercial entertainment industry is committed to consumer feedback. People were asked to watch pilots of television shows and rate them with a hand-held counter that registered whether they liked what they were seeing. Writers, directors, and producers are not always happy with the prospect of their shows being subjected to this simplistic evaluation system.

The commercial film industry uses test screenings and similar audience feedback methods to find out what people like or dislike. Films may be edited or even reshot if there are negative reactions at a test screening. Theme parks do extensive surveying to get feedback about rides, exhibits, and services. The economic pressure to have a hit in the entertainment industry will no doubt lead to the application of more intensive prescreening and testing. (See the Case Study at the end of this chapter for an opinion about surveying audiences.)

It is easy to see why there is so much suspicion about the place of marketing in the high-culture industry. As we will see, there are limits to how much consumer feedback is practical and how consumer-oriented an organization can be. For most arts organizations, being totally consumer driven in the choice of programs and presentations remains a totally alien concept.

Marketing Approaches

A company attempting to make a profit usually has different values and goals than a local nonprofit health care center or symphony, but both rely on establishing a positive relationship with individual consumers and the general public. Both private and public sector companies make plans and state their missions based on satisfying the public's wants and needs. The mission statement is the source of the organization's goals and strategic plans. The planning process includes defining the function of marketing in the organization. First, let us look at two approaches to marketing used by a great many arts organizations and then focus on customer-oriented marketing.

Product Orientation

Kotler and Scheff characterize the *product orientation* as one in which the organization believes that "consumers will favor those products that offer the most quality, performance, and features."[14] They cite as examples "a chamber music association that calls itself a 'society,' performs only traditional music, advertises in only a suburban weekly and doesn't understand why it doesn't attract a younger audience."[15] Other examples might be colleges and universities that continue to offer courses that are evaluated as being below standard or for which there is very low enrollment, or museums that feature specific works of art from the collection even when there is little public interest in the exhibit. Product-oriented organizations "have a love affair with their products."[16]

Sales Orientation

The organization with a *sales orientation* thinks that "consumers show buying inertia or resistance and have to be coaxed into buying more."[17] Most arts organizations engage in sales activities that they misidentify as marketing. Rather than make any changes in the product or how it is presented, they increase the resources allocated to advertising, direct mail, or telephone solicitations. These efforts usually result in short-term gains in audience. However, because it does not really adopt the consumer's perspective, the sales-oriented organization constantly has to replenish a large number of nonrenewing subscribers or members.

Customer Orientation

All of the marketing texts seem to agree that organizations that have evolved or start with a customer orientation have the best chance of competing in the world market today. An organization with a *customer orientation* must "systematically study customers' needs and wants, perceptions and attitudes, preferences and satisfactions."[18] To further clarify this definition as it applies to the arts, Kotler and Scheff go on to say:

> *This does not mean that artistic directors must compromise their artistic integrity.* Nor does it mean that an organization must cater to every consumer whim and fancy, as many managers fear. Those

who warn of such consequences if the devil (marketing) is let in the door simply misunderstand what a customer orientation truly means. To restate: marketing planning must *start* with the customer's perceptions, needs, and wants. Even if an organization ought not, will not, or cannot change the selection of the works it performs or presents, the highest volume of exchange will always be generated if the way the organization's offering is described, priced, packaged, enhanced, and delivered is fully responsive to the customer's needs, preferences, and interests. Furthermore, who the customer will be is largely up to the performing arts organization. Marketing will help maximize exchanges with targeted audiences.[19]

As this quote should make clear, an organization that takes a customer's perspective would, for example, use text to describe an upcoming performance in terms that an audience can respond to rather than in the jargon of the profession. If a potential ticket buyer believes that arts events are only for the wealthy and well educated, and everything the organization does with its promotional activity (ads, brochures, and so on) only reinforces this image, the arts promoter should not be surprised if the consumer feels reluctant to enter into the exchange process. On the other hand, arts organizations usually believe that they shouldn't have to describe a play like *Hamlet* as a "gut-wrenching tale of a family caught up in an whirlwind of lust and murder" in order to sell tickets. However, to discover the language that makes the most sense to its potential audience, the organization must engage in some basic consumer research. Research may show that a more dramatic description would make sense in their market.

An organization's key to successfully adopting a customer orientation resides in the research done on its community. What are people's attitudes and perceptions about the value of the music, opera, theater, dance, and art programs offered in your community? Based on that research, the customer-oriented arts organization would have several different approaches to communicating with the different audiences in the community. In some cases, the promotional campaign might be targeted to educating people about a new work or a new author. In other cases, the organization may focus on the strong emotions that a story or a piece of music conveys. For some potential audiences, *Hamlet* may spark their interest if described in more emotional terms. The arts marketer must of course be careful about crossing a line that distorts or debases the product. On the other hand, the risk of offending the sensibilities of a small number of the old guard patrons may prove worthwhile if it brings in new customers. However, unless the organization has a method for tracking the impact of different advertising tactics, these efforts will be wasted.

The problem that most customer- or audience-oriented arts organizations face when it comes time to communicate effectively about the product is a lack of money. The cost of multiple target promotional campaigns is usually well beyond the reach of most groups. However, a marketer would argue that this is money well spent because the objective is to build up long-term audience support and consumer identification with the product. Unfortunately, many arts organizations take a middle ground and ultimately communicate a bland image by trying to straddle too many marketing perspectives in their brochures and publications.

In the News—A Customer Orientation

The Milwaukee Art Museum provides a practical example of the successful adoption of a customer orientation in marketing.

Art Museum Thrives with Marketing
David I. Bednarek

Through aggressive marketing, the Milwaukee Art Museum is attracting more visitors and members at a time when attendance at art museums nationwide is declining.

Since 1984, attendance at art museums in the U.S. has gone down almost 5%, according to a Lou Harris poll, and is putting some museums on shaky footing because the higher cost of art and insurance demand greater attendance.

In the face of that national trend, attendance at the Milwaukee Art Museum has risen dramatically—from 129,000 in 1984 to 197,000 in 1989, an increase of 53%.

Membership went up 56%, from 6,500 to about 10,000.

The museum's success with marketing stands out as a model for other arts groups and similar organizations as leisure time becomes more scarce.

Rebecca Turner, director of marketing for the museum, attributed the increases to a decision in the early 1980s to get into marketing instead of simply relying on public relations to keep the museum going.

In addition to the increases in attendance and membership, Turner said the number of people taking classes at the museum went up from 771 to 2,000, the number attending special events increased from 9,000 to 49,000, and the number taking museum tours rose from 25,759 to 53,000.

Since 1984, the museum also has attracted more docents, the volunteers who work as guides.

In deciding what to do to sell the museum, the marketers first found out why people did not go and then set up programs to counter those reasons.

To the response, "I have no time for arts," for example, the museum set up mini-lectures on Gallery Nights, First Friday events with live jazz, "Bagels and Bach" on Sunday mornings and lunch-time lectures.

To those who say, "I don't know enough," the museum set up audio tours of exhibitions, using tapes to tell about the arts on display, the "Bluffer's Guide to Art," and Master of the Month gallery talks.

And to the complaint, "I won't fit in," the museum organized or helped organize Senior Days, Grandparents' Day, Free Days, Lakefront Festival of the Arts and Music in the Museum.

SOURCE: David I. Bednarek, "Art Museum Thrives with Marketing," *Milwaukee Journal* (April 11, 1990). Copyright © 1990 by the *Milwaukee Journal*. Used with permission.

Marketing Management

The Four Ps

Using these principles of marketing now allows us to move into the process of marketing management. To market its products or services effectively, an organization must carefully design its marketing mix. *Marketing mix* is defined as "the combination of activities involving *product, price, place,* and *promotion* that a firm undertakes in order to provide satisfaction to consumers in a given market."[20] Each of these elements will have an effect on the exchange process.

The *four Ps*, as they are often called, can be manipulated as part of the organization's overall strategy. For example, if you have a product with a brand name, such as the Metropolitan Opera, you may be able to manipulate the price based on the customer's perception of quality while stressing the place with its crystal chandeliers and red carpet in your promotional material.

The promotional aspect of the marketing mix is the most visible element, and it is usually divided into a further mix of types of advertising: newspaper, magazine, radio, television, direct mail, E-mail, a

website, raffles, and other public relations activities (e.g., having a soprano invited onto a local television talk show or radio program).

The overall marketing strategy for the organization may have several different marketing mixes. Depending on the target audience, you
may stress price or product. For example, a group sales flyer sent to a
retirement center may be accompanied by a letter that stresses price
first and then product. The same group flyer when sent to a college or
university drama department may be accompanied by a different letter
that stresses product first and then price.

Market Segments

The marketing manager or director is expected to have a good grasp of
the overall marketplace. As we discussed in Chapter 10, "Economics and
Financial Management," there are many markets in the system of supply and demand, and within the large markets, there are smaller markets for goods and services. Marketers use the term *market segment* to
identify "a group of buyers who have similar wants and needs."[21] Once
a market segment has been identified, the marketer begins the process
of *target marketing* by "developing a mix of the four P's aimed at that
market."[22]

In planning the marketing mix, information is the key ingredient
in designing a successfully targeted campaign. For example, if you buy
a mailing list from the state arts council with the names of 10,000 people interested in the arts in the state, you have identified a broad market segment. If this list of names is to be useful to you, it will need
further analysis. How many of these people attend particular types of
performing arts events? Narrowing the list further, how many of these
people are geographically close to your performance or exhibition space?
After you finish narrowing down the list to people within a three-hour
driving distance, are there enough names left to make it worthwhile
trying to target this group?

Mailing lists, which are purchased all the time in profit-sector marketing, may be far too costly for many arts organizations; for these
groups, the existing audience is the best and most cost-effective resource
for additional customers. The marketer's assumption is that if you
consume the arts product, your friends or colleagues may share similar
values.

Market Research

To engage effectively in target marketing, much detailed information
about the potential arts consumer must be known. Understanding the
demographics (age, income, education, gender, race) and having an
informed psychographic profile (consumer beliefs, values, attitudes) of
the potential consumer is crucial to designing the marketing mix for the
target market.

Marketing researchers in the profit sector have been developing
various behavioral and psychological models in an attempt to make target marketing as cost-effective as possible. The thrust of this work is to
divide consumers into lifestyle segments based on such things as activities, interests, and opinions. An example of the psychographic approach
(based on a behavioral profile) to understanding consumer behavior
can be found in the pioneering work in Arnold Mitchell's *The Nine
American Lifestyles*.[23] His research resulted in a more elaborate version
of Maslow's hierarchy of needs. Mitchell developed a hierarchy chart
representing segments of the population as a way to identify consumer

In the News—Price as a Marketing Tool

This article demonstrates the marketing principle of price manipulation as a method for attracting and increasing attendance.

This Theater Tells Patrons: Pay What You Can Afford
Scripps Howard News Service

PROVIDENCE, RI—At a time when the price of theater tickets is soaring beyond the reach of many, Trinity Repertory Theater will try a one-night experiment Tuesday of letting patrons pay what they will.

"The objective is to give every-one an opportunity to come to the theater," said E. Timothy Langan, managing director of the theater company.

The normal ticket price for the preview performance of Maxim Gorky's *Summerfolk*—a story Langan described as one about the Russian Empire's version of yuppies before the 1917 revolu-tion—is $24. Based on similar experiments in Baltimore and San Diego, Langan said he expected people would be willing to pay $3 to $4.

"But that's OK," he said. "The whole purpose of this is for someone to be comfortable in coming to the theater."

Trinity has set aside $5,000 from a grant to cover projected losses.

behavior. Mitchell called his chart a Values and Lifestyles Segment or VALS distribution.

The Association of Performing Arts Presenters (APAP) hired Mitchell in 1984 to conduct a study of arts audiences. In his report, *The Professional Performing Arts: Attendance Patterns, Preferences and Motives*,[24] he found that four groups, which at that time made up about 66 million people, were the primary market for arts organizations. He called these groups the Achievers, the Experientials, the Societally Conscious, and the Integrateds. Of these four groups, the Societally Conscious (12 percent of the population) were the best market per capita. Mitchell also found that among these four lifestyles, the most common reason cited for attending an arts event was to see a specific show, performer, or

Research Update

In an article in *American Demographics* magazine, questions were raised about market research techniques and the validity of certain assumptions about customers. The excerpts below will give you some ideas to ponder.

What Your Customers Can't Say
David B. Wolfe

Conventional marketing research depends on the assumption that people can accurately report their values, needs and motivations. But many scientists no longer believe this. "We have reason to doubt that full awareness of our motives, drives, and other mental activities may be possible," says neurologist Richard Restak. "Our inability to accurately report intentions and expectations may simply reflect the fact that they are not qualitatively conscious," adds Bernard J. Baars, author of *In the Theater of Consciousness*.

Consumer research's problems originate in psychology, a field that has long struggled to define human behavior with the same precision physicists use to describe the movement of bodies of atoms to stars. But

human behavior is too unpredictable to describe with such precision. An increasingly desperate search for cause-and effect explanations leads many psychologists to "retreat to abstract ideas that ignore contexts completely," writes Harvard psychologist Jerome Kagan. Consumer research reflects similar tendencies.

Models of consumer behavior tend to extract their subjects from the complex, often unpredictable, but completely natural contexts in which people live and make purchasing decisions.

Research Is Too Rational
For years marketers have complained that consumers often indicate one thing in research, yet behave differently in the marketplace. But consumers are not pathological liars. They have split personalities, according to University of Iowa neurologist Antonio Damasio. To be more specific, their decisions are split by the function of reason and emotion.

Damasio's research shows that different brain sites and different mental processes are involved with different kinds of decision-making. We use one set of mental tools when we consider hypothetical matters,

and another when we make personal decisions.

Emotions have a powerful effect on our consumer choices, because they push us toward decisions we think are best for us. We often bypass reason when making decisions because experience endows us with what Damasio calls "somatic markers." Somatic markers are like computer shortcuts that incorporate many keystrokes into one or two.

Many research questions fail to deeply stimulate consumers' somatic markers (or hot buttons). Instead, they invite respondents to develop a reason-based explanation that often distorts reality. Instead of the real reasons for buying or not buying something, researchers get a rationalization based on the respondent's idealized self-image. If they do not account for this bias, researchers are left with a model based on how people think they ought to be motivated, instead of a model based on their actual motivations.

group. He also found that even among these targeted groups, large percentages admitted that they never attended arts events. For example, an average of 28 percent never attended music concerts, 40 percent never attended theater productions, and 68 percent never attended dance events. His research found that lack of leisure time (30 percent), preferences for other leisure activities (34 percent), and not wanting to commit to season or series purchases (33 percent) were the primary reasons given for not attending.

Another approach to target marketing—one designed to help businesses connect with the consumer—is detailed in *The Clustered World* by Michael J. Weiss. Weiss's book, published in 2000, examines the work of a market research company. Claritas Corporation developed a system that uses a vast mix of census data to produce information that marketers buy to locate the people who might be disposed to buy their product. The Potential Rating Index for Zip Markets (PRIZM) system uses a zip code analysis of various neighborhood types. For example, Claritas' research has identified the two clusters for classical music and named them Blue Blood Estates and Executive Suites.[25] Blue Blood Estates represent a small percentage of households with median incomes of $113,000. The Executive Suites were listed with incomes of $58,000 and also liking espresso makers, dry cleaning, and *Cooking Light* magazine.[26]

The objective for an arts marketer using the Claritas system is to develop a database of the zip code distribution of its list of current subscribers and, at the same time, to gather information about the zip code distribution of the single-ticket buyers and to compare the data with the neighborhood types. At this point, the marketer could determine which areas the organization has not reached. Buying a list of labels from the local utility company would allow the organization to send targeted mailings to households in the zip code neighborhoods that the organization has identified as potential customers.

Ultimately, a system such as the one Claritas has developed should allow an arts marketer to target potential audiences by very narrow segments. After all, why should an arts organization waste its limited resources doing mass mailings when carefully targeted mailings to "the right people" will yield much more cost-effective results?

In 1996 NEA published a comprehensive report entitled "Age and Arts Participation."[27] The data was gathered as part of a Survey of Public Participation in the Arts (SPPA). The report identified seven age groupings, called cohorts, and analyzed the attendance patterns at classical music, opera, ballet, musicals, jazz, plays, and art museums. The highlights of their research included:

- The generation born 1936 to 1945 had very high attendance percentages at classical music concerts, opera, musicals, and plays.
- Younger cohorts (people born after 1946) had higher attendance percentages at jazz concerts and museums.
- Concerns were raised in the report about the fact that the generations born after World War II, despite better education levels, were not attending arts events to the same degree as the older generation.
- The report indicated that younger cohorts (after 1946) substituted television, cable, and radio broadcasts or videotapes and compact discs for live performing arts events.

Other Arts Research

The PRIZM and VALS approaches to market research can be very expensive to purchase and are out of reach for most small arts organizations. Although Mitchell's study for the Arts Presenters goes into great detail about such things as reactions to different types of advertising, audiences will react unpredictably to various marketing plans. Other sources to consider for marketing information include the research division of the National Endowment for the Arts (http://www.arts.endow.gov/pub/) that regularly publishes useful data. The *Journal of Arts Management, Law, and Society* and the *International Journal of Arts Management* also include articles on the latest arts marketing research. (Note: For more information go to http://www.heldref.org/html/body-jamls.html or http://www.hec.ca/ijam.) Another excellent source for marketing ideas is the comprehensive anthology published in 1995 by ARTS Action Issues entitled *Market the Arts!*

Arts organizations should regularly survey people in their community for feedback on new programs and on problems with existing operations. A properly designed survey can give an organization the opportunity to adjust and change its marketing mix. The use of the Internet and websites can be a low-cost way for arts organizations to gain continuing feedback from audiences. Online surveys or E-mail feedback about shows can be a useful way of keeping in touch with customers. The use of small *focus groups* is also a low-cost alternative for arts organizations. Focus groups of up to 10 or 12 may provide useful insights about the attitudes and perceptions of your audiences to your image and your advertising. Suggested resources for surveys are noted at the end of this chapter (see Additional Resources).

Marketing Ethics

Whatever approach is used in marketing research, the goal is to find out what the consumer thinks about the product or service. Marketers believe that with the right information they can better predict which combination of product, price, place, and promotion is needed to complete the exchange process on a regular basis with consumers. To bridge the information gap, marketers look to even more sophisticated applications of computers in their work. As a result, the line between market research and invading people's privacy has grown very thin. The selling of vast amounts of information about consumers is now a fact of life. Michael Weiss points out that "the information gathering business is booming, projected to grow to a $10 billion industry this year [2000]. Companies like Metromail and The Polk Company gather and sort information on the lifestyles and spending habits of most of the 100 million households in the nation."[28] As computers have increased in their data storage capabilities and programmers have become even more sophisticated in programming software, the ability to profile consumers will only continue to intensify.

Arts organizations, which depend on the sales of tickets and subscriptions for 60 percent or more of their operating budget, face a dilemma. How intrusive should they be when trying to reach potential arts consumers? Arts organizations want to identify and target people who are most likely to be long-term consumers of their product. Techniques such as telephone marketing, if handled properly, can lead to direct contact with consumers. On the other hand, people resent phone calls and "sales pitches" that intrude into their private lives. Marketers for arts organizations must also face the ethical issue of selling information about their customers to commercial firms. The arts consumer is a prime target for the marketer of upscale goods and services. Research has shown that arts consumers have more than the average amount of discretionary income and are therefore good targets for a wide variety of marketing assaults.

Strategic Marketing Plans

Now that the basic principles of marketing have been outlined, let us examine in more detail the critical planning process. As noted earlier in this chapter, if the marketing plan is to be effective, the entire organization must carefully consider how all phases of the operation relate to the dynamics of the marketplace. The simple fact facing all organizations is that new opportunities and new threats arise in the marketplace every day. An organization that can adjust to these changing conditions has the best chance of surviving in the long run.

Some board members may wonder why an organization such as a museum or some other well-established performing arts institution would need to worry about the changing dynamics of the marketplace. After all, won't people always go to the museum or to the symphony? Why should an organization spend time planning, reviewing its mission, devising strategies, and developing objectives when what it does is so obvious? Citing the examples of dance companies that have failed, museums that have had to reduce their hours and staff, and orchestras, theaters, and opera companies that have filed for bankruptcy should be enough to counter any argument that strategic marketing plans are a waste of time.

Planning Process

The organization's overall strategic plan (discussed in Chapter 5, "Planning and Decision Making") incorporates the marketing plan (see Figure 11-1). The organization's objectives drive the mission, goals, and objectives of its marketing plan. In addition, as noted in Chapter 4, "Arts Organizations in a Changing World," an analysis of opportunities and threats from the external environments (economic, demographic, political and legal, social and cultural, technological, and educational) is weighed against the organization's strengths and weaknesses. Once the basic mission and objectives of the organization have been defined in the strategic plan, the core marketing strategy can be developed. The target markets and the proposed marketing mix can be articulated. The process now moves to the final stage by providing the system for carrying out the marketing plan, including what performance criteria will be used to monitor progress. In addition, the specific tactics can be formed. Implementation plans and an evaluation system complete the process. The evaluation process should provide feedback to the core marketing strategy for long-term adjustments and directly back to specific tactics for short-term changes. For example, a short-term change might be to revise an advertisement in the paper when there is poor response to a particular offer. A long-term adjustment might be to evaluate all print media.

Marketing Audit

One method that an organization might use to assess its ability to carry out a marketing plan is to do a marketing audit. Essentially, an audit consists of asking and answering a series of questions that explore the

Marketer Profile

Danny Newman—Mr. Subscription Ticket Sales

Danny Newman's book *Subscribe Now!* is the source for many arts managers on a quest for how to sell subscriptions (see Additional Resources). Newman has been a working for the Chicago Lyric Opera since 1954 and has helped successfully lead their subscription sales efforts. In 1997 he was nominated for a National Medal of Arts for his efforts as a marketer and consultant. Despite the shift away from enlisting subscribers in favor of more flexible purchasing options, Newman remains firm in his belief that the best way to build a long-term relationship with audiences is through subscription plans. Many performing arts centers, college and university art departments, theaters, opera, dance companies and music groups copy Mr. Newman's approach to building audiences with much success. Gregory Mosher, a well-known theater director, noted in a September 23, 1997 article in the *New York Times* ["The Unsung Hero of Nonprofit Theater Is Still Selling"] on Newman that, "He's like Henry Ford . . . I must have read his book [*Subscribe Now!*] 100 times." Mosher went on to note that the subscription series was the cornerstone of the regional theater boom in the United States. The model was based on "a board of directors, a staff led by an artistic director and a managing director, and a six-play subscription series." The recent trend has been toward letting customers build their own series by mixing and matching a specific number of shows in a season. Exchange privileges become the cornerstone of the "Flex-packs," as they are often called.

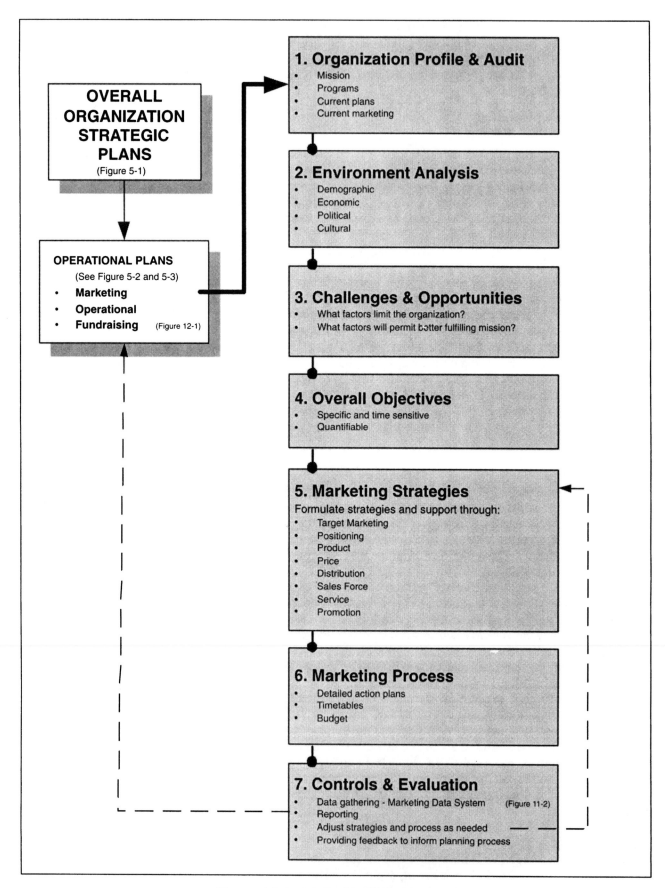

Figure 11-1 Marketing Planning Process

organization's markets, customers, objectives, organizational structure, marketing information system, and marketing mix. The Sample Marketing Plan in this chapter gives you a starting place for preparing an audit. The audit gives the staff and the board a common ground on which to build a marketing plan that fits the organization's mission and function.

Consultants

It is usually helpful to get the perspective of an outside consultant when formulating any strategic or marketing plan. Someone with expertise in planning can save an organization a great deal of valuable time struggling through the planning process. As noted in Chapter 5, planning is hard work, and because of the pressing daily needs of keeping the organization afloat, managers often assign this essential process a low priority. A consultant, if used effectively, can shake up the status quo and act as a catalyst to put planning at the top of the priority list. A word of caution, though: Consultants are not infallible, and they have been known to make mistakes. They can give bad advice and make recommendations that make conditions worse, not better. A background check of former clients is a requirement for organizations that want to protect themselves.

Strategies

The profit sector uses terminology borrowed from warfare when developing marketing strategies. Marketers use such terms as *frontal, encirclement, flanking,* and *bypass* attacks to describe marketing plans. Words such as *preemptive, counteroffensive,* and *contraction* are used to describe strategies.[29] Other options for organizations to explore include generic, market leader, market follower, and market niche strategies. Let us look briefly at the competitive environment facing many arts organizations and discuss strategy options.

The Competitive Marketplace and Core Strategies

When a community reaches the point in its growth where it has at least one professional arts organization from each of the major disciplines, the struggle for resources among these organizations will probably intensify. Arts people may carry on a cordial and friendly dialogue in public, but competition is tough and there are only so many dollars that people will spend on subscriptions, tickets, memberships, and donations. As we have seen, arts organizations also face competition for the entertainment dollar from videotape and DVD rentals, films, television, and amusement parks. Therefore, in formulating a plan of attack, an arts organization might consider a *niche strategy.* Such a strategy focuses on the qualities that make a live performing arts event or a trip to the museum a unique activity. The niche strategy can be combined with a *differentiation strategy* in an effort to feature those things that are unique about the product. This strategy combination allows the organization to concentrate on what is special about its product while appealing to a targeted market.

If the organization's planning process leads to a decision to expand its audience base beyond the typical demographic blend, a strategy to increase market share would be appropriate. In this *growth strategy*, the organization takes an aggressive advertising approach to reach new audiences. For example, if a theater company wanted to develop its market among African-Americans in the community, an advertising

In the News—Marketing Strategies

This newspaper article shows how an arts organization can expand consumer awareness for a very modest investment.

Toasting Cabbies to Tout Visitors
Associated Press

CHICAGO—The Art Institute of Chicago hopes a free breakfast will go a long way toward steering visitors in its direction.

The museum treated about 100 taxi drivers to Danish pastry, juice, coffee and a tour last week in the hope that the steering-wheel philosophers will talk up the place to their fares.

"Chicago taxi drivers really are roving ambassadors," museum spokeswoman Eileen Harakal said. "Not only do they answer passengers' questions on Chicago's attractions, but they help steer people to them."

"It's a great idea," said cab-driver Bill Hogan as he contemplated Henri Matisse's "Still Life With a Blue Table Cloth." "When people ask what there is to see in Chicago I usually say the Sears Tower, the Museum of Science and Industry and the Shedd Aquarium. Now I'll mention the Art Institute."

SOURCE: Associated Press, "Toasting Cabbies to Tout Visitors" (October 3, 1990). Copyright © 1990 by the Associated Press (AP). Used with permission.

Sample Marketing Plan

The first step in developing your marketing plan requires you to assess the current status of the organization. Depending on your organization, there may be additional questions you need to pose. Therefore, the items below should be viewed as a guide and not as the only questions you could raise.

1. **Organization Profile and Audit**
   - Name, type of arts organization, location, brief history, and years in existence
   - Programs and projects currently listed by the organization, or special performance or exhibition activities
   - Mission, goals, and/or objectives statements published? Is the mission clear? Are the goals connected to the mission, and do they seem achievable? Are the objectives and priorities clear about who, what, and when?
   - Is the organization operating under a current strategic organizational or marketing plan? If yes, what is its planning and implementation process? Review brochures, flyers, and other documents used by the organization in its current marketing activities. Are these pieces effective?
   - Is the organization operating within its budget? Is it a financially healthy organization? Does it have a budget surplus or deficit? Are the board and management functioning effectively?
2. **Environment Analysis**
   Demographic
   - What major regional and national demographic developments and trends pose opportunities or threats for this organization?
   - What actions, if any, has the organization taken in response to those developments?
   Economic
   - What major developments and trends in income, prices, savings, and interest rates are affecting the organization?
   - What major changes are taking place in the sources and amounts of contributed income (from individuals, corporations, private and public foundations, and government agencies)?
   - What actions has the organization taken in response to these developments and trends?
   Political
   - What recent local, state, or national legislation has affected this organization?
   - What federal, state, or local agencies should be monitored for future actions relating to the organization?
   - What actions has the organization taken in response to these developments?
   Cultural
   - What changes are occurring in consumer lifestyles, values, and educational opportunities that might affect this organization?
   - What actions has the organization taken in response to these developments?
3. **Challenges and Opportunities**
   Challenges: Depending on how you answered the questions above you may have a series of specific challenges facing the organization, such as but not limited to the following:
   - Declining subscriber base,
   - Increased competition from other arts organizations,
   - Lack of single-ticket buyers or members,
   - Need to diversify audiences,
   - Poorly focused target marketing,
   - Lack of commitment to customer orientation by the organization.
   Opportunities: State the opportunities you see that will help meet the challenges facing the organization. State these opportunities as facts, not strategies or objectives. For example, you found that a challenge facing the organization was a declining subscriber base. The opportunity is "potential exists to increase subscriber base." Even if your organization is "perfect" you may still have opportunities to venture into new areas such as merchandise or adding an experimental performance series.
4. **Objectives**
   Formulate objectives for the marketing plan based on the factual statements you have made. For example, if you stated, "opportunity exists to increase the subscriber base," you could state objectives for each of the areas below. For example:
   - Marketing: Objective will be to increase the subscriber base by a net of 5 percent in the next fiscal year.
   - Financial: Objective will be to increase earned income from subscriptions by 5 percent above the previous fiscal year.
5. **Marketing Strategy**
   In this section you outline your *game plan* for achieving all the objectives you set for yourself in:
   - Target Markets: Who will be targeted?
   - Positioning: What will be your positioning statement

campaign using specific media publications and radio stations with a high ratio of minority consumers would make sense. Also, targeting group sales by using the local network of African-American religious groups might prove successful. However, if the arts organization does not regularly offer a product that has some market appeal to members of various minorities, there is little chance that this strategy will succeed.

Whatever overall marketing strategy an arts organization selects, it is important to remember that it must fit with the mission of the organization. Care must be taken to avoid shifting the organization away from its mission to meet a market strategy. For example, museums are not in the gift shop business, but because these operations can become very healthy sources of cash, it is tempting to overemphasize their importance in marketing the organization.

Project Planning and Implementation

The details of preparing, budgeting, and implementing the marketing plan require careful attention. Decisions about where to put the usually very limited marketing resources available to the organization can make or break a plan. The work done on researching the community and a detailed cost analysis of various media campaigns will pay off in the project planning stage. Organization and project management skills are required to prepare the overall schedule and budget distribution for the marketing campaign.

Evaluation

After implementing the plan, the organization must carefully evaluate and monitor how well its objectives are being realized. For example, if the costs of implementing the strategy exceed the budget, and the number of new subscribers or members is below the levels established for success, the organization must be able to adjust its tactics or to revise the entire strategy before it is too late. As noted in Chapter 5, "Planning and Decision Making," the failure to abandon a plan that is not working can lead to numerous problems.

Marketing Data System

Within the organization's overall management information system and financial management information system, you should find a marketing data system (MDS). Its purpose is parallel to that of the MIS. The MDS should be designed to gather and analyze data regularly and to issue reports on the success of current campaigns. Figure 11-2 shows a typical MDS for an arts organization. The four major sources of data are the sales system (box office), audiences, staff, and various external environments. If the system is working properly, the feedback provided to the marketing staff will arrive in time to make corrections and adjustments in the marketing plan. With some sources of information, such as surveys, the data gathered could be translated into information that is useful in planning future seasons or programs.

Computers can play a central role in gathering and processing data for the MDS. As we saw in Chapter 9, "Organizational Controls and Budgets," the MIS and the FMIS must be linked with the marketing data system if the organization is to monitor its operations effectively. It is essential that the organization have a network of computers that share data among the marketing staff and other members of the management team to enable the marketing plans to be successfully evaluated. The complexity of such a system may require hiring outside

Sample Marketing Plan (cont.)

to sell to these target markets? "We are the only orchestra group performing the work of composer X in the tri-cities area."
- Product: Describe the product in customer terms that your research says these target markets find appealing.
- Price: How will you use price to achieve your objectives?
- Distribution: Will you expand access to tickets by selling through the organization's website, Ticketmaster, or Tickets.Com?
- Sales Force: Changes needed to achieve objectives? Hire more staff?
- Service: Any changes in how services are delivered? Extra hours? 800 number?
- Promotion: All forms of promotion. What specifically do you plan to do? Will you use direct mail or telemarketing, radio ads, PSAs, or what? In other words, what will be your media plan?

6. **Marketing Process**
   Detailed Action Plans
   - What will be done?
   - Who will do it?
   - What will be the benefit?
   Timetable
   - When will the action plan items be done? (Detail each action plan in a list or on a calendar.)
   Budget
   - How much will it cost? (Detail all the costs of the plan: graphics, printing, advertising, etc.)

7. **Controls and Evaluation**
   How will you monitor your progress? What kind and how frequent will be the reports? Create forms and reports for how you will measure your success in achieving the objectives you set for yourself and the organization.

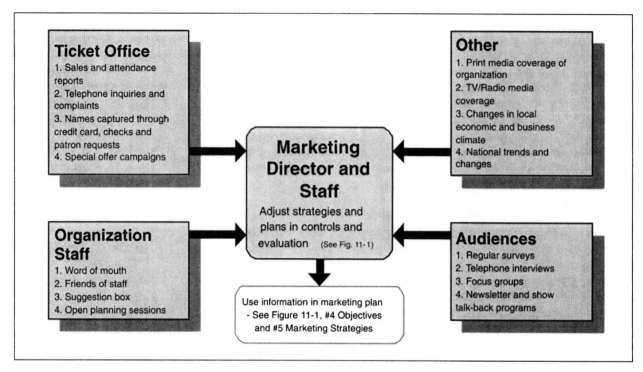

Figure 11-2   Marketing Data System

consultants to coordinate and advise the marketing manager. Without the ability to track all sales data quickly and accurately, the marketing manager's effectiveness will ultimately be seriously undermined.

Conclusion

Marketing can be an effective tool for keeping an organization growing and evolving. However, marketing is also a long-term investment. A well-organized marketing campaign should be integrated with operational and long-term organization plans. It makes no sense to attempt a marketing plan without having first clearly defined the mission and goals of the organization. Like any tool, marketing can be misused. Thousands of dollars can be wasted on advertising campaigns or printed brochures that have little or no impact on sales.

Ultimately, it is important to recognize how complex the purchase and attendance decision process is for the potential audience members. First they must achieve awareness of the event, then they have to decide if what you are offering is of interest to them. Next they must check their schedules to see if the dates and time you are performing fit in their schedule. Assuming all of those decision points are yes, then they must make contact with your ticket office and engage in the actual purchase process. They need to get dressed up, travel to your venue, find a place to park, find their way to their seat, and participate as an active audience member by enjoying your show. Then they have to negotiate the traffic and get back home before they can actually complete the experience. In other words, your average frequent attendee must be very well motivated to go through this process. Although we in the performing arts stress the "live performance" experience, it is also apparent that it is much easier to rent a video, DVD, or select a cable channel if one needs to satisfy a need for entertainment.

Unfortunately, there are no guarantees that your best plans to attract audiences will work. For organizations with limited resources, experimenting with different approaches to marketing is out of the question. However, finding the most cost-effective way to reach audiences when there are no funds for research also places impossible constraints on the marketing staff. It isn't surprising to find high turnover in an arts organization's marketing staff. Impossible goals, limited resources, and poorly conceived plans take their toll on even the most ambitious people. Upper management involvement and commitment to planning and implementation can go a long way toward remedying the problems that arts marketers face.

The most daunting task facing any arts marketer is the development of future audiences. The simple reality of a very limited audience base coupled with the ever-increasing competition from other entertainment options makes for a difficult mix of circumstances. As most arts marketers know, unless you can establish a pattern of arts consumption at an early age, it is both difficult and costly to change people's leisure behavior later in life. The arts marketing effort will no doubt continue, and wherever appropriate, the arts marketer will borrow from the commercial marketing world those techniques that work.

For students interested in a challenging field of work, arts or nonprofit marketing has a great deal of potential. The use of language and images to express an idea or to convey an organization's mission demands a great deal of skill and creativity. Because this chapter is just a glimpse into the world of marketing, students are urged to explore the readings listed in Additional Resources. A college undergraduate course in marketing would also be helpful to the future arts marketer.

Summary

The arts manager must plan, organize, implement, and evaluate marketing strategies to maximize revenue and meet the organization's objectives. Because of the bombardment of marketing efforts by a multitude of businesses and causes, the arts manager must dedicate significant resources to marketing if the organization is to be visible in the highly competitive entertainment marketplace. Marketing is a means to an end, and it should therefore be thought of as one more tool available to the arts manager to be used in realizing the overall goals of the organization.

Contemporary marketing attempts to match the wants and needs of consumers with products and services. Needs are physiological and psychological things that are lacking and are necessary for people's well-being. Wants are things that are lacking and that people find desirable or useful. People can gain functional and psychological satisfaction from tangible and intangible features of products or services.

Marketing activity is designed to facilitate the exchange process. This process involves a transfer of something of value between two or more parties or organizations. The exchange process is successful to the degree that the utilities of form, time, place, and possession can be satisfied through the exchange. The arts exchange usually involves satisfying a psychological want through the intangible features of an experience, which is modified by the inherent constraints placed on the four utilities by the delivery system (the performance or exhibition).

Marketing has evolved over the last 300 years. The production era, which grew out of the Industrial Revolution, concentrated on satisfying basic needs. It was assumed that people would buy whatever was manufactured. The sales era, which concentrated on increasing demand, began sometime after the Civil War. More emphasis was put on customers' wants, but the manufacturers still dictated what would be available to purchase. The marketing era, which came to the fore after World War II, reversed the relationship between the consumer and the manufacturer. The consumer-driven market relationship starts with what the consumer wants, not the product.

Marketing today is classified along the same historical line of evolution. A company may have a product, sales, or customer orientation. The product-oriented company assumes that its product is inherently good and needs no changes. The sales-oriented company concentrates on trying to increase demand for existing products and services. The customer-oriented company determines the perceptions, needs, and wants of the market and goes about creating a product to fit those needs. Arts organizations can and do use these three orientations. The market-oriented arts organization thrives if it understands the market's perception of its product and describes, prices, packages, and delivers its product to reflect those perceptions. It does not mean that the organization must change the product to attract customers.

Marketing management is based on the organization's manipulation of the four Ps—product, price, place, and promotion—or the market mix. The market mix can be adjusted to suit the target market. Market research has shown that people with various demographic and psychographic profiles react differently to various marketing mixes.

The entire marketing process is directly related to the organization's strategic plans. The main objectives of the strategic plan are incorporated into the marketing plan. An analysis of external environments and the strengths and weaknesses of the organization are also included. A detailed audit process may be used to assess the organization's capabilities to undertake an effective marketing campaign. From the marketing plan, specific strategies and detailed tactics can be designed to meet the defined objectives. The success of the marketing campaign depends on accurate and timely information gathered by the marketing data system.

Key Terms and Concepts

Marketing
Needs and wants
Functional satisfaction
Psychological satisfaction
Exchange
Form, time, place, and possession utilities
Production, sales, and marketing eras
Product, sales, and customer orientations
The four Ps: product, price, place, and promotion
Marketing mix
Market segments
Target marketing
Demographic profile

Psychographic profile
Focus groups
Strategic marketing plans
Marketing audit
Niche strategy
Differentiation strategy
Market share strategy
Marketing data system (MDS)

Questions

1. Define the term *marketing.*
2. What are some of the wants and needs satisfied by the following: a brand-name soft drink, a meal at a French restaurant, and a visit to an art museum?
3. Does marketing make you buy things that you don't need? Explain.
4. Give an example of an exchange process in which you recently participated that was not satisfying. What went wrong in the exchange? What would you change to make the exchange satisfying?
5. What suggestions would you offer about form, time, place, and possession utilities to a museum and a children's theater company that are each planning new community outreach programs?
6. When you are considering the purchase of an arts product, which of the four Ps is most important to you? Explain. Do you react differently to various marketing mixes? How?
7. What are some of the different market segments you would identify for theater, dance, opera, symphony, and museum organizations? How much attendance crossover do you think exists among the different segments? For example, do opera audiences go to the theater?
8. Do demographic and psychographic profiles of audiences match your perception of arts consumers? How do you think the profile of the audience will change over the next 20 years? How will changes in demographics affect arts organizations?
9. If you were managing a small modern dance company in a community with a well-established ballet company, what marketing strategy would you adopt to gain a market share?
10. According to "Art Museum Thrives with Marketing," what was the basic marketing strategy attempted by the Milwaukee Art Museum? Why was it so successful?

Portrait of the Artist As a Focus Group

Case Study

Too often these days, the creative types have only the courage of their audience's convictions.
  Michiko Kakutani

If you took a poll, what would America's best-loved painting look like? In their playful new book, "Painting by Numbers," two Russian emigré conceptual artists decided to find out. With a little help from some polling experts, Vitaly Komar and

Alexander Melamid queried 1,001 Americans about their tastes in color, form and style, and concluded that the most wanted painting in the country is a bluish landscape painting, populated by George Washington, a family of tourists and a pair of frolicking deer. The canvas is the size of a dishwasher and looks like something that might adorn the walls of a third-rate motel. It is the apotheosis of art created by consensus.

Komar and Melamid's exercise, of course, is a sly comment on the democratization of creativity and America's mania for polls. What is more disturbing is that their satiric project unwittingly underscores another trend at work in American culture: our eagerness to substitute public opinion for personal belief, market demands for authentic artistic and political vision.

From the world of advertising, consumer research has already spread to Washington, where President Clinton has rarely made a move without checking with his pollsters, and to Hollywood, where test audiences can affect the content, pacing and tone of big-budget pictures and determine which TV pilots get scheduled. From Hollywood, it is now spreading into music, theater, novels and journalism. The result is a brand of carefully positioned art and a culture-wide embrace of that old advertising slogan "The customer is always right"— even if that customer has no expertise, no knowledge, and no taste.

MTV's new show "12 Angry Viewers" gives audience members a chance to add a video to the station's playlist, and focus groups similarly determine what songs many radio stations will or will not play. In his insightful new book, "Dreaming Out Loud," Bruce Feiler points out that a growing number of country-music stations now employ market-research companies to tell them exactly what their audiences want. The process, he suggests, systematically excludes tracks that provoke the strongest reaction, positive as well as negative—and the resulting picks tend to be predictable, homogenized and cheerfully upbeat.

The sales imperative—be popular, be accessible, be liked —is also threatening to turn writing into another capitalist tool. In an effort to raise circulation, newspapers like *The Miami Herald* and *The Boca Raton News* have used reader-preference surveys to determine their "coverage priorities," and some novelists are adopting the literary equivalent of the applause-o-meter as well. The best-selling author Andrew Greeley has used focus groups to shape his marketing campaigns, and the novelist James Patterson has conscripted groups of test readers to analyze his books before publication. Patterson recently changed the ending of his new thriller, *Cat and Mouse*, in response to reader feedback; the novel reached No. 2 on *The Times* best-seller list.

This shameless second-guessing is not simply a money-grubbing attempt to give audiences what they think they want. It also represents the abdication by creative types of their artistic freedom and judgment. Just as today's politicians have elected to become mirrors of the national Zeitgeist rather than leaders, so have poll driven "artists" elected to become assembly-line manufacturers, in thrall to the opinions of mall rats deemed demographically correct.

No one has tried harder to turn the messy process of artistic creation into a systematic, risk-free proposition than Garth Drabinsky, the producer of the Broadway musical *Ragtime*. A 20-year veteran of the movie business, Drabinsky is methodically transferring Hollywood practices to the stage. He insists that a show's prospective book writer submit an initial treatment to insure that the writer is not "going off on a tangent and doing something that is incongruous to the philosophy or ideas of the producer." For *Ragtime*, he hired a polling firm to help calibrate audience reactions. The show's book eventually went through some 20 drafts.

"We want to hear what audiences have to say about what they're seeing," Drabinsky says, "and most importantly; we want to find out if the work is coherent—if it's making sense emotionally and dramatically." The *Ragtime* focus groups, he argues, helped his creative team "learn about the response of audiences to the characters we've chosen to put in the show," as well as "whether they feel the show is too long."

So what if critics complained that *Ragtime* lacked a distinctive voice? So what if they thought it had the feel of a corporate committee? *Ragtime* has already racked up a $17.5 million advance, and other producers and theater owners are being encouraged to use surveys and exit polls as a means of boosting business. In an article in the theatrical magazine *Back Stage*, George A. Wachtel, president of a firm called Audience Research & Analysis, writes: "Response cards distributed during previews can produce objective feedback from which the creative team can learn what is working and what isn't." In five years, Wachtel says, "When you open the Playbill for a show and it says, advertising by . . . , publicity by . . . , it will also say market research by . . . , because it's going to become part of what happens on Broadway. In five years, I predict that most shows will be doing audience surveys and will be better understanding their audience from the get-go, and that the majority of new shows will have some kind of preview research."

Such predictions eerily limn a future in which Pop Art gives way to Poll Art—a future in which reproductions of Komar and Melamid's cloying painting will hang on every museum's walls.

Questions

1. Compare and contrast the point of view of this article with the quote from Kotler and Scheff beginning "This does not mean that artistic directors must compromise. . . ."

    a. Discuss the differences in the positive and negative effects of marketing research and polling.

    b. What is your conclusion about the prediction that marketing research firms will be credited in programs in

Broadway theaters in the future? Is this a good or bad thing? Why?

c. The "Artist As a Focus Group" article assumes that arts marketing is geared toward "shamelessly second-guessing" and is an "attempt to give audiences what they think they want." Kotler and Scheff argue that this approach isn't necessary to market your event and that understanding your audience will only help you better communicate what you are offering. Is it possible to not give audiences what they want and still expect them to attend your arts event? Discuss.

References

1. Marshall Sella, "The 150-Second Sell: Take 34," *New York Times Magazine* (July 28, 2002), p. 34.
2. Philip Kotler and Joanne Scheff, *Standing Room Only* (Boston: Harvard Business School Press, 1997), p. 44.
3. "AMA Board Approves New Marketing Definition," *Marketing News* (March 1, 1985), p. 1.
4. Charles D. Schewe, *Marketing Principles and Strategies* (New York: Random House, 1987), p. 5.
5. Ibid., p. 5.
6. Ibid., p. 7.
7. Ibid., p. 7.
8. Ibid., p. 7.
9. Ibid., p. 8.
10. Ibid., p. 10.
11. Ibid., p. 19.
12. Ibid., pp. 14–16.
13. Joy Horowitz, "Off the Street and into the Audience: Tourists Help Pick Fall TV Schedule," *New York Times* (July 7, 1991).
14. Kotler and Scheff, *Standing Room Only*, p. 33.
15. Ibid., p. 33.
16. Ibid., p. 33.
17. Ibid., p. 33.
18. Ibid., p. 34.
19. Ibid., pp. 34–35.
20. Charles D. Schewe, *Marketing Principles and Strategies*, p. 33.
21. Ibid., p. 36.
22. Ibid., p. 36.
23. Arnold Mitchell, *The Nine American Lifestyles* (New York: Warner Books, 1983), pp. 13–24.
24. Arnold Mitchell, *The Professional Performing Arts: Attendance Patterns, Preferences and Motives* (Washington, D.C.: Association of Performing Arts Presenters, 1984), pp. ES-1 to ES-4, 21–24.
25. Michael J. Weiss, *The Clustered World* (New York: Little, Brown and Company, 2000), p. 79.
26. Ibid., pp. 180, 194.
27. Richard A. Peterson, Darren E. Sherkat, Judith Huggins Balfe, and Rolf Meyrson; Erin V. Lehman, ed., *Age and Arts Participation,*

NEA Research Division Report #34 (Santa Ana, Calif.: Seven Locks Press, 1996), pp. 1–5.
28. Weiss, *The Clustered World*, p. 39.
29. Schewe, *Marketing Principles and Strategies*, p. 55.

Additional Resources

There is no shortage of books on marketing. A quick trip to a bookstore should turn up numerous titles on marketing and marketing research. Listed below are some additional resources that will prove helpful in your arts marketing efforts.

David H. Bangs, Jr. *The Marketing Planning Guide*, 4th ed. Chicago: Upstart Publishing Company, 1995.

Michael Blimes and Ron Sproat. *More Dialing, More Dollars: 12 Steps to Successful Telemarketing*. New York: American Council for the Arts, 1984.

Fred E. Hahn and Kenneth G. Mangun. *Do It Yourself Advertising and Promotion*, 2nd ed. New York: John Wiley & Sons, 1997.

Roman G. Hiebing, Jr. and Scott W. Cooper. *The Successful Marketing Plan*, 2nd ed., Lincolnwood, Ill.: NTC Business Books, 1997.

Neil Kotler and Philip Kotler. *Museum Strategy and Marketing*. San Francisco: Jossey-Bass Publishers, 1998.

Jay Levinson and Seth Godin. *The Guerrilla Marketing Handbook*. New York: Houghton Mifflin Company, 1994.

Bradley G. Morison and Julie Gordon Dalgleish. *Waiting in the Wings*. New York: American Council for the Arts, 1987.

Danny Newman. *Subscribe Now!* New York: Theatre Communications Group, 1977.

Surveying Your Arts Audience. NEA Research Division Manual. Washington, D.C., 1985.

David Parmerlee. *Preparing the Marketing Plan*. Lincolnwood, Ill.: NTC Business Books, 1995.

Priscilla Salant and Don A. Dillman. *How to Conduct Your Own Survey*. New York: John Wiley & Sons, 1994.

12
□ □ □ □ □

Fundraising

Philanthropic behavior is motivated by values. Board member commitment to serve and ask, volunteer enthusiasm, a funder's sense of satisfaction in giving are based in an implicit search for a way to act on their values.
Kay Spring Grace, *Beyond Fund Raising*

The act of giving to good causes is well established in U.S. culture. The charitable system developed by various religious organizations to provide social services in the United States still depends on individual donations of funds, goods, and services. The intervention of direct government support in this system is a fairly recent phenomenon. U.S. government subsidies only became widely institutionalized after 1933. Today, the United States has a unique mixture of public and private support for health, education, social services, and culture (sometimes referred to as nongovernmental agencies). Government support of giving is also reflected in the tax benefits available when a person files a tax form and itemizes expenses.

Organized fundraising by entities other than churches dates back to the nineteenth century. For instance, the International Red Cross operated the first disaster relief fund drives as early as 1859.[1] One source cites Lyman L. Pierce and Charles S. Ward as the fathers of modern fundraising, based on their work for the YMCA in the 1890s. The techniques they developed were used in 1905 to raise money for a new building in Washington, D.C., and these techniques made them pioneers of the major capital campaign. In fact, they may have been the first fundraising consultants, judging by the work they did assisting the U.S. government sell war bonds to help finance World War I.[2]

From these humble beginnings has risen a multibillion dollar industry. In 2001, for example, the *Giving USA 2002* report estimated that $212 billion was given to nonprofit and charity organizations by individuals, corporations, and foundations. This represented a 2.3 percent decline from 2000 after adjusting for inflation. The report goes on to note, "Charitable giving for the arts, culture, and humanities rose to an estimated $12.14 billion in 2001."[3] This represented a 2.7 percent increase over the previous year, when adjusted for inflation. The arts accounted for 5.7 percent of the total contributions in 2001, as reported in research done by the Center for Philanthropy at Indiana University.

Why Do People Give?

The act of giving is a particular behavior that is motivated by a complex set of reasons and emotions. Although the giving process mirrors the exchange concept we discussed in Chapter 11, "Marketing and the Arts," there is another layer of behavior reflected in donor behavior. The personal satisfaction people derive from giving is difficult to quantify, but fundraisers must carefully consider this factor in how they formulate their approach to seeking support in the community. People give to particular causes or organizations because they believe that what is being done is helping society in some way. Joseph R. Mixer's book *Principles of Professional Fundraising*[4] cites numerous surveys and theories about giving behavior. Mixer focuses on the "Social Exchange Model for Giving"[5] to detail the individual giving process. He goes on to say:

> The charitable organization or agency presents client needs and services to a prospect along with a request for funds. If the request is favorably received, the prospect responds with a donation of funds and possibly time. To continue the relationship, the recipient provides some form of satisfaction to the donor.
>
> The essence of what is returned to the donor is not a commodity or service that can be used profitably by the giver, but an intangible, psychic satisfaction that relates to the donor's personal motivations. An enhanced degree of self-esteem, a feeling of achievement, a new status, and a sense of belonging are among the most powerful rewards donors can receive. Giving satisfies donors' fundamental human needs and desires.[6]

Fundraising and the Arts

Fundraising is an everyday activity for an arts organization. Whether it is called fundraising, development, advancement, or community relations, the basic objective is the same. The quest to build, maintain, and enlarge an organization's base of donors who routinely support and believe in your organization is a full-time challenge. Perhaps no area of managing an arts organization comes under closer scrutiny or is subject to more pressure than fundraising. For many organizations, 40 percent or more of the yearly operating budget may come from gifts or grants by individuals, foundations, arts councils, and corporations. If there is a decline in gifts from any of these sources, arts organizations with little or no cash reserves often find themselves in serious financial difficulty. This "unearned income," as it is sometimes called, is very much earned through the hard work of the staff and the board of directors.

As we have discussed, the changing external environments (economic, political and legal, cultural and social, demographic, technological, and educational) create opportunities and pose threats for arts organizations. Each of these environments may have an impact on the organization's fundraising efforts. A recession will probably signal a slowdown in giving because people feel they need to retain more of their discretionary income. In an election year, major donors may give more to candidates and less to cultural organizations. Changes in the tax laws could also affect giving. If people gain a benefit by making a donation to an arts organization and thereby lowering their overall tax liability, they will become donors. However, the cause-and-effect relationship between these environments and donations is very unpredictable. Therefore, the arts manager must keep a watchful eye on donation flow.

Direct government support of the arts in the United States still represents a very minimal commitment of resources even after almost 40 years since the establishment of the National Endowment for the Arts. Direct government subsidies of the arts in many parts of the world are hundreds of times greater per capita than in the United States. The unique partnership of individual and private support for the arts defines the conditions in which all fundraisers must work.

Fundraising Plans

Because fundraising is so closely linked to the overall fiscal health of the organization, management of fundraising activities must be thoroughly integrated into the strategic planning process. In fact, many arts organizations place marketing and fundraising under the control of a development director. This person hires specialists in each area of development to realize the objectives formulated in the short- and long-term organizational plans.

In organizations with inadequate staffing (which describes many arts organizations), one person may try to manage and implement annual giving, develop major gifts or a capital campaign (e.g., for a new building), cultivate foundation contacts, and engage in grant writing to local, state, and federal agencies. It becomes very difficult for one person on staff to meet these diverse fundraising objectives. As we have seen in the chapters on planning, organization, and control, a manager needs adequate resources to carry out the organization's overall objectives. Because each of these fundraising areas requires a working knowledge of a vast amount of detail, it is unrealistic to expect one person to keep up with this impossible workload. Of course a supportive and active board of directors can be of assistance in the effort. However, the staff person usually ends up being the one everyone looks to when the fundraising goals are not achieved.

As we will see, much of the work involved in fundraising is research and writing. Work needs to be done in advance to carefully cultivate a match between the organization and the donor. On the other hand, a great deal of fundraising also involves social interaction with donors and potential donors. Without the time and help to research and cultivate donors, the fundraiser's success rate will be very limited. Seldom are the benefits immediate to the organization. Years may go by before an individual finally makes a major donation to the organization. People who seek instant gratification will probably find development a very frustrating area in which to work.

On the whole, fundraising seems to be a growth industry. There is a constant high demand for people who can organize and effectively manage the fundraising activities of a nonprofit corporation. The downside of this high demand is the often-unrealistic expectations about how much money can actually be raised. The tendency to overestimate eventually leads an organization into a deficit operating mode. The net result is often a high level of turnover in the development area in the nonprofit sector. An article entitled "Revolving-Door Dilemma" in the April 18, 2002, issue of the *Chronicle of Philanthropy* concluded that there was indeed significant turnover, but found no studies in existence that quantified the scope of the problem.

In this chapter, we explore the requirements an organization must meet before it tries to raise money. We also discuss strategies to use in approaching different target donors and organizations that specialize in giving to the arts.

Preparing Fundraising Plans

James Gregory Lord, a recognized expert in the field of fundraising, notes that, "people give to people." He goes on to say, "People don't give to an institution. They give to the person who asks them. Often, a contribution is made because of how one person feels about another. The institution may be almost incidental. People also give for people—not for endowments or swimming pools."[7]

If fundraising managers keep this fundamental fact in the forefront of all planning and solicitation efforts, they will probably be successful in establishing in donors a lifelong pattern of giving. No matter what strategy an organization plans to adopt in its fundraising efforts, the bottom line depends on regular donations. Without the regular support of individuals, corporations, foundations, and government (even if it is only in the form of a tax break), most organizations would not be able to survive. Let us examine in more detail how to go about establishing a pattern of regular giving.

Strategic Planning and Fundraising

As noted, most fundraising activity begins with a great deal of background work. Unless the organization happens to have a wealthy benefactor who hands out money with no questions asked, countless hours must be spent preparing to ask people for their support. The flow chart in Figure 12-1 depicts a typical system for organizing the fundraising for an organization.

An organization's strategic plan normally contains a specific operational plan for the proposed fundraising efforts. In Chapter 5, "Planning and Decision Making," the concepts of the overall organizational strategy and the operational strategies for special areas were discussed. In Chapter 11, "Marketing and the Arts," we saw how the marketing plan would be integrated with the strategic plan. Now we consider how the fundraising needs would be integrated into the overall strategic plans.

The overall strategy the organization adopts will of course effect the development of the organization's profile and audit. Take the example of an organization that adopts a growth strategy. It is safe to assume that the fundraising staff would need to address the issue of finding more new sources of funds for the organization. This requires that time be spent on donor research. On the other hand, if the organization adopts a stability strategy, the fundraisers might concentrate their efforts on the current donor base. As with any planning process, multiple strategies probably should be incorporated into the overall master plan. However, the staff and budget resources required to support multiple approaches can become burdensome.

Profile and Audit

The fundraising process shown in Figure 12-1 is broken down into five major activity areas. Of course the starting and ending points in any process are not always clear and distinct. Assessment must be taken before action.

The organization's mission and programs are the source for all fundraising activities. These elements are the core from which you build

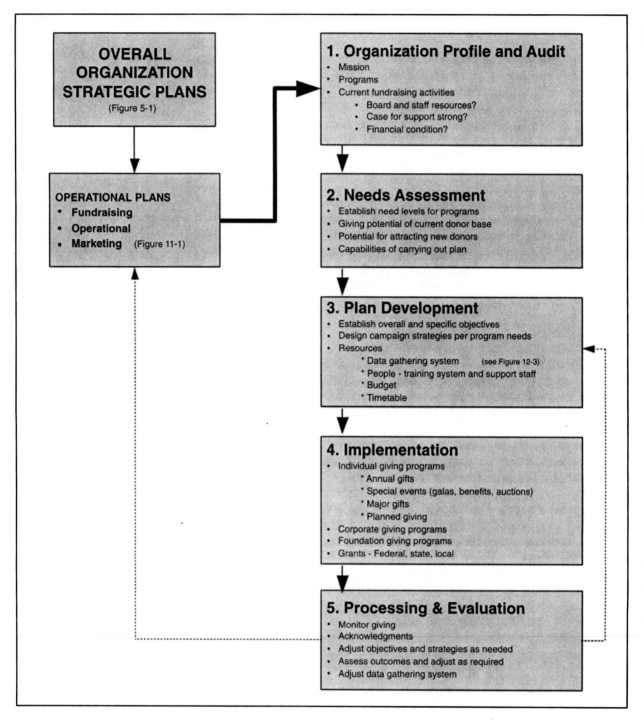

Figure 12-1 Fundraising Planning and Process

your fundraising goals. If your goals include bringing opera to school-children in your community, then it will be clear to donors why you need funding for a truck or a van. In addition, you more than likely engage in fundraising now. The common questions that the fundraising staff starts with include: How well is the current process working? Do you have a clear and strong case for support? Is the financial condition of the organization healthy? Focus groups from the community may be helpful in gathering outside input about your organization. For example, organizations tend to think people in the community know more about them than they do.

As we noted in Chapter 11, marketing and fundraising are usually less successful when presented in a product- or sales-oriented manner. A general appeal that says, "Give to us because we make great music and we are worldclass," will not promote the exchange process. A letter mailed to a parent that says, "Your gift will help a child experience the wonder and joy of music," might prove to be more successful.

The next step, determining the amount needed, is based on a careful analysis of the budget and the fiscal health of the organization. For example, if the strategic plan called for establishing an operating endowment fund to provide an annual income of $50,000, the fundraising goal could be as high as $1.25 million. This figure assumes that the $1.25 million would earn an interest rate of 8 percent, thus yielding $100,000 per year. After deducting $50,000 for the operating fund, the remaining $50,000 would be reinvested in the endowment to overcome the annual effects of inflation, which is assumed to be 4 percent in this example.

The actual campaign planning and development involves formulating written material, creating the graphics and brochures to communicate the project or program, planning special fundraising events (e.g., auctions, dinners, and costume balls), and tactics such as telephoning donors to ask for support. The training of staff and volunteers, establishing a detailed timetable, and donor research all must be done before launching a campaign.

The implementation stage typically is on several fronts. Gifts from all categories of donors are solicited with the intent of building the long-term relationships necessary for future campaigns. The cycle of preparing, asking, evaluating, and starting to plan all over again is inherent in the fundraising function of an arts organization.

Funding Pyramid

The capital campaign funding pyramid shown in Figure 12-2 is one approach used to establish how many gifts at which amounts will be needed to meet a specific goal. A major capital campaign with a goal of $5 million usually concentrates its initial efforts on raising at least half of the money before publicly announcing the campaign effort. A lead gift of $250,000 and gifts of at least $25,000 are secured before the campaign is announced in order to build momentum. With at least half of the money raised, fundraisers can tell people, "Here's a project that others are willing to support."

To succeed in building the pyramid from the top down, the fundraisers must do their homework. Identifying possible funding sources, evaluating their giving potential, ranking them within the pyramid, and finding the right contact person could take a year or more. All of this work can amount to nothing if the wrong person asks for the gift. As James Lord says, "People give to people." It is critical that the fundraising staff educate board members and other volunteers about how and when to ask for support. As we will see later in this chapter, the entire fundraising effort is a marketing effort. The fundraiser tries to match the wants and needs of the donor with the goods and services of the organization.

Assuming success, the process is completed by legally accounting for the gift and acknowledging the support. As with the marketing

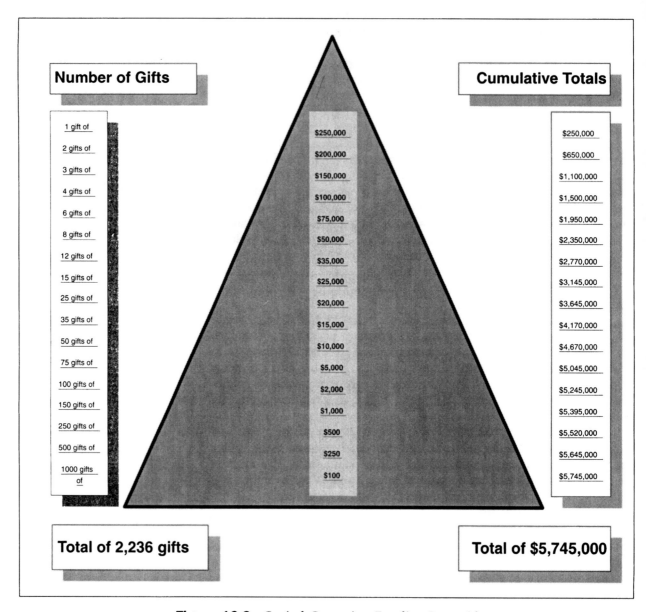

Figure 12-2   Capital Campaign Funding Pyramid

campaign, evaluation and adjustment go on constantly in an effort to fine-tune and maximize the gift-giving program.

Marketing and Fundraising

An effective fundraising campaign requires the implementation of a well-organized marketing system. As in the marketing campaign, the goal is to achieve a close match between the donor and the funding need. In this case, the exchange process should make donors feel that the money, goods, or services they are donating will help solve a specific problem. For example, the money they donate to the operating endowment, if marketed properly, becomes a gift that supports any number of aspects of the organization. Finding the proper "hot button" for each donor—for example, the young artists' program or the museum arts classes for children—is a way to maximize the satisfaction of giving. The fact is, if the fundraising campaign is not donor-driven in the way it is packaged and presented, it will probably not be as effective or successful.

Fundraising Management

Fundraising involves what by now should be the familiar aspects of project management: budgets, schedules, timetables, problem solving, and group leadership techniques. An individual with excellent group and project management skills is required for a successful campaign. Excellent communication skills are a must for the development personnel.

Thousands of details must be coordinated into a unified whole if the organization is to reach its fundraising goals. We begin by examining the background work required for getting ready to ask for support. Then, we review the techniques and tools used to maximize the possibility of support from various funding entities.

Background Work

What Does the Organization Do?

After completing the fundraising audit and assessment, the process should shift to formulating what the organization can do to address a range of needs in the community. How does the symphony orchestra, museum, or dance, theater, or opera company satisfy the current needs of the community? What needs are not being met? Can the arts organization fulfill any of these needs? In *Managing a Nonprofit Organization*, Thomas Wolf identifies three important steps in this process, which he calls the case for support:[8]

1. Identify the important problems or needs that the organization intends to address with the help of the contributions.
2. Demonstrate the organization's ability to address these needs.
3. Match the proposed areas of organizational activity with the funder's own philanthropic interests.

The obvious starting point for an organization attempting to identify problems or needs is to address the current programs and projects. For example, the fictitious theater company examined in Chapter 9, "Organizational Controls and Budgets," had established a home season, touring operation, education program, and building fund (capital campaign) to meet the various needs of the community. To make its case for support, the theater company would offer proof of how it is uniquely qualified to meet the community's needs through its regular season, which enriches the cultural life of the community by presenting quality productions. The theater could argue that the touring operation provides a service to a wide geographical area and a diverse audience and that the education program offers a school or apprentice program to teach acting skills to young people. The building fund is targeted to provide a permanent home for the theater company so that it may increase its effectiveness in presenting its season and its projects in the community.

After the theater company outlines what it is doing and how it is effectively addressing the community's needs, the important process of matching activities to funders takes place.

Accurate research about potential donors is critical to making the optimal match. For example, a foundation may focus on education, a corporation may support high-visibility activities such as touring, and

Study Philanthropy?

A recent article in the *New York Times* noted that there were over 75 graduate schools offering masters programs in philanthropy in America. Schools such as Yale, Indiana University–Purdue University, and numerous centers for not-for-profit study have proliferated over the last 20 years. The article also points out that salaries for professionals are generally one-third lower in general for the not-for-profit sector.

SOURCE: Dirk Johnson, "A Master's Degree in Philanthropy Teaches the Business of Doing Good," *New York Times* (December 24, 1997), p. C-19.

Study to Give Away Money?

Another newspaper article focused on teaching the rich how to give money away. The Rockefeller Foundation offers a course in Practical Philanthropy. Tuition is $10,000 for a week-long series of courses on reading financial statements to sharing information with guest speakers about the need and impact of giving. Weekend training sessions by consulting firms in Boston were also noted.

SOURCE: Alex Kuczynski, "The Very Rich Pay to Learn How to Give Money Away," *New York Times* (May 3, 1998), p. A-1.

individual donors may want to be associated with a new facility. A significant amount of time can be wasted if the wrong donor is approached. Even worse, a potential donor may be turned off to your organization because of an inappropriate approach. A closer examination of this matching process is presented later in this chapter when various funding sources are discussed.

Staff and Board Participation

One of the expectations of any fundraising campaign is that staff and board members will actively participate to help reach the goal. Potential donors may ask how much support staff and board members provide to the organization. Answers about the average contribution per staff or board member must be at hand. After all, why should donors give to an organization that does not have the support of its own people?

Many nonprofit organizations expect their board members to contribute a particular amount each year. This could range from a few hundred to many thousands of dollars. For some organizations, especially organizations made up of board members selected for their expertise and not for their wealth, there are expectations about contributing specific amounts of time to projects each year. In addition, nonprofit organizations are now asking staff members to make an annual donation. The amount is usually significantly smaller on average than the board member's gift, but the demonstration of strong internal support for the organization is important when talking to outside donors.

Data Management

A well-designed management information system to gather data about potential donors is critical if the organization is to organize its fundraising campaigns. Chapters 9 and 11 provide examples of management information systems designed for the overall operation, the financial system, and marketing. In arts organizations, which usually have very limited staff resources, the data gathered about donors should be integrated with the sales and marketing systems. This integration can be achieved if the computer software is designed to capture and store information about sales and giving. Several companies specialize in fundraising software for nonprofit organizations. Any issue of the *Chronicle of Philanthropy* will contain advertisements for such systems. A careful analysis of the software's capabilities is required, and the support available from the company after the system is purchased should be explored to ensure that the organization's data management needs will be met in the long-term. For example, the fundraising financial record-keeping system must be able to track revenue through the entire accounting system. As we saw in Chapter 10, "Economics and Financial Management," the balance sheet and account statements must reflect changes in the fund balances based on these donations. The donor tracking system must therefore be integrated with the accounting software used by the organization.

Data System Needs   Members of the development staff should be able to sit down at a computer terminal, enter the name of a subscriber, single-ticket buyer, or member, and pull up a complete list of all transactions or donations made by that person. Staff members might also want to identify everyone who donated more than $50 and less than $250 in the last year. Donor tracking systems usually contain data fields about the estimated salary and giving potential for each subscriber or

In the News

An article in the *Chronicle of Philanthropy* pointed out that more fundraisers in resource-strapped organizations are using the Internet as a tool to assist in fundraising research. The ability to download foundation reports, application forms, and other relevant information represents a major shift in the whole information-gathering process. The ability to secure frequent updates from funding entities, to participate in electronic discussion groups, and to locate new sources of funding help make the Internet a useful tool for an arts manager. The major challenge in using the Internet is that too much data is available. It is therefore easy to become overwhelmed with data or to waste time looking for yet one more website. The article did list several websites for organizations such as the Foundation Center, the Grantsmanship Center, as well as various grants discussion groups.

SOURCE: Marilyn Dickey, "Fundraisers Turn to the Internet," *Chronicle of Philanthropy* (May 1, 1997), p. 23.

member. Staff members might also want to know who gave from a particular range of zip codes. The ability to cross-reference donors with sales of subscriptions or memberships is also important. For example, if some patrons only purchased single tickets to the musicals that the theater company performed, this information could be effectively incorporated in a fundraising letter. The letter would mention the individuals' fondness for musicals and suggest that they make a donation to support the production fund so more great shows could be produced for their enjoyment.

The donor data management system is also critical in developing confidential financial information. For example, if the business section of the local newspaper announces that one of your patrons just received a promotion, this information should find its way into the data file. A promotion probably means a larger paycheck. This information is noted so that the next time a solicitation is made, a higher gift amount is requested.

A word of caution is in order about confidential information. The tendency to put large amounts of irrelevant personal data in a computer is directly proportional to the ease with which the data can be entered. A clear policy about what information may be kept in the donor file and who may have access to these data is important if the organization is to have any credibility in the community. Policies about the

Web Resources

The computer software to manage donor data range in price from a few hundred dollars to many thousands. Many smaller organizations use MS Excel or MS Access or Filemaker Pro to develop their own home-grown donor records system. Some sample websites to explore include: http://www.donorperfect.com/, http://www.blackbaud.com/solutions/fundraising.asp, http://www.linkedsoftware.com/, http://fundtracksoftware.com/, or try http://www.fundraiser-software.com/.

Donor Bill of Rights

The Donor Bill of Rights was created by the American Association of Fundraising Counsel (AAFRC), Association for Healthcare Philanthropy (AHP), the Association of Fundraising Professionals (AFP), and the Council for Advancement and Support of Education (CASE). It has been endorsed by numerous organizations.

The Donor Bill of Rights

Philanthropy is based on voluntary action for the common good. It is a tradition of giving and sharing that is primary to the quality of life. To ensure that philanthropy merits the respect and trust of the general public, and that donors and prospective donors can have full confidence in the nonprofit organizations and causes they are asked to support, we declare that all donors have these rights:

I. To be informed of the organization's mission, of the way the organization intends to use donated resources, and of its capacity to use donations effectively for their intended purposes.

II. To be informed of the identity of those serving on the organization's governing board, and to expect the board to exercise prudent judgment in its stewardship responsibilities.

III. To have access to the organization's most recent financial statements.

IV. To be assured their gifts will be used for the purposes for which they were given.

V. To receive appropriate acknowledgement and recognition.

VI. To be assured that information about their donation is handled with respect and with confidentiality to the extent provided by law.

VII. To expect that all relationships with individuals representing organizations of interest to the donor will be professional in nature.

VIII. To be informed whether those seeking donations are volunteers, employees of the organization, or hired solicitors.

IX. To have the opportunity for their names to be deleted from mailing lists that an organization may intend to share.

X. To feel free to ask questions when making a donation and to receive prompt, truthful, and forthright answers.

SOURCE: National Society of Fundraising Executive website: http://www.afpnet.org/.

confidentiality of the data gathered by the development staff must also be enforced. Passwords or security codes to access the donor data will be meaningless if staff members sit around the lounge discussing how much someone gave to the operation. Any breach in security should be dealt with quickly and visibly.

Fundraising Costs and Control

The annual campaign and the various capital fund drives contain a mix of activities designed to reach as many potential donors as the budget will permit. Development managers always seek ways to keep the costs of raising money as low as possible. The impact of these costs cannot be ignored. Potential donors want to know whether the organization is capable of using their gift efficiently. Although fundraising costs may vary with different types of campaigns, if they reach 20 percent of the total raised, it is time for the organization to reassess its methods. Organizations that can keep fundraising costs under 10 percent are usually viewed favorably by donors.

An effective budget control system must be in place before an organization undertakes any fundraising activity. In addition, legal requirements must be met when reporting income raised through donations on federal and state tax forms. Some states require special licenses before any fundraising may begin.

Direct and Indirect Costs   Arts organizations usually have direct fundraising costs for salaries, wages, and benefits. These costs should be distributed across the budget if several fundraising activities are supervised by one staff. Developing a project budget such as the one shown in Figure 9-8 makes it easier to track costs. Consultant fees would also be listed as a direct cost to the project. Other costs include supplies and services (paper, copying, printing, telephones), equipment (computers), and travel. Indirect fundraising costs reflect such items as a portion of the rent, lease, or mortgage, utilities, and the maintenance of general office equipment used for fundraising activities. For the purposes of budgeting, the financial manager must calculate the various costs of each area's use of the common resources and formulate a distribution that can be used to prepare fundraising budgets.

When applying for government grants, the organization can be reimbursed for indirect costs if these costs are reflected in the budget. For example, if a museum gets a grant for $1 million to run an educational program, 30 to 50 percent of the budget could be allocated for indirect costs. The organization could therefore expect that an additional $300,000 to $500,000 would be provided above the $1 million to support the costs of supporting the project. Grant applications to foundations and corporations normally show indirect costs as part of the overall project budget. Foundations and corporations may place restrictions on or refuse to support indirect costs. The application guidelines for these granting agencies normally outline the costs they consider to be legitimate.

Fundraising Techniques and Tools

A successful fundraising campaign never ends. Most organizations must continually seek donations if they are to survive financially. As soon as the annual campaign has been completed for one fiscal year, it is time to get started on next year's fund drive. The overall goal remains the same each year: to establish a regular pattern of giving to the organization. Let us examine some of the specific details of the various ongoing campaigns that an organization must maintain. In addition to the occasional large capital campaign (usually conducted every three to five years), annual campaigns targeted to individuals, corporations, foundations, and government agencies require constant attention and fine-tuning.

Individual Donors

All organizations want to have a substantial number of individual donors who make regular unrestricted gifts to the organization. An unrestricted gift carries no stipulation as to how the funds may be spent. Unrestricted gifts give the organization the flexibility to shift funds to fill the greatest need. Restricted gifts, on the other hand, are given on the assumption that the funds will be used for a specific project or program. The organization has a legal obligation to use restricted funds in the manner designated by the donor. An unrestricted gift might be added to the operating fund balance or be used to cover the expenses of a specific production or project. A restricted gift might be designated only for the building fund endowment. Because solicitations to corporations, foundations, and the government often carry distribution restrictions, the more unrestricted gifts the organization can regularly gather, the better.

The actual percentages of your audience who may donate to your organization will vary with how effective you are in making your case. For example, if you have 1,500 regular season subscribers you might have between 10 percent and 30 percent that regularly donate to your annual fund. Obviously the fundraiser's goal is to achieve the highest percentage of donors from the subscriber base as possible. As you see in "FYI—Giving," the mainstay of support comes from individuals.

Because regular giving is the lifeblood of many organizations, it is fairly common for organizations to maintain a standing committee of board members and staff to coordinate the fundraising activity. Yearly funding goals and objectives are set, a detailed timetable is created, specific details—such as who makes the calls and who signs the letters—are worked out, and assignments are distributed to the board and the staff. This is an example of all of the management theories coming together. The fundraising committee must plan, organize, and lead effectively if the organization is to remain strong.

The techniques for building a large base of individual donors include donor research, offering numerous funding options, personal contact, telephone solicitation, direct mail, and special events.

Donor Research   Many of the techniques used to develop an audience are used in donor research. The current subscribers, members, and single-ticket buyers form the core of the active donor base. This core group should be subjected to the most intense research, and as complete a donor file as possible should be compiled on each person (see Figure 12-3).

The next level of research focuses on less active supporters and prospects. Vast amounts of data about prospective donors must be gathered and rated in terms of potential for further use. As Thomas Wolf says, "Only prospectors find gold."[9] The organization must commit personnel to go through lists of former subscribers, patrons of other arts organizations, country club members, and members of social or business organizations. They must also explore school phone directories (including college or university phone books), references given by current

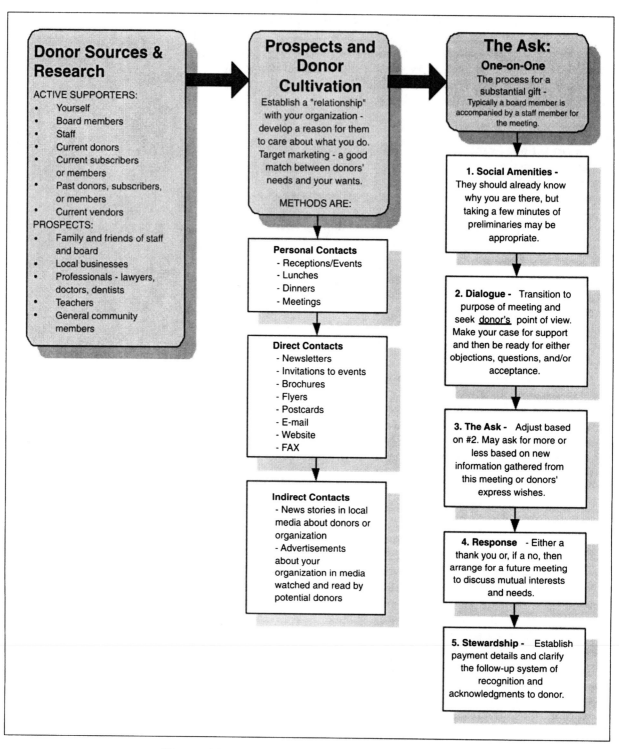

Figure 12-3 Donor Cultivation and Solicitation

donors, and published social registers. Sources such as *Who's Who in America*, which publishes regional directories, may also be of use.

Funding Options Fundraisers like to speak of gift giving as an "opportunity" or a chance to make an "investment in the future." Well-organized development managers design several choices for donors using a concept not unlike a menu. For example, gifts can be targeted for the current operating fund for those people who want their gifts to be put to use immediately. Others may want their gift to go to an endowment fund, which is invested, and only a portion of the interest is used to fund operations or special programs. A scholarship fund is a good choice for donors who want their gifts to have maximum longevity. Others may want to offer their funds in the form of a deferred gift, that is, a promise to provide funds, property, stocks, bonds, life insurance, property, or jewelry at some future date. Another form of deferred giving is a bequest, which is a gift that is distributed through the donor's will. Some donors specify that a portion of their life insurance will be donated to an organization.

Figure 12-4 shows one possible rating system for evaluating major gift prospects. Although there are no hard and fast rules here, the organization must have a rating system in place for every donor. Without this information the fundraiser is operating in the dark. Asking for too much or too little money can have equally negative outcomes. Donors who consider a major gift $500 may be frightened away from the organization if you ask them for $5,000. At the same time, donors capable of giving $50,000 may be insulted if you ask them for only $5,000.

As with any menu, it should be possible for the donor to combine several options. For example, an organization with annual donors who make bequests and give regularly to an endowed fund is in a fortunate position. Offering a selection of donor options is taking the principles of being a customer-driven, marketing-oriented organization to its logical conclusion. The donor programs must be designed to provide the maximum exchange satisfaction for donors who write that check or sign a document giving something to the organization.

Donor Ratings (Sample)	Gift Request if (To be given over 5 years)	Minimum income is .... and	Minimum Net Assets
When cultivating a long-term donor you will need to establish a target for the maximum you think is achievable over 5 years.	$7,500	$30,000	$375,000
	$12,500	$50,000	$625,000
	$18,750	$75,000	$1,000,000
The factors that may alter this rating system, which is based on 5% of the income or 10% of the net worth, include	$25,000	$100,000	$1,250,000
	$37,500	$150,000	$1,875,000
	$50,000	$200,000	$2,500,000
* Giving history	$62,5000	$250,000	$3,125,000
* Timing	$125,000	$500,000	$6,250,000
* Financial stability	$250,000	$1,000,000	$12,500,000

Figure 12-4 Donor Rating Matrix

Personal Contacts   Personal contact is the preferred method for cultivation and for securing larger gifts because fundraising is most effective when people ask other people for their support. The management of public events such as meetings, receptions, lunches, and dinners give the fundraiser the opportunity to keep in direct contact without directly asking for money. Some donors like the social aspects of seeing and being seen at various public functions. Helping them realize their need to be seen will probably pay off later when making the more personal one-on-one solicitation.

In a typical major gifts or capital campaign in which large sums of money are sought, the organization usually engages in a long courtship with the donor. Let us assume that a museum's donor research targets a local business executive for a gift to the building fund. On paper, this person looks like a good candidate, but without an introduction, the organization might get a firm refusal. If the research indicates that a current member of the board knows the executive, a valuable link exists. If there is no existing contact, an appointment should be made to get things rolling. The first meeting will probably be brief and informational. The board member who knows the executive should attend the meeting to help smooth out the initial communication. A staff member might accompany the board member to be introduced and answer questions, but his or her presence is merely functional. A package of information about the organization and a brief outline of how the current fundraising drive is doing would probably be enough for this first visit.

The key goal in making the first contact is for each party to learn more about the other. Followup meetings, invitations to various events sponsored by the organization, lunch at a local restaurant, informative notes, and updates by telephone would round out the process. When the fundraising committee feels that the time is right, the designated contact makes the request. The staff member should not actually ask for the gift. It is unethical for staff members to make such requests because they are paid by the organization. The board member or a volunteer should do the asking.

Communication Tools   In order to keep donors informed and aware of your programs and needs a series of carefully planned communications must be part of the cultivation process (see Figure 12-3). For example, newsletters, brochures, flyers, postcards, and even group E-mail can prove useful in keeping your current and potential donors informed. Keeping an active website updated also helps deliver news to interested parties faster than print media or letters. In addition, the public relations and marketing staff must have a plan to ensure that news stories or advertisements keep the organization visible in the community. Donors like seeing the organization they support being seen by others as an effective member of the community.

Telephone Solicitations   As shown in Figure 12-2, the typical funding pyramid includes many gifts valued at $500 or less. Personal contact is not an effective way to reach all of these donors. One of the most cost-effective alternatives is to make phone calls to as many prospects as possible.

Enthusiastic leadership is a must when motivating the board and other volunteers to ask for money over the telephone. This is especially true because the process of asking people for money can be very discouraging. Fundraisers always tell volunteers, "Don't take that 'no' personally!" However, it is only human nature to feel as if your request was rejected because you did not ask in the right way or you were not convincing enough.

Small organizations normally schedule a week or two each year for telephone fundraising campaigns. Banks of telephones, eager volunteers, and a little training with a well-written and flexible script can translate into thousands of dollars for an organization. Again, solid research can pay off for the organization. When a caller begins talking with a prospect, an information card or computer screen should help guide the interaction. Potential donors are initially very hesitant about getting a phone call from a stranger, so the first 20 seconds of the conversation is usually scripted to ask questions designed to get the prospect to respond. Assuming that the information about the potential donors is correct, it should be possible to establish what they thought of the last performance they saw or the last exhibit they attended. The key is engaging the person and building to the request in a timely manner. If the caller is able to connect with the prospect, the typical tactic is to ask for a bit more than the donor research indicates. For example, if it is possible that the potential donor might give $150, the caller might be scripted to suggest initially an "investment" of $500. Eventually, an amount with which the donor feels comfortable will be reached, and the "closing" can take place. The logistics of getting the gift information and payment method correct and thanking the donor concludes the process.

Advances in technology have permitted computers to dial automatically and play prerecorded sales messages, but many donors hang up as soon as they realize that someone has invaded their privacy with a request for money. However, the benefit for nonprofit organizations is a cost savings when they use this technology.

Direct Mail   Direct mail marketing and fundraising is a big business in the United States. Every day, high-speed computer printers merge-print millions of pieces of what most people call "junk mail" with names and addresses purchased from list brokers. Many people never open the handiwork of the direct mail marketer, but enough people respond to these offers to convince businesses that the cost is worth incurring.

Arts organizations have used the techniques of the direct mail marketer for years in attempting to build a subscriber or member base. The mailing of a solicitation for funds follows the basic direct mail principles and is traditionally part of the mix of options used by the development staff.

The outer envelope represents the critical first contact with potential donors. The envelope must communicate a short, strong, and clear message that something of interest is inside. A popular technique uses the word *Free* on the envelope with the assumption that people will be curious to see what the offer is. If the fundraiser can get potential donors to open the envelope, the combination of a well-written letter and an informative brochure will bring readers further into the solicitation. Because most people initially scan the text of the letter and brochure, the copy must be written and laid out in such a way as to get the message across in as few words as possible. The response device (the piece returned to the organization) and the reply envelope should provide a fast and easy way of completing the solicitation.

Tracking Responses   Direct mail is a long-term investment. Organizations that expect much more than a 1 or 2 percent response rate may be in for a surprise. For example, a 1.5 percent response rate for a 10,000-piece mailing would yield 150 donations. Let's say the average donation is $25. The first mailing thus yields $3,750. First-class postage, letter, brochure, reply device, and reply envelope cost an average of 60¢ per unit. The first mailing therefore costs $6,000 and only raises $3,750. However, if you view these 150 donors as a long-term investment, the $2,250 loss will eventually be recouped. Suppose that the arts fundraiser tracks these donors as a target group that responded to a particular campaign. In the next year, a telephone solicitation of these 150 people yields a 40 percent response rate, and the average donation is $75. The organization has gained $4,500 minus the cost of telephone solicitation. Let's say it costs $150 to get this next $4,500. This leaves the organization ahead by $2,100 on its total investment of $6,150. In the third and fourth years, 50 percent of the remaining donors from the first year's campaign give an average of $125 each. The net yield now increases to $7,635 in donations after subtracting $6,240 in solicitation costs over four years. If carefully monitored and tracked, the organization should be able to create an overall system of periodic direct mail solicitations that yield a regular cash flow.

Note that this simplified example of a direct mail cost analysis is used to illustrate a point. Direct mail marketers have very comprehensive formulas for calculating campaign costs. For example, the data in this example does not take into account inflation, which is a cost to the campaign. In addition, the cost of raising money is fairly high in this example. Costs of 20¢ or less per dollar raised would be more appropriate. Of course, if just one of those few donors you recruited five years ago makes a major gift to the organization for $250,000, the direct mail costs can become a minor issue.

Special Events Arts organizations usually try to hold at least one event a year as a fundraiser. A group of volunteers coordinates and produces a costume ball, a silent or live auction, a raffle, or a benefit performance. The effort and time required to produce a major event can be overwhelming if the organization does not have the resources to make it happen. The costs of producing an event like a costume ball may run into the tens of thousands of dollars. Careful control of the budget is required, or the event may end up costing the organization more than it earns in donations. However, with a good planning committee and a realistic schedule, it is possible to earn thousands regularly for the organization and to provide a memorable experience for the donors.

These events can also provide visibility in the community for the organization. Raffles, for example, can be a way of involving the local business community in the arts by persuading business owners to donate goods and services. State and local governments may place restrictions on certain types of events, so it is always a good idea to consult with a lawyer before proceeding.

Corporate Giving

As pointed out earlier in this chapter corporations donated $8.2 billion to charities in 1997. Although this is a substantial amount, it represents less than 6 percent of the $143.5 billion given by all funders to charities in 1997. Typically, there is also a strong relationship between the economy and corporate giving. In addition, corporations undergo constant changes in ownership as they are bought, sold, and merged. Nonprofit organizations must adapt to the changing business environment if they

In the News

An article in the *New York Times* entitled "We Paid How Much for Dinner?" pointed out the reality that the pricing of special event or gala tickets often does not cover all the costs. The article specifically notes that the tickets for the Conservatory Ball for the New York Botanical Garden, which were $1,000 each, stated that "all but $150 of each ticket" is tax-deductible. However, the author of the article discovered that the cost of the event actually came out to be $461.50 per person. According to IRS regulations, the deduction the ticket buyer is able to claim should only be for the difference between $461.50 and $1,000. However, the article points out that in this case, the Botanical Garden covered the difference through the overall operating budget for the event. Regardless of the difference, an arts organization needs to be careful to design special events that return an agreed upon percentage above costs. Ideally, the board should be aware of the return and have in place policies about the cost of sponsoring events. It is also important to calculate the staff time as a cost of doing the event. Often this is overlooked when glowing reports are made about how little was spent on a special event.

SOURCE: Stephanie Strom, "We Paid How Much for Dinner?" *New York Times* (May 19, 2002), p. 9-1.

intend to capitalize on the available funds. In the best of times, arts and cultural organizations are usually not at the top of the corporate funding priority list, but regular support can be found if fundraisers are willing to make the effort to track down the sources.

Corporate support is based in large part on the concept of *reciprocity*: What will the corporation gain by supporting a performance or an exhibition? A company may have motives for funding a specific event because of its public relations value, marketing potential, or benefits to its employees. The fundraiser's research must focus on trying to fit the organization into the corporation's donor strategy. The lack of a good strategic fit, as it is called, is the primary reason why support is not given to an organization. Arts organizations must remember that establishing a good strategic match is part of their marketing process. The packaging and emphasis of a proposal may need to be adjusted as the priorities of corporations change.

Corporate support is usually restricted to the immediate community because businesses are concerned about raising their profile in their immediate market. Larger corporations sometimes sponsor performances or major exhibits that have a highly visible national tour program. For the most part, a regional arts group has little chance of attracting national corporate support unless there is an active branch of the corporation in the area.

A method once used to raise corporate support in some communities was to develop a United Way–type fundraising campaign for the arts. However, for many nonprofit organizations, the benefits of a regular funding source were offset by a drop in overall corporate giving. Companies no longer had to give as many grants because they consolidated their giving and reduced their overall commitment of funds. Corporations saw an opportunity to continue to do good, but for less.

Potential Problems The most problematic issue related to corporate support is the conditions (some direct, some implied) that may be attached to a gift. For example, a performing arts group or museum may find its corporate support quickly withdrawn at the first sign of controversy. Once withdrawn, the chances of getting this support back may be very limited.

There may also be ethical considerations that the organization must take into account before applying for corporate support. For example, seeking funds from companies that produce products thought to be harmful to the environment or to people, or from companies that have holdings in politically repressive countries, could be detrimental to the community perception of the arts organization.

Fundraising Process The overall planning and research process for corporate fundraising is not greatly different from the one used for individuals or foundations. Corporations that make direct grants are listed in publications such as the *National Guide to Funding in Arts and Culture*. They number slightly more than 300.[10] The Internet may also prove useful when seeking information about potential corporate donors. Corporations generally establish foundations to distribute their gifts.

One of the most important steps in this process is the direct contact with an individual in the corporation or business. In this simplified model, if there is no existing contact, then a courtship process is undertaken. In many cases, the organization rewrites the proposal before asking for the gift because the initial meeting with the corporate contact made it clear that the original proposal did not address the company's current funding interests. In other cases, contact occurs before the proposal is written.

Whatever the situation, the overall process of corporate fundraising must be integrated within the master plan (see Figure 12-1). The funding manager for a nonprofit organization should read the business section of the daily paper and follow national trends in the business publications in an effort to stay in tune with the opportunities that may arise.

Foundations

A foundation is defined as a "nonprofit, non-governmental organization with a principal fund or endowment of its own that maintains or aids charitable, educational, religious, or other activities serving the public good, primarily by making grants to other organizations."[11] *The National Guide to Funding in Arts and Culture,* 5th Edition, lists 5,237 entries. They are distributed as follows:[12]

Grant-making foundations	4,618
Community foundations	223
Direct corporate-giving programs	342

The National Guide is an excellent research source for information about types of grants, amounts granted, purposes, limitations, publications, and application procedures. The inside front cover of the guide provides the reader with a key to the funding organization profiles. The website at http://www.fdncenter.org/ is also an excellent entry into the world of grants. Many other resource books are available as well, two of which are listed under Additional Resources.

As with corporate fundraising, a good match between an organization and foundation must exist. Foundations usually fund specific types of activities. For example, the Ticketmaster Foundation supports arts and culture programs and health care associations in California. They do not make grants to individuals, and they contribute only to preselected organizations. *The National Guide to Funding in Arts and Culture* indicates that in 1995 they gave grants up to $25,000.[13]

As always, a clear, concise proposal and ability statement is the first step in the application process. Because many small foundations have little or no staffing, the application procedure may be as simple as a cover letter, a one-page proposal, and a budget. A large foundation may require a proposal of eight to ten pages, and a screening committee may review applications before referring them to a grants committee. Regardless of the length of the proposal, the applicant must state the problem, describe how the organization is qualified to solve the problem, explain the benefits to the community, and outline how the effectiveness of the project will be measured and evaluated. Fundraising activity remains a person-to-person business, and without the proper introductions, the applying organization is an unknown entity. The greater the depth of involvement of the board in the community, the better the chances that the organization will be able to make itself a part of the grant-making network that exists in foundation funding.

Government Funding

It is possible to find funding for the arts at all levels of government in the United States. Local arts agencies usually have limited funds, but if an organization is trying to establish a positive record of effectively using grant money, the local level is a good starting point. For example, local agencies often provide funding for outreach programs into the schools. They may also help sponsor programming, assist with advertising to bring in out of town audiences, or subsidize ticket discounts to students or older audiences. The application procedures are usually simple, and the amount of time and money spent administering the support is minimal.

State arts councils usually have permanent staffs, standard application procedures, formal review panels, and standard evaluation and reporting procedures. They generally offer numerous types of grants, including grants for programming, new works, outreach touring, and individual artists. In many cases, the state agencies parallel the National Endowment for the Arts. Funding research is again required to achieve the best match between the arts organization and the granting agency.

The National Assembly of Local Arts Agencies located in Washington, D.C., sponsors an annual meeting and offers their members regular workshops on many areas of operation. Because NASAA (http://www.nasaa-arts.org/) members form the core of agencies that distribute state and federal funds, an arts organization would be wise to cultivate a relationship with these organizations.

The National Endowment for the Arts   As noted in Chapter 4, "Arts Organizations in a Changing World," the National Endowment for the Arts is the major source for funding and recognition in the arts community. The NEA website publishes information that gives applicants an overview of the major grant areas. Each program area and division of the NEA publishes detailed guidelines to help applicants through the process.

The 2000 annual report by the NEA indicates that approximately $83 million in grants were awarded.[14] NEA matching grants programs help stimulate an important partnership between arts organizations and donors. Organizations that receive funds from the NEA also benefit from the recognition. Having received a grant adds to the legitimacy of the enterprise and, though the NEA never intended it, creates a "stamp of approval" for the arts group. Donors assume that if a group or an artist had successfully passed through the grant review process, the work must be worthy of merit. As discussed in Chapter 4, the political turmoil that invaded the NEA's operation in the late 1980s and the 1990s affected the agency's image and its ability to support the arts in America. While the public's attention was focused on a limited number of controversial grants, thousands of grant requests were being reviewed, processed, and funded.

The Peer Review Process   The core of the NEA granting process is the peer review. A panel of experts are assembled at specific times during the year to review applications. Members of the committee are assigned specific grants to study in detail and to discuss at the panel meetings. The time for each presentation is limited, and the competition for support is intense. Each year, the NEA receives thousands of grant applications. The average grant application receives only a few minutes of discussion. Therefore, the proposal must be brief and to the point. The NEA staff reviews the details of the application, but the opening proposal, which is very limited in space, is what is most often read. If the reader's interest is not captured immediately or if the proposal raises more questions than it answers, the request will be pushed to the bottom of the stack. Consulting with the NEA staff may help when researching the kinds of key words, phrases, or concepts that are likely to catch the panelists' attention. At the same time, a brilliant proposal may fail because an organization has no track record, meaning that it has no previous history of having effectively used donated funds.

Applying for NEA funding is not very different from the corporate and foundation process. Establishing contacts within the agency and cultivating relationships with key people will help to establish the arts organization as a viable target for funding.

Other Government Sources   Up to this point, our discussion of grants and the government has focused on the performing arts. The National Endowment for the Humanities also provides grants covering such areas as design, museums, research, music history, and interdisciplinary projects. In fact, thousands of grants are available from the federal government. Many of these grants have criteria that may make it difficult for an arts organization to qualify, but occasionally an opportunity arises that is worth pursuing.

The key to finding government support is research. One helpful source is the *Federal Register*, which is a very thoroughly indexed and cross-referenced publication that lists all federal grant programs. The *Catalog of Federal Domestic Assistance* (http://www.cfda.gov/) contains information on government funding programs and is indexed by agency and subject area. The Federal government makes extensive use of its websites and the Internet to make much of this information available. Patience is required when wading through the myriad of choices, but vast amounts of information about Federal programs can prove helpful.

Conclusion

Arts organizations have come to depend on funds from a mix of donors. Funding levels from individuals, corporations, foundations, and government agencies are subject to changing environments. For example, support for arts and culture changes as the economy improves or declines, as public attitudes about censorship shift, as government support for social services declines, as state arts budgets are slashed, and as companies disappear through mergers. Because the funding arena can be so volatile, arts groups are usually advised to avoid becoming dependent on any one source of funds.

The situation of too many nonprofit groups chasing too few donations by foundations and corporations probably will not improve in the next few years. In fact, as the demands for private support increase to cover the budget restrictions on government support for needed social and medical services, the actual amounts available to distribute to arts and culture groups may decline significantly. In fact, the privatization movement in government has put additional strains on nonprofit organizations as local arts and cultural organizations struggle for attention and resources. Funding cuts for activities that do not directly serve the public with services place a strain on many arts groups. In this situation, the pressure to "downsize" government comes into conflict with the economic benefits that the arts can bring to a community, to say nothing of the improved quality of life. Self-reliance and reducing the number of people and organizations receiving entitlements became the priorities in the 1990s and continue into the 2000s. The criteria for what constitutes "public benefit" has been raised, and arts organizations have found it necessary to reframe their message about the benefits they provide to the community.

Individual donors find themselves inundated with direct mail appeals and regular telephone solicitations from every conceivable cause. As more organizations learn the tricks of the fundraising trade, individual donors will be asked to support even more groups. Arts organizations may find a backlash from donors, which then cuts into their major source of support. The fundraising staffs and the board of directors for many organizations will have to continually reevaluate their fundraising strategies. The trend may be toward more personal appeals in an attempt to form a tighter bond with donors. This has become especially critical as donors have become more assertive about how their funds are used.

The concepts of *venture philanthropy* and donor contracts have found their way into more support exchanges. The venture philanthropist is coming to the funding relationship with the organization from the point of view that his or her donation is an investment in the organization's future. This type of donor expects results or some kind of definitive measurable outcome. As the Case Study points out, control over how a donation is used has become a big concern among fundraisers.

Summary

Arts organizations in the United States depend heavily on the support of individuals, foundations, corporations, and the government to achieve their objectives. Traditionally, U.S. government involvement in the arts has been minimal.

People give for a variety of reasons based on the concept that they receive intangible benefits in a social exchange with the organization. Giving, which is a person-to-person business, depends on the careful design and integration of the organization's strategic and operational plans. Auditing the organization's readiness to undertake a campaign includes analyzing its mission, objectives, resources, activities, and programs. The fundraising process requires a marketing orientation directed at donors to be effective.

The case for support is a key element in the organization's overall fundraising strategy. Board and staff support are needed to demonstrate to donors the commitment in the organization. An effective data gathering and management system is also needed. Careful control of the costs of raising money and disbursing funds are required for legal reasons.

Campaigns are designed to target funding groups, which include individuals, corporations, foundations, and government agencies. Donor research leads to designing different funding options to fit the needs of different funders. Gift programs are designed to accept current support, deferred giving, and bequests. Personal contact is the most effective way to solicit large gifts from a limited number of wealthy individuals. Telephone and direct mail campaigns are used to reach a wider audience. Donors are also becoming more demanding regarding how their gifts are used.

Corporations and foundations are usually approached based on the strategic fit between the donor's objectives and the organization's needs. Campaigns for government support usually involve meeting program requirements and criteria established by agency staff members.

Key Terms and Concepts

Social exchange model for giving
Funding pyramid
Fundraising audit
Case for support
Fundraising data management
Direct and indirect costs
Capital campaign
Annual campaign
Restricted and unrestricted gifts
Deferred gift
Bequest
Direct mail promotion
Reciprocity
Strategic fit
Foundation

Questions

1. What impact will the change in U.S. demographics have on giving over the next 20 years?

2. Do you agree with the concept of expecting staff to donate regularly to the arts organization for which they work? Explain.

3. Do you think it is appropriate for arts organizations to gather personal data on potential donors for future use? What data would be inappropriate to keep? Why?

4. Have you ever been approached to make a gift to an arts organization? What techniques were used to solicit the donation? Did those techniques work? Explain.

5. Should arts organizations reject donations from corporations because of what the company manufactures or the politicians it supports? Explain.

6. If an arts organization unknowingly received donations from an individual later found guilty of defrauding people out of their money, should the organization return the gifts for redistribution back to the people who were defrauded? Defend your position.

Case Study

As this March 2002 article in the *Chronicle of Philanthropy* points out, major gift donors are taking an active role in how their support is being used by organizations.

Donors Increasingly Use Legal Contracts to Stipulate Demands on Charities
Debra E. Blum

More and more donors not only want control over the gifts they make to charity, legal and fund-raising experts say, but they also are demanding that the terms of that control be put in binding, sometimes exhaustive, contracts.

The written agreements often contain a host of provisions beyond those that spell out how and when donors will make their contributions and how charities will spend the money.

For example, a contract may include a backup plan in case the charity ceases to exist or changes its mission. Or a contract may state that the institution will not challenge the right of the donor, or a representative of the donor, to sue to enforce the terms of the contract—a right typically reserved for state attorneys general.

A contract may also include what is known as a most-favored-nation clause, a provision directing an institution never to treat the gift or the project the gift underwrote any less favorably than other gifts or projects, such as when it comes to publicity or future upkeep.

Some contracts also stipulate how the proceeds gleaned from research projects financed by donations will be split and spent.

Provisions setting out penalties if beneficiaries do not meet the contracts' terms also are becoming more common. Such provisions, called Sword of Damocles clauses—after the threat faced by the Greek courtier Damocles, who, legend says, was seated at a banquet beneath a sword suspended by a single hair—may require gifts to be returned to donors' foundations, or be transferred to other charities.

Case Western Reserve University, for example, is bound by a contract with a donor to select for an endowed professorship a faculty member who belongs to a particular association of physicians. If the university does not choose a qualified individual for the post, the contract says, the money for the endowed position must be transferred to a similar institution that will appoint such a person. The contract even specifies who will judge whether a faculty member fits the criteria.

Duncan Hartley, associate vice president for development and alumni affairs at Case Western, says that the university found the conditions of the gift acceptable. Key, he says, is that the qualifications for the professorship spelled out in the contract are compatible with the university's standards.

We wouldn't agree to something we wouldn't feel perfectly comfortable carrying out," Mr. Hartley says. "And if it is something we believe in and the donor believes in, there's no reason not to feel comfortable making written assurances. It makes perfect sense that donors would want complete confidence that their money will be spent as they wished."

Protecting Charities

Still, Mr. Hartley and other charity officials say, nonprofit groups have to make sure their interests are protected, especially when donors make specific demands.

Frank J. Connors, a lawyer at Harvard University, says he favors adding language to gift agreements that give Harvard wiggle room in the event that it becomes impossible or overly burdensome to carry out a donor's wishes. For example, he says, an institution would need to maintain some discretion if a donor specifies that a gift be used exclusively for scholarships for students entering Harvard who have graduated from a certain secondary school.

Years after the gift is made, Mr. Connors says, the university could have "a scholarship fund generating a couple of million dollars, but you have only five people graduating from the school, or there no longer is a school." In those circumstances, he says, "The university has to be able to use that money as it sees fit for other scholarships."

David W. Lawrence, a longtime fundraiser who retired this year as president of the Northwestern Memorial Foundation, in Chicago, says that while many gift agreements protect the interests of contributors, they also can be shaped to help institutions handle what he describes as zealous donors.

"Some donors become more and more involved with a project, and come up with more ideas down the line," he says. "You want to try to put guidelines up front in the agreement so that you don't put the institution in the position of releasing too much control as the donor wants to become more involved."

For example, he says, an agreement could provide for the creation of a committee to hear the donor's future suggestions.

"That puts some insulation between the development officer and the donor," Mr. Lawrence says. "The donor reserves the right to enter into discussions about additional elements of the project, the acceptance of which would be determined through an established process. You wouldn't have a development officer out there having to say yes or no."

Overall, he says, a thorough gift agreement helps strike the right balance between donor and beneficiary.

"Everyone has a chance to buy into the particulars of the gift," Mr. Lawrence says. "Everyone knows what to expect."

Questions

1. Do you think the use of donor contracts is a positive or negative trend in the process of arts fundraising? Explain.

2. What are some positive or negative stipulations donors might place on arts organizations regarding the use of their gift?

3. If you were the Executive Director of an arts organization how would you respond to a major donor asking to have some input on the season titles you selected or the exhibitions presented?

References

1. Melissa Mince, "History of Nonprofit Organizations: Summary," in *Nonprofit Corporations, Organizations and Associations*, 5th ed., edited by Howard L. Oleck (Englewood Cliffs, N.J.: Prentice-Hall, 1988), p. 41.

2. Neil Pendleton, *Fundraising* (Englewood Cliffs, N.J.: Prentice-Hall, Spectrum Books, 1981), p. xi.

3. *Giving USA 2002* (Indianapolis, Ind.: AAFRC Trust for Philanthropy, 2002), pp. 6, 11, 129.

4. Joesph R. Mixer, *Principles of Professional Fundraising* (San Francisco: Jossey-Bass Publishers, 1993).

5. Ibid., p. 10.

6. Ibid., pp. 10, 11.

7. James Gregory Lord, *The Raising of Money* (Cleveland: Third Sector Press, 1986), p. 75.

8. Thomas Wolf, *Managing a Nonprofit Organization* (Englewood Cliffs, N.J.: Prentice-Hall, 1990), p. 211.

9. Ibid., p. 225.

10. Loren Renz, "Foundation and Corporate Support," *National Guide to Funding in Arts and Culture* (New York): The Foundation Center, 1990), p. vii.

11. Ibid., p. vii.

12. Ibid., p. vii.

13. Ibid., p. 26.

14. National Endowment for the Arts, Annual Report 2000, p. 50.

Additional Resources

Albert Anderson. *Ethics for Fundraisers*. Bloomington: Indiana University Press, 1996.

Mim Carlson. *Winning Grants Step by Step*. San Francisco: Jossey-Bass, 1996.

Kent E. Dove. *Conducting a Successful Fundraising Program*. San Francisco: Jossey-Bass, 2001.

Joan Flanagan. *Successful Fundraising*, 2nd ed. Chicago: Contemporary Books, 2000.

James M. Greenfield. *Fundraising Fundamentals*. New York: John Wiley & Sons, 1994.

Dennis P. McIlnay. *How Foundations Work*. San Francisco: Jossey-Bass, 1998.

Mal Warwick. *How to Write Successful Fundraising Letters*. San Francisco: Jossey-Bass, 2001.

Douglas E. White. *The Art of Planned Giving*. New York: John Wiley & Sons, 1995.

13

□ □ □ □ □

Integrating Management Styles and Theories

Throughout this book, the emphasis has been on applying business theory and practice to managing an arts organization. In this chapter, we summarize different styles of management and various strategies for integrating management systems into the operation of an organization. We also review the specific functions of arts management and see how they can be applied to various management styles and systems. The goal of this chapter is to give the reader a model from which to work.

Management Styles

As discussed in Chapter 8, "Fundamentals of Leadership and Group Dynamics," management styles have a profound impact on the way an organization functions. We have also seen that leadership and management are often different activities. There is clearly a need for leaders who can manage and managers who can lead. Since people usually are not as effective at everything they attempt, it is important for the arts manager to recognize his or her strengths and weaknesses. Leaders have a better opportunity for success if they put together a management team that compliments their strengths and compensates for their weaknesses.

There are as many different ways to run an organization as there are people in this world. Everyone has a slightly different view of what techniques work best in managing an arts organization. In the interest of developing some practical approaches to management, we examine three basic styles of management that can be used to lead an organization: the rational, institutional, and organic approaches. Obviously, many other management styles may be applicable. Flexibility remains the foundation of any style of management. It is important to develop a repertory of responses from which to choose as operational situations change.

Before we focus on three management styles that can help keep an organization operating effectively, let us visit with an arts manager struggling with a dysfunctional work situation. There is always something to learn—even from bad examples.

The Dysfunctional Arts Manager: A Model Rooted in Overextension

No one starts off in management with the goal of becoming a dysfunctional manager. A manager may become dysfunctional as a by-product of an organization with a culture that thrives on disorder as the standard operating mode. Organizations usually become dysfunctional either through evolutionary development or when an individual with a strong dysfunctional personality is allowed to take control of the management. We here trace the development of an organization that becomes dysfunctional or that creates a dysfunctional manager.

Dysfunctional Organizations   In Chapter 2, "The Evolution of Arts Organizations and Arts Management," we saw that when an organization starts up, there is usually a small group of extraordinary people willing to spend 18 hours a day doing everything, including marketing, advertising, contracts, schedules, budgets, and stuffing envelopes. Fayol's organizational *esprit de corps* is seen everywhere. Ambition, optimism, ceaseless energy, and a degree of ignorance about how impossible the job really is—all these elements are mixed together in a flurry of high-speed activity.

The volume of work increases as the number of productions, programs, or exhibits grows each year. Because everyone is so busy working, no one notices the gradual increase in the workload. New tasks and projects are added, and staff members groan but accept the added work. The promise of more help and more money is held out as a goal to work toward. However, planning, if it is done at all, is never for more than a few days or a few weeks at a time. Little crises are put aside until they become big enough to disrupt operations. Before long, the problems multiply until the small staff spends all of its time solving one organization-threatening crisis after another. For example, one month the funds in the bank suddenly are insufficient to cover the payroll. "How could this happen?" everyone asks. No one is really certain because the payroll always managed to get done. Someone points out that it isn't a payroll problem; rather, the issue is cash flow. The investigation into the problem leads to the discovery that everyone was so busy last week dealing with a different crisis that no one deposited the box office receipts in the bank.

This example may seem extreme, but unfortunately it isn't. Overextended staff members who sometimes handle three or four major functional areas are often the norm in arts organizations. The corporate culture often found might be summed up as follows: "Because you love the arts, you will have the privilege of working long hours at low pay." Arts groups often thrive on having a work force "addicted" to the organization and the constant adrenaline-producing excitement associated with getting the show, special event, or exhibit finished minutes before it opens to the public.

The dysfunctional manager is a product of this type of organizational system. The stress levels are high, so reason and logic are in short supply. Decisions are made and then quickly reversed because no one thought through the consequences. On any given day, no one knows what is really going on in the organization because of a lack of clear-headed thinking.

One obvious symptom of an organization suffering from dysfunctional management is frequent staff turnover. High-energy people burn out quickly in a culture that requires them to sacrifice their private lives. Workaholic managers who drive their staffs to exhaustion assume that everyone is capable of matching their own work level. A newly hired employee is expected to adopt the intense work ethic immediately and the value system quietly, no matter how unpleasant. The beginning operations-level staff person, with no point of comparison, accepts the required work level as the norm. A staff member without the power to effect a change in the work ethic usually opts to resign. The employee who resigns is immediately identified by the remaining staff as someone who "just didn't like to work hard," thus carrying on the cultural values of the organization.

The Dysfunctional Manager An organization can also become dysfunctional when the management team itself is dysfunctional. The cause of this problem is that the person in the role of manager is simply not suited for the job. In reality, some people were never intended to be managers. Their basic personalities, for whatever reason, are inadequately formed. These individuals may have a whole range of character flaws, including excessive defensiveness, aggressiveness, or passivity, verbal abusiveness, or being withdrawn. Unfortunately, the list could go on. Everyone has problems, but the inescapable fact is that the managing process of the organization tends to reflect the personality of the manager. As character flaws become more pronounced and, in some cases, are manifested in severe psychological problems, the workplace becomes dysfunctional.

Unfortunately, a person hired into this situation is usually not aware that there is a problem until a few weeks have passed. After the first few explosions reveal the true personality of the manager and the character of the organization, the new employee has the option of adapting to this dysfunctional culture, trying to change it, or leaving.

How important is it that a manager be able to exhibit a positive personality profile and possess skills and expertise to help further the goals of the organization? It is central to the success or failure of the entire operation! No matter how beautifully crafted the mission statement or how detailed and comprehensive the strategic, marketing, or fundraising plans may be, if the individuals hired as managers cannot work with people in a way that promotes commitment, responsibility, and a sense of enjoyment about the work to be done, then the chances of ever achieving anything more than mediocrity are slim. It is important to remember that an organization is only as good as the people it employs. There is no escaping the fact that organizations can become dysfunctional because of the people who work within them, and not always because of outside forces.

We now turn to three positive management approaches and contrast them with the dysfunctional manager. One of these three approaches, depending on the situation, may be more appropriate for effective leadership and management. The lines between one style or another are usually blurry, and on any given day a leader or manager may put any one or more of these styles to good use. When you are reviewing the information in Figure 13-1, keep in mind that any one or a combination of all three styles may be used on a given day.

The Analytical Manager: Changing the Culture

Applying an analytical style of management takes persistence on the part of the manager. The first step in the process is to identify the steps that will be most effective in accelerating change where it is needed most. Some parts of the organization will be impossible to change quickly, and others may be ready and willing to assist with making things different. There are no rules or guidelines that apply universally when trying to change a culture that has grown self-destructive. However, one obvious point to keep in mind is that changes are usually a great deal easier to instigate by moving with the flow of the organization rather than against it. This simply means that changing the attitudes

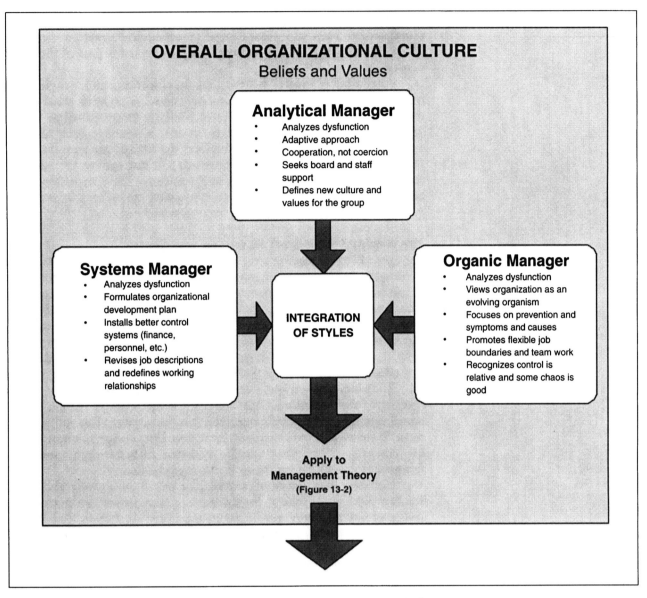

Figure 13-1 Management Styles

and values of people by cooperation rather than coercion will greatly accelerate the acceptance of the analytical manager's point of view.

One strategy to pursue is to enlist the support of the other senior staff and the board to undertake an organizational assessment and audit modeled after the marketing audit that was outlined in Chapter 11, "Marketing and the Arts." The objective is to make board and staff members more aware of how the organization behaves and where the values and beliefs need to be changed to make the operation more effective and humane. Making sweeping changes to an organization is a daunting task, especially when it is dysfunctional. It can be done, but it may take longer than anticipated. After all, it usually takes years for an organization to develop a culture of elaborate values and beliefs.

Cultures in conflict have been illustrated in numerous examples in this book. For instance, bringing in new artistic leadership is an opportunity for change, but it can also lead to counterproductive disruption.

Analytical managers understand that rapid change in any organizational system leads to a great deal of psychological stress on everyone. Being able to gauge how fast change can be effected is part of the art of managing.

Analytical managers believe that organizations and people learn from their experiences and mature over time. A creative artist and a manager (perhaps the same person), working in cooperation with a board of directors, can use the functions of management to chart a course for the organization that replaces the state of constant crisis and anxiety with controlled growth. Granted, it is not easy to set aside the time for planning and organizing in the midst of the unremitting press of daily business, but once a system is in place, the difficulties every organization expects to go through are smoothed out a bit.

The Systems Manager: Structure and Control

The systems management style emphasizes organizational development techniques and control systems to help reach the stated objectives. Part of the rise of the systems manager can be attributed to the change from founder-driven arts groups to board-driven arts institutions. The museums, performing arts centers, operas, theaters, and dance companies that started off with one or two people 30 or 40 years ago may now employ 50 to 100 people and have multimillion-dollar budgets and extensive office, production, and performance facilities.

With this growth and increasing complexity has come the development of the professional arts manager. When a board hires a professional manager, it is usually expected that the organization will adopt a more "businesslike" or corporate structure. The change to a more businesslike style of operation usually follows a crisis brought about by a financial or personnel problem in the organization.

Not everyone greets what could be called the *managerization* of the arts with enthusiasm. For example, some critics say that adding layers of management produces bureaucratic structures that hinder the accomplishment of objectives and add to the operating costs. Although unplanned growth can indeed create such situations, the reality is that most arts organizations tend to function with very limited staff resources; therefore, it is a common practice to give people two, three, or four job titles—any one of which could be a full-time job. What is seen by some as too many managers is often the organization's way of finding a reasonable balance between the number of people required to do the tasks and the organization's stated mission, goals, and objectives.

At another level, the role of the systems manager has grown in response to the increased pressure to produce a balanced budget and the funding community's desire to see its money used responsibly. To cope with the issues of fiscal accountability and increasing organizational complexity, the two- and three-headed management structures are also finding their way into larger arts organizations.

Regardless of the debate about the increasing number of middle- and upper-level managers in arts organizations, what was once a novel idea is now a multimillion-dollar institution in the community. The time and money given by the board of directors, often the most influential people in the community, frequently carry subtle and not so subtle restrictions that can redirect the organization to a safer or less controversial path. A vigilant management and artistic team can work with the board to keep the art alive and challenging. However, given the economic and political pressures, it is not hard to see why many arts institutions begin to engage in forms of self-censorship. If the community support for the organization is strong enough, the artistic reasons for performing a particular play or mounting a particular exhibit should outweigh the financial or political pressure placed on the organization.

The Organic Manager: Adjustment and Adaptation

The organic management style recognizes that a changing dynamic exists in organizations, and that, like a living organism, the group will grow and change over time. In some ways, the organic manager functions like a doctor who practices preventive medicine. The organic manager works with a dynamic system and focuses on spotting problems that could affect the health of the organization. Intervention is designed to treat the symptoms and the causes. In this case, the tools used to practice this preventive medicine are the theories and practices of management, economics, marketing, and so forth, which have proved to work in given specific circumstances.

Organic managers realize that they are working with very distinct groups, and that these groups have flexible boundaries of skills and interests that overlap. The ability to give each group a sense of its own importance in the whole, while at the same time promoting communication and understanding, is the most important job facing the organization's leadership.

The organic manager also recognizes that there is an element of chaos in any organizational system. However, chaos doesn't necessarily mean that the organization is out of control. In the context of an arts enterprise, chaos is recognized as an element of creative unpredictability. No one is ever sure that an arts event or exhibition will really work as planned. Giving artists the freedom to experiment carries with it risks that an organic manager recognizes. The organic manager makes allowances for the different levels of structure required for the various parts of the organization. The accounting department has rules and regulations restricting what can be done, but curators, directors, choreographers, and designers are given more freedom to explore alternative solutions. Recognizing the differences in the way subunits need to operate does not mean abdicating control. The latitude given to creative artists and scholars still fits within the overall control system that everyone agrees is necessary.

Management Theories

Having established a management style, which may include a combination of analytical, systems, and organic techniques, the manager can turn to adapting various management theories to arrive at an overall operating approach to the organization (see Figure 13-2).

Process Management

Many of the fiscal and production aspects of an arts organization can benefit from the application of quantitative procedures and ongoing statistical analysis borrowed from the scientific and process theories of management. There are potential gains in productivity if constant monitoring of routine procedures is a part of the organization's culture. Is there a more effective way to go about the process of constructing, storing, or rigging scenery? Can money be saved if a rehearsal sequence is altered? Is the method used to enter sales data producing the timely information management needs to quickly spot financial problems? Is the procedure for processing an order organized so as to reduce the number of steps required? Nearly all of the tracking of responses to mailings, donation requests, marketing, and sales campaigns relies heavily on techniques related to process management. As we saw in Chapter 9, "Organizational Controls and Budgets," and Chapter 10, "Economics and Financial Management," an organization's MIS and FMIS require the vigorous application of quantitative systems if the organization is to stay informed about its fiscal health.

One clear signal that it is appropriate to undertake a more process-oriented approach to aspects of the operation is when you hear the phrase, "But we have always done it that way around here." There may be good reasons why certain procedures are accomplished in specific ways, but nearly everything that is done routinely can usually be done more efficiently if given some thought.

Human Relations

As we saw in Chapter 3, "Evolution of Management," and Chapter 8, "Fundamentals of Leadership and Group Dynamics," the human relations approach to management grew out of McGregor's Theory X and Theory Y, Maslow's hierarchy of needs, behaviorist theory, and other psychological approaches to the workplace. Because the product of a performing arts organization is the work of people, there is a natural fit between human resource management and an arts organization. The arts manager must realize that each employee group has its own set of behaviors and expectations about the work of the organization. For example, the stagehands working on a show will have a very different perspective about their job and their place in the organization than that of fundraising assistants. Both support jobs are needed to make the organization work, but employees in each category need different types of recognition and rewards for their contributions to the organization.

Developing performance standards and an appraisal system that recognizes the similarities and differences in employee groups while keeping employees focused on the defined objectives requires a significant commitment of the manager's time. Given the dynamics of an arts organization, once-a-year job reviews will simply not monitor adequately the work output of employees. In fact, this approach would amount to "management by neglect" of your employees. Daily, weekly, or monthly reviews, mostly informal in nature, of employee performance may be more appropriate, depending on the type of work being done.

Attention must also be paid to how effectively the organization's communication and management information systems are working. Information is often equated with power. Those who have the information have power over those who do not. However, this is a very destructive approach to information management. As we saw in Chapter 6, "Fundamentals of Organizing and Organizational Design," all organizations have formal and informal structures and communication systems. If any employee group is excluded from the communication system, the risk of rumors and the harmful distortion of information increases in great leaps. No employee communication system is perfect, but it makes little sense to establish communication approaches guaranteed to alienate people.

The Open System

The organizational model of the open system and its ability to adjust to changing circumstances have been stressed in many chapters in this text. Input from clients, audiences, donors, staff, and so on, is combined with input from the external environments—the economic, political and legal, cultural and social, demographic, technological, and educational environments—to produce an organization that constantly changes and adjusts to the world around it. The open system approach to management does not mean that the organization's mission undergoes constant change. Rather, the open system allows the organization to capitalize on opportunities that support its mission while minimizing the impact of threats to the enterprise. For example, new digital video and Internet technology may provide additional cash flow opportunities for the arts by opening up new markets for distribution of the product and by creating new viewing audiences. At the same time, an adverse tax ruling by the IRS or a proposed Federal law that affects labor practices can be addressed through active participation in the political system.

The Contingency System: An Integrating Approach

The approaches and theories reviewed thus far are all directed at finding a way to integrate the various styles and theories of management into a workable system. Combinations of analytical, systems, and organic management techniques applied to theories of process management, human relations, and the open system can help a manager achieve results when carrying out the functions of management.

One model that meshes these styles and theories is shown in Figure 13-2. The integration of these styles and theories into what is called a contingency system holds much promise. The important point to remember with this system is that, depending on the circumstances and the nature of the problem, the manager can pick and choose options, combining some portion of each approach. Sometimes, it is a human resource problem; at other times, it is a quantitative problem; and on other occasions, the problem relates back to a change in one or more of the environments or input groups. Each individual will feel comfortable with different applications of a contingency system; however, the central point is that a manager must actively choose the particular combination of styles and theories that will best solve the organization's problems.

Let us review the functional areas of management from the perspective of applying this overall contingency system of management.

The Management Functions

The center of the arts organization's operational system is found in the functions listed in this section. The goal of the entire organization should be to take the contingency system, which integrates management styles and theories, and apply it to the operational areas in ways that achieve the organization's stated goals and objectives.

Planning and Development

Looking toward the future is a major responsibility of a manager in any organization. As we saw in Chapter 5, "Planning and Decision Making," the ability to plan requires no special genius. The key ingredients are self-discipline and an established process. Of course, the underlying culture of the organization must value looking ahead and should stress the

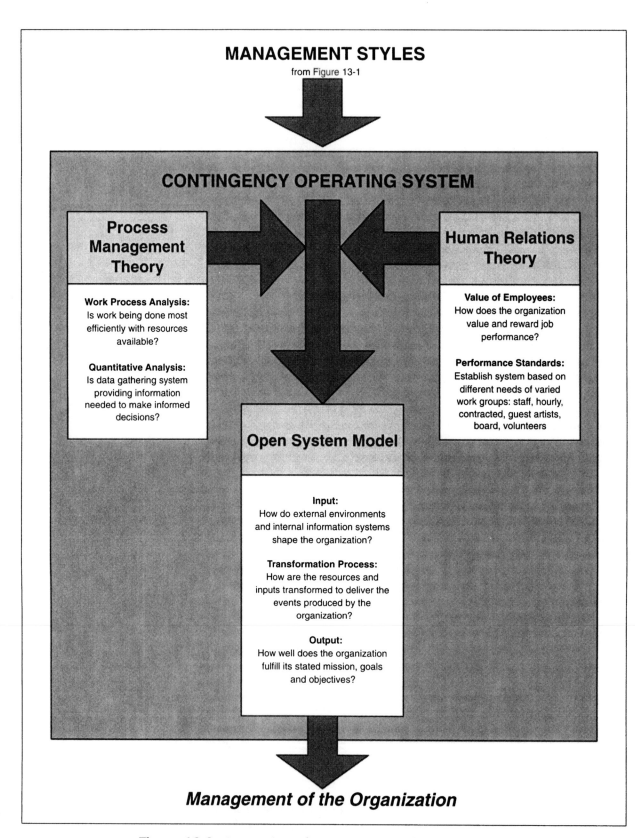

Figure 13-2 Integration of Management Styles with Theories

involvement of the board and all levels of staff in the process. Every action that an organization takes must relate to the overall master plan. If it doesn't, human and other resources will be misdirected and ultimately wasted.

Types of Plans   All managers, including overextended managers, engage in short-term and crisis planning. Problems such as cash flow difficulties, a show that might have to be canceled, a tour cut short because presenters backed out at the last minute, a work of art damaged at an exhibit, and the death of a member of the cast are part of the business. Managers with a methodology in place for quick problem-solving identify the source of the difficulty, generate alternatives, and implement and evaluate decisions before a crisis develops that threatens the operation of the organization. Written outlines and procedures to follow when a crisis does strike can help the organization keep its balance.

Intermediate-range planning (one to three years) is integral to the program development and fundraising activities of an arts group. Launching any fundraising campaign requires coordinated planning to organize resources and people in cost-effective ways. The case must be strong and the reasons for giving must be clear to potential donors. The need for the funds must relate directly to the organization's strategic planning.

Long-range strategic planning and development (four to ten years), although always subject to revision, are also important processes in helping to shape the organization's future. Long-term planning is a serious business, but the enjoyable and creative side of the process should not be overlooked. "What if" discussions among the board, the artists, and the staff can lead to new ideas and directions. In fact, planning is a break from the routine of day-to-day work, and it should be a strong selling point for potential board members. After all, would you rather be on a board of directors that was actively engaged in charting the future of the organization, or would you prefer to sit through yet another report detailing fund balance transfers?

Marketing and Public Relations

Arts organizations are businesses that must function in the highly competitive entertainment industry. Effective marketing and positive public relations can help any enterprise target and inform people of goods and services designed to meet their wants and needs. The key to success, especially given the very limited resources that most arts groups have to work with, lies with making sure that you are talking to the right people.

The universe of goods and services seems to be expanding as thousands of new products come on the market every month, making the task of keeping an arts organization visible even more exacting. Therefore, expanded press and media relations must be a central part of the organization's strategic plan if the organization is to command any attention.

As we saw in Chapter 11, "Marketing and the Arts," marketing is an organizational orientation that places the consumer at the beginning of the process. To be truly customer-driven is seen as an ideal in establishing a long-term relationship between product and consumer. However, many arts organizations equate being "customer-driven" with lower artistic standards and pandering to the public. They therefore engage in what is more accurately described as a "selling orientation" toward the public. The selling approach assumes that if consumers are made aware of the product, they will buy it. In more extreme cases, organizations adopt a product orientation, which assumes that because the product is so inherently good, people will want to buy it.

Marketing Strategies   As was pointed out in Chapter 11, adoption of a marketing orientation for an arts organization requires a careful analysis of the four Ps (product, price, promotion, and place) and, at the same time, an understanding of the limits of marketing. For example, no marketing campaign will suddenly create an arts audience by changing the well-established behavior of masses of people overnight. As we have seen, the audience for high-culture events is a by-product of the education system, especially at the college and university level. Arts marketers interested in building a long-term purchase and donation relationship with consumers would assemble demographic and psychographic profiles of the community, and a distribution of neighborhoods by spending type (e.g., money and furs, pools and patios) in an effort to piece together the most effective campaign that the available resources permit. The objective is to get inside the consumer's head to find out what combination of the four Ps will lead to the exchange process: money in exchange for the arts experience.

Of course, marketing strategies need not be targeted to only a limited segment of the population. Marketing to reach a diverse audience is important and will become critical as the demographic composition of America continues to change. The key to reaching people lies with how and what you communicate about the product to the public. Reaching new audiences, especially minorities, depends on the mix of programs and community outreach, the right price, and access to the facility.

It must be stressed again that all of the innovative marketing strategies in the world cannot create an arts consumer overnight. Marketing is a long-term investment of the organization's resources. Results should be measured over three- to five-year periods of time, not just one season.

Finally, it is also important to remember that marketing and fundraising share the similar goal of establishing an exchange relationship with audiences and donors. The progression from single-ticket buyer to subscriber or member and finally to long-term donor dictates an integrated plan under the general heading of development.

Personnel Management Staff, Labor, and Board Relations

Even when the manager adopts a human resource management strategy that takes into account the various attitudes and values of the different work groups within the organization, being able to keep employees happy and productive is still an enormous challenge. Establishing working conditions that support the creative process and encourage artists and scholars, the board, and staff members is one of the manager's primary objectives. This would seem to be self-evident, but judging by the stories of performers, designers, staff, and technicians about the abuses of management—which also includes directors, conductors, and choreographers—it is a miracle that there isn't more strife in arts organizations.

Unions   The abusive past practices of management were a primary reason for the establishment of unions in the arts. Although managers and unions may never see eye-to-eye about how the organization operates, the fact remains that it is management's job to establish the criteria for performance. For the arts manager, defining acceptable practices is at the heart of the relationship with the union because, when both sides sit down to negotiate a contract, the odds are very high that labor and management will not agree about levels of compensation, benefits, and work rules. The arts manager who does not understand how the "backstage" really works in a theater, concert hall, or museum will be placed at a huge disadvantage when it comes time to evaluate the rules written into a contract. A lack of appreciation for the work environment could cost the organization thousands of dollars every time a show is performed or an event takes place. In addition, an arts manager must remember that a union is also a complex organization and is therefore subject to the same external and internal forces that shape the arts group. Understanding the perspective of union members and the union organization can make the arts manager's job a little easier.

Board of Directors   Managing relations with the board is just as important to senior- and middle-level staff members as is a successful contract negotiation with a union. The board, which could be made up of anywhere from 8 to 50 or more people, has its power blocs, hard workers, and deadwood, just like any other organization. A powerful finance committee, for example, could prevent a manager from implementing new programs by not approving a budget. A board personnel committee could hold up a key appointment or lobby for a candidate of the board's choosing. Approval of a season might be held up if the board has doubts about title selection.

For the arts manager, a clear picture of the scope of the board's power and responsibility is of primary importance if the organization is to function effectively. In numerous case studies in this book, we have seen board actions both strengthen and undermine arts groups. There never seems to be a shortage of stories about the communication gap between artistic directors and the board. The Case Study in this chapter provides a good example of board-staff challenges.

Personnel Management   Meanwhile, as organizations mature, issues of salaries, staff training, and renewal will become more important. Finding new challenges, revising job descriptions, reorganizing departments, and combining or separating jobs should all become part of the overall operation of the personnel area.

When adding up all of the work required to manage the personnel functions of an arts organization, artistic directors or museum directors might wonder when they will have time to direct a production or engage in scholarly research. In reality, there is no time. Upper-level managers, like artistic directors who involve themselves in production, find that, more often than not, one or more functional areas are left unattended. What strategy can an artistic director use to resolve this conflict? One obvious approach has been to split the job into different positions based on operations and product development. This explains why more organizations are creating two or three upper-level management positions to supervise the fiscal, planning, and operational aspects of the arts enterprise. The tradeoff for some artistic directors is that they must share their power with others. At some future date, should conflict arise with the board, artistic directors might find that one of their operational peers is undermining their credibility and forming a power bloc against them.

Fiscal Management

The area of fiscal planning and control is also at the core of the arts organization. A large portion of a manager's time will probably be spent on this area, often at the expense of such equally important areas as planning, programming, and staff development. Financial management is at the center of so much attention because expectations about the amount of money that can be generated through sales and donations are often unrealistic. At the same time, prices, labor, and operating costs continue to escalate higher than anticipated. The combination of these two elements establishes a perpetual deficit hanging over many organizations.

In *The Quiet Crisis in the Arts*, Nello McDaniel and George Thorn note that arts organizations are in a state of constant debt crisis, which produces an unbelievable amount of personal stress on the staff.[1] The cycle of overspending followed by painful budget cutting takes its toll on people. When artistic directors speak of maintaining quality even in the face of budget cuts of tens of thousands of dollars, people know that it is simply impossible. If you cut the budget, you reduce the quality. The expectation that the performers, designers, technicians, museum preparators, and others will somehow be able to create the same quality product with fewer rehearsals, less money for resources, and so forth, is total nonsense. The assumption seems to be, "If we say often enough that we aren't going to lose quality by cutting budgets, then maybe everyone will begin to believe it."

Managing and leading by fiscal self-delusion is hardly the most effective way to build board and staff confidence. In fact, a board member asked to raise yet another million dollars might respond, "Well, if we can do the same quality with a million-dollar budget cut, why did we go a million dollars in debt in the first place?" The answer usually comes back, "Because we are dedicated to pursuing excellence in the arts." The more accurate answer would be, "Because we didn't know how to effectively manage the human and production resources we had available to us." Needless to say, the latter reason usually isn't a discussion item for staff and board meetings.

Financial Strategies   There are a few fiscal management strategies that are likely to keep the organization solvent and the board confident. They include the following:

- Realistic budget planning procedures for revenue first, then expenses;
- Organizational attitudes and values that stress that budgets are not to be exceeded;
- Very tight control and oversight systems for expenditures;
- A clear picture of the cash flow needs of the organization;
- A system for accounts payable activity that pays no bill before its time except when there is a discount for early payment;
- A very aggressive "asset management program" that involves investment in a wide range of financial instruments.

Government Relations

As we learned in Chapter 4, "Arts Organizations in a Changing World," government relations extend from the federal to the local level. A manager's involvement in the political arena is usually fairly limited. However, as we have seen in the last few years, without the support of the people who make the laws and sit on the appropriations committees, arts organizations will suffer. Arts groups must earn the support of elected officials at all levels of government. Support is not given just because the arts organizations and artists think their enterprise is nobler than other agencies established for a public good.

The first step for successfully interacting with the government system is education. The arts manager must learn how the various local, state, and federal systems work. The second step involves learning about the power brokers and the issues close to them and their constituents. The third step requires the arts manager to visit the various representatives in an effort to become visible. The fourth step involves making the newfound visibility mean something by updating the representatives about the organization's important activities and the positive impact of the arts on the community.

For a weary arts manager trying to cover all of the management functions described in this section, the political system, with its complex subculture, is not always the highest priority. If the arts manager is too busy to have lunch with the local director of cultural affairs or to go to a candidate's fundraising dinner, there should be no surprise when politicians don't spring to the rescue when the arts group has a budget crisis or some other problem.

Conclusion

The goal of developing an integrated approach to management styles and theories is to help the organization succeed at whatever it attempts. As we have seen, managing is an intensely personal process. The theories may provide the overall structure, but the effectiveness of any management system ultimately depends on the people who are doing the managing. The ability to establish an overall work environment where people can express a point of view without fearing for their jobs, or where they can make suggestions that will be heard, is often overlooked when it comes to designing an organization. Of course, people who work in any organization want to earn enough money to live comfortably, and they want to have the support of health benefits should they have an accident or become ill, but on a day-to-day basis, people also have an intense desire to believe that their work is making a worthwhile contribution and that their effort is being recognized in some way. Therefore, a manager must always remember that it is the people who are important to the organization, not just the product. Treating people with respect and recognizing their daily contribution to the enterprise are key ingredients in successful organizations.

To integrate management styles and theories, managers must also know their own strengths and weaknesses. Undertaking a personal inventory helps a manager to see more clearly the things he or she does well and to identify the areas that need improvement. The advantage of using this approach is that it keeps the manager and the organization renewed. It is also important for the manager to reap a sense of personal satisfaction when it comes time to evaluate how well things are working. Success is a great motivating force, especially when it is widely recognized throughout an organization.

Running an arts organization never was and never will be easy. Although arts organizations can benefit from applying management theory and practice to become better organized and more efficient, there is still no single element that guarantees survival. Getting better at doing well is an ambitious goal that any arts manager should be proud to work toward. To achieve that goal, an arts manager should be prepared to borrow any techniques that work from business, government, educational institutions, or other nonprofit organizations. Successfully integrating these different approaches to effectively manage an organization requires as much creativity as any visual or performing artist. Forging a successful partnership of manager and artist is therefore predicated on each party's recognizing the other's creative contribution to one goal: creating a world in which life is enriched by the accomplishments of both parties.

Questions

1. Based on your own experiences, can you cite examples of situations in which analytical, systems, or organic management styles were used to solve a problem effectively?

2. With proven approaches to managing, such as scientific and human relations management, and organizational models, such as the open system, to help guide operations, why do so many arts groups have trouble with their management structures?

3. Use any of the case studies in this text to provide examples of the effective use of the following functional areas:
   - Planning and development.
   - Marketing and public relations.
   - Personnel management.
   - Fiscal management.
   - Government relations.

Case Study

As this article points out, when a communication gap between the staff and the board reaches a certain point, dire results may ensue.

A Dramatic Disagreement: Did the Rep Have to Die?
Yes, says the board; no way, says the staff.
Barry Johnson

Most of the facts involved in the January 22 decision to close the doors at Portland Repertory Theatre aren't in dispute.

The company was carrying a sizable debt, and cash-flow problems were so acute that it was going to miss at least one payroll.

But did the theater need to die? On that crucial point, the staff and board of Portland's second-largest theater company are completely at odds.

And local actors who have been part of artistic director Dennis Bigelow's splendid unofficial company are outraged at the board's decision.

"I think that these people just plain wanted out," said David Meyers, one of the actors in the Rep's production of

"Old Wicked Songs" that was closed down by the board in the middle of its run.

"They were just tired of playing with it and decided to kill it," he continued. "They killed a vital organization for their convenience."

Board members such as Bill Coniff have a different view: "We had no choice," Conniff said. "We held it off as long as we could."

The Rep's death leaves a gaping hole in Portland's arts scene. During the past three years under Bigelow, the Rep has been the home of some of the best theater in town—such productions as "Three Tall Women," "Two Trains Running" and "Arcadia." And it's been an important home for many of the city's best actors, many of whom may not be able to stay here without the work the Rep provided.

But no matter who is right, the essential fact is that Portland Repertory Theatre is gone.

What went wrong behind the scenes while the company was moving from success to success onstage?

The Rep's troubles didn't start yesterday. It had been struggling with a large deficit long before Bigelow was named artistic director three years ago—nearly $500,000 for a non-profit that brought in little more than $1 million in its best years.

And the deficit had grown in the two years before Bigelow arrived while the company, under Geoffrey Sherman's leadership, had anticipated to upgrade itself and become a player in the regional theater world. When Sherman left to become artistic director of Meadow Brook Theatre in Michigan, the board had serious discussions about closing the theater.

But it decided to carry on, choosing Bigelow to help it put its financial and artistic house in order.

Bigelow actually began to shrink the deficit. But a double whammy brought his financial juggling to a halt in October. The company owed significant sums of money to both its bank, U.S. Bank, and its landlord, the World Trade Center. It was broke, it couldn't borrow money, and the new season's expenses were about to pile up in earnest.

Bigelow went public with his plight, telling *The Oregonian* that if a significant rescue attempt wasn't mounted the theater would have to close.

The Regional Arts and Culture Council and the Northwest Business Committee for the Arts responded by hiring well-regarded arts consultant George Thorn.

Thorn's conclusions were surprisingly optimistic. The company had already taken major steps to cut its expenses, trimming staff and moving to smaller, cheaper quarters. It had just finished its fiscal year with a small surplus. Its artistic achievements had just been recognized with the local Drammy Award for best show of the year for its production of "Arcadia." Thorn thought that if the company could start an aggressive fund-raising campaign to help it through its cash-flow difficulties, its long-term prospects were good.

Good Signs

Sure enough, when the staff went to its subscribers with a plea for money, they responded surprisingly well. Since October, the Rep had raised more than $170,000, much of it in small contributions from subscribers.

"I think it's significant that our Community stepped forward for us, and for the first time we didn't borrow money in October, November or December," Bigelow said. The Rep had frequently used its line of credit with U.S. Bank to get through those high-expense, low-income months. Traditionally, the company was flush with cash in the spring, when its subscribers signed on for the next year. Last year's receipts for those months were more than $280,000, Bigelow said.

So, the game was to get through the lean months until the spring's cash infusion.

Living today on tomorrow's receipts can be a dangerous sport. The subscribers, after all, were paying for shows they wouldn't see until next year. Allen Nause, artistic director of Artists Repertory Theatre, the city's third-largest theater, said his company tries never to use its subscription income on anything but expenses for the upcoming season. But it's still a common practice. Artists Rep, known for its conservative financial philosophy, has done it in bad years. And it's simply a fact of life for many other arts organizations with subscription seasons to sell.

"In this day and age, when arts organizations aren't carrying huge cash reserves, there's always the need to finance your work from a cash-flow standpoint," said Cynthia M. Fuhrman, director of public relations and marketing at the city's biggest theater, Portland Center Stage. "It's not just theaters; it's symphonies, operas and ballets, too."

January Slump

Money from the Rep's contributions dried up in January. And although both "Molly Sweeney" and "Putting It Together," the company's fall and Christmas shows, were critical hits and did reasonably well at the box office, they didn't meet the Rep's projections. Bigelow and board members say the box office was hurt because the company didn't have enough money to advertise them well.

Last season, the company used a Meyers Memorial Trust grant quite successfully to boost single-ticket sales. Its "Arcadia" did about $70,000 worth of single-ticket sales. The advertising money wasn't available for this season.

"We faced the immediate cash flow crisis of not being able to meet payroll," Bigelow said. "It caught the staff a little off guard when we missed payroll, but to a person they were willing to work to make the season happen. Everyone knew we were about to mail next season's renewal form."

After that, things moved fast. The board met January 20 and 22 to deal with the problem of missing the payroll. At the first meeting, the board decided to consult a bankruptcy attorney. At the second, it voted to close the theater's doors.

Board President Avery Loschen said the board looked at the staff's projections of revenues and expenses as well as cash flow. Board members estimated the percentage of outstanding grants that were likely to come through. And they came to a stark conclusion. "It was not prudent for us to accept donations or start a subscription campaign if we didn't believe we could mount a new season. And we don't believe we could have mounted a new season. Given the numbers we were given by the staff, anybody who would have made the decision to go forward would not have been making a prudent business decision."

Another Interpretation

The staff has a completely different assessment. It argued that the situation wasn't as dire as the board made it sound, and that the board did a dismal job of raising money.

"They are confusing cash flow, the immediate problem, with end-of-the-year performance," said Michelle Schneiter, the company's director of development. "Our projections all showed we were going to do $30,000 better than last year, which was our first season in the black."

Schneiter said the company had received positive signals on two pending grants, one for $50,000 and another for $10,000. News from the foundations was expected by the end of January or early February, she said.

"I can tell you in the past we've been led to believe we were going to get grants and they didn't come through," Loschen responded. "Anyway, the money wasn't enough to solve the problems."

The staff, Schneiter said, was hoping board members would solve the immediate cash-flow problem by lending the company money to meet payroll. Then the company would use income from season subscriptions to repay the board.

But Schneiter's critique of the board didn't stop there. "January was a challenge, and we really needed the board to fundraise. They just didn't," she said.

"Since we went public in mid-October, they raised very little money, less than 10 grand. That was pretty frustrating. I chalk that up to poor leadership on the board."

Board President Loschen disagreed. "Many, many of those checks were solicited by board members during that urgent campaign," he said.

Thorn's report on the company had suggested that expanding the company's circle of significant donors, traditionally a function of the board, was crucial to its success.

"Generally, we did not have enough contacts to broaden our base of funders," Bigelow said. "That was going to be the key to the Rep's future." He said only one of 19 board members was doing a good job in this area, though the board did raise $40,000, including one $10,000 gift, from among its members before it went public with its problems in October.

Ask Schneiter, should the Rep have closed its doors, and her response is succinct. "Yes, we did have to close, because the board didn't want to fund-raise. *Should* it have closed? No."

From the Outside

It's difficult to sort out this profound disagreement between staff and board. Both sides agree that the company had a large deficit and severe cash-flow problems. They even agree that substantive steps had been taken to correct the problems.

But the board decided that those steps were not enough. "We kept hoping an angel would appear, but it never happened," Coniff said.

Bill Bulick, executive director of the Regional Arts and Culture Council and a longtime audience member of Portland Rep, followed the company closely the past few months.

"There was a rallying around the company," he said. "Money came in, and it seemed there was a possibility to dig the company out of its cash-flow crisis and its deficit. The board had to be aware of the heavy lifting this would involve and didn't think it was up to it."

But the larger community is also complicit, he said. "It always seems like there should be more resources than there are out there because this community says it cares about having these vital, creative people in its midst."

Aftermath

For the actors who frequently worked at Portland Center Stage, the closing of the company is disastrous. As one of two full Equity companies in town (Artists Repertory Theatre recently joined this small group, but it is operating under special rules for the next three years) Portland Rep was an important source of employment for the city's best actors.

Actors David Meyers and Sharonlee McLean are maintaining a wait-and-see attitude. McLean has started regular gatherings of actors to talk about what happened and begin to think about starting a new theater along the lines of Portland Rep, But just about everyone in the theater community worries about what might happen to the scene here.

During the past few years, the number of talented, accomplished actors in Portland has increased dramatically. Portland Rep, using locally based actors for nearly all its shows, was one of the major reasons for this growth. Without the Rep, those actors have far fewer chances to work—and actors from other cities one less reason for coming.

For audiences, the niche the Rep filled, bringing recent American plays to Portland for sharp, professional productions, is empty. It's difficult to imagine the fall season this year without the powerful performances of Gretchen Corbett, David Ivers and Wayne Ballantyne in Brian Friel's delicate "Molly Sweeney." In thinking about theater in Portland without experiences like this one, the magnitude of the loss of Portland Repertory Theatre begins to sink home.

Questions

1. Identify and summarize the major differences between the board and the staff over the closing of the theater.

2. Based on the facts as they are stated in this article, do you believe the board was correct in taking the action it did? Why?

3. What would be a better business practice than paying for current year expenses with next season subscription sales? What suggestions do you have for this or any arts organization about managing cash flow?

4. The article stresses the importance of the board fundraising function. However, it would appear that the $500,000 deficit played a factor in bringing the company to a close. What overall leadership and management styles do you suggest could have been adopted by the Portland Rep to have averted this closing?

Reference

1. Nello McDaniel and George Thorn, *The Quiet Crisis in the Arts* (New York: ARTS Action Issues, 1991).

14
□ □ □ □ □

Career Options and Preparing for the Job Market

The arts management workplace is undergoing an evolution that parallels the changes occurring in arts organizations, as we discussed in Chapter 1, "Management and the Arts," and Chapter 4, "Arts Organizations in a Changing World." As arts organizations have matured so has the workforce. Many of the senior managers and leaders of today either brought their management training and experience with them from the business sector or they developed as managers through an informal process that is akin to on-the-job training. Many others in the field started either in the performance, production, operations, or design side of the arts and made a transition into management.

The relatively recent advent of university programs offering majors or courses in arts management or administration is continuing to have an impact on the quality and quantity of the labor pool. A new supply of college- or university-trained arts managers are finding their way into arts organizations around the world. Of course, one needs to keep this growth of the college-educated arts management workforce in perspective. Most universities with colleges or schools of business typically have hundreds of majors in comparison to the handful of majors interested in the management of the arts.

For this edition of *Management and the Arts* it seemed appropriate to add a chapter on the next steps to pursue if you are truly interested in arts management or administration. Having studied arts organizations for the last few weeks, you should have a much better understanding of the field itself and the issues that face arts organizations. At the same time you should now be fluent in the vocabulary of arts management as well as the business side of the arts. It is important for you to have a little direction about how to fulfill the passion you have for the arts by using your new-found knowledge, skills, and abilities as a potential manager and leader. Let us take a look at some of the steps you will need to take.

Where the Jobs Are

As you would expect, the opportunities for employment in the field of arts management are often tied to the geographical distribution of arts organizations. The bigger the population base the more likely you will find a wider distribution of all types of arts organizations. This does not mean that there are no arts management jobs in the rural areas of

America or Canada. But common sense dictates that the arts population base will be higher in larger metropolitan areas.

As you know, museums and performing arts organizations are dependent on members, audiences, patrons, and donors in order to sustain themselves. Not only must the area have the population base to ensure a certain level of support, but as we have seen, there needs to be a sufficient number of people with the educational level, time, and disposable income to form a core audience. Demand for the arts product requires a sufficient supply of arts consumers. In order for arts consumers to satisfy their demand for entertainment there must also be a sufficient supply of arts organizations providing that product. The balance of the supply of and demand for the arts needs to be a factor in your process of considering job opportunities.

As we saw in Chapter 10, "Economics and Financial Management," the expansion in the number of arts organizations since the 1960s has been supported by the population growth. And while there has been tremendous growth in the number of arts organizations paralleling this population growth, the actual percentage of people who consume the fine arts product has not significantly increased in the last 50 years. It is unlikely, therefore, that there will be a big increase in demand for arts managers any time in the near future. On the other hand, if one moves beyond the not-for-profit arts and culture field to the larger marketplace for entertainment, demand for managers seems to be increasing. Whether you decide to work in the not-for-profit arts and culture side of the industry or the for-profit entertainment industry, you will need the same skills as a manager and a leader.

Personal Choices and Selection Criteria

Your options for employment in the field are dictated by a number of choices you need to make. The focus here is on a geographical approach to arts management jobs, but your selection process will be further narrowed by the criteria you set for yourself, such as the type of arts organization you may want to work for, your range of skills and specialization, and fundamental economic survival issues. For example, you may love dance and have as your goal being a marketing director for a dance company that produces new work. However, the number of jobs in a given area for marketing directors of dance companies may be very limited. Are you willing to do arts marketing for an orchestra, theater company, or museum? Have you prepared yourself for working outside the arts in a related field until that job you really want with the dance company becomes available? Maybe you'll take the route of finding a non-arts-related job that provides enough compensation to allow you to volunteer to help the dance company.

So where does this leave you? Do you want to go to larger metropolitan areas such as New York City, San Francisco, Chicago, Los Angles, Seattle, Denver, Atlanta, or Washington, D.C.? Do you feel more comfortable in slightly smaller cities, or perhaps a university arts environment? If so, you may want to seek out employment in a university performing arts center or in a fine arts college or school. Perhaps you would prefer going to work for a bigger company in the field of television, or for a cable TV company or a multimedia company. Perhaps you will explore a job with a corporation as an events planner or manager, or move into managing an artist or a touring music group. Obviously, all of these choices carry pluses and minuses depending on your individual goals.

Develop a Personal Plan

A student with thousands of dollars of loans to repay has one set of decision-making criteria for employment. An individual who worked for years before going back to school to seek a degree in arts management has a different set of goals and expectations. Some of you may seek more experience and find yourself in circumstances that permit pursuing an internship after you finish school. Regardless of your situation, the need to establish a plan is important. The process discussed in Chapter 5, "Planning and Decision Making," is easily transferred to your own circumstances. You need to use the same five steps we touched on in making a plan: (1) define your objectives, (2) assess your situation, (3) formulate outcome options, (4) make your choices and implement your plan, and then (5) continue to evaluate your choices. You need to write your plan out and remain flexible as new opportunities arise. If you follow this process you will already be far ahead of many people you will be competing with in the job market. In other words, you need to do your homework.

From the Employer's Perspective

If you have spent any time around people in the arts you are no doubt aware of how much the element of "networking" is stressed. You may assume that you will be hired for a position entirely on the merits of your application and qualifications, but the fact is that employers are looking for other clues about your potential for success as a future employee. For example, if, all other things being equal, an employer recognizes the name of one of the references in your résumé, you have a better chance of getting the follow-up contact on your application. The process of hiring someone is, as pointed out in Chapter 7, "Staffing the Organization," a very complex and somewhat risky activity. The wrong hire can lead to numerous problems for an organization, beyond the obvious one of not getting the work done at the level of quality expected. Similarly, your career development and reputation may be harmed by accepting a position in which you are not going to be able to succeed. Therefore, employers are usually looking for references to give them information about the quality of your work, your skills and abilities, and how well you work with others—your interpersonal skills. A positive reference from someone the employer knows and trusts can be a critical part of the hiring process. Experienced employers know that people may exaggerate their accomplishments on a résumé and references are not always the most forthcoming when providing information about an applicant.

Compensation Issues

One of the key questions you are often told *not* to ask about too early in the process of seeking a job is "How much does the position pay?" A potential employer usually controls the timing of the offering of the compensation and benefits package. Sometimes an employer will list a salary range for a position to clarify for applicants what they can expect. However, the trend in recent years has been to not list salary information, which leaves applicants in the dark about how much the position they are seeking will pay. You can list your salary requirements in your cover letter, but then you run the risk of being eliminated for a job you may really want because the employer cannot meet your salary needs. If you get a follow-up call from an employer, you might then ask about the salary range. The employer might give you some numbers or may simply say the salary is negotiable. This delicate process can be made a little less mysterious if you do a little research.

As pointed out in Chapter 2, "The Evolution of Arts Organizations and Arts Management," detailed salary surveys are few and far between in the arts. Sources such as *The NonProfit Times* can be a place to start in gathering information; its "2002 Salary Survey" provides national and regional salaries for ten types of positions. The positions profiled are middle- and upper-level management positions, however, so the salaries are well above the starting salaries one can expect as a recent graduate. For example, a development director working in the South averages $47,359 versus $64,068 for the New England area. When cost-of-living adjustments are factored in, the New England salary is probably not as high as it appears. (For more information on the survey go to http://www.nptimes.com.)

The overall operating budget of an organization is a major determining factor of compensation. *The NonProfit Times* survey noted that the national salary average for the development director of an organization with a budget of $500,000 to $999,999 was $43,033. As you would expect, the bigger the overall budget, the higher the average salary. But what about entry-level positions? Based on reports from recent graduates of arts administration programs, the salary offers being made for new hires are significantly lower than these averages. For example, an entry-level grant writing position for an organization with a budget under $10 million might range from as little as $18,000 to as much as $28,000.

In the early twenty-first century a recent graduate of a master's program would probably receive salary offers for a position like "development assistant" in the mid- to high 20s in the not-for-profit arts field. Many recently hired arts administration students report getting offers in the mid- to high 20s and low 30s. What about salaries in the arts jobs working at colleges and universities or the for-profit entertainment industry? Little hard evidence exists in the form of higher education arts salary surveys. University administrator salaries are often published in the *Chronicle of Higher Education*. However, these salary averages are often for more senior level positions, and therefore the rates are far above those of starting salaries. Positions such as marketing directors or ticket office managers typically pay in the 30s and low 40s in university settings. The benefits packages are often better at universities due to the larger number of employees paying into the insurance system, thus spreading costs out for everyone.

An October 2001 survey published by INTIX (http://www.intix.org/October2001_p1.pdf), the association representing the ticketing industry, gives some insight into salaries beyond the arts sector. Many of the INTIX members include large civic centers and sports teams. Combined box office manager average salaries for men and women were $39,330. Directors of ticket sales positions were paying a combined average of $54,842. Starting ticket office salaries in the low to mid-20s are not uncommon.

A helpful tool for determining the adequacy of a salary may be found on the many websites that allow you to enter a salary and compare it to the cost of living in various parts of the country (e.g., http://www.salary.com). Common sense should prevail when weighing an offer to take an arts management position for $28,000 in New York City, for example, versus Dallas or Atlanta. The cost of living in New York City makes it an economic fact of life that a $28,000 salary is not going to allow you to have the same standard of living as other cities.

As you saw in Chapter 7, "Staffing the Organization," there are more costs related to being hired for a position than the salary. The scope and level of benefits that go along with a position are also a cost to the organization and must be factored into any hiring process. Health insurance is one of the most expensive benefits to offer employees. Many small arts organizations either forego this benefit entirely or hold off giving the benefit until you have passed a six-month probationary period. Insurance, if it is offered, is typically a shared cost with the employee. The actual percentages or amounts may vary, but it is not unusual for employees to pay 20 percent to 50 percent of the cost of their health insurance. Other perks, such as dental and eye insurance or retirement benefits, will vary greatly depending on the organization's budget. From your perspective as a job seeker, many of these benefits will be costs deducted from your gross salary along with a variety of taxes.

In conclusion to this discussion of salaries let me offer the following advice. The important point to remember is that there are so many variables influencing an actual offer that it is dangerous to assume numbers published in this book, or in any survey, are hard and fast. The recent graduate seeking employment needs to keep in mind two basic salary negotiating strategies. The first approach is to try to get the highest salary you can walking in the door. Employers may indicate that you'll be eligible for a salary increase after a year, but the reality is that most arts organization barely keep up with a cost of living increase to keep pace with inflation.

The second approach to a salary offer is to look at the offer being made as an investment in yourself with an initial low return that will have a large payoff later. For example, you are hired as an assistant marketing director at $25,000, which may be below what you really wanted. When you are hired you make it known that if you prove yourself capable, you would like to be the first one considered if there are any internal promotions available in the organization. After three years of hard work you have proven yourself to be marketing director material, and when your current boss leaves you are promoted to the position with a $15,000 increase in your salary. Of course, many workplace complications could intervene and sidetrack you from this strategy. In any case, you need to reconcile what you feel you should be paid based on your sense of your worth, with what the salary market will bear in the area and, of course, the basic economic facts of life such as the cost of living in the area.

Career Development Options

Spending time reviewing a few issues of *ArtSEARCH* can be a good way to develop a better sense of what the job market in various aspects of arts management and administration looks like. Larger organizations can afford to hire assistants or associates in many of the departments. These types of jobs provide an excellent way to get a career established. Smaller organizations are often looking for staff members who will be willing to take on two or more department areas of major functions in the organization. As we have seen in Chapters 4 and 7 arts organization are typically understaffed, and the culture of the organizations tends to reinforce the expectation that you will work harder and longer for the good of the arts.

To some extent, developing a career in general requires a willingness to sacrifice something in return for achieving the goals you set for yourself. Therefore, the sacrifices you have to make to be successful in a career in arts management are not any different from any other field. Your success will depend on a mixture of the special skills and talents you possess, your interpersonal abilities, and your willingness to be adaptable and open to change. Of course there are choices you can make to assist you in your career development. Your educational background, internships, and life experiences are all factors that help contribute to your potential for success.

Education

How important is it to have a degree in arts management to get a job in the field? That depends to some extent on the hiring philosophy of the organization. First and foremost the organization has the goal of finding someone who can quickly assimilate the requirements of a job and who can start being productive as soon as possible. Typically, organizations are looking for people with some experience, usually at least five years or more, for positions that involve running a department or an area. Positions with titles like marketing or development director, production manager, or ticket office manager fall into this category. Although the organization looks at what school you went to and what your degree area was, it is more interested in where your last job was and the scope of your previous duties and responsibilities. The closer the match between what you did before and what the hiring organization wants you to do, the better the odds that you will make it to the short list. Similarly, the hiring organization will be more likely to pursue you if they are familiar with your references.

Whatever your educational background has been, making a career shift can be problematic. For example, if you were a marketing director for a large regional opera company and you now want to shift gears and do development for a small children's theater company, your application will probably not move to the top of the pile. Like it or not, managers are often typecast in much the same way a performer is. An employer will ask, "Why does this person want to make this switch?"

Likewise, if there are networking connections based on your references most likely the hiring organization will pursue you. Therefore, if you were a marketing director for a large regional opera company and you think you want to shift gears and do development for a small children's theater company your application will probably not move to the top of the pile. Like it or not, managers are often typecast in just the same way a performer is. An employer would ask "Why does this person want to make this switch?"

If you are someone who is just entering the field, your degree area takes a little more importance. You may not have the work experience, but it is assumed that you have learned some skills in school. As we saw in Chapter 2, "The Evolution of Arts Organizations and Arts Management," organizations give some clues about the critical management skills they believe are required to work in the arts (see Figure 2-2), but at the same time indicate that on-the-job training is still needed. If you have taken course work in which you produced projects that you can show prospective employers—in areas such as ticketing sales and customer relations, marketing, public relations, fundraising, event planning, budgeting, or grant writing—this will help your application surface for further consideration. The transition from student to staff member is greatly enhanced if you can demonstrate skills and accomplishments that match the needs of the position the organization is trying to fill. Ultimately, employers want to know if you can do the job and are likely to fit in with the mix of people they already have on staff. Ultimately, they really do not care a great deal what your grades were in your classes.

Internships

One of the proven ways to make the transition from the world of being a student to being on the staff of an arts organization is through an internship. If everything works properly, the arrangement is mutually beneficial. You gain valuable experience and expand the scope of your skills and abilities, and the organization gains from your work effort while investing next to nothing in employee overhead. Publications such as *ArtSEARCH* contain a special section under "Career Development" for internship opportunities. Some of these internships offer a small stipend or living expenses, but many do not. Regardless of the financial considerations, students typically look upon an internship as an investment in themselves and as a good way to further their education.

There are some obvious considerations to make when contemplating the internship option. Beyond your personal costs (getting to the internship site, daily living expenses, and the hours you will be expected to work), you must consider the potential for the internship to further your goal of achieving full-time employment. Unless you are independently wealthy, internships are obviously a short-term arrangement. The duration can be for a few weeks in the summer to a year that coincides with the organization's program schedule.

The process of getting an internship is not unlike seeking a job. Applications, résumés, cover letters, and samples of your work may be required. Many arts organizations have formal internship programs with staff directors or coordinators assigned to manage the activities of a group of interns. Organizations operating at this level will more than likely have a developed set of expectations and duties for the interns. Some may even have job descriptions and ongoing evaluation systems. As you would expect, the better organized internship programs are typically found in the larger arts organizations with the budgetary resources to support the program. This does not mean that all larger arts organizations have attained a fully functioning intern program. Unfortunately, some of the larger arts organizations have internship programs that are less than effective, and some organizations are not ready for or equipped to effectively manage interns. The skills and abilities required of someone to effectively supervise an intern are not found universally in the workplace. Being relegated to only menial tasks such as making copies and collating mailings can occur. In fact, in some workplace situations the student intern may be perceived as a threat to the job security of some of the staff. This kind of environment of course undercuts the whole notion that the intern is there to learn as well as assist.

Many of the potential problems or misunderstandings that can develop when doing an internship can be alleviated with some basic written documents. When doing any internship it is usually advisable to draw up an agreement with the organization about the basic work conditions and expectations. Having some written goals and objectives for your internship can be very useful and can offer you some protection if the arrangement becomes problematic. Even if it is only a bullet list of goals, it is better than nothing. Of course the ideal circumstance would be to have an internship that allows the student to experience a range of opportunities working for the arts organization while aiding it in fulfilling its mission.

Organizing Your Job Search

There is no shortage of how-to books when it comes to job seeking, résumés, and cover letters. A quick trip to a local bookstore will give you a good idea of just how much is available out there. Websites have also created more opportunities to seek out employment opportunities. However, your search for a job in the arts management sector narrows your field very quickly. *ArtSEARCH*, the *Chronicle of Philanthropy*, and other specialized not-for-profit publications are a good place to start. Getting on E-mail lists of job openings and making use of your alumni connections through your university can also be of assistance. If there is a particular organization that you are interested in working for, a phone call to whomever handles the hiring is in order. Asking if they are willing to accept your résumé for future reference is not a bad place to start.

As with any goal you wish to achieve, you need to apply the same management techniques talked about in Chapter 5, "Planning and Decision Making." Establishing in writing what your objectives are in this job search is an important part of the process. Developing a timetable and a task list to accomplish your objective is required.

Analyzing what an organization seems to be seeking in its search, and then assessing your match to its needs is an essential first step. I have received a phenomenal number of cover letters and résumés from applicants that prompted me to wonder if they had even read the job ad. Tailoring your application to highlight the areas in your résumé and experience that match the employer's needs often promotes the call to you for an interview.

Developing Your Résumé

Résumés have undergone quite a transformation in the last 10 to 15 years as the personal computer has been enlisted to create interesting layouts and informative content. The simple chronological listing of jobs or internships has been supplanted by a more skills-based résumé. As we saw in Chapter 11, "Marketing and the Arts," target marketing for an arts organization consists of trying to reach the right people with the right message. The same holds true in the job search. The more targeted the cover letter and résumé is to the employer and the organization, the better the chance you will attract their attention.

See "Skills-Based Résumé Structure" and the sample résumé shown in Figure 14-1 for a place to start. Recognizing that your skill sets are transferable to different types of arts organizations is important if you wish to sustain a life in the field of arts management. In fact, it is critical to present your range of skills in such a way that you do not cause potential employers to exclude you from an applicant pool. Like it or not, employers generally make very quick initial judgments about your suitability for the position. If they have to work to see whether what you have listed in your résumé applies to their position, they are much less likely to seek you out. The simplest adjustment in your résumé can make all the difference. If you are applying for a marketing job, for example, and your résumé lists development and marketing experience in that order, simply switching the order of these items can make your résumé more effective. Such adjustments are quite easy now, with word-processing programs.

Developing Your Cover Letter

Your cover letter should be an enhancement to your résumé and needs to be directly related to the particular job you are seeking.[2] The generic cover letter of three sentences addressed to "Dear Sir or Madam" is very ineffective as a personal marketing tool. The effective cover letter, which is typically one page for most entry-level and middle-management jobs (longer for more middle and senior-management positions), should be targeted to the job and should enhance the information in your résumé. Assume that you are applying for a grant writing job and have adjusted your résumé so that your skill sets in grant writing are now at the top of the page. Your cover letter should then take one or more of your skills and provide an additional level of detail for the employer. For example, if you indicate that you have successfully written grants for touring performance programs, use the cover letter to let the

---

Skills-Based Résumé Structure

The skills-based résumé is created with the premise that an employer is seeking someone with the capabilities to supervise a functional area and accomplish a set of tasks in support of the organization.[1] If you have a limited work history, the skills-based résumé allows you to focus on what you can do, not how long you worked for your previous employer. A chronological résumé mixed with a skills format may be appropriate for someone with more experience in the workplace. A skills-based résumé also helps to minimize the fact that you just graduated, if that is the case. Another assumption in this résumé format is that you would adjust your skills to match the priority or expectations noted in the employment advertisement or job posting.

The following outline is intended to serve as a starting place. The résumé in Figure 14-1 is a simple example of a skills-based résumé.

Title: Arts Manager or Arts Administrator or Production Manager (or whatever title fits what you are)

Contact Information:
Name
Current address
City, State, Zip plus 4
Phone, fax, mobile, and E-mail contact information

Objective: (Optional) This can be useful is cases where you can offer some overview of what you are seeking

Major Functional Area 1: (E.g., Marketing and PR, Fundraising, Production Management, Event Planning, etc.)

- Bullet list of your accomplishments using the skills and action verbs (accomplished, achieved, attained, arranged, built, chaired, composed,

coordinated, created, devised, demonstrated, etc.)

Major Functional Area 2, 3, or more:

- Bullet list of accomplishments with action verbs

Special Skills:
Awards:
Education: List schools, degree, major areas. (You are not required to list graduation dates if you do not want to. Employers may remove you from their short list despite your skills if they see you just graduated from college.)

References: List names, phone numbers, and E-mail addresses. (If you say "Furnished Upon Request," you are adding a barrier between you and the potential employer. If someone is interested in your résumé make it easier, not harder, to consider your application.)

Hopefully Employed

1234 Happy Place Trail, Apt 11c
Tallahassee, FL 32312
(850) 555-1212 ** hopeful@urcool.job

Arts Management

Professional Skills

- Leadership and personnel management
- Project management
- Fundraising
- Marketing and public relations
- Contracts and nonprofit legal issues

- Corporate financial management
- Economic forecasting tools
- Arts event production management
- Website design and development
- Production management

Experience

Business Management & Computer Support

- Create and maintain vendor and invoice database for accounts payable department
- Assist with integration of accounting and reporting software
- Network and email support with Novell and Microsoft systems
- Create and file Articles of Incorporation for nonprofit corporations
- Positions Held
    - Administrative Assistant, No Such Associates, Inc.
    - Research and Computer Support Assist. Medium Size Arts Org., Inc.

Marketing & Promotion

- Design and graphic layout of Arts Newsletter
- Design and layout newspaper ads for arts series
- Design television ad campaign for PSA on local PBS station
- Compile and update media lists and database
- Positions Held
    - Intern, Really Cool Theatre Company
    - Production Assistant, Sort of Cool Opera Company

Computer Skills

- Ticketing Systems (TicketMaster, PASS 3), * Database (Access, FileMaker Pro), * Project Management (MS project), * HTML (Dreamwaver, FrontPage)

Education

MA, Arts Administration, Pretty Big University
BS, Business Administration and Communications, Smaller University

Figure 14-1 Skills-Based Résumé

reader know how successful the program was ("We toured 30 schools during the year and performed for 10,000 students in the district"). It is equally important to identify the facts of your experience and their relationship to this job. (See "Sample Cover Letter.") Remember, the employer is typically seeking someone who can do the things it needs to have done. It may be wonderful that you were able to secure a grant for a summer workshop in visual arts, but if I already have a successful program in that area, I am not going to be as interested in you. On the other hand, if you say you were able to add to the curatorial staff of the museum and that's what my organization is trying to do, you are much more interesting to me as an employer.

Doing job research has been made easier as websites have begun to post a great deal of information about the organization and its program. This research can help you further focus on important issues you can address should you be considered for the job.

Portfolios and Other Ways to Demonstrate Your Skills

Let us assume you have been able to attract the employer's interest based on your résumé and cover letter. Now what? You can further help your application for a job if you have examples of your best work. Creating a CD-ROM or a personal website offers many new opportunities as an

---

Sample Cover Letter

First Paragraph: Express your interest in the job and where you heard about it.

Second Paragraph: Here is your opportunity to sell yourself. Help the employer find the key points in your résumé that support the position being offered and the qualifications being sought.

Third Paragraph: Remind the employer that you have many skills by providing a little more background information on yourself.

Fourth Paragraph: Establish that you are ready to take action and that you have even more good skills to show them. Also make it clear that you will respond to a phone call or an E-mail query if they need more information.

Fifth Paragraph: Close with a thank-you and express your interest in the job.

Date
Ms. Good Job
First Arts Organization
1234 Nice Street
Good Place, Somewhere Zip code

Dear Ms. Job:

I am interested in the marketing assistant position at the First Choice Arts Organization recently advertised online at Cool Arts Jobs. I have enclosed my résumé and references that you may contact at your convenience.

As you will see in my résumé, I have recently worked on the marketing campaign for the summer arts in the park program. We were able to increase the summer arts sales by 20 percent this year. I believe I can contribute to the marketing efforts of the First Arts Organization through my writing and my extensive graphic design skills. I understand you are also seeking

someone to develop a budget system for your marketing office. While I was in graduate school I assisted on revamping our departmental budget system.

My degree program stressed the importance of fundraising and special event planning in the arts. I feel I am very skilled in these areas. I assisted on several big events held at the summer festival.

I would appreciate the opportunity to meet with you to review my portfolio of recent arts administration projects. Please feel free to call me or send me an E-mail if you need any more information about my previous experience.

Thank your for your time and consideration. I look forward to hearing from you.

Sincerely,
Hopefully Employed
Enclosure: Résumé

employment tool when you seek a job. Too much information can work against you, but striking the right balance of information by creating a sample of your work electronically could be critical for getting noticed in a crowded field of applicants. If you send samples with your application materials, be sure to keep them minimal and representative. If the employer wants more information, you can follow up with details. For example, including the executive summary of a grant application, the summary points of a marketing or fundraising plan, or samples of other graphics or writing samples can serve to move you ahead of the other applicants. The goal, as always, is to establish the best match between you and the organization.

Interviewing

Seeking out resources about interview techniques is worth the effort. If you are able to advance in the application process to the interview state, you want to be as effective as possible, so take the time to read a book like David Eyler's *Job Interviews That Mean Business*[3] or to find interview tips on a website such as Monster.com. Chapter 7, "Staffing the Organization," pointed out the differing styles found in the interview process. Some organizations are going to have prepared questions they ask all the applicants in a formal setting. Other organizations may have one person conduct the interview, then let others meet you informally for the rest of the process. Since there are no hard and fast rules about how an organization will approach this process, it is incumbent upon you to research the organization and gain as much information as you can about the process the organization plans to use in making its hire.

A follow-up interview may take place if the search is local or regional. Should this be the case, you will probably have the salary and benefits discussion mentioned earlier in this chapter. Being prepared with the right questions and listening for the details of an offer will save you a great deal of time later. Many people new to the job market do not find out the details of benefits, vacation time, and policies about sick leave and travel until after they are hired. Asking about benefits, for example, may reveal potential problems with taking the job. The organization may not offer health insurance until you have worked there for six months.

Getting Hired

Should you be fortunate enough to be hired, the process of making the transition to a new organization, coworkers, and supervisors, and adapting to the culture of the organization, goes on for some time. Depending on the job, it often takes one full business cycle (or a year) with the organization to become familiar with all of the challenges facing you in the job. As a new employee you often have a grace period in which to operate with minimal judgments being made about you by the people you work with and report to. However, after as little time as a week on the job people are already forming perceptions about you and your work. It is the nature of the workplace and the acculturation process that you will be judged as a success or not based on what may seem to you to be rather superficial criteria.

Managing your job and career success remains your responsibility, and the amount of guidance and support you receive will vary with the type of organization. Finding a mentor in the organization or being assigned a more senior staff member to communicate with can be of great assistance in the early stages of a new job. However, this may not happen, and you will be on your own a great deal. Unlike your teachers and advisors when you were a student, people in the workplace are not necessarily as concerned about how you are doing. That is not to say that the workplace you encounter will be a hostile environment, but the workplace is a social environment as much as it is a place of business. If you are to succeed in your job, your social skills will be as important as your job skills in some circumstances.

Building a Career

In the early stages of your career you will discover that ideas you had about what you wanted to do and where you wanted to work will go through several transitions. Most students find new opportunities and experiences in the workplace that lead to new directions or even new jobs. The excitement of learning new skills and successfully meeting big deadlines or completing important projects will create a rewarding cycle of personal development. The normal frustrations of the workplace will be put aside when you see the positive results of your work or the work of a team you led. Your success will also no doubt lead to your being asked to do more for the organization. Then you will face your first critical career development hurdle. Taking on too many projects or too much work—which is very easy to do in the arts organizations that are strapped for human resources—can undermine your effectiveness and lower the estimates of your capabilities in the eyes of management. Being able to keep enough objective distance between your long-term career goals and the day-to-day challenges of work will become increasingly difficult as you find yourself taking on more responsibility in your job.

How do you stay focused on building a rewarding career for yourself in the arts? Most long-term success lies in applying the same skills you use to be successful in your job to your own the personal career plans. You need to be set goals, develop objectives, implement action plans, and then evaluate the results and adjust for changing circumstances. Taking some time to analyze your own situation and formulate action plans can really pay off when an unexpected opportunity or a crisis arises. As you will soon find out, the career path you take often does not follow a straight line. For example, internal promotions or lateral moves to other arts organizations in your community may provide you with unexpected opportunities to advance your career. You may also find yourself unemployed when an organization runs into trouble, or worse yet, you may be fired from your job. Being prepared for the worst is very much like having contingency plans in place for an organization, as discussed in Chapter 5, "Planning and Decision Making." Recognizing that not all work-related outcomes will be positive, and having a plan in place should an event such as losing your job occur, can actually provide a degree of security.

As you will no doubt discover, many people in the workplace are driven by real or imagined fears that inhibit them from thinking clearly about the situation they may be in and the choices they have. An effective manager realizes, as we discussed in Chapter 8, "Fundamentals of Leadership and Group Dynamics," that many of the problems and crises one faces in the workplace are part of the context of the work and the working relationships among the staff. Applying situational leadership and management techniques to your own career development can be a very good way to advance yourself to whatever level in the organization you choose.

Career Goal

As I noted in the Preface, one of my goals in writing this book was to help develop arts managers who support and collaborate with artists to help fulfill the mission of the organization. Establishing yourself as a leader and manager in the arts will take no less work than it does to become a recognized performer, writer, designer, or scholar in the arts. The discipline and drive needed to excel in the arts are just as important for the staff in the office as they are for the chorus of the opera or the violin section of the orchestra.

Think about your job as an arts manager in the same way you think about what a conductor of an orchestra does. As you work with the staff of an arts organization, try to achieve the exquisite harmony and unity of purpose of a beautifully sounding symphony orchestra. For example, it makes sense to have the customer service aspects of your ticket office working in cooperation with your marketing, public relations, and fundraising functions. You need to have each of these sections of the organization "in tune" with each other. If you agree with this analogy, you can see the necessity for investing a lot of time and energy in your career path. It takes a great deal of hard work to achieve the kind of excellence people have come to expect from the arts and artists in their community.

Good luck and best wishes in your choice to make a life in the arts.

Career Development Work Plan

1. Develop a bullet list of your major employment and career goals for the next two to five years. Indicate the type of organization you would like to work for, the type of job title you are seeking, and any other key factors that describe your employment objectives.

2. Develop a draft of a skills-based résumé. Focus on the items noted in the reading and develop your list of action verbs to describe what skills and abilities you possess. Do not become too eager to do the graphic layout for the entire résumé. First work on key phrases to describe what makes you a potential outstanding employee. Write up a skills and abilities inventory. Try to develop a priority ranking of your strengths.

3. Next, using a recent issues of *ArtSEARCH*, or a similar publication, analyze the types of job titles, qualifications, duties, and salary information found in the job listings. Look for information in the ad about the size of the organization, its overall operating budget, and the number of staff or season of events performed. Are there phrases used in the ads such as "an ideal candidate," or "successful candidate"? Develop your own bullet list of key duties in the "responsible for" or "oversees" or "experienced in" sections of the ads.

4. Begin putting together several versions of your skills-based résumé that address the kind of ideal candidate with the applicable experiences that will allow you to successfully assume the desired responsibilities. Refine and focus the résumé to the major types of positions that interest you. Develop a layout template for the résumé that provides for maximum readability (i.e., leave some white space) with basic graphic design elements (shading, bold type, boxes, frames, or other interesting graphic tools) to create an interesting looking résumé.

Proofread your résumé for any errors or typos and have others proofread as well.

5. Draft a cover letter of the jobs that interest you the most. Tailor the cover letter to the job ad and provide additional details about the scope and scale of the projects you successfully completed to add to the depth of your application. Have someone else proofread the letter for you.

6. If you are contacted, follow up with the employers immediately. Review David Eyler's *Job Interviews That Mean Business* in preparation for a potential phone interview. Often the first approach of interest will come in the form of a telephone interview. If the employer likes what he or she hears on the phone, it may lead to more contact. Should the employer wish to set up a personal interview, you need to do your research on the organization and brush up on your interview answers to the typical questions employers pose.

References

1. Susan Britton Whitcomb, *Résumé Magic* (Indianapolis: JIST Works, 1999).
2. Richard H. Beatty, *The Perfect Cover Letter*, 2nd ed. (New York: John Wiley & Sons, 1997).
3. David R. Eyler, *Job Interviews That Mean Business* (New York: Random House, 1999).

Index

Page numbers followed by "f" denote figures, "t" denote tables, and "b" denote sidebars or boxes.

A

Acceptance theory, 163
Accounting
  accrual-based, 240–241
  cash-based, 239
  definition of, 239
  fund-based, 241
  overview of, 240f, 241–242
Accounting formula, 242
Accrual-based accounting, 240–241
Acquired-needs theory, 172
Action plans, 93
Actor's Equity Association, 151
Ad hoc committee, 178
Administrative assistant, 115, 123
Administrative management
  arts application of, 52–53
  history of, 51–52
Administrator, 9
Advertising, 232
Age Discrimination Act, 142
Agency organization, 119
Aggressiveness, 180
American Ballet Theatre, 23
American Federation of Musicians, 151
American Federation of Television and
    Radio Artists, 151
American Guild of Musical Artists, 151
American Guild of Variety Artists, 151
American Marketing Association, 254
Americans with Disabilities Act, 143
Analytical manager, 306–308, 307f
Applications, for employment, 145–147
Apprenticeships, 148
Artist-manager
  description of, 18
  history of, 21
Arts
  in ancient civilizations, 19–20
  as institutions, 18–19
  audience for, 223–224
  broadcast media effects, 71
  business growth in, 3, 5
  content sources, 67
  economy and, 68b, 227, 236

environment effects. *See*
    Environment(s)
  expansion period for, 24
  fundraising and, 279–280
  future of, 5–6, 79
  government support for, 19, 32–33
  growth of, 28, 36
  lobbying for, 70b
  managerization of, 308
  market demand effects on, 232
  organizing for, 109
  post–World War II boom of, 74
  research regarding, 264
  technology effects, 6
  trend shifts in, 223
Arts councils, 297
Arts festivals, 20
Arts groups. *See also* Group
  interactions among, 76
  synergy among, 76–77
Arts management
  in ancient civilizations, 19–20
  education opportunities, 35–36
  in Greek civilization, 19–20
  growth of, 37–38, 325
  during Middle Ages, 20–21
  opportunities in, 2f
  during Renaissance, 21–22
  in Roman civilization, 20
  in seventeenth to nineteenth
    centuries, 22–23
  in twentieth century, 23–24
Arts manager. *See also* Manager
  audience development, 271
  classroom training of, 29–30
  content analysis by, 66–67
  functions of, 14–15
  information sources for. *See*
    Information sources
  jobs for, 30–31
  National Endowment for the Arts
    and, 34–35
  on-the-job training, 29–30, 46
  organizational design perspectives,
    118–121

Arts manager, *continued*
  personal mission of, 31
  profile of, 28–30, 37
  salary of, 30–31
  women as, 30
Arts organization. *See also*
    Organization
  as institution, 11–12
  audience-oriented, 259
  business plan for, 27b
  components of, 177
  contingency approach, 56
  core values of, 14b
  cultural network connection for, 130
  culture of, 10–11
  customer-oriented, 259
  definition of, 6, 108
  diversification of, 30
  division of labor in, 10
  economic impact of, 227, 228b–229b
  elements of, 10–11
  environment interactions, 11, 11f
  founder-director, 11
  goals statement, 14b
  hierarchy of authority in, 9
  informal structure of, 10
  marketing ethics of, 264–265
  matrix structure of, 120–121, 122f
  mission statement of, 14b
  monitoring of, 66
  nonprofit. *See* Nonprofit arts
    organization
  open system model of, 7f, 110f
  planning effects on, 97–98
  scientific management principles
    applied to, 50–51
  strategies used by, 14b
  structure of. *See* Organizational
    structure
  tax-exempt status, 25–26
Arts subsidy, 5
Assets, 241
Associate artistic director, 115–116
Association of Arts Administration
    Educators, 35
Association of Performing Arts
    Presenters, 36, 262
Audience, 75–77, 223–224
Audit
  description of, 26
  fundraising, 285
  marketing, 265, 267
  organizational, 307
Auditions, 145
Authority, hierarchy of, 10
Average total costs, 230

B
Babbage, Charles, 48
Baby Boomers, 72

Balance sheet, 242–243, 243f
Barnard, Chester, 52
Behavior modification, organizational,
    175
Behavioral decision theory, 100
Benefits, 140–141, 328
Bet-your-company culture, 126
Blocking, 180
Board of Directors
  description of, 150–151, 151b, 177
  effectiveness strategies for, 181–182
  financial statements reviewed by, 245
  fundraising by, 286, 289
  investment policy, 246–247
  manager's interactions with, 315
  staff interactions with, 181
Bookkeeping, 239
Bottom-up planning, 95–96
Broadcast media
  information gathering from, 77–78
  socialization effects, 71
Budget
  balancing of, 245
  capital, 209
  cash flow projections, 215–217, 216f
  centers for, 208
  compensation amounts and, 327
  controls for, 210
  definition of, 87, 206–207
  description of, 205–206
  detailed, 211, 213f
  elements of, 210–215
  fixed, 208
  flexible, 209
  information resources, 209b
  operating, 209
  overview of, 217
  preliminary control use of, 208
  process of, 209–210
  project, 209, 211, 214f, 215
  reality of, 210
  schematic diagram of, 207f
  summary, 211, 212f
  top secret document status of, 208
  zero-based, 209
Bureaucracy, 111–112
Business manager, 237
Business plan
  description of, 27b
  developing of, 94–95

C
Capital budget, 209
Career. *See also* Employment; Job(s)
  development of
    education, 329–330
    fears that affect, 336
    focus on, 336
    internships, 330–331
    overview of, 328–329

sacrifices required, 329
stages of, 336
work plan, 337–338
goal for, 337
management of, 155
Cash flow projections, 215–217, 216f
Cash-based accounting, 239
Catholic Church, 20–21
Censorship, 21–22
Central Opera Service, 23
Centralization–decentralization, 124
Chain of command, 121, 123
Change
artists and, 72
in environments, 64–66
growing into, 65–66
legal environment, 69
political environment, 69
responses to, 65
unpredicted, 75b
Chicago Lyric Opera, 23
Child labor, 48–49
Civil Rights Acts, 142–143
Claritas Corporation, 263
Coaching, 148
Coercive power, 161
Cognitive-based motivation theories
description of, 170
equity theory, 172–173
expectancy theory, 173–174
Cohesiveness of group, 179
Combination strategy, 92
Command group, 177–178
Commercial theater production, 3, 4f
Committee
ad hoc, 178
definition of, 178
disruptive behaviors, 180–181
efficiency of, 178
management by, 169–170
standing, 178
Communication
assessment of, 310
case study of, 318–322
definition of, 182
description of, 182
formal, 184
informal, 184
internal, 128
lines of, 116–117, 310
management information system, 202
perception of, 183–184
schematic diagram of, 183f
Compensation, 140, 152b, 326–328
Competing, 180
Competitive marketplace, 267, 269
Complementary good, 231
Computers
accounting uses of, 242
fundraising uses of, 286–288, 293

management information system use
of, 203
marketing data system use of,
269–270
marketing uses of, 257
Consultants, 78
Content analysis, 66–67
Contingency approach, 56
Contingency leadership, 165–166
Contingency planning, 96
Contingency system, 311
Continual evaluation, 66
Contracts
union negotiation of, 151–152
with volunteers, 150b
wording of, 152b
Control process
in arts setting, 196
description of, 193
elements of, 194–198
input standards, 196
leadership influences, 195
limitations, 194
performance measures, 196
schematic diagram of, 195f
steps involved in, 194–195
summary overview of, 217
Control system
accounting areas, 200
areas for, 195
in arts setting, 200
case study of, 218–220
description of, 193
establishment of, 200
financial areas, 200
management by exception, 197–198
management by objectives, 198
performance appraisal systems,
198–199
summary of, 199–200, 217
Coordination
horizontal, 121, 124–125
vertical
centralization–decentralization, 124
chain of command, 121, 123
definition of, 121
delegation, 123–124
span of control, 123
Core values, 14b
Corporate culture
bet-your-company, 126
business environment, 126–127
cultural network, 128–130
description of, 10–11
heroes, 127–128
hidden hierarchy in, 128
leadership loss effects, 127–128
process, 126
real world and, 130
rites and rituals of, 128

Corporate culture, *continued*
  theory vs. reality, 125–126
  tough-guy, 126
  types of, 126
  values supported by, 127, 154
  work hard–play hard, 126
Corporate fundraising. *See also*
      Fundraising
  problems associated with, 295
  process of, 295–296
  reciprocity principle for, 295
  statistics regarding, 294–295
  techniques for, 295
Costs
  fundraising, 288
  marginal, 228–229
  total fixed, 228
  total variable, 228
Cover letter, 332, 334, 334b
Creative class, 72, 73b
Crisis planning, 96, 313
Critical incident appraisal, 199
Critical path method, 55
Cross-training, 148
Cultural boom, 223
Cultural environment
  case study of, 81–83
  description of, 71–72
Cultural network, 128–130
Culture of organization
  analytical manager's effect on,
      306–307
  description of, 10–11
Curator, 39–40
Customer orientation, 258–259, 260b

D
Dance chart, 115f
Dance companies
  in twentieth century, 23
  in United States, 23–24
Decision making, 98
Decision theory, 100
Delegation, 123–124
Demand. *See also* Supply and demand
  advertising effects, 232
  arts and, 232
  consumer tastes effect on, 232
  expectations effect on, 232
  income effects, 231–232
  law of, 230–232
  price of other goods effect on, 231
Demographic environment, 71–73
Departmentalization, 119–120
Differentiation strategy, 267
Direct mail fundraising, 293–294
Diseconomies of scale, 230
Disposable personal income, 223
Distributed leadership, 182
Divisions of labor, 10

Divisions of work, 112, 113f–116f
Donors, fundraising
  communication with, 292
  data management regarding, 286–287,
      287b
  funding options for, 290–291
  personal contact with, 292
  ratings matrix, 291f
  research of, 289–290
  restricted gift, 289
  solicitation strategies for, 290f, 299
  unrestricted gift, 289
DVDs, 74
Dysfunctional manager, 304–306
Dysfunctional organization, 304–306

E
Economic environment, 68
Economics
  arts and, 68b, 227, 236
  arts organization and, 222–223
  entertainment business effects, 68
  financial management and, 248
  issues regarding, 226
  organizational impact and, 227
  principles of, 225–227
  productivity issues, 224–225
  questions regarding, 222
  technology applied to, 225
Economies of scale, 230
Education
  art involvement in, 75
  arts consumer and, 75
  career development, 329–330
  opportunities for, 35–36
Educational environment, 75
EEOC. *See* Equal Employment
      Opportunity Commission
Effort-performance expectancy, 173
Eighteenth century, 22–23
Employee(s). *See also* Staff
  career management system for,
      155
  developing of, 154–155
  firing of, 149
  hiring of, 335–336. *See also* Staffing
  maintaining of, 154–155
  management of, 315–316
  organizational values communicated
      to, 127
  performance standards for, 310
  replacement of, 148–149
  socialization of, 147
Employee manual, 156b
Employment. *See also* Career; Job(s)
  Employer's perspective, 326
  geographical considerations, 325
  organization size and, 328–329
  personal plan for, 326
Employment-at-will, 149

Entertainment business
  creation of, 1
  economy effects, 68
  government policy effects, 5–6
  growing of, 3, 5
  marketing, 253, 257–258
  profit-making ventures, 3
  technology effects, 6
Environment
  business, 126–127
  changing of, 64–66
  content analysis, 66–67
  cultural, 71–72, 81–82
  demographic, 72–73
  description of, 10, 11f, 62–63
  economic, 68
  educational, 75
  legal, 68–70
  management information system and,
    203
  organizational design and, 119
  political, 68–70
  schematic diagram of, 63f
  social, 71–72
  technological, 73–75
  types of, 62, 63f
Equal Employment Opportunity
    Commission, 142
Equal Pay Act, 142
Equity theory of motivation, 172–173
ERG Theory, 171
Ethics
  fundraising, 295
  marketing, 264–265
Exchange process, 255–256
Exit surveys, 76
Expectancy theory of motivation,
    173–174
Expectations, 232
Expenses centers, 208
Expert power, 162
Extrinsic rewards, 173–174

F
Factors of production, 233
Fads, 66
Family and Medical Leave Act, 143
Family-oriented theme parks, 1
Fayol, Henri, 51–52
Featherbedding, 153
Federal Register, 298
Feedback, 109, 199
Film industry, 257
Financial Accounting Standards Board,
    239
Financial management
  business manager's role in, 237
  description of, 236–237
  economics and, 248
  investments, 245–247

nonprofit, 237
  reserve funds, 249
  summary of, 247
Financial management information
    system
  description of, 26, 237
  development of, 239
  purposes of, 238–239, 248
  schematic diagram of, 238f
Financial manager, 237
Financial report, 249–251
Financial statements
  balance sheet, 242–243, 243f
  description of, 24–25, 242
  statement of activity, 243–245
Firing of staff, 149
Fiscal management, 316
Fiscal planning, 316
Fiscal year, 210–211
Fixed budget, 208
Flexible budget, 209
Follett, Mary Parker, 53
Form 990, 242
Form utility, 255
Formal communication, 184
Formal group, 177
Formal leadership, 160
For-profit arts organizations, 1
Foundations, 296
Founder-director organization, 10,
    24–25, 126–127
Frustration-regression principle, 171
Functional manager, 9
Functional satisfaction, 254
Fund reserves, 249
Fund-based accounting, 241
Funding pyramid, 283–284, 284f
Fundraisers, 86
Fundraising
  amounts needed, 283
  arts and, 279–280
  audit, 285
  Board of Directors participation in,
    286, 289
  case study of, 300–302
  computers for, 286–288, 293
  confidentiality issues, 287–288
  control of, 288
  corporate
    problems associated with, 295
    process of, 295–296
    reciprocity principle for, 295
    statistics regarding, 294–295
    techniques for, 295
  costs of, 288
  credibility, 169
  data management system, 286–288
  description of, 150, 278
  donors
    communication with, 292

Fundraising, *continued*
    data management regarding,
      286–287, 287b
    funding options for, 290–291
    personal contact with, 292
    ratings matrix, 291f
    research of, 289–290
    restricted gift, 289
    solicitation strategies for, 290f,
      299
    unrestricted gift, 289
  ethics, 295
  foundations, 296
  goals for, 282, 314
  governmental, 296–298
  growth in, 280
  history of, 278
  management of, 285
  marketing and, 284–285
  mission statement and, 281–282
  motivation for, 278–279
  National Endowment for the Arts,
    297
  organization's role in, 285–286
  plans for, 280–285
  process of, 281, 282f
  revenue obtained from, 279
  schedule for, 293
  staff participation in, 280, 286, 289
  statistics regarding, 278
  strategic planning and, 281, 282f
  summary overview of, 298–300
  techniques and tools for
    description of, 288–289
    direct mail, 293–294
    donors. *See* Fundraising, donors
    special events, 294
    telephone solicitations, 292–293
  web resources for, 287b
Funds
  expending of, 210
  reserve, 249

G
General manager, 9
Generally accepted accounting
    principles, 239
Goals
  arts organization, 14b
  career, 337
  description of, 14b, 86
  fundraising, 282, 314
Government
  arts supported by, 19, 32–33
  entertainment business regulations,
    5–6
  fundraising sources, 296–298
  information sources, 78
  management relations with, 316–317
  staffing regulations, 142–143

Greek civilization, 19–20
Group
  adjourning stage of, 179
  cohesiveness of, 179
  command, 177–178
  definition of, 177
  development stages of, 178–179
  disruptive behaviors, 180–181
  dynamics of, 167f
  dysfunctional activities of, 179–180
  effectiveness strategies for, 180–182
  formal, 177
  forming stage of, 178
  informal, 177
  interest, 178
  norming stage of, 178
  norms of, 179
  performing stage of, 178–179
  storming stage of, 178
  summary overview of, 186
  task, 178
  temporary, 177
  types of, 177–178
Groupthink, 179–180
Growth strategy, 92, 267, 269

H
Halo effect, 184
Hawthorne effect, 53–55
Hierarchy of authority, 10
High-definition television, 74
History
  Greek civilization, 19–20
  Middle Ages, 20–21
  Renaissance, 21–22
  Roman civilization, 20
Horizontal coordination, 121,
    124–125
Horsing around, 180
Human relations management
  arts application of, 54–55
  description of, 53, 310, 312f
  Hawthorne effect, 53–55
  Maslow's hierarchy of needs, 54–55
  McGregor's Theory X and Theory Y,
    54–55

I
Immigration Reform and Control Act,
    143
Income, 231–232
Income effect, 236
Incorporation, 25
Industrial Revolution, 47–48
Inferior goods or services, 232
Inflation, 224
Informal communication, 184
Informal group, 177
Informal leadership, 160
Informal organizational structure, 117

Information sources
  arts groups, 76–77
  associations, 78
  audiences, 75–77
  board of directors. *See* Board of
    Directors
  consultants, 78
  description of, 75
  government, 78
  media, 77–78
  professional meetings, 78
  staff members. *See* Staff
  suppliers, 78–79
Input standards, 196
Interest groups, 178
Intermediate-range plans, 86
Internal Revenue Service 501(c)(3), 25
Internet, 67
Internship, 330–331
Interviewing, 146, 156, 335
Intrinsic rewards, 173–174
Investments, 245–247

J
Job(s). *See also* Career; Employment
  compensation issues, 140, 152b,
    326–328
  considerations in selecting, 325–326
  geographical considerations, 325
  interviewing for, 335
  locating of, 324–325
  matrix of, 141–142
  organization size and, 328–329
  search for. *See* Job search
Job analysis
  description of, 137
  job context, 139
  personnel qualifications, 139
  schematic diagram of, 138f
  standards, 139
  work activities, 137–139
  work tools, 139
Job context, 139
Job description
  application method, 141
  benefits, 140–141
  compensation, 140
  description of, 139
  employment requirements, 140
  general description, 140
  responsibilities, 140
  sample, 141b
  specific duties, 140
Job rotation, 148
Job search
  cover letter, 332, 334, 334b
  hiring after, 335–336
  organizing of, 331
  portfolio, 334–335
  résumé, 331–332, 332b, 333f

L
Labor disputes, 152–154, 154b
Labor divisions, 52
Law of contingent reinforcement, 175
Law of demand, 230–232
Law of diminishing returns, 229
Law of immediate reinforcement, 175
Law of supply
  description of, 232–233
  price of resources effect, 233
  suppliers effect on, 233–234
Leadership
  arts application, 169
  behavioral approach to, 164
  case study of, 187–189
  contingency approach to, 165–166
  control system influenced by,
    195–196
  definition of, 160
  description of, 13
  distributed, 182
  formal, 160
  fundamentals of, 159–161
  future of, 169–170
  ineffective, 177
  informal, 160
  loss of, 127
  managerial success and, 160
  news stories regarding, 170b
  normative model of, 166, 168
  power
    acceptance theory of, 163
    description of, 160
    expert, 162
    guidelines for using, 163–164
    limits to, 162–163
    personal, 161–162
    position, 161
    questions regarding, 161
    reference, 162
    sources of, 161–162
    zone of indifference, 163
  situational theory of, 168
  standards set by, 127
  styles of, 165f
  summary overview of, 185–186
  theories of, 167f
  theory X, 160
  theory Y, 160
  trait approach to, 164
  transactional, 168–169
  transformational, 168–169
Legal environment, 68–70
Legitimate power, 161
Liabilities, 241
Line manager, 9
Lines of communication, 116–117,
  310
Lobbying, 70b
Long-range plans, 86

M
Mailing lists, 261
Maintenance activities, 181
Management
  administrative, 51–53
  as art, 45–46
  Board of Directors interactions, 315
  case study of, 131–135
  classical perspectives of, 50–51
  committee-style, 169–170
  contingency system of, 311
  control functions of, 13–14
  development function of, 311, 313
  emerging view of, 57–58
  evolution of, 47–49
  example of, 9b
  financial. *See* Financial management
  fiscal, 316
  functions of, 12b
  government relations with, 316–317
  history of, 47
  human relations, 53–55, 310, 312f
  Industrial Revolution effects on,
    47–48
  leading by, 13
  levels of, 7–8, 8f, 113–116
  managerial level of, 8–9
  middle, 8
  on-the-job theory of, 46
  open system model of, 311, 312f
  operational level of, 8
  organization size and, 8f, 10
  organizing by, 13
  personnel, 315–316
  philosophy of, 47
  planning by, 12–13, 311, 313
  principles of, 51f
  process, 309–310, 312f
  as science, 45–46
  scientific. *See* Scientific management
  staff, 315–316
  strategic level of, 8–9
  styles of, 304–309, 317
  theories of, 309–311, 317
  timeline of, 49f
  total quality, 57
  unions and, 154, 314–315
  in United States, 48–49
Management by exception, 197–198
Management by objectives, 198
Management information system
  arts organization application of,
    201–202
  business environment effects, 203
  components of, 202f
  computers, 203
  data and information, 201, 205, 206f
  definition of, 200
  establishment of, 200–201
  factors that affect, 203–204

  future of, 205
  implementation-related problems,
    204–205
  importance of, 201
  mistakes associated with, 204–205
  organizational design effects, 202
  purpose of, 203
  schematic diagram of, 202f
  summary overview of, 205
  terminology, 201
Manager
  analytical, 306–308, 307f
  arts. *See* Arts manager
  definition of, 6, 108–109
  dysfunctional, 304–306
  functional, 9
  functions of, 14–15
  general, 9
  job responsibilities of, 6
  line, 9
  organic, 307f, 309
  personality of, 306
  professional, 308
  salaries of, 31
  staff, 9
  stage, 152b
  systems, 307f, 308–309
Mandatory Retirement Act, 142–143
Marginal costs, 228–229
Market failure, 226
Market research, 261–264
Market segment, 261
Marketer, 265b
Marketing
  advent of, 253
  approaches for, 258–259
  audit, 265, 267
  case study of, 273–276
  Claritas system for, 263
  computer uses for, 257
  consultants for, 267
  customer orientation, 258–259, 260b
  definition of, 254
  description of, 313–314
  entertainment and, 257–258
  ethics of, 264–265
  evolution of, 256–258
  exchange process and utilities,
    255–256
  functional satisfaction and, 254
  fundraising and, 284–285
  methods of, 252–253
  modern, 257
  needs and wants, 254–255
  overview of, 252–253
  planning process, 265, 266f
  price as tool for, 261b
  principles of, 260–261
  product orientation, 258
  promotional aspects of, 260–261

psychological satisfaction and, 254
sales orientation, 258
strategic plans for, 265–270, 314
summary overview of, 270–272
target, 261–263
Marketing data system, 269–270, 270f
Marketing plan, 268b–269b
Maslow's hierarchy of needs
   human relations management,
      54–55
   motivation and, 170–171
Mass media audience, 1
Matrix structure of organization,
   120–121, 122f
McCallum, Daniel Craig, 48
McGregor's Theory X and Theory Y,
   54–55
Mechanistic organizational design, 110
Meetings, 180–181
Mentor, 335–336
Metropolitan Opera, 62
Middle Ages, 20–21
Middle management, 8
MIS. *See* Management information
   system
Miscommunication, 182
Mission statement, 14b, 87–90
Modeling, 148
Motivation
   in arts work setting, 170
   summary overview of, 185–186
Motivation theories
   cognitive-based
      description of, 170
      equity theory, 172–173
      expectancy theory, 173–174
   description of, 167f, 170
   integration of, 176
   need-based
      acquired-needs theory, 172
      description of, 170
      Maslow's hierarchy of needs,
         170–171
      two-factor theory, 171–172
   reinforcement-based
      description of, 170, 174
      organizational behavior
         modification, 175
   social learning theory-based, 170,
      176
Museums
   curator of, 39–40
   in Greek civilization, 20
   jobs with, 325
   organizational chart of, 116f
Music industry, 74

N
National Assembly of Local Arts
   Agencies, 297

National Endowment for the Arts
   appropriations for, 31, 34f
   arts audience statistics, 223–224
   arts manager and, 34–35
   board of directors, 35
   budget battles, 33
   censorship, 33, 78
   chairperson of, 34
   creation of, 31, 37
   description of, 3, 23–24
   founding of, 31
   grant funding by, 32, 297
   information resources regarding, 33b
   mission statement of, 32
   peer review process, 297–298
   planning contributions by, 96–97
   reauthorization hearings, 34
   state agencies, 35
   vision of, 32
National Labor Relations Board, 152
NEA. *See* National Endowment for the
   Arts
Need-based motivation theories
   acquired-needs theory, 172
   description of, 170
   Maslow's hierarchy of needs, 170–171
   two-factor theory, 171–172
Needs, 254
Negative reinforcement, 175
Net assets, 241, 244–245
Niche strategy, 267
Nineteenth century, 22–23
Nonprofit arts organizations
   description of, 1, 3
   filings by, 26
   financial manager's role in, 237
   financial statements, 24–25
   fundraising by. *See* Fundraising
   incorporation, 25
   IRS filings, 242
   legal status, 24–25
   motivation of, 226
   tax exemption, 25–26, 227
Nonprofit financial management, 237
Normative leadership model, 166, 168

O
Objectives, 86, 93
Occupational Safety and Health
   Administration, 69
Off-Broadway theater, 23
Older Workers Benefit Protection Act,
   143
On-the-job management theory, 46
On-the-job training, 148
Open system model, 7f, 110f, 311
Opera
   in nineteenth century, 22
   in twentieth century, 23
Operant conditioning, 175

Operating budget, 209
Operational plan, 86
Operations research, 55
Orchestras
description of, 24
organizational chart, 114f
Organic manager, 307f, 309
Organic organizational design, 110
Organization. *See also* Arts organization
agency, 119
audit of, 307
definition of, 6, 108
dysfunctional, 304–306
fundraising role of, 285–286
growth of, 125
mechanistic, 110
structure of, 112. *See* Organizational
structure
theory vs. reality in, 125–126
values of, 127, 154
Organizational behavior modification,
175
Organizational chart
adherence to, 112
art museum, 116f
dance company, 115f
definition of, 112
departments or work groups,
112–113
divisions of work, 112, 113f–116f
lines of communication, 116–117
management levels, 113–116
matrix, 122f
symphony orchestra, 114f
theater company, 113f
work performed, 112
working relationships, 112
Organizational design
approaches for, 109–110
art manager's perspective, 118–121
bureaucratic, 111–112
description of, 109–110
environment effects, 119
informal, 117
management information system and,
202
mechanistic, 110
organic, 110
staffing needs and, 138–139
technology effects, 119
Organizational structure
art manager's perspective, 118–121
departmentalization, 119–120
informal, 117
matrix, 120–121, 122f
people and, 118
strategy supported by, 118
Organized labor, 143
Organizing
for arts, 109

benefits of, 109
coordination. *See* Coordination
definition of, 108
description of, 7, 13, 108
management function of, 108–109
Owen, Robert, 48

P
Paper trail, 242
Paradigm shifts, 57
Participative management, 54
Path-Goal theory, 168
Pay equity, 173
Peer groups, 71–72
Performance appraisal systems, 198–199,
217
Performance standards, 310
Performance-outcome expectancy, 173
Philanthropy, 285b
Place utility, 255
Plan
fundraising, 280–281, 282f
intermediate-range, 86
long-range, 86
marketing, 265, 266f
operational, 86
as organization map, 85
short-range, 86
single-use, 87
standing-use, 87
strategic. *See* Strategic plan and
planning
Planning
arts and, 84–85
bottom-up, 95–96
business plan. *See* Business plan
case study example of, 102–106
contingency, 96
crisis, 96, 313
effects of, 97–98
failure of, 97
importance of, 12–13
limits of, 96–98
manager's role in, 313
necessity of, 85
organization effects, 97
process of
action plans, 93
description of, 87
goals, 93
mission statement, 87–90
objectives, 93
resource analysis, 91
sample, 95b
schematic diagram of, 88f
situation analysis, 90–91
strategy. *See* Strategic plan and
planning
questions answered by, 85–86
resources for, 85b

sample document for, 93f
short-term, 313
strategic. *See* Strategic plan and
  planning
summary overview of, 100–102
terminology associated with,
  85–87
top-down, 95
Point-of-purchase systems, 257
Political environment, 68–70, 70b
Poor, Henry Varnum, 48–49
Portfolio, 334–335
Position power, 161
Possession utility, 256
Potential Rating Index for Zip Markets,
  263. *See also* Claritas
  Corporation
Power
  acceptance theory of, 163
  description of, 160
  expert, 162
  guidelines for using, 163–164
  limits to, 162–163
  personal, 161–162
  position, 161
  questions regarding, 161
  reference, 162
  sources of, 161–162
  zone of indifference, 163
Pregnancy Discrimination Act, 143
Press release, 253
Price matrix, 234f
Print media, 77–78
Privacy Act, 143
Problem solving
  defining of problem, 99
  definition of, 98
  expected vs. unexpected problems,
    98
  risk and, 99–100
  steps involved in, 98–99
  styles of, 98
  techniques for, 99–100
Process culture, 126
Process management theory, 309–310,
  312f
Product orientation, 258
Professional manager, 308
Profit-making, 229–230
Project budget, 209, 211, 214f, 215
Projection, 184
Promotional activities, 252–253
Psychological satisfaction, 254
Public relations, 313

R
Ratio analysis, 245
Ratio of expendable net assets, 245
Reciprocity, 295
Recognition seeking, 181

Recruitment of staff
  difficulties associated with, 144–145
  external, 144
  internal, 143–144
  philosophy of, 144
Reference power, 162
Rehabilitation Act, 142
Reinforcement-based motivation
    theories
  description of, 170, 174
  organizational behavior modification,
    175
Renaissance, 21–22
Research
  arts, 264
  market, 261–264
Research and development department,
  120
Reserve funds, 249
Resource analysis, 91
Restricted fund, 241
Résumé, 331–332, 332b, 333f
Retrenchment strategy, 92
Revenue
  description of, 210
  fundraising, 279
  matrix for, 234f
  maximization of, 234–236
Revenue centers, 208
Reward power, 161
Risk
  problem solving and, 99–100
  volunteers and, 149–150
Rites, 128
Rituals, 128
Romans, 20

S
Salaries
  budget and, 327
  funding for, 139
  range of, 326–327
Sales orientation, 258
Scalar principle, 121
Scaling, 235, 235f
Schedule, 87
Scientific management
  arts application of, 56–57
  contingency approach, 56
  description of, 45–46
  quantitative approaches, 55–56
  systems theory, 56
Screening of applicants, 146
Selective perception, 184
Self-confessing, 180
Self-control, 176
Self-efficacy, 176
Self-fulfilling prophecies, 160
Seventeenth century, 22–23
Shoe leather network, 204

Short-range plans, 86
Short-term planning, 313
Single-use plan, 87
Situation analysis, 90–91
Situational leadership theory, 168
Six Sigma, 57–58
Smithsonian, 24
Social environment, 71–72
Social learning theory, 170, 176
Span of control, 123
Special pleading, 180
Stability strategy, 92
Staff. *See also* Employee(s)
    Board of Directors and, 181
    compensation for, 140
    developing of, 10, 154–155
    firing of, 149
    funding for, 139
    fundraising by, 280, 286, 289
    information gathering from, 77
    maintaining of, 154–155
    management of, 315–316
    orientation of, 147
    overextended, 305
    performance standards for, 310
    qualifications of, 139
    recruitment of. *See* Recruitment of
        staff
    replacement of, 148–149
    selection of, 155
    training and development of,
        147–148
    turnover of, 147, 305–306
    working conditions for, 315
Staff manager, 9
Staffing
    application process for, 145–147
    challenges associated with, 136
    constraints on, 142–143
    costs associated with, 142
    description of, 136
    government regulations, 142–143
    importance of, 155
    job analysis. *See* Job analysis
    job description. *See* Job description
    job matrix, 141–142
    laws regarding, 136, 143–144
    needs for, 137
    organizational design and,
        138–139
    organized labor effects, 143
    process of, 137–149, 138f
    recruitment for, 143–145
    schematic representation of, 138f
    selection process
        application, 145–147
        auditions, 145
        interviewing, 146, 156
        legal considerations, 147
        screening, 146

tests, 146–147
    summary overview of, 155–157
Stage manager, 152b
Standing committee, 178
Standing-use plan, 87
Statement of activity, 243–245
Stereotypes, 184
Storytellers, 128–129
Strategic plan and planning
    definition of, 86
    description of, 97
    formulation of, 91–93
    fundraising, 281, 282f
    growth, 92
    market-based, 256
    marketing, 265, 266f
    organizational structure support of,
        118
    retrenchment, 92
    revising of, 313
    stability, 92
Stress, 305
Substitute goods or services, 231
Summary budget, 211, 212f
Supply and demand
    description of, 230
    law of demand, 230–232
    law of supply. *See* Law of supply
    revenue maximization and,
        234–236
Survey of Public Participation in the
    Arts, 263
SWOT analysis, 63, 90–91, 91b
Symbolic processes, 176
Sympathy seeking, 180
Symphony orchestra
    description of, 24
    organizational chart, 114f
Synergy, 76
Systems manager, 307f, 308–309
Systems theory, 56

T
Target marketing, 261–263
Task activities, 181
Task behavior, 168
Task group, 178
Tax exemption, 25–26, 227
Taylor, Frederick W., 50
Technological environment, 73–75
Telephone solicitations, 292–293
Temporary group, 177
Testing, 111–112
Theater company organizational chart,
    113f
Theater productions
    in eighteenth century, 22
    off-Broadway, 23
    steps involved in, 3, 4f
Theory X, 54–55, 160

Theory Y, 54–55, 160
Theory Z, 57
Ticket office manager, 52
Ticket pricing, 235–236
Time utility, 255
Top-down planning, 95
Total fixed costs, 228
Total quality management, 57
Total variable costs, 228
Tough-guy culture, 126
Training of staff, 147–148
Trait approach to leadership, 164
Transaction, 239
Transactional leadership, 168–169
Transformational leadership,
    168–169
Trends
    definition of, 66
    impact of, 79
Turnover of staff, 147, 305–306
Twentieth century, 23
Two-factor theory, 171–172

U
Unions
    contract negotiations, 151–152,
        152b–153b
    definition of, 151
    description of, 143
    disputes, 152–154, 154b
    management vs., 154, 314–315
    purpose of, 151–152
    types of, 151
United Scenic Artists, 151
University business schools, 58
Unrelated business income tax, 26
Unrestricted fund, 241

V
Valence, 174
VCRs, 74
Vertical coordination
    centralization–decentralization, 124
    chain of command, 121, 123
    definition of, 121
    delegation, 123–124
    span of control, 123
Virtual reality, 74
Volunteers
    Board of Directors. *See* Board of
        Directors
    commitment of, 150
    contracts for, 150b
    description of, 149
    disadvantages associated with, 150
    management of, 149
    risk considerations, 149–150

W
Wants, 254
Work
    activities of, 137–139
    standards for, 139
    tools necessary for, 139
Work groups, 112–113
Work hard–play hard culture, 126
Workforce
    staff. *See* Employee(s); Staff
    volunteers, 149–150
World Wide Web, 67
Wrongful-discharge lawsuit, 149

Z
Zero-based budget, 209
Zone of indifference, 163

Printed in the United States
127640LV00001BA/1-16/P

9 780240 805375